THE EVOLUTION OF OPERATIONAL ART

THE EVOLUTION OF OPERATIONAL ART

FROM NAPOLEON TO THE PRESENT

Edited by
JOHN ANDREAS OLSEN
AND
MARTIN VAN CREVELD

OXFORD
UNIVERSITY PRESS

OXFORD
UNIVERSITY PRESS

Great Clarendon Street, Oxford OX2 6DP

Oxford University Press is a department of the University of Oxford.
It furthers the University's objective of excellence in research, scholarship,
and education by publishing worldwide in

Oxford New York

Auckland Cape Town Dar es Salaam Hong Kong Karachi
Kuala Lumpur Madrid Melbourne Mexico City Nairobi
New Delhi Shanghai Taipei Toronto

With offices in

Argentina Austria Brazil Chile Czech Republic France Greece
Guatemala Hungary Italy Japan Poland Portugal Singapore
South Korea Switzerland Thailand Turkey Ukraine Vietnam

Oxford is a registered trade mark of Oxford University Press
in the UK and in certain other countries

Published in the United States
by Oxford University Press Inc., New York

First published 2011

British Library Cataloguing in Publication Data
Data available

Library of Congress Cataloging in Publication Data
Data available

Typeset by SPI Publisher Services, Pondicherry, India
Printed in Great Britain
on acid-free paper by
MPG Book Group, Bodmin and King's Lynn

ISBN 978–0–19–959948–6

1 3 5 7 9 10 8 6 4 2

Preface

This book project, initiated and sponsored by the Swedish National Defence College's Department of Military Studies, began in the summer of 2008 with the objective of producing a one-volume anthology that would focus on the essence and development of operational art, with equal attention to theory, practice, and utility. The book would be intended primarily for specialists—military professionals, 'officer-scholars', and postgraduate students—but at the same time be of interest to readers with a generalist's interest in military history, strategy, and operations.

To meet these objectives, and strike the balance among depth, width, and context—the framework recommended by Sir Michael Howard in his classic work, *The Causes of Wars*—I contacted one of the most prolific writers on the subject, Professor Martin van Creveld. We quickly recognized that the natural and inevitable starting point was Napoleon Bonaparte and that the book should be based on country-specific case studies. After selecting the cases themselves, we identified the leading experts on each topic. We also agreed that ideally the book should begin and conclude with chapters by Professor Sir Michael Howard and General Sir Rupert Smith, respectively: two figures who have significantly shaped contemporary thinking on the use of military force. In the process of contacting potential authors, we discussed the substance and form of the book with Professor Hew Strachan of Oxford University. As a result, the project became part of its Changing Character of War Programme.

I am deeply grateful to all the contributing authors for responding to the general guidance they received. They performed independent scholarship that resulted in new insights, and demonstrated their complete professionalism throughout the editorial process. I am also grateful to Harald Høiback, Margaret S. MacDonald, Simon Moores, H. P. Willmott, and Palle Ydstebø for reading through and commenting on the manuscript at various stages. In addition, I would like to thank Dominic Byatt, Jenny Lunsford, and Lizzy Suffling at Oxford University Press for their professionalism in seeing the publication through.

Most importantly, it has been a true pleasure to co-edit this work with Martin van Creveld. Never withholding his opinions, and offering them in a refreshingly sharp fashion, he made the book much better through his analytical insight, focus, and determination. I deeply value the strong friendship that we have developed through this and other projects.

John Andreas Olsen
Sarajevo

Contents

Prologue

Professor Sir Michael Howard

'Operational art', so the editors of this book point out, 'is the grey area between strategy and tactics'. Recently, this grey area has been the subject of intensive study, but, for the best part of two centuries, military theorists ignored it. They concentrated on 'strategy', the business of the high command, and 'tactics', the means of defeating enemy forces once battle was joined, which was the concern of the commander in the field. For many of them, indeed, 'strategy' and 'operations' were the same thing: deciding where to give battle, and then, in the immortal words of Nathaniel Bedford Forrest, 'gitting tha fustest with the mostest men'. Antoine de Jomini phrased it more elegantly: 'to operate, with the largest number of forces, in a combined effort on the decisive point'. In any event, the object of the strategist was to bring his forces to battle under the best possible circumstances. It was 'the battle' that ultimately counted.

But strategy is about *thinking* and *planning*. Operations are about *doing*: hence the phrase 'operational art'. It has been truly, if unkindly, said that amateurs do strategy but professionals do logistics. Without logistics, there can be no operations, and, without operations, strategy remains so much hot air. But further, without effective *tactics* even the most effective operations are a tragic waste of effort. To take an example from the Second World War: Winston Churchill might conceive strategies for the defeat of the Axis powers but his military advisers had to determine which were operationally possible. Even when they were possible they came to grief, whether in Norway in 1940, the Western Desert in 1941–2, or Anzio in 1944, because of tactical failure once battle was joined. Churchill's American allies may have been less imaginative so far as strategy was concerned, but they were brilliant at logistics. As Dr Echevarria points out in this volume, the American way of warfare was, and remains, as 'battle-oriented' as that of Napoleon. For General George Marshall in 1942, strategy consisted simply in identifying the main enemy force and destroying it in a 'decisive battle'. Its style, as he puts it, is 'more about winning battles than winning wars'. 'Operations' were thus largely a matter of logistics, which itself was largely a matter of management. If the logisticians can deliver a sufficient superiority of force, tactical incompetence does not matter all that much. American forces could afford to learn, however expensively, on the job, and wear down their adversary through sheer force of numbers. This perhaps explains, as Avi Kober points out in his critique of the

Israeli army, why the American military and its imitators have produced many competent managers but very few 'great captains'.

German military doctrine, as Professor Showalter explains in his chapter, was also 'battle-oriented', but their battles, unlike those of the Americans, could not be ones of attrition. Faced with enemies on all sides, Helmuth von Moltke and his successors had to secure a decisive victory against one adversary before turning against another, and that decision had to be predetermined by skilful operational combinations before the hazards of the tactical encounter. Moltke achieved this in 1866 at Königgrätz and in 1870 at Sedan. It disastrously failed to deliver von Schlieffen's *Schlacht ohne Morgen* in 1914 but worked brilliantly in 1940, when German strategy, operations, and tactics combined seamlessly to produce a victory that astounded the world.

But operations not only need effective tactics to be successful: they have to be guided by an effective strategy. Dennis Showalter shows us how, in spite of brilliant tactics, Ludendorff's great offensive in March 1918 led nowhere and brought no strategic results. The same applied on the Eastern Front in the Second World War, when German operational art and tactical expertise delivered millions of prisoners and conquered half a continent, but produced no decisive victory. The strategy it served was flawed by faulty political judgement that neither the operational efficiency nor the tactical skill of the *Wehrmacht* could correct.

'Operational art' flourished in the era between Napoleon and Eisenhower; generals who had to move, supply, and command armies numbering hundreds of thousands in campaigns covering entire continents and their adjacent oceans and ultimately the air above both: campaigns that could and did result in 'decisive' battles that owed their success rather to logistical superiority than to tactical skill. But after that, things became more complicated. In the 1950s, it became clear that a decisive victory in a 'conventional' campaign, whether in Europe or in Asia, could always be trumped by the use of nuclear weapons. So could operational art be used to avoid both defeat and nuclear Armageddon? Paradoxically, as Hew Strachan shows us, it was the British, who had barely begun to think about, let alone practise, operational art before the Second World War, who pioneered thinking on how to solve this problem, before the collapse of the Soviet Union ended—at least, for the time being—any need to do so.

Simultaneously, the Americans were confronting another kind of problem in Vietnam. There their conduct of 'operations' was, as ever, masterly. Vast quantities of men and equipment were ferried across the Pacific and delivered to the fighting zone. It enabled them to win all their battles. Nonetheless, they lost the war.

In his contribution to this volume General Rupert Smith tells us why. The era of 'industrial war' is over—at least, for the time being. Wars are no longer fought between peoples, but among peoples. Their object is no longer the conquest of territory, but the winning of loyalties. For this, we still need strategies, though ones embracing far more than military means, and tactics, though of a subtle and discriminating kind. In between there still remains the indispensable grey area of operations. But we need to think of them all in rather a different way, and General Smith, who has vast experience of the problem, suggests how this should be done.

In short, this volume is both instructive and thought-provoking. I feel highly privileged to have been invited to introduce it.

List of Abbreviations

ACTS	Air Corps Tactical School
AEF	American Expeditionary Force
ARRC	Ace Rapid Reaction Corps
AWRD	Authority for Weapon Research and Development
BESA	Begin–Sadat Center for Strategic Studies
CCP	Chinese Communist Party
CPV	Chinese People's Volunteers
DBK	Dominance in Battlefield Knowledge
DFID	Department for International Development
EBO	Effects-Based Operations
FM	Field Manual
GLCMs	Ground-Launched Cruise Missiles
GRU	Main Intelligence Directorate
GSS	General Security Service
GTF	General Tactical Functions of Larger Units
HIC	High-Intensity Conflict
IAF	Israeli Air Force
IDF	Israel Defense Forces
IGO	Intergovernmental Organization
ISAF	International Security Assistance Force
KMT	Kuomintang
LIC	Low-Intensity Conflict
MOOTW	Military Operations Other than War
NARKOMO	People's Commissariat of Defence
NCW	Network-Centric Warfare
NEP	New Economic Policy
NGO	Non-Governmental Organization
NORTHAG	Northern Army Group
OGPU	Unified State Political Administration
OKH	Oberkommando des Heeres
OMG	Operational Manoeuvre Group
OSCE	Organization for Security and Co-operation in Europe
OTRI	Operational Theory Research Institute
PKO	Peacekeeping Operation

PLA	People's Liberation Army
PLO	Palestine Liberation Organization
PRC	People's Republic of China
PU-36	Temporary Field Regulation-36
PVO	Air Defence Forces
R&D	Research and Development
RAF	Royal Air Force
RKKA	Red Army's Main Staff
RMA	Revolution in Military Affairs
RPG	Rocket-Propelled Grenade
SAM	Surface-to-Air Missile
SSI	Strategic Studies Institute
TTP	Tactics, Techniques, and Procedures
UNC	United Nations Command
UNDP	United Nations Development Programme
UNPROFOR	United Nations Protection Force
USAID	United States Agency for International Development

Introduction

John Andreas Olsen and Martin van Creveld

Operational art emerged as a new and distinct component of warfare in the nineteenth century.[1] Broadly defined as the grey area between strategy and tactics, operational art spans the theory and practice of planning and conducting campaigns and major operations aimed at accomplishing strategic and operational objectives in a given theatre of operations.[2] An intermediate link between strategy and tactics has always existed, but a distinct concept that encompasses a systematic and deliberate plan of campaign for major operations is a mere 200 years old.

The forces unleashed in 1648 by the Treaty of Westphalia and the creation of the modern state, combined with the political, social, and economic upheaval of the French Revolution and the age of Napoleon, contributed in no small part to creating the conditions that in turn led to a new approach to the conduct of war. Napoleon's extraordinary ability to mobilize his forces, deploy them into the theatre of war, and then manoeuvre large independent formations to concentrate them at the critical moment of battle set a new operational tone.[3] The Napoleonic Wars, based as they were on armies so large that they had to be divided into separate corps, came to represent a transformation of war in terms of goals, broad participation, scale, accelerated tempo, and the roles that battle and manoeuvre played in the operational repertoire.

Throughout the nineteenth century that repertoire was extended by technological advances: most notably the railroad, but also new means of communication in the form of the telegraph and the telephone, as well as weapons such as rifled small arms, breech-loading rifled guns, and machine guns.[4] The cumulative effect of technological progress, together with organizational improvements based on corps-sized formations, revealed that the tactical framework was too narrow, and strategic perspectives were too broad, to ensure effective orchestration of military forces.

This realization, and the resulting institution of an intermediate level of military theory and practice, came about at different times and in different forms in various states around the world. In Europe and the United States they were influenced, directly or indirectly, by the writings of Carl von Clausewitz and Henri Antoine Jomini, both of whom took the Napoleonic Wars as their point of reference for their analyses. Neither of them used the term 'operational art', or referred to a separate level between strategy and tactics, but they did discuss campaigns and theatres of war. Hence, the concept was implicit in their theories, which served as a foundation for successive generations of military commanders who were to extend modern military theory.

Field Marshal Helmuth von Moltke the Elder, for thirty years the chief of staff of the Prussian Army, no doubt viewed his actions in terms of achieving military victory rather than in the more abstract light of using military means to attain strategic goals, but he was one of the first commanders to grasp the significance of linking strategy with tactics. His new method of directing armies in the field found its best expression in the Franco-Prussian War of 1870–1, which marked the end of French hegemony in continental Europe and resulted in the creation of a unified Germany. Operational art also played an important part in the First World War, especially on the Eastern Front and under Field Marshal Edmund Allenby in Palestine. For most countries, however, the Second World War provides the most significant point of departure for contemporary studies of operational art, not least because of its material scale and geographic scope. The legacy of that war in the sphere of operational art includes successive and deep operations, flank manoeuvres, and encirclement, all executed with relatively high speed and with the objective of destroying the enemy's army. In the subsequent decades, as nuclear theory came to dominate both political and military thinking, some armed forces downplayed the significance of the operational level; in others the concept lingered in the background; and yet others discovered operational art for the first time and gave it new expression through doctrine and teaching.[5] That the United States began to study operational art systematically in the 1980s ensured that the concept would receive considerable attention among its allies.

Operational art is currently taught at most command and staff colleges throughout the Western world. Small-scale versions—'small' because the opponents are not regular forces but terrorists, guerrillas, and insurgents of every kind—are practised at US, NATO, and EU headquarters and command posts. Procedures for operational planning and guidance of operations include key elements expressed in terms such as centre of gravity, decisive points, critical strengths, critical vulnerabilities, critical requirements, lines of operations, *Schwerpunkt* (weight of effort), culmination point, and operational deception. Other important terms include advance, retreat, exterior and interior lines, breakthrough, flanking movement, and pivots. Military colleges and operational headquarters abound with manuals, procedures, and checklists for dealing with the operational level of war and operational art. These materials provide a common, coherent set of references covering a logical framework, proven methodologies, and a standardized vocabulary. Hence, they are indispensable for commanders, especially in a day and age when various countries with very different experiences must work together in alliances and coalitions.

It is, therefore, a paradox that operational art, though acknowledged as an important element in the planning and execution of military operations at home and abroad, remains under-researched and relatively poorly understood. Simply put, manuals, procedures, and checklists cannot substitute for in-depth studies. They must be accompanied by records and analyses of campaigns that define important milestones in the evolution of operational art: not only the flashes of genius and intellectual apexes, but also the periods devoid of creative thinking; not only successful campaigns, but also those that lacked appropriate theoretical underpinnings or operational excellence. The historical record tracing the evolution of operational art can best be understood through studies that cover both theory and practice. This book is intended to provide military professionals, officer-scholars, and graduate students that wider framework and contextualization of operational art by tracing its roots and development in various countries.

BRIEF SUMMARY

The book's point of departure is the last decades of the eighteenth century. In Chapter 1, Professor Martin van Creveld demonstrates that the emergence of campaigns, made possible by a certain size of military formations, in essence opened the way for the operational level of war, operational warfare, and operational art. The complexity of campaigns, especially those that took place along broad fronts and covered large distances, accentuated the role of effective control, which, in turn, brought into play a new dimension of warfare. The historical factors that ushered the operational dimension into the world were the French Revolution and the *levée en masse*, and the man who presided over its birth was Napoleon Bonaparte.

Professor van Creveld suggests that this revolution in military affairs was made possible by three factors that owed very little to technology per se. First, the *corps d'armée* system ensured armies of a certain size, within which each corps could operate under unified and central direction and therefore undertake unprecedented manoeuvres in terms of speed and range. Second, the imperial headquarters ensured that the emperor received timely and relevant information in a systematic fashion, and in turn provided the corps with a plan of campaign. Third, the 'directed telescope' provided the link between the two, supplementing information on the ground from 'intelligent captains' with assessments from senior officers. The combination of these three factors, together with the genius and energy of Napoleon, led to an outcome that represented 'an increase, indeed, almost an explosion, in the speed, extent, range, and flexibility of military operations'. The author emphasizes that this outcome did not result from Napoleon having better or simply more information than his opponents, but from the system he had put in place, which ensured that he and the *Grande Armée* 'were able to function *without* having such information'.

In the next case study, Professor Dennis Showalter focuses on the rise and fall of operational art in the Prussian-German context. For three decades, following Napoleon's defeat at Waterloo in June 1815, Prussia assumed a rather low-key position in Europe, viewing itself more as a *Kleinstaat* than as a great power. The Second Industrial Revolution and the re-emergence of a French empire redefined Prussia's ambitions. Two significant military successes marked the Prussian return to power: the defeat of Austria in 1866 by Prussia and the defeat of France in 1870–1 by a Prussian-led alliance. Field Marshal Helmuth von Moltke, who directed these campaigns, sought to bring 'the army to the right place at the right time and in the right combination to avoid stalemate in the field to sustain the commander's synergistic relationship with political authority'. His ability to take advantage of the railroad system, thereby enabling large numbers of troops to engage in battle under favourable circumstances, and his pursuit of quick and decisive victories by going on the offensive, meant that he in effect elevated tactical and logistical considerations into what we now define as operational art.

Erich von Ludendorff's operations on the Eastern Front (1914–17) notwithstanding, it would take another seventy years before the Germans again managed to take full advantage of operational art, in this case in the form of *Blitzkrieg*. These 'lightning wars' forced Germany's enemies off-balance through sophisticated planning and creative implementation that focused on gaining and maintaining the initiative. This was accomplished by a series of well-coordinated offensive actions, making the most of speed, daring, and the combination of firepower and manoeuvre to strike decisively. The German invasions of Poland, France, Norway, Denmark, and the Low Countries in 1939 and 1940 reflected operational art at its best, with execution now augmented by air power to support ground forces.

But Germany's experience showed that operational art by itself cannot ensure success; instead, it must be coupled with a reasonable strategy and policy. Operation Barbarossa, the invasion of Russia in June 1941, marked 'imperial overreach' and demonstrated the insufficiency of German operational art. Thus, Showalter's story is one in which operational art found its place and was carried out superbly, only to fall victim to unrealistic aims. The founding of the Bundeswehr and the downsizing of the German armed forces currently leave little scope for Germany to practise operational art in the tradition of von Moltke's Prussia.

In Chapter 3, Dr Jacob W. Kipp analyses the evolution of Soviet-Russian operational art from the perspectives of both war and society, since the military dimensions cannot be understood without recognizing the revolutionary political and societal factors at play in the Soviet Union prior to the Second World War. The chapter begins by examining the ideas developed by officer-scholars such as Aleksandr A. Svechin and Mikhail Tukhachevsky, the former emphasizing a form of attrition as an alternative to destruction of the enemy army and the latter focusing on 'deep operations' and their linkage to the strategy of annihilation.

With the theoretical framework in place, Kipp next examines operational art in various campaigns and battles during the Second World War, beginning with the Soviet–Finnish War of 1939–40. This war exposed Soviet military weaknesses that the Wehrmacht was able to exploit, but the Red Army proved very capable of learning. Thus, Operation Uranus, the Soviet counter-offensive at Stalingrad that was launched in November 1942, is often hailed as the turning point of the war; Russian military commentators today still point to the Battle of Kursk as a classic example of a successful 'premeditated defence' and the 'point when Germany finally lost the strategic-operational initiative'; and the author considers the linked operations Bagration and Lvov-Sandomierz in the summer of 1944 an 'outstanding example of Soviet operational art'.

Although all of these operations included elements of manoeuvre, deep operations, envelopments, encirclements, shock and awe, surprise, and other features of operational art, there is no doubt that mass was significant in distinguishing victory from defeat: the Soviets simply overwhelmed the Germans with superior numbers of aircraft, tanks, artillery, and men. Neither can there be any doubt that the objective of the campaigns was the enemy army: when Stalin spoke of breaking 'the spine of Japan' at the very end of the war, he was referring to the Kwantung Army. Like Showalter, Kipp concludes that operational art found its place in the Second World War at various fronts, but, as happened in Germany, has become a lost form of art in post-war Soviet-Russian armed forces, which have never engaged in large-scale operations against a regular enemy.

In Chapter 4, Professor Hew Strachan examines the origins, development, and implications of operational art in the British armed forces. During the nineteenth century, most British officers used the word 'operations', as Clausewitz did, to describe military activity in general. Some, however, followed Jomini, who had begun to develop a specific vocabulary to describe the links between 'strategy' and 'tactics'. Jomini's most obvious influence on British military theory was found in the notion that operational thought rested on the application of principles. Caught between the expectations of major European wars and the realities of colonial soldiering, the British army was wary of adopting a fixed doctrine, but welcomed the 'principles of war' as a way of acknowledging its need to be flexible and adaptable. The *Field Service Regulations* of 1909 represented the first official attempt to encapsulate this approach within operational art—one that survived the First World War and was endorsed by J. F. C. Fuller. But the war also made clear that traditional definitions of strategy did not apply during a coalition conflict requiring full national mobilization. Fuller, who introduced the term 'grand strategy', therefore opened the way for 'operations' to be recognized as an independent and subordinate level of war. Nonetheless, the establishment of doctrine remained anathema, and without it operational art was driven by tactics rather than by strategy. This, according to Professor Strachan, was a key reason why the British army tended to perform poorly at the operational level in the Second World War.

When the operational level of war re-emerged in Great Britain during the 1980s, it was accompanied by doctrine for the first time. The linkage between doctrine and operational art was inspired less by the US army's response to Vietnam than by responses to Soviet and German practice and theory going back to lessons from the First and Second World Wars. During the 1990s, doctrine, originally based upon Britain's need to compensate for inferiority in numbers in the Cold War, became the basis of dogma. 'Manoeuvre' became applicable to almost all aspects of war at many different levels, and was increasingly applied in contexts where Western forces now enjoyed overwhelmingly superior firepower. The old tensions between building capacity for large-scale war (army corps) and smaller actions (Northern Ireland, Bosnia, etc.) reappeared as the British armed forces strove to become truly joint. The former requirement pulled operational thought in a more tactical direction; the latter gave it a more strategic—and even political—aspect.

Dr Antulio Echevarria's point of departure is that US operational art has essentially focused on perfecting war's 'first grammar'—the principles and procedures related to defeating an opponent by armed force—while struggling to come to grips with war's 'second grammar'—the handling of insurgencies, guerrilla warfare, and irregular warfare. In Echevarria's opinion, a preoccupation with destroying the enemy's military forces has led the United States to adopt a battle-centric view of warfare. Consequently, American operational art over the last century has concentrated on fighting battles rather than on waging wars, and rests on the flawed assumption that winning battles can easily translate into winning the peace for which the wars were waged. By tracing doctrines and manuals, as well as actual operations from the First World War to the present, Echevarria demonstrates that all US armed services—land, sea, and air—shared this outlook.

It was during the Cold War era, when scholars and practitioners were about to lose faith in the relevance of operational art, that the concept actually blossomed in the US: introduced in 1982 in the form of AirLand Battle, revised and improved in 1986, and executed with great success (albeit against an opponent who proved much weaker than expected) in the Gulf War of 1991. Echevarria notes that US forces performed operational art with excellence during the invasions of Afghanistan in 2001 and Iraq in 2003, as these campaigns were based on an understanding of war's 'first grammar', only to falter as these campaigns made the transition from regular warfare to war's 'second grammar', which demands knowledge of how to design, plan, and conduct counter-insurgency operations.

Supplementing the Euro-Atlantic perspective, Dr Avi Kober examines the rise and fall of operational art in the Israeli armed forces. Chapter 6 argues that until the early 1970s the dominance of high-intensity conflicts, with their relatively favourable conditions for battlefield manoeuvre, enabled Israeli operational art to flourish. Combining an indirect approach with a domestically developed form of *Blitzkrieg*, Israeli operational art reached its high points in 1956 and 1967. Since the early 1970s, however, new conditions have affected Israeli operational art negatively. First, with low-intensity conflicts becoming the only type of warfare in which Israel has engaged since the 1980s, the importance of the operational level of war has decreased, primarily because such confrontations tend to take place at the two extremes of the levels of war spectrum—tactics on the one hand, and strategy, or even grand strategy, on the other. At the same time, experience in high-intensity conflicts, which traditionally provided the central source of inspiration for Israeli commanders and their operational art, has almost disappeared among the military leadership. Second, given the close linkage between operational art and manoeuvre, the ascendancy of firepower over manoeuvre and the strong belief that superior weapon-system technology can decide battles, campaigns, and even wars have had a detrimental effect on Israeli operational art. A by-product has been a greater tendency to think linearly at the expense of the non-linear and creative thinking on which Israeli operational art at its finest was traditionally based. Third, the post-heroic state of mind that has characterized Israeli society and its political and military echelons since the late 1970s has also de-emphasized the significance of manoeuvre.

By establishing the Operational Theory Research Institute in 1995, Israel sought to overcome this decline. The institute was touted as a renaissance for operational art, but Kober maintains that the effort failed miserably because it created a postmodern theoretical construct and terminology that few could understand and relate to. Furthermore, in terms of leadership training the Israel Defense Forces (IDF) focused more on equipping commanders with managerial skills than on grooming great captains. The inadequate professional training of IDF commanders—for reasons Kober explains in his chapter—has prevented commanders from becoming familiar with the best theoretical materials on classical and modern military theory in general and operational art in particular. Kober concludes that Israel's return to a high standard of operational art will depend on getting back to the basics of military thinking, and on a military leadership that understands the value of a higher standard of professional education and training.

In Chapter 7, Dr Andrew Scobell examines the Chinese way of war, focusing on the rise of the Communist movement in the 1920s and the founding of the People's Republic of China in 1949. However, he suggests that key elements of operational art have been at the heart of the Chinese form of war for centuries. Furthermore, while the Chinese strategic tradition contains distinctive cultural elements, it exhibits greater commonalities with other traditions than are often recognized, especially when one looks beyond written texts and at the actual conduct of operations. Drawing on the writings of Sun Tzu, Zhuge Liang, and Mao Zedong, and on contemporary doctrines and experiences from both conventional war and guerrilla warfare, Scobell identifies the hallmarks of China's operational art as the combination of orthodox and unorthodox elements, a mixture of human factors and technology, and a blend of offensive and defensive priorities, as well as mobile and positional warfare. In addition, Chinese forces sometimes fight for show, sometimes for military victory, and sometimes for both.

In Scobell's view, since modern Chinese operational art sees these characteristics as *yin* and *yang* rather than as absolutes, it resembles Western thinking more than the school of 'Chinese uniqueness' suggests. This is especially true at a time when China's armed forces seek to become both combined and joint so that they can potentially deal with the full spectrum of armed conflict: from war for national survival to peace operations abroad to local disturbances. While operational thought in Europe and the United States has been characterized by high and low points, the Chinese have been relatively consistent at keeping the tenets of operational art alive, both in theory and in practice.

Finally, in the Epilogue, General Sir Rupert Smith argues that we have moved from 'industrial war' to 'war amongst the people' emphasizing that this change of paradigms has strong implications for the operational artist and his or her practice of operational art. Collectively, these chapters describe how the concepts that underpin operational art originated, how they received practical expression in various campaigns, and, perhaps most importantly, how they developed over time. Theory is critical to refining and improving existing methods of applying operational warfare,[6] and its importance cannot be overstated; however, to be useful, theory and its accompanying vocabulary must be combined with a proper examination of historical trends and practical experience. The present volume attempts to achieve that combination.

NOTES

1. John English, 'The Operational Art: Developments in the Theories of War', in B. J. C. Kercher and Michael A. Hennessy (eds.), *The Operational Art: Developments in the Theories of War* (Westport, CT: Praeger, 1996), 7.
2. For simplicity, 'planning and conducting campaigns' refers to the whole spectrum of 'design, preparation, organization, sustainment and termination of campaigns'. See, for example, Milan N. Vego, *Joint Operational Warfare* (Newport, RI: US Naval War College, 2007), I-4 and GL-12.
3. Michael D. Krause and R. Cody Phillips, *Historical Perspectives on the Operational Art* (Washington, DC: Center of Military History, United States Army, 2005), 25.
4. Vego, *Joint Operational Warfare*, I-16.
5. See Edward N. Luttwak, 'The Operational Level of War', *International Security*, vol. 5, no. 3 (Winter 1980–1), 61–78.
6. Vego, *Joint Operational Warfare*, I-6.

1

Napoleon and the Dawn of Operational Warfare

Martin van Creveld

INTRODUCTION

It is usually possible to analyse the conduct of wars, and especially the larger ones among them, on three separate levels. At the bottom are tactics; that is, the use of the available military means in order to win battles. At the top is strategy; that is, the use of *all* available means (not merely military ones) in order to win the war. Somewhere in between lies the operational level, which might be defined as the use of the available military means in order to win campaigns. Implicit in these distinctions is the assumption that a war may very well see several campaigns unfold at the same time. For example, during the First World War, it was the government in London that ran the war as a whole; the commanders in France, Palestine, and Iraq engaged in what little operational art there was; and the corps, division, and regimental commanders took care of tactics. In this chapter, what concerns us is the second, or middle, of these three levels.

Before proceeding further, it is necessary to emphasize one absolutely essential point: whatever the differences that separate the three levels—and there is, however, no doubt that they merge into each other to some extent—they have one thing in common; namely, the fact that they both describe and prescribe how to deal with an acting, reacting enemy; and that, as a result, the medium in which they move, so to speak, consists of uncertainty. To paraphrase a famous sixteenth-century phrase referring to the tendency of Swiss mercenaries to melt away when they were not paid, *pas d'enemi, pas de la guerre; pas d'incertitude, pas de guerre aussi* (no enemy, no war; no uncertainty, no war either). Any attempt to understand war at any level, including the operational one, without taking this fact into account might just as well be consigned to the dustbin before the first word is even put on paper.

FROM THE STONE AGE OF CAMPAIGNING TO NAPOLEON

During most of history, operational art did not exist. This was not necessarily because the above-mentioned distinction between battle, campaign, and war as a whole was not understood. For example, an examination of the Peloponnesian War (431–404 BC) will show that, at times, it was waged in several separate theatres at once. The chain of command went down from the *ecclesia*, or popular assembly, which made all the most important decisions, to the *strategoi*, or commanders on the spot. From them, it extended to the *hegemonoi*, or officers, of the tactical units. The same is true of the Second Punic War (218–201 BC). The Senate in Rome sent instructions to the theatre commanders, who were either consuls or proconsuls, in charge of the armies in such places as northern Italy, southern Italy, Spain, and, later, North Africa. The theatre commanders, in turn, had legionary commanders (either praetors or legates), military tribunes, and centurions serving under them. An examination of the fifth-century-BC Greek historian Thucydides and the first-century-AD Roman one Livy will show that neither of them had any difficulty in understanding the difference between the overall direction of the war on one hand and exercising command over one of its theatres on the other.

Instead, what prevented operational art from developing was *the inability of most forms of information to move much faster than the troops themselves.* Consider an army commander—we shall not deal with navies here—preparing to wage a campaign at any time and place before 1800 or so. Let us ignore the question of how to acquire information concerning the theatre itself. In case he was operating in friendly territory he would, of course, be expected to be familiar with it. In case he was planning to invade enemy territory, he would have to prepare ahead of time by reading the available books, interviewing travellers, and the like.[1] A commander who did not study the country ahead sufficiently thoroughly could very well put his army at risk. This was what happened to Alexander the Great when he marched back from India in 322 BC and to Napoleon when he marched across the Sinai in 1798 AD; on both occasions, a lack of the appropriate information all but caused the troops involved to die of thirst along with their commander.

More pertinent to our topic, such a commander would need enemy information: his whereabouts, his numbers, his composition, his capabilities, and, perhaps most important of all, his intentions. Supposing the enemy to be beyond immediate visual range, such information might reach him from one of two sources. On the one hand, there was 'passive' information in the form of the reports of travellers, deserters, etc. Its principal advantage was that it might (but need not) reach him while the enemy was still a considerable distance away; its principal disadvantage, in that its contents, instead of being tuned to meet the commander's exact requirements, were the product of accident. In addition, the very real possibility that travellers and deserters, acting either deliberately or out of ignorance, might bring false information had to be taken into account.

To overcome these problems, any commander worth his salt would engage in an active quest for information of the kind that, in Rome, was known as *exploratio*. Spies, often wearing some kind of disguise, would be dispatched. If they succeeded in entering the enemy camp and emerging alive, they might report back with many kinds of useful information. Patrols might be sent out and subject the enemy to direct observation, as well as bringing back prisoners for interrogation. Barring actual treachery, the information these instruments might provide would probably be more focused and more reliable than that derived from 'passive' sources.[2] On the other hand, spies and patrols differed from travellers and deserters in that they would have to cover the distance between their employer and the enemy twice; once on their way out, once on their return.

In today's networked world, all but the most unimportant information moves at the speed of light. Delays, of course, are anything but unusual. However, they are normally the result of inefficient procedures or congestion. Hence, they are much more likely to ensue at the points of departure and arrival than on the way; however long or short it may be, that way itself is literally covered in a flash. This was not true in the pre-industrial world, when the speed at which news was transmitted could vary tremendously in accordance with the weather, the topography, the state of the roads, and so on. Owing to the all-but-seamless way in which it was passed from mouth to ear, the kind of news that moved fastest of all was rumour. Speeds of up to 250 miles per twenty-four hours are on record. However, of all forms of information, rumour was the most problematic. Its origins were unknown and its reliability uncertain; in Caesar's words, very often *fama* far outstripped the facts.[3] Furthermore, it only brought the kind of news that happened to be floating around, as it were, not that which the commander needed.

Other kinds of information moved much more slowly. To stick to the above categories, travellers and deserters probably only made their way more or less at the same speed as armies did, rarely exceeding twenty-five miles per day. This meant that any enemy information they could provide a commander with would only arrive a fairly short time before that enemy himself came into view. Of course, small groups of military men on a special mission could move much faster, especially if they were mounted. However, as already noted, they would have to make their way to and fro, moving first forward and then back to the rear so as to submit their report. As a result, the effective range at which they could operate was limited indeed. Modern historians put it at two to seven miles, though, here and there, longer ones are recorded.[4] Reading Caesar's *Bellum Africanum* in particular, one gets the distinct impression that, very often, precise information concerning the enemy's whereabouts only reached him at the very last moment. Even as the vanguard riding ahead of his army reported his presence, the commander himself could see a cloud of dust rising on the horizon.[5] In this sense, when Napoleon, asked how one fights a battle, answered that 'on s'engage, puis on voit' (first you engage, then you see), he came close to summing up all previous military practices.

It is true that, from the earliest days on, some methods existed that could transmit information faster than men travelling either on foot or on horseback could. Some were acoustic—one thinks of tam-tams, or of the messages that men stationed in posts established by the Persian emperors used to shout to each other across the desert, or of the cannon shots that Napoleon used at the time of the Battle of Marengo. Others were visual: smoke signals (by day), fire signals (by night), and the kind of signals that are transmitted by mirrors. Here and there, one finds stories about other kinds of visual signals. Thus, the Bible explains how Joshua during the Battle of Ai waved a javelin as a sign for the ambush he had mounted to be sprung.[6] All these methods were used on occasions, sometimes with success, sometimes without. However, all suffered from obvious limitations in regard to range as well as the kind of information they could transmit.

Finally, it is necessary to say something about relay systems. Such systems, consisting of mounted messengers stationed in fixed positions and taking over from each other, were no mystery to the Hellenistic kingdoms, the Roman Empire, and, much later, the Mongols.[7] They are capable of transmitting information almost as fast as rumour does—speeds of up to 200 miles per day are on record. Unlike acoustic or optical systems, they place no limits on the kind of information that may be transmitted (though there *will* be a problem in obtaining further clarification, which the messenger who delivers the message will be unable to provide) or any difficulty concerning reliability. Still such systems suffer from two grave disadvantages. First, the stations of which they consist are fixed in geographical space. They are, therefore, more useful in friendly territory than in an enemy one. More on the defence than on the offence (when one would have to construct a new chain of stations as one advances); more on the strategic level than on the operational one. Second, they are enormously expensive to build and maintain.

Perhaps even more interesting than the problem of gathering information about the enemy is that of staying in touch with, and directing the operations of, friendly ones. Today we are used to a situation where, picking up a hand-held gadget, we can form near-instant communication with anyone we want almost regardless of distance, relative geographical position, relative movement, and topographical obstacles that may separate him from us. That, however, is a recent development; after all, mobile phones are barely a quarter-century old. Even if we push things as far back as we can, they will go no further than the invention of radio during the early years of the twentieth century. For half a century or so before radio, there was only the telegraph, an instrument that is dependent on wire and, therefore, not nearly as mobile and nearly as flexible as radio is. This explains why, originally, at any rate, the impact of the telegraph was only felt at the highest levels; that is, when it was a question of establishing communications between the capital and general headquarters in the field. As one Austrian officer wrote in 1861, only rarely was it of any use to the tactician.[8] Before the telegraph, there was literally nothing.

Probably, the best analysis of the possibilities and limitations of operational warfare as it was waged under such conditions comes from the pen of an outstanding Israeli scholar, Yuval Harari, who has analysed the English armies during the Hundred Years War (1337–1453).[9] Since the king acted as his own commander-in-chief in the field, we shall ignore the problem of maintaining communications between France, the theatre of war in which he operated, and London, from which reinforcements and, at times, money would have to come. Instead, we shall focus on the conduct of operations inside France itself.

In 1346, the year in which the famous Battle of Crecy was fought, Edward III was based west of Paris. From there, Harari says, the king would have needed about a week to pass an order to his lieutenant in Flanders or receive a report from him. Let us assume that, to exercise effective command over a distant subordinate, a commander-in-chief has to go through four stages. First, he has to send a message to that subordinate, who presumably is more familiar with local conditions, and ask him for a plan. Second, he must have that plan submitted to him; third, he must transmit his orders back to the subordinate; and, fourth, he must receive confirmation that those orders have been understood and will be carried out. Still assuming the king is based in the region west of Paris, and his subordinate in Flanders, the entire cycle will require a full month to go through. Of course, this is an ideal cycle and one that was rarely completed in this precise form. Shortcuts were made, the subordinate's initiative and ability to look out for himself taken into account. Even if we reduce it to a minimum, though, a week is a long time to receive a piece of information or to send out an order before it can arrive and be obeyed.

Other English armies operating in France at the time were even further away and, consequently, even harder to reach. Thus, a considerable force was stationed in Gascony; however, communicating with it took about twice as long as with the one in Flanders. As a result, Harari tells us, 'for armies coming from different fronts to join hands [was usually possible] only when they were not opposed by a strong hostile army . . . how each [local commander] conducted operations on his front was affected to only a small degree by [the king's] plan or by operations on other fronts'.[10] As a matter of fact, we have reason to think that Edward, who was an excellent commander, *did* intend to have three armies meet before fighting the battle. However, communication difficulties seem to have interfered and prevented the juncture from being brought about.

When the time came in August, all the king could do was take up a defensive position between two woods. There, his front covered by a muddy field, he stood and fought outnumbered, man against man, with only the forces immediately available to him. There certainly was a question of tactics, which turned out to be superb and led to the French army being routed, but hardly one of operational art. Indeed, one could almost say that the dire situation in which he found himself on this occasion was the result of the failure of operational art, to the extent that he understood it and tried to exercise it.

Over thousands of years, the technology of transportation and communication changed hardly at all—men could not walk faster or further in AD 1346 than in 1346 BC, and horses remained horses. Accordingly, it is perhaps not surprising that this statement can be generalized. The wars of Alexander the Great, of the Hellenistic kingdoms, and of Rome all point to the same conclusion.[11] It was, of course, always possible to create a diversion by sending a force to some remote theatre of war, as the Romans did when they sent Scipio to fight in Spain; however, a commander could only exercise effective command over the forces that formed part of his own army and marched with him. As a result, commanders who knew what they were doing took good care not to disperse their forces or make them move by different routes far apart from each other, unless they could be pretty certain that no enemy was likely to attack those forces in detail.

A contributing factor to this may have been the absence of good large-scale maps, especially of the kind that can cover entire theatres of war in some detail. To convince oneself of this fact, one only has to see a Roman itinerary or the rough sketch that late-sixteenth-century Spanish commanders used in order to march their forces from their assembly place in northern Italy around the frontiers of France towards the theatre of war in the Netherlands.[12] Some historians have gone further still, arguing that the absence of maps itself indicates the inability of pre-modern people to visualize the world in terms of the two-dimensional space so vital to operational art.[13] However, this is uncertain.

As late as the second half of the eighteenth century, Frederick the Great, one of history's great commanders, is still found using similar methods and labouring under similar constraints. While maps were improving—triangulation, introduced after the invention of the telescope around the middle of the eighteenth century, was now used to make them—on occasions, he still considered it necessary to rely on sketches made by his own hand. Concerning enemy information, as the king himself wrote,[14] the most important sources remained travellers, local inhabitants (meaning, any halfway intelligent peasant), deserters, and prisoners. To these would be added the spies sent out to explore the enemy camp, and—something he does not say, probably because he took it for granted—the cavalry patrols that went to observe it and that might take the prisoners. On any given day, even the fastest of those could only cover twice or thrice the distance the army itself could. However, since messages had to be physically transmitted from mouth to mouth or from hand to hand, 'active' methods of obtaining information had their effective range cut in half, owing to the need to make a return journey.

For the same reason, that is, the slow pace at which information travelled, the distance from headquarters at which it was possible to exercise effective command was also limited. Again, relying on the words of Frederick himself, we find that normally it was no more than about two miles, which meant that fronts were limited to about four miles.[15] In fact, the one campaign when he tried to carry out a concentric advance on two separate fronts, during his invasion of Bohemia in 1757, ended in failure. Contemporary critics were not slow to blame him for even making the attempt.[16] At a time when battles were still being fought by long lines of men standing shoulder to shoulder, such short fronts limited the number of troops an army might comprise. This, in turn, explains why, in the view of Turenne, exercising command over more than 50,000 men was beyond the capability of a single person.[17] As if to confirm this analysis, bodies of troops operating beyond the commander-in-chief's immediate control were known as 'detachments'. Various considerations, including, above all, the need to expand the area in which supplies might be gathered and to provide flank security, might compel a commander to form them and use them. However, doing so always carried the risk that, when battle was imminent, they would not be available to participate in it.

As long as this remained the case, the possibilities open to operational art were limited. On occasions, armies simply blundered about, groping for the enemy until they found him. This is what happened, we are told, on the eve of the Battle of Cynoscephalae in 197 BC and also formed the prelude to many a medieval battle. On other occasions, they might deliberately advance towards each other or retreat from each other. Under commanders, such as Conde, Turenne, Marlborough, and the Marshal de Saxe, they might also circle one another as dogs do. Sometimes they did so in an attempt to press the enemy against some kind of natural or artificial obstacle, such as a river, a mountain range, a fortress, or a moat, and force him to give battle under unfavourable circumstances. On other occasions, it was a question of compelling him to abandon, not his lines of communications—there were none—but the area from which he drew his supplies. Yet if only because changing from an order of march, which required depth, into an order of battle, which demanded width, took a considerable time, in the end, it was almost always a question of forming two lines. Depending on equipment and tactics, those lines might be thick or thin. However, almost certainly they would confront one another for a time, perhaps even a considerable time, before coming to grips. Indeed, cases are on record when armies faced one another for several days on end.

Under such circumstances, the logic behind Clausewitz's somewhat puzzling statement that most battles took place by a sort of tacit agreement between the opposing commanders becomes clear.[18] As he says, battle was something that one side, hoping for victory, offered, and the other, hoping for victory or fearing defeat, either accepted or declined. Once it was accepted, everything depended on what happened on the field itself; that is, on the tactics both sides might use. One might, indeed, go further. The logic could be taken as the explanation for the master's famous claim that, in war, the best *modus operandi* is always to be very strong—first in general and then at the decisive point—and that the decisive point in question always ought to be the enemy's army.[19] If this interpretation is accepted, it shows Clausewitz in a surprisingly backward-looking light. Here, however, we are concerned not with the way Clausewitz understood war as it was waged during the centuries before 1800, but with the manner in which it developed after that date.

ENTER 'THE GOD OF WAR'

To bring about a revolution in military affairs, two things are normally needed: an objective development that will make it possible, and a man who will seize that development by the horns, ride it, and direct it. In the last decade of the eighteenth century, both things happened to coincide. Together, they produced a sea change in warfare that was to dominate the field until 1945 and whose consequences are still with us today.

Nowadays, perhaps because so many people in the humanities and the social sciences have developed an inferiority complex vis-à-vis their colleagues in the natural sciences, there is a tendency to assume that all-important developments are, essentially, technological ones.[20] Whether this idea is broadly correct—whether, for example, Rome's victories over Carthage and the Hellenistic kingdoms can really be attributed to technological superiority—will not be disputed here. Suffice it to say that, referring to the period around 1800 in which we are interested here, it is definitely *not* correct. It is *not* correct that military technology made any great strides between the end of the Seven Years War in 1756 (perhaps, the end of the War of the Spanish Succession in 1714) and the outbreak of the French Revolutionary Wars; for example, in 1815, the British 'Brown Bess' musket had been in service for a hundred years. Nor is it true that Napoleon's armies, whatever their other virtues, enjoyed any real technological advantage over their opponents.

To prove the last-named fact, it is enough to recall the way Napoleon, the future emperor, laying siege to Acre in 1799, commanded his troops to gather spent enemy cannon balls and bring them to general headquarters. Evidently, the artillery pieces of the 'progressive' French and of the 'backward' Turks were interchangeable. Similarly, in the wake of the victorious 1805 campaign against Austria, Napoleon incorporated the entire artillery park of his defeated enemy, lock, stock, and barrel. The next year, the muskets with which the Prussian army fought and lost the Battle of Jena were actually somewhat superior to their French counterparts. Later, the emperor used captured ones to equip the troops he raised in Poland. At the time when he was finally sent to Saint Helena in 1815, the Industrial Revolution, while in full swing, had not yet reached the battlefield. Most of the important technological developments that were to revolutionize nineteenth-century warfare, such as percussion caps, rifled, breach-loading small arms and cannon, railroads, and telegraphs, let alone machine guns, were still in the future. Even as late as 1830, Clausewitz in his *magnum opus* does not mention a single one of them.

This is not to say there were no improvements of any kind. We have already referred to maps. Assisted by the telescope and by triangulation—starting in the second half of the seventeenth century, the former made it possible to carry out the latter over large areas—they underwent considerable development. Conversely, it was the lack of adequate maps that almost caused the French expeditionary force in the north-western Sinai to die of thirst in 1798 and contributed to Napoleon's defeat in Russia in 1812. Roads improved—Napoleon himself once estimated that he was able to cover long distances twice as fast as Caesar had—and so did carriages which were now equipped with springs. Perhaps the most important improvement was introduced during the French Revolution itself. The idea of building an optical telegraph that would use various kinds of signals to transmit messages is an ancient one and is mentioned by Polybios among others. It may even have been realized along the Roman *limes*, or border.[21] However, prior to the introduction of telescopes, such systems suffered from the disadvantage that the relay stations had to be built closely together, making them prohibitively expensive. Perhaps surprisingly, from the moment telescopes *did* become available to the time they were used for the purpose about a century and a half had to pass.

The net of optical telegraph lines that France started building in 1794 is known as the Chappe system, after the brothers who invented it.[22] It consisted of a series of towers, each so situated as to be visible from the ones adjacent to it on both sides. Some of the towers made use of existing structures, such as church spires, whereas others were specially constructed. Each tower was staffed by two men, a receiver and a transmitter. Each one was surmounted by a large movable beam with a shorter beam, also pivoted and movable, attached to each of its ends. The beams were attached to ropes, which were worked from inside the tower, enabling them to be set into 196 different positions representing different letters, words, or even entire phrases. Messages could be transmitted either *en clair* or in code, by day or by night (when the beams were illuminated). Depending on the weather and also on the length of each message (the shorter the message, the faster it could be transmitted), speeds of up to 250 miles per day could be achieved. At first, there was just one line that led from Paris towards the Pas de Calais, its function being to warn of a possible British landing. Under Napoleon, several others were built, radiating from the capital towards Germany and Italy.

In the summer of 1809, it was the telegraph that warned Napoleon that the Austrians had invaded Bavaria. This marked the opening move of the wars of the Fourth Coalition. It enabled the emperor, who was in Paris, to alert his forces, which were scattered over much of Germany, thus laying the foundation for what turned into perhaps the greatest strategic masterpiece of his entire career. We, however, are interested in the operational level; that is, the one where armies, or part of armies, manoeuvre against each other in the field. At this level, the optical telegraph, being immobile in space, had even less to offer than the electrical one that followed it. An attempt to organize mobile signalling towers mounted on carts came to nothing. All this goes far to show that, although there had been some technical progress, its extent was rather limited. It cannot really explain the invention of operational art that Napoleon wrought.

Napoleon himself was a phenomenon *sui generis*; one of those compact men who seem so energetic that, had an electric bulb been thrust into their mouth, it would have lit up. His nerves were outstanding—cases are on record when he spent the last hours before 'one of those tremendous battles on which the fate of countries, peoples and crowns depends', as he put it, fast asleep. By nature, he was an optimist, always believing in his own star and that things would turn out well in the end. A commander, indeed, cannot afford to behave in any other way. Combined with an encyclopedic memory for faces as well as considerable verbal and theatrical gifts, these qualities enabled him, time after time, to create a situation where men fought to the death for him, cheering.

On a campaign, this prodigy would spend the night wherever was convenient. Normally, this would be some country house that had been set apart for him ahead of time (complete with a willing woman to entertain him). If necessary, however, he would sleep in a tent or bivouac on the ground. He only slept four or five hours in twenty-four, in addition to sometimes taking a nap at convenient times. The days were filled with travel—as much as fifty miles per day, either by carriage or on horseback—during which he reviewed troops, carried out personal reconnaissance, met with subordinates, and occasionally issued an order. Serious staff work, the kind of work on which the course of the campaign and the fate of the army depended, was done in the evenings and early in the mornings. These were the times when maps were laid out, messages received, and orders dictated, often to four secretaries trying to keep up at once.

Would operational art have seen the light of day even without Napoleon? Given the other factors that were involved, on which more presently, the answer is almost certainly yes. Would it have done so in the same form and, above all, with the same force? The answer is almost certainly no. To understand the man, it is perhaps best to read his letters in general and his military ones in particular. They are written in fairly simple, often extremely colourful, if sometimes somewhat ungrammatical, French. Sometimes they go into fairly great, sometimes even excessive, detail; on other occasions, they are exceedingly short and to the point, telling subordinates what to do and leaving the rest to them. Invariably, they are infused with a sense of urgency and dynamism that are *sans pareil.* There are no lengthy theoretical expositions, often not even numbered paragraphs. To peruse them, to understand them, and to appreciate the enormous powers of memory and concentration on which they are based, is to sense oneself in the presence of perhaps the most competent person who ever lived.

THE GREATEST ARMY ON EARTH

While certain technological developments were indispensable in forming the background to operational warfare, the *effective* cause which made that warfare both possible and necessary, and which was the one on which Napoleon seized, was the growth in the size of armies. We have already noted that, during the eighteenth century, it was considered beyond any man's capability to command more than 50,000 men or so. Comparing theory with reality, we find that some armies were larger than this; at Malplaquet, in 1709, the allies had 86,000 men, the French 75,000. This, however, was exceptional. Though subsequent eighteenth-century battlefields occasionally saw armies numbering 60,000 men, almost a century had to pass until forces of this size were again assembled.

For about a century and a half before 1789, the armies of the *ancien regime* consisted of long-serving professionals, which meant that they remained relatively small. By contrast, the French Revolution brought into being the *levée en masse*—the first time anything similar had been seen in Europe for about a thousand years. Neither the feudal lords of the Middle Ages, nor the Italian city states, nor the absolute monarchies that dominated the continent from about 1500 on had used anything of the kind. Conscripted at the age of nineteen, the number of men under arms underwent a spectacular increase. By 1798, France, whose forces were being organized by Lazare Carnot, had approximately 800,000 of them. Though it took time, others were forced to follow. From about 1805 on, 200,000 men operating in a single theatre of war were nothing unusual, and by 1812 Napoleon even mustered 600,000 for his Russian campaign, and this apart from the forces needed to garrison Germany and hold down Spain.

If only for logistic reasons, such forces could no longer be concentrated along narrow fronts as their predecessors had been. If only because they spread out, the old methods whereby the bulk of them came under the direct control of the commander-in-chief who directed them by way of messengers or else by acoustical and visual means, such as bugles, drums, flags, and standards, were no longer appropriate. A method had to be found, and urgently found, by which they could spread out *and* continue to operate under a unified, central direction—without, that is, becoming 'detached' as they used to. Ultimately, that method was found in the *corps d'armée* system. The more time passes and the better positioned we are to appreciate the nature of the change, the more apparent its importance becomes not merely to Napoleonic warfare but to everything that followed.

Considering how simple the idea is, the fact that it took so long to be implemented appears surprising. Judging by archaeological evidence and by what we know of tribal warfare, even during the Stone Age, many war parties were not homogenous. Some braves carried edged weapons—knives, spears, and the like—others, bows, others still slings. By the end of the second millennium BC, heavy infantry, light infantry, heavy cavalry, light cavalry, and many intermediate types were all in existence. Shortly after 400 BC, artillery, in the form of torsion-operated engines, some of which were light and mobile enough to be used not merely during siege warfare but in the field,[23] was added. From that time on, arguably no further change took place for over 2,000 years. Yet, with the exception of the Roman legions, which *did* comprise different kinds of units armed with different kinds of weapons, it does not seem to have occurred to anybody to combine the various arms under a single unified headquarters. And even the legions were mainly administrative formations, not tactical ones.

Commanders from Alexander in the fourth-century BC to Scipio in the third-century BC all the way to Richard the Lionheart in the twelfth-century AD certainly understood combined-arms warfare and often engaged in it. So did Prince Maurice and Gustavus Adolphus in the seventeenth century and Marlborough and Frederick the Great in the eighteenth century. One only has to think of the way in which, in countless Hellenistic battles, the cavalry, acting as the hammer in the commander's hand, was used to press the enemy against the anvil in the form of the infantry. Perhaps the real reason why combined formations suitable for waging such warfare were not created at a much earlier date was social. Since the men brought along their own arms, and since the kind of arms they brought often reflected class differences, those of them who were mounted and carried the more expensive weapons may well have refused to serve with, or under, their less well-to-do comrades. However that may be, the troops of each arm were organized in their own units—regiments of infantry, squadrons of cavalry, batteries of artillery, and so on.

After 1650 or so, when things became more institutionalized, each unit formed part of its respective arm. Each came under its own commander who was himself commissioned into the arm in question. There, things rested until the eve of battle itself. At that point, the commander-in-chief worked out the *ordre de battaile* and assembled his subordinates to explain it to them. A 'general'—meaning, originally, an officer senior enough not to be tied to one arm only—would be put in charge of units of different kinds constituting the right wing, the left wing, the reserve, and so on. However, the commands in question were not intended to be permanent. When the battle was over, they were dissolved almost immediately so that things reverted to their normal state.

The Marshal de Saxe in his *Reveries on the Art of War*, which were written in 1732, played with the idea of re-establishing 'legions' more or less on the Roman model. Each one was to be 'furnished with everything that can be required to fortify itself', and each one was to come with its own permanent commander and headquarters as a way to facilitate command and control. Hence, 'if the commander in chief . . . wants to occupy a post, to obstruct the enemy in their projects, or in a hundred different situations which are found in war, he has only to order a particular legion to march'.[24] However, nothing seems to have come out of it. In any case, Saxe's work remained unpublished for twenty-five years after his death, when it was rescued from oblivion.

Apparently, the first to experiment with permanent formations combining the various arms was the Duc de Broglie during the Seven Years War in Germany. Yet, the real changes in organization that opened the door to operational warfare, as it were, were only made by the National Assembly in 1794. Even so, they remained incomplete. Here, we shall not trace developments in detail, and, indeed, this is a field on which much research remains to be done. Suffice it to say that, in 1805, the first consul, as Napoleon then was, was experimenting with them;[25] five years later, the system had reached maturity.

At the heart of the new system stood the *corps d'armée*, a permanent formation made up of all three arms: that is, infantry, cavalry, and artillery. It was provided with its own engineering service, intelligence service (each marshal, or corps commander, had at his disposal a fund on which he could draw to engage spies), medical service, and, of course, headquarters. That headquarters, in turn, came complete with the necessary staff officers, secretarial personnel, messengers (everything still depended on messengers, who were always in short supply; as a result, commanders often 'borrowed' each other's messengers), and the like. Depending on the number of divisions it contained—the divisions themselves were miniature corps—normally each corps was 20,000 to 30,000 men strong. Here and there, even larger ones, comprising as many as 40,000 men, were created. Simply by adding or detaching divisions, the corps could be adapted to the mission at hand.

Perhaps most important of all, the corps were roughly *interchangeable*. As a result, they were able to step into each other's shoes without any need for changes in organization. Previously, waging combined-arms warfare meant that units of each arm had to be carefully pre-positioned before, besides, and behind each other, so they could play their allocated role in the commander's plan. An excellent example is the Battle of Arsouf in 1189, where Richard the Lionheart personally placed each of his cavalry and infantry units. Should that plan go wrong, or should troops of the various arms be separated from each other (as, e.g., was always happening during the battles that the Hellenistic monarchs fought against the Romans, and as also happened at Hattin in 1187), disaster would stare the commander in the face. Now, with every corps able to take over from every other almost at a moment's notice and wage combined-arms warfare in turn, such planning became unnecessary. The result was that, even as the width of the front across which the army operated grew, that army also made vast gains in flexibility.

Gone were the days when vanguards, flank guards, rearguards, wings, reserves, and the like had to be put together each time there was a mission to be accomplished or an engagement fought. Gone, too, were the days when such bodies of troops, lacking a combination of the three arms, a permanent headquarters, and the necessary services, were only able to look after themselves to a very limited extent and, therefore, had to be kept fairly close to general headquarters so as to submit their reports and receive their orders. Instead, contemporary wisdom, as exemplified by Clausewitz himself, considered that each corps should be able to fight independently, even when outnumbered two or three to one, for long enough to be stationed a day's march away from its neighbour.[26] As a result, the width of the front across which an army could safely operate went up as if by a stroke of magic, from about four miles to several times that number.

Like Athene leaping out of Zeus' head, all these developments came together for the first time in the campaign of 1805; as they did so, the world held its breath. On this occasion, the *Grande Armée*, as it was known, numbered approximately 170,000 men. Herodotus' mythological 1,500,000 Persian soldiers apart, this was probably the largest number that had been brought together for a single campaign in history until that time. They were divided into seven corps, each with its own Roman number, though, in practice, there was always a tendency to call each corps after its commander. Having arrived at their jumping-off positions on the Rhine—some of the corps came from Boulogne, where they had been preparing to invade England, whereas others came from the Netherlands—they stretched from Koblenz in the north all the way to Freiburg in the south. The distance between the wings was about 200 miles. However, since just one corps was deployed south of Strasbourg, where it acted as a decoy, the average distance between the six remaining ones amounted to twenty-five miles—exactly as Clausewitz recommended. Crossing the Rhine on 25–6 September, each corps marched by a separate road and was assigned a foraging area to its left.[27] Later, as the campaign unfolded, geographical realities and operational requirements caused both the distance between the corps and the front as a whole to become progressively smaller.

From the description so far, one might think that the *Grande Armée*, propelled by the emperor's orders as if by a huge spring, simply formed a phalanx vastly larger than, but not essentially different from, anything that had been conceived from the time of Leuctra (371 BC) on. That is the truth, but it is only a half-truth. What is really impressive about the campaign is both the good order with which it proceeded *and* its flexibility—the way in which the corps kept changing roles with each other as operations unfolded. So important was this aspect of the matter that, in time, it became standard practice to judge the military power of a country by the number of corps it could field.

Now a corps acted as a vanguard, now as a pivot. Now it served as a flank guard in relation to the army as a whole, now as a rearguard. A corps might very well find itself acting as a hammer on one day, then serving as the anvil on the next. War itself became a question of managing time and space; as the Confederate commander Nathan Bedford allegedly put it at a later time, succinctly but not at all inaccurately, one had to 'gitting tha fustest with the mostest'. All this presupposed very good staff work and traffic control, or else the endless columns of marching men and the trains of guns and carriages that followed them would quickly become hopelessly entangled. It is a tribute to the *Grande Armée*, and to the new system of operational warfare that it invented and waged, that this control and this staff work were usually, though not invariably, achieved.

To illustrate how things worked out in practice, take the movements of the 7th Corps. Commanded by Marshal Joachim Murat, the emperor's brother-in-law, it differed from the rest in that it was made up mainly of cavalry. Originally, as the only one of the corps stationed south of Strasbourg, its role was to mount a demonstration in the Black Forest region. After all, as Freiburg's *Alte Franzosenweg* reminds visitors to this day, for centuries this had been the route that French armies took on their way to invade southern Germany. The trick worked, helping to explain why the Austrians remained at Ulm as if mesmerized, allowing themselves to be surrounded by the rest of the *Grande Armée* which was marching further to the north. Later, the corps started advancing east along the Danube Valley so as to form the anvil against which the Austrians at Ulm were pressed. Later, its mission was changed again. Now, it formed the vanguard, marching straight eastward along the Danube Valley until it reached, and entered, Vienna.

Or take the 3rd Corps. Its commander was Marshal Louis Nicolas Davout, who was probably the most capable of all Napoleon's subordinates and the only one whose grasp of operational warfare rivalled the emperor's own. During the first stage of the campaign, the one that culminated in Ulm, it joined the 2nd Corps in providing cover to the *Grande Armée*'s exposed northern flank against possible Prussian intervention. At Ulm itself, it formed the outer (easternmost) part of the ring that closed on 'the unfortunate General Mack'. Meanwhile, the 2nd Corps, having parted company with it, had gone to Munich, seventy-five miles to the east as the crow flies. There, its task was to wait for, and if necessary halt, an anticipated attack by Austria's Russian allies. Next, during the advance along the Danube towards Vienna, the 3rd Corps found itself in the vanguard directly behind Murat. Having followed the latter into the Austrian capital, it was left to garrison the city but did not remain there for long. On the night of 30 November–1 December, an imperial summons arrived, sending it on a thirty-six-hour, sixty-mile, march to Austerlitz, where it did, in fact, arrive in time to play a critical part in the battle.

Acting on the defence, a corps that ran into the enemy might call for assistance and hold out until it arrived. Acting on the offence, it could tie down the enemy until its neighbours received the call and converged on him. Either he would be forced to beat a hasty retreat, or else he would be threatened with annihilation. Most importantly of all, the system put Napoleon in a position where he was often able to accomplish what previous commanders only seldom succeeded in doing—namely, *force* the enemy to give battle at a time and place of his own choosing. The days when, to quote Clausewitz again, 'war [was] nothing but a duel on a large scale' were coming to an end. As Napoleon himself put it in a famous bulletin, 'it is said that the Emperor invented a new method of waging war, making use of the soldiers' legs instead of their muskets'.[28]

While operational warfare increased, siege warfare decreased—the two modes balanced one another like an elevator and the counterweight that is attached to the cables. From the beginning of history, a well-situated, well-constructed, and garrisoned and provisioned fortress or town had often been able to hold up an army for days, weeks, or even months. Cases when sieges lasted for years are on record. Especially during the early modern age, siege warfare, pitting itself against the large numbers of powerful fortresses by which Europe was covered, played just as important a role in war as battles did. The advent of the new system of war, together with the vast armies on which it ultimately rested, changed this situation. Fronts as wide as the ones on which Napoleon and, not long after, his opponents deployed meant that practically any fortress could be bypassed and left behind. In a sense, the relationship between field- and siege warfare was inverted. From the time of the biblical Joshua to that of Frederick the Great, a country could not be said to be truly conquered as long as its fortresses still held out. Now, to the contrary, most fortresses were only taken after the occupation and as a result of it. From the beginning of his career, Napoleon, who at one point boasted of having commanded in sixty *battailles rangées*, only conducted four sieges.

The emperor's formidable personality apart, the capstone that held the entire system together was the imperial headquarters. Its composition and functioning have been described many times;[29] here, we shall limit ourselves to essentials. It was made up of three parts with only the emperor himself to link them. They were, first, the Maison, an ancient institution taken over from royal times, the État Major de l'Armée, and an administrative headquarters. The Maison, divided into a cabinet, a secretariat, a statistical bureau, and a topographical bureau, was where all intelligence reports arrived and were put in a form suitable for the emperor's scrutiny (sometimes, however, he would cut through the organization, going on reconnaissance or personally interrogating prisoners himself). It was there, too, that information about all subordinate formations was stored and kept up to date, and the maps needed for planning the campaign prepared.

The État Major received the corps' daily and periodical situation reports, and presented them to the emperor. Its chief, Berthier, helped him work out his next moves, translated them into detailed orders (normally, the corps commander could expect to receive two messages: a brief, often personal, one from Napoleon and another from Berthier which amplified it), and made sure that they reached the corps. Especially at night, which was when much of the real work of planning and commanding was done, both these organizations were always located close to the emperor himself. By contrast, the administrative headquarters, which was responsible for such matters as reinforcements, prisoners, the wounded, and the administration (read, exploitation) of the theatre of war, might be located dozens, even hundreds, of miles to the rear; while Napoleon recognized the need for military administrators, he did not like them and felt they were 'repugnant'.[30]

One part of the command system to which I myself have drawn attention in the past,[31] and whose importance cannot be overestimated, was the 'directed telescope'. In fact, there was not one 'telescope' but two. One consisted of eight to twelve *adjutants genereaux*, senior officers with the rank of colonel or brigadier. The other, of about double that number of *officiers d'ordonance*, intelligent captains whom the emperor once defined as 'jeuns gens qu'on peut faire courir' ('young men whom one can make run').[32] Both groups were used to cut through the mass of information regularly passed upward by the subordinate units, which by the nature of things tended to become standardized and highly profiled. Both enabled Napoleon to obtain what information he needed at the time he needed it, while, at the same time, decreasing his dependence on the general staff. The difference between the two groups was that the *adjutants*, as senior personnel, were sent on missions that required independent judgement, including the compilation of reports on the corps and their *prima donna* commanders, the marshals. By contrast, the *officiers* were used to gather information on more limited, though scarcely less important, matters, such as the state of roads, bridges, fortresses, and so on.

As Plato wrote in the *Republic* around 420 BC, to describe a dead animal is one thing, to gain an idea of the harmonious way in which all its parts work together, another. By 1805, the elements of the system that Saxe had 'dreamt' about, that de Broglie (along with several others) had experimented with, that the national assembly developed, and that Napoleon perfected were in place. The outcome was the spectacular campaign culminating in the so-called Three Emperors' Battle at Austerlitz on 2 December 1805. To see how things worked out in practice, I have selected the 1806 campaign against Prussia.

A NEW METHOD OF MAKING WAR[33]

After 1792–3, when its army invaded France as part of the First Coalition and was repulsed at Valmy, Prussia took no further part in the French Revolutionary and Napoleonic Wars. Still, friction between the two countries, the one ruled by Napoleon and the other by Frederick William III (reigned 1797–1840), was not lacking. In 1805, on his way to fight the Austrians, Napoleon had Bernadotte's corps cross the Prussian territory of Ansbach without so much as asking for permission. The next year, wishing to make peace with England, he dangled Hanover before the eyes of the Court of St James. Offended by this, as well as by Napoleon's insistence that it cede some territory so as to create principalities for Murat and Berthier, Prussia prepared to go to war.

As far as Napoleon was concerned, preparations got under way at the end of August. Working at the Palace of St. Cloud, he pored over his maps (he had a hand-painted, 1:100,000 set that covered the whole of Europe, a rare achievement for those days). Within days, he had formed a preliminary plan for concentrating the *Grande Armée* at Bamberg. Berthier, who was not yet aware of the secret, was asked to present a comprehensive report on the state of the army. Similar reports, concerning munitions and supplies, were demanded of Dejean. Since the French army had never taken this particular route when fighting in Germany, not much information was available on towns, villages, rivers, fortresses, and the like. Hence, officers of the statistical bureau were sent to visit the French embassies at Leipzig and Berlin, travelling slowly to explore the roads that led through the Frankenwald and Saxony towards Prussia further north. Indeed, as long as the campaign lasted, Napoleon was constantly asking the marshals to present him with any piece of topographical information that might prove useful to him.

On 10 September, Marshal Bessieres, who commanded the Imperial Guard, was ordered to prepare his force for the field.[34] Precautionary orders also went out for three other corps to be concentrated at Würzburg as soon as the news of a Prussian declaration of war arrived. On 18 September, the day when Napoleon learnt that Prussia had declared war and invaded Saxony (the news had taken five days to cover the 600 miles from Berlin to Paris), the iron dice were cast. Three days later, informed by Berthier that the Prussians, moving faster than expected, had crossed the Elbe and were marching south-west towards Hof and Hanover, he departed for Mainz, on the river Rhine, which at that time marked the frontier between France and Germany. Having taken leave of the empress there, on 2 October, he reached Würzburg, the town he had designated as the westernmost point of the front behind which the *Grande Armée* was to assemble. As he arrived, Murat, having received news from his cavalry patrols operating in Saxony, informed him that he had located the 150,000-strong Prussian army at Erfurt.[35]

By this time, Napoleon had made up his mind as to the way he wanted the campaign to develop. In a letter to his brother, King Louis of Holland, he explained:

> It is my intention to concentrate all my forces on my extreme right, leaving all the country between the Rhine and Bamberg completely uncovered in such a way as to have almost 200,000 men united in the battlefield. If the enemy [assumed to be moving slowly west from Erfurt] sends detachments into the area between Mainz and Bamberg I shall not be bothered, since my line of communications goes back to Forchheim, which is a little fortress close to Würzburg. . . . [The enemy, who does not know this] believes my left to be on the Rhine and my right on the Bohemian border, and that my line of operations is thus parallel to my front. He may therefore try to attack my left, in which case I shall throw him into the Rhine.[36]

He also took the opportunity to review the *Grande Armée*, 180,000 men divided into eight numbered corps, who were now well on their way to the pre-selected starting positions.

On their side, the Prussians were equally clueless to what their enemy was planning to do. To a large extent, this was because of the French cavalry patrols which covered their army's exposed northern flank, hiding its movements and preventing any news of them from leaking out. But whereas the French, with their *corps d'armée* organization, felt equal to any eventuality and were developing a prodigious activity, the Prussians tarried and hesitated. For thirteen days, they milled about at Erfurt, holding councils of war and waiting for the last 'detachment' to join them, so they could give battle. They expected the emperor to advance from the west; not only was it the shortest road to Berlin, but it was the one Marshal Soubisse, on his way to the great French defeat at Rossbach, had taken in 1757. If Clausewitz, who had access to the archives, may be believed, so strong was the obstacle presented by the river Saale that the thought that he might come for them from that direction never entered the Prussians' heads.[37] Fearful of making a move in any direction lest the boa constrictor come and catch them, according to Hermann von Boyen, an eyewitness who was later to become his country's minister of war, they busied themselves with minor matters of protocol.[38]

By 5 October, the emperor had completed his dispositions and the campaign proper got under way. The *Grande Armée* was launched forward, marching in a general north-east-north direction along three separate roads. The 4th Corps (Soult), followed by the 6th (Ney) and another formation consisting of 10,000 Bavarian allies, made up the right. In the centre, 1st Corps (Bernadotte) led the way with 3rd (Davout), a heavy cavalry corps, and the Guard (Lefebvre), which formed the general reserve, following. The left consisted of the 5th Corps (Lannes) and, behind it, the 7th (Augereau); he himself, along with several thousand men comprising the Maison, the État Major, and an escort, marched with Bernadotte in the centre. By Napoleon's normal standards, the distance between the army's wings was rather small, extending over no more than sixty miles from Schweinfurt to Bayreuth with Bamberg almost exactly in the centre. Still, this was *fifteen times* as much as Frederick the Great had recommended forty years earlier. As had happened in the previous year, later during the campaign the figure went down. Overcrowding meant that the troops had to carry along more supplies than usual. In the sparsely populated Frankenwald, there could be no question of feeding the army by the usual method of requisitioning; however, overcrowding was made inevitable by the nature of the country and by the need to keep Austria neutral by scrupulously staying away from the border between Franconia and Bohemia. At the head of each column rode a cavalry brigade that screened its moves, marked the roads, and explored the country ahead.

Even now the emperor, while informed of the enemy's whereabouts, still had no idea of what he might do next. Mainly, this was because King Frederick III, who was present, and the Duke of Brunswick, the 80-year-old veteran of the Seven Years War who was serving as his commander-in-chief, had not yet made up their minds on how to pursue the campaign. As long as they remained inside the Frankenwald, the French columns, though more or less out of touch with each other, were safe. Partly for this reason, partly because of the paucity of traverse communications, very few orders went out to the marshals during this period. The moment of real danger came when they debouched from the forest. Given the latest reports concerning the Prussian dispositions, this was especially true of Lannes' corps forming the vanguard of the column on the left. Who knew what might be waiting for him there? To guard against this danger, Napoleon planned the corps' movements in such a way that, marching in parallel, they should do so roughly at the same time. To Soult, who was leading the other wing, he wrote: 'once at Hof [on the other side of the Frankenwald], your first concern is to establish communication with Lobenstein, Ebersdorf, and Schleiz'.[39] All of these were places where the *Grande Armée* had to pass and where the enemy, assuming he had finally understood what was going on, might present himself to oppose it.

In the event, the cavalry brigade and Lannes' corps on the left *did* come under enemy attack at the time when, tired after weeks of almost non-stop marching and out of touch with the imperial headquarters, they emerged from the forest at Saalfeld. The emperor, who was still inside it, could hear the ensuing cannonade; however, since it did not last for very long, he did not allow it to perturb him.[40] On 9 October, with the *Grande Armée* now operating on Saxon territory, the centre column, with Murat at its head, met a Prussian detachment at Schleiz. He defeated it, making it fall back, and sent back news to Napoleon who was marching directly behind him at Ebersdorf.

Throughout these days, the riddle of where the Prussian army was, and, even more so, what its intentions were, remained unsolved. It is true that, on paper, the French enjoyed a small numerical advantage over their enemy. However, they were now far away from their bases at Bamberg and even further from their starting positions on the Rhine. Some of Napoleon's corps, notably the Guard, were still dozens of miles behind, desperately trying to catch up. By contrast, the Prussians were already concentrated and operating not far from their own border. To use the terminology developed by the greatest contemporary expert, Antoine Jomini,[41] the emperor only had one possible line of retreat open to him. Had he been forced to take it, he would have been pressed against the Saale and might have been annihilated; not so the Prussians who had two or three. A lesser commander less certain of his troops' ability to fight, even if outnumbered, might have allowed these facts to delay operations or even bring them to a temporary halt until the situation clarified itself. Not so, of course, in this case.

The news of the engagement at Schleiz, which was brought to Napoleon by one of his senior *adjutants genereaux*, clarified the situation to a certain extent. From it, as well as some prisoners' reports that were attached to it, he was finally able to cobble together what he thought was a coherent estimate of where the enemy was, and what he was up to. To Soult, who was leading the right wing and thus almost as likely to come under Prussian attack as Lannes had been, he wrote:

> It seems clear to me that the Prussians were planning to attack; their left was going to debouch through Jena, Saalfeld, and Coburg, commanded by Prince Louis at Saalfeld. The other column was going to proceed via Meiningen and Fulda. The Prussians being located further to the west than had been anticipated, it thus seems you have nothing between you [at Plauen] and Dresden, perhaps not even 10,000 men.

To this missive, which was written at 08.00 hours on 10 October, he appended another:

I have just received your dispatch of 9 October, 18.00 hours [as the crow flies the distance between Plauen and Ebersdorf is less than twenty miles, which gives us an idea of how fast, or how slow, news travelled in those days]. . . . The news that 1,000 Prussians are retreating from Plauen to Gera leaves no doubt in my mind that Gera is the meeting point selected by the enemy. I doubt whether they can concentrate there before I get there first. I hope that the day will bring information that will give me a better idea of their plans.[42]

Yet, at this time, he had not yet re-established communications with two out of his eight corps operating on the left.

The day passed without further enemy news. 'Once we arrive at Gera', Napoleon wrote to Soult at 18.00 hours, 'things will clarify themselves'.[43] Meanwhile, acting on the little information he had, he issued a series of orders that would have led to the concentration of all his forces in a semicircle around Gera by noon on 11 October. This proved to be a blow in the air; when Murat's cavalry, closely followed by Bernadotte's corps, entered Gera in the morning, it found the place empty. Only around midnight did two other reports arrive. One, coming from Soult, said that the enemy had left Gera (in fact, only small forces had taken up positions there; the bulk of their army was between Erfurt and Jena, much further to the west). The other, written by Murat, gave a more correct picture by explaining that a captured Saxon officer had placed the king of Prussia with 200,000 men at Erfurt. Clearly, Brunswick was not going to exploit the opportunity and offer battle as far south as Napoleon had feared. For all he knew, the Prussians might be preparing to retreat north, in the direction of Magdeburg, or east, towards Dresden: wrong again. In fact, the Prussians had been as much in the dark as he had been, perhaps more so. On 10 October, they had only just become alerted to the danger to their southern (left) flank. They were forced to give up whatever plan they may have had to attack west towards Gotha, but there still could be no question of a general retreat.[44]

At this point, based solely on two reports and a hurried glance at the map, the great manoeuvre that was to place the *Grande Armée* across the Prussian communications and force Brunswick to give battle with his front inverted got under way. Between 02.30 and 06.00 hours on 12 October, a series of curt orders went out to the marshals. While Napoleon personally wrote to those in the forefront of the advance, he left it to Berthier to inform the rest. On average, the orders moved at 5.6 miles an hour,[45] a rather slow pace that was probably a result of the fact that they were travelling at night over unfamiliar terrain. What *is* impressive, and seems to confirm everything said about the *corps d'armée* system so far, is the speed with which they were carried out. Again, on average, just two hours passed from the moment each one was received to the moment execution began. For all the electronic marvels at its disposal, no modern force of similar size could have done better and a great many do very much worse.

Following its orders, the entire *Grande Armée* swung to the north-east. Proceeding, this time, from the army's left wing to its right, Lannes was ordered to march directly north-east towards Jena with Augereau following him as far as Khala. In the centre, Murat was to proceed to Zeitz, on the road to Dresden. Bernadotte and Davout, who previously had been marching right behind Murat, were to overtake him and march all the way to Naumburg and Auerstadt. There, turning about and facing west, they would form the army's new right (northern) flank. Finally, Soult and Ney, marching right across Murat's, Bernadotte's, and Davout's communications, were to approach Jena from the east, even as Lannes was advancing towards it from the south. Again, one can only admire the quality of the staff work and traffic discipline that went into these orders and made the complicated moves possible. Except for Bernadotte, whose 1st Corps got lost at Naumburg and was not heard of again until after the Prussian army had been brought to battle and destroyed, everything went like clockwork.

This is not the place to analyse the double battle of Jena–Auerstadt, a subject that belongs more to tactics than to operational art. Suffice it to say that, contrary to the opinion of most subsequent historians, the Prussian infantry—so often described as consisting of yokels forcibly enlisted and kept in place by means of the knout and the lash—stood its ground and fought magnificently. Drilled until they could perform with machine-like precision, they loaded and fired and loaded and fired until they literally dropped; in the whole world, probably no troops could have done more.[46] If there was a failure of fighting spirit on the Prussian side, it affected the officers and not the famous *Kantonisten*. An examination of the respective numbers of both groups who were killed in the two battles will confirm this point.[47] Nor was Napoleon's victory due to any superior information at his disposal. In fact, the problems with information, concerning both the enemy and the whereabouts of the various French corps and their activities, that had bedevilled the campaign right from the beginning still continued.

Remarkable as it sounds, when the Battle of Jena ended in victory early in the evening of 14 October, the emperor *still* had no idea what was going on. Throughout the day, he had simply forgotten about several of his own corps, neither sending orders to them nor receiving their reports. Instead of commanding the campaign, he took charge of the battle. If he had once written that each one of his marshals thought that the point where *he* was operating was the most important of all, now he himself was guilty of the same fault. Much worse still, the information at his disposal, which was two days old, led him to think that the forces he had just defeated constituted the main Prussian army. In fact, they were no more than a flank guard with 60,000 men; meanwhile, the main Prussian force, numbering around 100,000, was situated further north-east and remained untouched by the battle. When an orderly, sent by Davout, informed Napoleon that the 3rd Corps had just defeated the Prussians at Auerstadt, he snapped back that 'your marshal must be seeing double today'.[48]

CONCLUSIONS: THE NEW METHOD UNLEASHED

Revolutions in military affairs are tremendous events. Like bursting supernovae, they light up the sky; the particular revolution we are discussing here enabled one ruler/commander, Napoleon, and one country, France, to overrun practically the whole of Europe within a few short years. But whereas supernovae disappear when their fuel runs out, revolutions in military affairs follow a different course. They end, if they ever do, when other nations, armed forces, and commanders wake up to the possibilities they open.[49] To use the language of Thomas Kuhn in *The Structure of Scientific Revolutions*, each 'revolution' is succeeded by a period of 'normal' warfare. But not before it has left indelible traces behind it, forcing anybody who comes after it to adapt to it.

As noted above, the particular revolution with which we are concerned here, and which led to the emergence of 'operational' warfare, owed very little to technological factors. No great and important inventions preceded it. Personally, Napoleon tended to be on the conservative side, technologically speaking. He did away with the French balloon units, and he also refused to subsidize the American inventor of the submarine and the steamboat, Robert Fulton. Instead, the revolution was made possible by the development of three interrelated institutions that contradicted one another in some ways but complemented one another in others. The first was the *corps d'armée* system, which began to develop from the 1760s on, until, in 1805, it burst on an unsuspecting world. The second was the imperial headquarters; the third, which until two and a half decades ago had been largely ignored by the literature, was the 'directed telescope'.

The corps *d'armée system*, by creating formations that were both able to look after themselves for a time and interchangeable, led to a sharp decrease in the amount of information that, per mile of front and per manoeuvre planned or executed, armies needed in order to move, operate, and engage the enemy. The imperial headquarters, crowned by the emperor's own formidable intellect, allowed the information that operations *did* require to be processed in an efficient and timely, if not always orderly, manner. The 'directed telescope' provided the link between the two, acting as the emperor's eyes and ears both when it came to obtaining information about the enemy and the environment and when it was a question of finding out what his own forces were up to. Even more importantly, it prevented the emperor from becoming the prisoner of his own general staff. Whereas the first of these three elements minimized the need for information, the second and the third were responsible for processing and transmitting that part of it which was still needed. The outcome was a vast increase, indeed, almost an explosion, in the speed, extent, range, and flexibility of military operations. To the point where, for the first time in history, it often became possible to compel an enemy to give battle, even if there were no borders or natural obstacles against which he could be forced.

Subsequent historians have often accused Napoleon of over-centralization, claiming that he did not share his plans with any of his subordinates and treated them almost like puppets on a string. The charge is not entirely unfounded. Though the emperor was the first important commander in history to employ a chief of staff in the modern manner, Berthier was very far from being his coequal partner. Besides, he controlled neither the Maison nor the administrative headquarters where much of the work of directing the *Grande Armée* and looking after its needs was done. He was excellent in caring about a myriad of details, but totally unfit for operational command; 'a goose whom I have turned into an eagle of sorts', was Napoleon's own cruel, but not unjust, description of him. While some of the marshals, Soult in particular, were closer to the emperor than others, almost as long as the campaign lasted none of them was given full insight into their master's plans. Such an insight was granted only to King Louis of Holland, and then at a very early stage when the emperor still had no idea where in Germany the clash of arms would take place. Presumably, he thought that, since the king remained safely in his palace in Holland, letting him in on the secret could do no harm.

On the other hand, in making this assessment, historians have been guilty of confusing Napoleon's time with their own—of looking at things through the wrong end of the field glasses, so to speak. Whether through their work or through personal experience, those historians have long been familiar with combined-arms formations and the staffs that make them work. Not so Napoleon who, although he was not entirely without forerunners, had to create them almost *ex novo*. As he was well aware and occasionally said, the machine that Berthier ran was incomparably larger and more complicated than anything ever seen in history until that time. Taking into account the size of the formations the marshals led and the distances at which they operated from the imperial headquarters, they were given greater independence, and carried greater responsibilities, than almost any of their predecessors. Certainly, they were not without their shortcomings, idiosyncrasies, and petty jealousies. A very good example comes from the Jena campaign itself. At Auerstadt, Bernadotte, taking offence at not being given separate orders and being told to follow in Davout's wake, sulked and delayed. The result was the near destruction of the 3rd French corps by the Prussians. Nevertheless, on the whole, they served their master as well as any similar group of men in history did.

As this episode and many similar ones show, the system was far from perfect—what machine, made of fallible human parts, operating against an enemy who is free to act as he sees fit, and engaged in the most stressful human activity of all, ever was? Quite a number of the shortcomings were the emperor's own fault. Though he was undoubtedly a genius, throughout the campaigns he seems to have sent out his orders with no kind of system whatsoever. He personally analysed bits and pieces of intelligence as they came in and responded to them, wrote to whomever he thought necessary at that moment, put into his messages whatever part of his plan he thought fit, and informed only those others whose names happened to occur to him at that particular time.

Particularly in view of the slow pace at which they travelled, greater attention could have been paid to the sequence in which orders were written and sent so as to make sure that all the marshals should get theirs on time. Nor did Napoleon, working incessantly, always distinguish between operational command and attention to all kinds of administrative and logistic details; had he done so, he would have been able to concentrate on the former and leave more of the latter to his subordinates, especially Berthier and Dejean. Further savings could have been made, and errors avoided, by systematically providing Berthier and the État

Major with a comprehensive order valid for all the corps. This done, they could have used his directive as a basis for writing to each marshal separately. As it was, the corps often received double and sometimes conflicting orders, one from Napoleon and the other from Berthier. Indeed, it was precisely the function of the latter, struggling manfully, to try and put some kind of order in this; usually, he succeeded well enough for things to proceed, but sometimes he did not.

With this we come to the last, and most important, point. Well matched against his opponents, technologically speaking, Napoleon's secret in bringing about operational warfare was not that he had at his disposal more, or better, information than those opponents did. Instead, it is found in the fact that, thanks to the three above-mentioned institutions and the way he made them work together, he and the *Grande Armée* were able to function *without* having such information. In fact, it would hardly be an exaggeration to say that the ability to do so is the supreme test by which any military organization must ultimately be measured. The following poem, attributed to the Chinese sage Lao Tzu ('the Old Master', who probably lived in the sixth-century BC), sums up the matter as well as anybody can:

> Thirty spokes are joined together in a wheel,
> but it is the center hole that allows the wheel to function.
> We mold clay into a pot,
> but it is the emptiness inside that makes the vessel useful.
> We fashion wood for a house,
> but it is the emptiness inside that makes it livable.
> We work with the substantial,
> but the emptiness is what we use.[50]

NOTES

1. On the way Alexander, for example, did these things; see D. W. Engels, 'Alexander's Intelligence System', *Classical Quarterly*, 74, 2, 1980, 327–40.
2. For the way the Romans, for example, used all these sources, see N. J. E. Austin and M. B. Rankov, *Exploratio: Military and Political Intelligence in the Roman World from the Second Punic War to the Battle of Adrianople* (London: Routledge, 1995), 64–85.
3. *Bellum Civile* (London: Heinemann, Loeb Classical Library, 1963), III. 36.1.
4. Ibid., 45.
5. *Bellum Africanum* (London: Heinemann, Loeb Classical Library, 1946), 12.
6. Joshua 8:15.
7. On such systems, see the Book of Esther, 3:13, 8:10, 8:14; Herodotus, *The Histories* (London: Heinemann, Loeb Classical Library, 1961–6), viii. 98; Xenopohon, *Cyropaedia* (London: Heinemann, Loeb Classical Library, 1949), 6.17; Procopius, *Anecdota* (London: Heinemann, Loeb Classical Library, 1953–4); H. C. Bräuer, 'Die Entwicklung des Nachrichtenverkehrs: Eigenarten, Mittel und Organisation der Nachrichtenbeförderung', Diss. (Friedrich-Alexander-Universität, Nürnberg, 1957), 56ff.; and A. M. Ramsay, 'The Speed of the Roman Imperial Post', *Journal of Roman Studies*, 15, 1929, 60–74.

8. L. von M., 'Review of *Über der Einfluss der Eisenbahnen und Telegraphen auf die Kriegsoperationen*', *Österreichische Militärische Zeitschrift*, ii, 1861, 150–4.
9. Y. Harari, 'Inter-Frontal Cooperation in the Fourteenth Century and Edward's 1346 Campaign', *War in History*, 6, 1999, 379–95.
10. Ibid., 386.
11. See Martin van Creveld, *Command in War* (Cambridge, MA: Harvard University Press, 1985), 25–6.
12. Reproduced in G. Parker, *The Army of Flanders and the Spanish Road, 1567–1659* (Cambridge: Cambridge University Press, 1972), 104.
13. On this, see C. Adams and R. Laurence, *Travel and Geography in the Roman Empire* (London: Taylor and Francis, 2007); P. Janni, *La Mappa e Il periplo: Cartografia antica e spazio odologico* (Rome: Giorgio Bretschneider, 1984).
14. Frederick the Great, *Militärische Schriften*, ed. G. B. Holz (Berlin: Mittler, 1913), chapter 4.
15. Ibid., chapter 18.
16. See W. Erfurt, *Der Vernichtungssieg. Eine Studie über das Zusammenwirken getrennter Heeresteile* (Berlin: Mittler, 1939), 2–9.
17. Napoleon as quoted in C. J. F. T. Montholon (ed.), *Recits de la captivite de l'empereur Napoleon a Sainte Helene*, vol. ii (Paris: Paulin, 1847), 133–4.
18. Carl von Clausewitz, *On War*, eds. M. Howard and P. Paret (Princeton, NJ: Princeton University Press, 1976), 245–6, 297.
19. Ibid., 204, 290.
20. For a good recent example, see M. Boot, *War Made New: Technology, Warfare, and the Course of History: 1500 to Today* (New York, NY: Gotham, 2006).
21. See J. Donaldson, 'Signalling Communications and the Roman Imperial Army', *Britannia*, 19, 1988, 349ff.
22. A short description of the system will be found in Martin van Creveld, *Technology and War: From 2000 B.C. to the Present* (New York, NY: Free Press, 1989), 153–6. See also J. R. Elting, *Swords around a Throne: Napoleon's Grande Armée* (New York, NY: Free Press, 1988), 103–5.
23. For this entire subject, see E. W. Marsden, *Greek and Roman Artillery* (Oxford: Clarendon, 1971), 206–33, 227, 238–40; for a specific case when artillery was used in the field, see Tacitus, *The Histories* (London: Penguin, 1986), iii. 23.
24. M. de Saxe, *Reveries on the Art of War* (Mineola, NY: Dover, [1757]/2007), 52–3.
25. 'Plan de campagne pour l'armée du Rhin', 22 March 1800, *Correspondance de Napoleon Ier* (Paris: Plon, 1863), vol. vi, no. 4694, 201.
26. Clausewitz, *On War*, 301.
27. Napoleon to Murat, 21 September 1805, *Correspondance*, xi, 232–3.
28. Sixth Bulletin of the Grande Armée, 18 October 1805, *Correspondance*, xi, 340.
29. Elting, *Swords Around a Throne*, 81–102; van Creveld, *Command in War*, 65–8; D. Chandler, *The Campaigns of Napoleon* (New York, NY: Macmillan, 1966), 367–80.
30. C. J. T. de Montholon (ed.), *Recits de la captivite de l'empereur* (London: Ridgway, 1820), vol. I, 453.
31. van Creveld, *Command in War*, 75–8.
32. Napoleon to Berthier, 17 September 1806, *Correspondance*, vol. xiii, no. 10804, 201–2.
33. Napoleon to Murat, 21 September 1805, *Correspondence*, xi, 232–3.
34. Napoleon to Bessieres, 12 September 1806, *Correspondance*, vol. xiii, no. 10768, 174–5.
35. Murat's reports are printed in H. Bonnall, *La Manoeuvre de Jena* (Paris: Libraire militaire, 1904), 193.

36. Napoleon to Louis of Holland, 30 September 1806, *Correspondance*, vol. xiii, no. 10920, 292–6.
37. Clausewitz, *On War*, 494.
38. See H. Otto, *Gneisenau: Preussens unbequemer Patriot* (Bonn: Keil, 1979), 178–9.
39. Napoleon to Lannes, 7 October 1806, *Correspondance*, vol. xiii, no. 10961, 320–1.
40. Napoleon to Soult, 10 October 1806, *Correspondance*, vol. xiii, no. 10980, 335–6.
41. Above all, in *Précis de l'Art de la Guerre: Des Principales Combinaisons de la Stratégie, de la Grande Tactique et de la Politique Militaire* (Brussels: Meline, Cans et Copagnie, 1838).
42. Napoleon to Soult, 10 October 1806, *Correspondance*, vol. xiii, no. 10977, 332–4.
43. Ibid., vol. xiii, no. 10980.
44. On their deliberations, see *Notes on the Battle of Jena*, by an Officer of the R. Staff Corps (London: Naval and Military Press, n.d. [1827]), 11–17.
45. Based on van Creveld, *Command in War*, table 1, 88.
46. On the way the Prussians fought, see F. N. Maude, *The Jena Campaign* (London: Sonnenschein, 1909), 156.
47. See Martin van Creveld, *The Culture of War* (New York, NY: Presidio, 2008), 359–60.
48. Quoted in Chandler, *The Campaigns of Napoleon*, 488.
49. In the case under consideration this started happening from 1809 onwards; on this, see R. M. Epstein, *Napoleon's Last Victory and the Emergence of Modern War* (Lawrence, KS: University Press of Kansas, 1994). By 1813, even Napoleon conceded that '*ces animaux* [i.e. the enemy] *ont apprenu q'uelques choses*' (these animals have learnt something).
50. Lao Tzu, *Tao Te Chin*, trans. S. Mitchell, verse no. 11 ⟨http://acc6.its.brooklyn.cuny.edu/phalsall/texts/taote-v3.html⟩.

2

Prussian–German Operational Art, 1740–1943

Dennis E. Showalter

INTRODUCTION: MATRICES

'Operational art' is usually and reasonably defined in general terms as the intermediate area between tactics and strategy, involving the use of large military forces to decide campaigns in the context of a theatre of war. Along with counter-insurgency, its mastery is a contemporary touchstone of military effectiveness.[1] And operational art is also linked inextricably with Prussia and Germany.[2]

The Western world has developed three intellectual approaches to war. The first is the 'scientific'. The scientists interpret war as subject to abstract laws and principles. Systematically studied and properly applied, these principles enable anticipating the consequences of decisions, behaviours—even attitudes. The Soviet Union offers the best example of a military system built around the scientific approach. Marxism–Leninism, the USSR's legitimating ideology, was a science. The Soviet state and Soviet society were organized on scientific principles. War making too was a science. The application of its objective principles by trained and skilled engineers was the best predictor of victory.

The second approach to war is the 'managerial'. Managers understand war in terms of organization and administration. Military effectiveness depends on the rational mobilization and application of human and material resources. Battle does not exactly take care of itself, but its uncertainties are best addressed in managerial contexts. The United States has been the most distinguished, and successful, exemplar of managerial war. In part, that reflects its underlying pragmatism: an ethic of getting on with the job. In part, it reflects a historical geography that since the revolution has impelled America to export its conflicts—in turn, making administration a *sine qua non*. From the disasters suffered by Harmar and St. Clair in the 1790s to the catastrophe of Task Force Smith in Korea in 1950, without effective management successful fighting has been impossible.

The Germans, for their part, have understood war as fundamentally an art form. Though requiring basic craft skills, war defied reduction to rules and principles. Its mastery demanded study and reflection, but depended ultimately on two virtually untranslatable concepts: *Fingerspitzengefühl* and *Tuchfühling*. The closest English equivalent is the more sterile phrase 'situational awareness'. The German concept incorporated as well the importance of panache—the difference, in horsemen's language, between a hunter and a hack—or in contemporary terms, the difference between a family saloon car and a muscle car. It emphasized speed and daring, manoeuvring to strike as hard a blow as possible from a direction as unexpected as possible. That mentality depended on, and in turn fostered, particular institutional characteristics: a flexible command system, high levels of aggressiveness, and an officer corps with a common perspective on war making.

Robert Citino describes the genesis of this 'German way of war' in a Prussian state located in the centre of Europe, ringed by potential enemies, lacking both natural boundaries and natural resources. Unable to wage and win a long war, Prussia had to develop a way to fight front-loaded conflicts: short, intense, and ending with a battlefield victory leaving the enemy sufficiently weakened and intimidated to forgo a second round.[3]

Prussia's situation in turn not merely generated but required the tactical orientation of its military mentality. This is in direct contrast to the United States, whose fundamental military problems since at least the Mexican War have been on the level of strategy and grand strategy: where to go and how to sustain the effort. Actual fighting has been a secondary concern, which is why so many of America's first battles have been disasters.[4] Prussia, on the other hand, was unlikely to recover from an initial defeat.

That was the lesson and the legacy of Frederick the Great. Frederick's concept of rational war leadership institutionalized the strategic principle that Prussia must fight short, decisive wars. That meant developing a forward-loaded military system, an army able to go to war from a standing start with its effectiveness highest at the beginning. It meant that nothing should be wasted on secondary concerns. Skirmishing, scouting, all the other elements of 'little wars' increasingly present in the eighteenth century, were, in Frederick's mind, above all, wasted time. And time was the one thing Prussia did not possess.

Frederick's emphasis on time required not merely seeking battle, but holding nothing back once the fighting started. The West's experience since the Middle Ages, however, had consistently demonstrated the randomness of combat. The collective wisdom of eighteenth-century war making responded by minimizing Fortuna's opportunities: marching and fighting only under perceived favourable conditions. Denied that option, Frederick lived on the edge. At Mollwitz in 1741, the day seemed thoroughly lost until the final advance of the Prussian infantry turned the tide. The Battle of Soor in 1745 began when the Austrians surprised his camp and ended when Frederick improvised victory from the fighting power of his men.[5]

As a consequence, the king became committed to minimizing what Clausewitz would call fog and friction by making Prussia impervious to shock and surprise. In the aftermath of the Silesian Wars (1740–8), Frederick increasingly integrated the state's economy into its war-making function.[6] The annual manoeuvres, involving as many men as a fair-sized battle—44,000 in 1753—were meant to test formations and tactics, to practise large-scale evolutions, and to accustom senior officers to handling large bodies of troops under stress. This last, though

Frederick never made the point explicit, may well have been his justification for the devastating, and career-destroying, critiques that accompanied the exercises. To a degree, they replicated the unpredictable, high-risk conditions of command in an eighteenth-century battle.[7]

The Seven Years War tested Frederick's approach to its limits. Instead of ending quickly, decisively, and positively, the conflict dragged on into unpredictability. In less than a year, the painstakingly prepared Prussian army suffered heavy and irreplaceable casualties at Lobositz, Kolin, and outside Prague. Russian troops invaded East Prussia while a massive French army supplemented by contingents from the Holy Roman Empire advanced from the west. Frederick's only ally was a Britain unwilling to commit more than minimal financial and military resources to the continent.

The king rallied, kept his army in the field and his people paying taxes, shifted troops from sector to sector of his threatened kingdom, masterminded dazzling triumphs, and recovered from catastrophic defeats. But there was no room to develop a concept of operational art.[8] Rossbach, Leuthen, Zorndorf, Hochkirch, Kunersdorf, Torgau—each is commemorated in its own monographs. But their usual objective was to expel invading armies. They were victories won in vacuums and arguably sterile. Prussia, by the end of the Seven Years War, was on the point of conquering itself to death. The kingdom was shaken to its physical and moral foundations. As many as 180,000 Prussians had died in uniform, to say nothing of civilian losses from disease and privation. Provinces were devastated, populations scattered, currency debased. The social contract of the Prussian state, service and loyalty in return for stability and protection, was shaken to its foundations.[9]

Frederick addressed the consequences of a tactical focus in policy terms by developing and projecting the post-war Prussian army as a deterrent force, and by successfully establishing himself as the defender of Central Europe's status quo against a disruptive Austrian.[10] His successors during the French Revolutionary Wars, however, fell back into a tactical, opportunist mode at all levels. The failure of this approach was demonstrated in 1806. Prussia went to war for a policy reason, in order to avoid relegation to client-state status. It took the field in a tactical context. Just enough time remained in the normal campaigning season for one major battle. Even then the Prussian army had to do no more than bloody Napoleon's nose as a gesture of good faith to an embryonic Fourth Coalition, buying time for British guineas and Russian bayonets to bring to bear their respective influences.[11]

This was not an optimal situation, but neither did it seem obviously beyond the army's capacities—until Jena and Auerstedt. As Martin van Creveld's contribution to this volume demonstrates, the only operational art practised on that brief campaign was on the other side. Prussia's response was to retool its army to fight in the context of a coalition. Its basic organization was the medium-sized combined-arms brigade. Its tactics stressed wearing down an enemy by extended firefights, then using small flexible columns to determine weak spots, and, finally, developing opportunities through small-scale attacks. It was not a doctrine encouraging the striking of decisive, independent blows in the operational contexts Napoleon was introducing.

The Prussian army of the Wars of Liberation remained more the force of a German *Kleinstaat* than of a great power. The increasing tendency towards mass that characterized its tactics from Dresden to Waterloo in good part reflected limited ability at brigade and battalion levels to execute the sophisticated combination punches of a tactical concept designed to maximize the effectiveness of a numerically limited force.[12] And in a wider context, Prussia in 1813 became part of an alliance whose sheer size combined with its fear of Napoleon to produce a simulacrum of operational thinking: evade the emperor and advance where he was not. But mutual mistrust, bad staff work, and simple lack of vision prevented anything like a coherent theatre-level planning.[13]

The army of 1813–15 might not have matched its Frederickian predecessor in size or effectiveness. It was at the top of the list in fighting spirit. Its tone was set in allied councils by Marshal Gebhard von Blücher, a fierce old soldier whose character and behaviour harked back to the Thirty Years War. He knew only one way of making war: fight without let-up. Prussian diplomacy followed a similar line. It was Prussia that took a consistent lead in demanding action in the months after Leipzig. It was Prussia that successfully reminded the Fourth Coalition that peace was contingent on victory, and victory meant Napoleon's removal.[14] During the Hundred Days it was Prussia, personified once more by Blücher, pulling the Duke of Wellington's chestnuts from the fire of Waterloo and transforming 'a damned near-run thing' into a decisive victory.[15]

What these achievements had in common is that none of them had anything to do with operational art except in retrospect. Prussia's post-war army was no less tactically oriented. Its order of battle totalled just over 100 infantry battalions. About the same size as its Frederickian predecessor, it was no numerical match for post-Napoleonic French and Austrian armies that each had over 250 battalions, to say nothing of a tsarist Russia that counted over 700. Even the post-war British army, starved of funds and hidden away in the far corners of the empire, stabilized at around 100 battalions.

That reflected a synergy of economic limitations and diplomatic moderation. For three decades after Waterloo, Prussia consciously assumed a facilitator's role in the Concert of Europe, the Holy Alliance of the three eastern empires, and the German Confederation. It would take a second European revolution, the re-emergence of a French empire, and a near-tectonic shift in Austria's German policy for Prussia to redefine its position.[16]

THE GENESIS: THE PRUSSIAN ARMY AND HELMUTH VON MOLTKE

That redefinition marked the emergence of operational art in the Prussian army. Its emergence was a breech birth; the midwife was Helmuth von Moltke. Clausewitz is credited with making a clear distinction between strategy and tactics.

Whether he actually defined a third interim level or used 'strategy' in a way that today would mean 'operational art' is often debated.[17] Prussia's current and historical contexts, however, left little room for an operational sphere during Clausewitz's era. Only by the 1840s did the Industrial Revolution begin highlighting the limits of the tactical paradigm institutionalized since the Era of Reform.

Those limits developed on two levels. The first was control. Even in the later stages of the Napoleonic Wars, armies had metastasized beyond the capacities of their nervous systems. That held for battles: Borodino, Leipzig, Dresden, and even more for campaigns, as illustrated by the repeated fiascos of Napoleon's marshals when left to their own devices in Germany during 1813.[18] As populations increased and administrations improved, forces sent to war could expect to grow larger and the entropy inherent to war making increase.

The second problem facing European armies was the growing effect of firepower. Flintlocks were giving way to percussion caps and muskets to rifles. Cannon were growing deadlier both at long ranges and point-blank. As killing zones became larger and deadlier, how could men and units best respond? Was it still possible to manoeuvre effectively on the modern battlefield? Or would the gridlocks already nurtured by a lack of control be exacerbated by concern for bare survival?

Moltke was only one of a generation of staff officers and commanders constrained to address Prussia's historical problem in new contexts. The state still needed to fight short, decisive wars—more than ever as after 1848 the diplomatic environments of Europe and the German Confederation moved away from collectivity and cooperation.[19] One way of addressing the synergistic challenges of control and firepower, implemented in France and Austria, was to improve morale, training, and leadership. Prussia followed suit in the military reorganization of the early 1860s, which essentially replicated the front-loaded system of Frederick the Great.[20] Moltke was an artist and a novelist, a man of letters as well as arms. Perhaps that creative element of his personality encouraged him to expand his approach—to think outside the box on two levels.[21]

The first was tactical. Moltke understood that Prussia confronted a paradox that was approaching a dichotomy. The state's policy and strategic requirements for short wars depended on offensive action. But battlefields increasingly dominated by firepower facilitated defence. The man who had only to stand his ground, load, and fire had a basic advantage over the man who had to fire and move. When *élan* met steadfastness, firepower determined the outcome. His advocacy of flank attacks was scarcely original. Their value was likely to be even greater in the opening stages of a campaign—in the words of Confederate general James Longstreet, inexperienced troops tended to be 'sensitive around the flanks as a virgin'. Frederick the Great's famous oblique order was essentially nothing more than a last-minute flank attack. But the increasing range of rifles and artillery constrained the modern flanking movement to move wider and deeper to envelop an enemy whose own reserves would be positioned further in the rear to keep them out of range. The increased size of armies also meant the flanking force must be larger than previously accepted—an army corps at least. The larger the numbers, the more the possibilities of 'fog and friction'. And in Moltke's words, a good horseman does not drive even the boldest steed against an insurmountable obstacle.[22]

Moltke's solution was to mount the flank attack outside the tactical level—in what hindsight calls an operational context. Prospects for success improved exponentially when forces could be concentrated on the field from different points against the enemy front and flank. It should be noted that Moltke still presented that process as strategy. But events in 1866 and 1870 demonstrated that a distinction was emerging between movement to theatre and advance to contact.[23]

Moltke understood from the 1850s that railroads made possible the movement of large forces in short time periods to a common destination, with men and animals arriving in good condition: neither softened by long stretches in freight wagons nor worn out by long approach marches. Railroads also facilitated systematic resupply even into the war zone, diminishing the strain on traditional logistic systems. Initially, he processed this development in a tactical context of bringing superior numbers to a decisive point. Increasingly as well he addressed the problems generated by an embarrassment of riches: how best to move a large force brought to one place forward on what were still very limited road networks while keeping it out of its own way.[24]

Prussia's use of railroads in 1866 to deploy forces simultaneously to widely separated areas outside the zone of operations, then advancing to concentration, was not a grand plan. It reflected rather King William's reluctance to authorize mobilization for a 'brothers' war', and the limits of Prussia's railway system in terms of layout and track mileage. When Prussia's concentration was complete, the Elbe Army's three divisions were at Torgau, the 1st Army's six divisions were 150 kilometres further east at Görlitz, and eight more were in Silesia with the 2nd Army, almost 200 kilometres' distance from the 1st Army. Prussia would have to advance into Bohemia, no matter what Benedek decided to do, in order to have any hope of concentrating its forces. Not to worry, Moltke assured William. No matter which way the Austrians turned, towards Silesia or to meet the threat from Prussian Saxony, he would be enmeshed in an operational net, with the unengaged elements of the Prussian army closing on his flanks and rear.

The Prussians fought their way into Bohemia in a series of blistering encounter battles that constrained their opponents to fall back on the fortress of Königgrätz on the Elbe River. By 2 July, Moltke's subordinates and their chiefs of staff were convinced they had taken as much risk as was acceptable in marching divided into the theatre of war. The time had come to fight united. He insisted on the continuing advantages of separate, simultaneous advances against the Austrians' front and flanks. King William decided in Moltke's favour—not least because he seemed the most sure of himself with the clearest sense of what to do next. In fact, what Moltke had was a good card player's poker face. Not until a patrol brought definitive information on the enemy position later that night was Moltke able to issue final orders for the next day: the 1st Army was to pin the Austrians frontally, while the 2nd advanced on their left flank. The rest is familiar history: 3 July 1866 witnessed arguably the most decisive and significant battle between the Napoleonic Wars and the Second World War.[25]

From Prussia's perspective, the run-up to Königgrätz is best understood in terms of imposing will on circumstances. An evaluation of the evidence suggests that both the campaign and the battle were near-run things. Moltke's reliance on the railroads to deploy his armies was a calculated risk committing Prussia to an operational approach offering a reasonably enterprising enemy significant opportunities to decide the issue by defeating the advancing armies in detail. Königgrätz itself was essentially a tactical victory. Prussia's success owed more than is generally understood to the principal field commanders, Crown Prince Frederick and Prince Frederick Charles, and to the fighting power of the men they led. The implications and the possibilities of a forward strategic concentration and an operationally structured campaign were clearer in retrospect than in prospect even to Moltke. But the results had been decisive, and the chief of staff saw the prospects of their systematic repetition.

The 'Instructions for Higher Troop Commanders' were issued in 1869 with the king's approval, summarizing the lessons of the previous campaign in the context of the necessity for breaking the enemy's will by destroying his force as quickly as possible: *Vernichtungsschlacht*. That was a combined-arms process, involving a synergy of manoeuvre, firepower, and pursuit. It was also, Moltke declared, the operational objective of the campaign, which, on one hand, served the ends of strategy and, on the other, would be completed tactically.[26]

Moltke's concept of operations was also shaped by his understanding of the relationship between war and policy. As chief of staff, he accepted a sharp distinction between the two spheres. In peacetime, the army's job was to plan and prepare for the next war. It was the government's task to establish that conflict's paradigm and define its parameters.[27] That yin–yang symbiosis gave Moltke after 1866 a single-contingency situation: planning a war against France. Like all of Prussia's wars, it would have to be decided quickly. That depended on the railroads. Where in 1866 he had improvised existing lines and based his plan on the extrinsic deployment that resulted, his concern from 1867 to 1870 was to funnel as many men and horses as possible into the Rhineland–Palatinate area of Prussia as quickly as possible. A military transportation plan established rail schedules for the entire army. Tested in a November 1867 war game, it required thirty-two days to move the Prussian field army into its designated zone of operations in the west. A year later, that time had been reduced to twenty-four days. By 1870, it was twenty days. The railway system had no fewer than six organized rail routes, each able to handle two or three corps in succession: eighteen trains a day over double-track lines, twelve on single-track routes. By 3 August, the nineteenth day of mobilization, the field force was ready to advance.[28]

The purpose of this rapid concentration in such a relatively small and limited area was to enable a march on Paris. Paris was the heart of France, and of the Second Empire: it could not be sacrificed in a strategic withdrawal. To threaten it was to make possible the campaign's operational goal: engaging and destroying the French army. A decisive victory would put pay to French military power. Of no less significance, it would convince other powers, Austria in particular, to let half-drawn swords return to their scabbards.

Moltke expected to have about 360,000 men for his offensive; superior numbers, but not exactly overwhelming, especially for an attacker. His corresponding decision was to concentrate two armies—in the event a single, oversized 2nd Army—that would advance in two echelons, ready to attack to its front or swing to either flank. On the right, a 1st Army of two corps would cover the 2nd's advance and be ready to strike against the French left flank should an opportunity arise. The 3rd Army, with a final strength of three Prussian and two-and-a-half South German corps, was to serve as a left-flank guard and itself engage a French flank should opportunity offer.

In specific terms, Moltke planned to swing south of the French fortress of Metz, then advance on the Moselle. A major battle should take place before reaching the river, and 'thereafter nothing can be predicted in detail'. This approach is often cited in general works as illustrating Moltke's aphorism that no plan survives contact with the enemy. It also illustrates the chief of staff's contention that, therefore, the initial plan must be a good one! He provided regularly updated timetables for the advance of each corps—detailed to a point of specifying what locations each formation would reach on a particular day. He insisted as well that the corps' marches on entering the theatre of operations be specifically regulated from above: strict control of the campaign's initial stages. Control was the best available measure against the development of something like a continuous front; with Prussia's three armies pushing the French back steadily—but too slowly to fulfil the war's policy objectives.[29]

Once the campaign began, its circumstances changed as the opposing armies manoeuvred, engaged, and reacted. Calling this the collapse of Moltke's war plan may be a bit strong.[30] But certainly the chief of staff repeatedly confronted the unexpected. Like the fine whist player he was, Moltke kept his head and read his cards even when Prussia's government, in the persons of its king and its Chancellor, Otto von Bismarck, was looking over his shoulder. If his game plan varied from hand to hand, the changes were in a consistent context: maintaining the goal of destroying the French army.

After the initial battles on the frontier at Spicheren, Wissembourg, and Wörth, the French retreated in two directions.[31] Five corps fell back towards the fortress of Metz. Three others withdrew in the direction of the fortified camp of Chalons. Moltke concentrated on the larger force. The 1st Army and part of the 2nd would push the French directly. The 3rd Army reinforced by two of the 2nd's corps would swing up from the left into their flank and rear. When the French slowed to engage in a half-hearted rearguard fight at Borny on 14 August, Moltke reacted by designating the 2nd Army as the pivot of a flank movement around the fortress of Metz and against the main French line of retreat towards Verdun. The chief of staff's concept remained operational. He had no plans for a major battle on 16 August. Vionville–Mars-la-Tour was the consequence of an aggressive corps commander implementing his notion of initiative and mission tactics by throwing his two divisions across an entire army's axis of movement.[32] The tactical outcome depended essentially on the quality of the Prussian army at all levels. But Moltke quickly understood its operational implications. France's main army was cut off, and Moltke's revised intention was to turn the 2nd Army to the north, face it to the rear, and use it to drive the French either back into Metz or across the border into neutral Luxemburg and internment.

Gravelotte–St. Privat, fought on 20 August, was another soldiers' battle, whose heavy casualties resulted in a tactical victory but an operational dead end. The immediate opponents shut themselves up in Metz. Moltke and Bismarck alike, however, understood not merely the desirability, but the necessity, of a quick and decisive end to a war whose continuation carried an increasing risk of destroying the European balance instead of adjusting it in Prussia's favour. The general and the Chancellor correspondingly agreed on the next military objective. The new French army forming at Chalons was the last of the Second Empire's front-line forces. Defeating it called for refocusing operational concepts that had temporarily devolved to serving tactical objectives. Moltke took the 3rd Army, formed a new Army of the Meuse from three corps of the 2nd Army, and headed west.

Moltke expected the Army of Chalons to retreat towards Paris. Instead, it lurched forward with the ostensible goal of relieving Metz by marching around Moltke's right flank. 'The dummies will pay for this', remarked Moltke as he swung his armies north, into the Argonne Forest.[33] Surprised and badly shaken in preliminary fighting, the Army of Chalons fell back on the old fortress of Sedan to 'regroup'. The Germans followed up and closed in, moving smoothly through thick forests on poor roads, the corps marching separately but positioned by Moltke and his staff subordinates to fight united. By the night of 31 August, German bivouac fires formed an almost unbroken circle around the French positions. 'We have them in a mousetrap', rejoiced Moltke. A hardbitten French general found another metaphor: 'we're in a chamber pot, and tomorrow we're going to be shit on'. Both men were correct.

Sedan was Moltke's last chance to make war at the operational level. Against the revolutionary French Republic, the German forces were split three ways: pinned down in a siege of Paris, fending off the improvised Republican armies' effort at relieving the city, dealing with an increasingly comprehensive guerrilla war, and able to decide none of the situations. His intellectual response was the 'Essay on Strategy' he composed in 1871. In it, he borrowed the familiar aphorism of Austria's Archduke Charles: 'strategy is a science; tactics is an art'. But between them was emerging a third category, a new reality. He wrote of 'strategy' as a system of expedients—not a pure science but the application of science to practical purposes: particularly maintaining an objective under the pressure of constantly changing circumstances. What he was describing, however, was operational art: bringing the army to the right place at the right time and in the right combinations to avoid stalemate in the field and sustain the commander's synergistic relationship with political authority.[34]

For the next twenty years, Moltke developed the distinction between the aim of war and the object of operations. The former was determined by the state. The latter usually meant the enemy army, although that too could be defined in policy contexts, as had been the case against Denmark in 1864 and Austria in 1866. He also developed the concept of operations as war's offensive element. Railroads had increased the strength of the strategic defensive. Firepower dominated tactics. In both cases, logic, reinforced by friction, tended towards stagnation. The operational sphere was the province of will, planning, and insight. Prussia and Germany's enduring need for quick, decisive victory correspondingly rendered imperative the cultivation of operational art.[35]

Metaphorically speaking, Alfred von Schlieffen was not a whist player. If this narrowly focused man had a defining game, it was chess. In contrast to Moltke, Schlieffen sought to integrate strategy, operations, and tactics in a seamless web. His goal was a 'total battle', *Gesamtschlacht*, that would begin with mobilization, move through concentration, deployment, and advance to contact, then culminate in a battle of envelopment built around flanking manoeuvres and flank attacks. Not for him the random fall of the cards, the acceptance of strategy as a system of expedients. Schlieffen believed that strategy drove operations and operations drove strategy. He believed, moreover, that the entire process must proceed as quickly as possible. The sheer size of modern armies exponentially exacerbated the problem of control, and correspondingly nurtured entropy. Citizen armies built around mobilized civilians would inevitably be unprepared for combat. Victory was disproportionally likely to go to the side best able to exploit an opponent's unreadiness by throwing him off balance and keeping him confused.[36]

This need for haste had two taproots. One was the diplomatic fecklessness of the post-Bismarckian Reich: Germany's diplomats and leaders were alike, inexperienced in the nuances of world power politics. Theirs was the heritage of Prussia, a regional power with limited interests beyond Germany and Poland. Germany had neither treaty rights nor historical precedents to support too many of her claims. Nor did she have statesmen able to play second-best hands into winners at an international poker table against reasonably competent rivals holding better cards.[37]

The results were an increasingly shaky Austrian alliance, an increasingly alienated Great Britain, and, above all, a Republican France and an Imperial Russia brought together by mutual fear of what Michael Stürmer appropriately calls 'the restless Reich'. That alliance was the bedrock of European diplomacy for twenty years, and its increasing stability made the prospects of a two-front war more and more a reality.

The spectre of one kind of war, that theory and experience alike agreed Germany could not win, shaped and drove Schlieffen's concept of a total battle won from as close to a standing start as possible against France, the enemy that could not trade space for time.[38] But most immediately that concept in turn ran into a technological imperative generating the second kind of war Germany could not win: a deadlock. The heavy losses incurred by Prussian attackers in 1870 encouraged in the next decade comprehensive revision of infantry tactics to incorporate and emphasize the advantages associated with defence: planning, cover, and firepower.

It encouraged the introduction of heavy guns into field warfare, to facilitate breaking through the kinds of fixed defences the French were constructing. By the mid-1890s, however, fortress technology had moved well ahead of the destructive power of mobile heavy artillery. Pessimists—or realists, depending on one's perspective—advised forgetting about anything but a slow, costly, episodic advance.[39]

The implications for a short, victorious war were obvious. Schlieffen's response was to turn from breakthrough to envelopment: the sweep through Belgium that became the focal point of German war planning. This revised operational concept has been shown as less a doomsday machine in the literal sense than Schlieffen himself might have preferred. Instead, his memoranda reveal an almost Moltkean acceptance of contingency at the sharp end, with specific courses of events depending on French behaviour and German success. He had the uncomfortable habit of assuming divisions and army corps would emerge as needed, like warriors from the dragon's teeth sowed by Cadmus. Schlieffen's own scenarios frequently involved a series of rapid victories on the frontier that would cripple the French army and set the stage for further operations in the interior over six to nine months.[40] By 1914, that period was being extended to as long as two years in some general staff circles.[41]

Germany's defeat in the West in the autumn of 1914 has been explained in terms of policy, strategy, operations, tactics, and a near-infinite number of combinations. Its principal operational weakness was not its neglect of contingency, but the fact that it had no room for friction. Everything at all levels had to go preternaturally right for the whole to work. Even a little grit gridlocked the system beyond its ability to repair itself or the high command's capacity to retune it.[42]

Considered in retrospect, however, the 1914 campaign also illustrated a gap in the German concept of operations: a neglect of mobility. From ancient times to the present day, pursuit and exploitation at the operational level turn a victorious battle into a victorious campaign. Eighteenth-century Prussian cavalry was essentially a tactical instrument. In the Wars of Liberation, it was deployed by regiments and brigades. In the Wars of Unification, larger formations were only organized on mobilization. Moltke the Elder focused on reconnaissance and screening.[43] Schlieffen insisted on strong cavalry forces on the flanks of the German advance. Instead, however, in 1914 half the cavalry of Germany's active army was directly assigned to infantry divisions. Of the ten cavalry divisions deployed on the Western Front, five were deployed to cover the advance in such unlikely cavalry country as the Vosges and the Ardennes.

The German cavalry division of 1914 was a potentially effective combined-arms team. Its six regiments, 4,500 troopers, had twelve field pieces and half-a-dozen mobile machine guns as organic fire support. They depended on horses, but were by no means helpless on foot. Regiments were extensively trained in marksmanship and skirmishing. Officers did not ignore the potential of dismounted fire action. The division had its own bridging train, and even a radio detachment. Most divisions either had attached or could call on a battalion or two of *Jäger.* These elite light infantry formations included a cyclist company, a machine-gun company, and a small motor-transport column whose ten trucks could be used to shuttle infantry forward much like the truck companies attached to US infantry divisions in the Second World War.

One need not assume that German cavalry utilized as an early version of the Soviet operational manoeuvre group would have somehow averted stagnation. The high force-to-space ratios of the Western Front, combined with the historically unique imbalance among firepower, mobility, and protection, would, in all probability, have ended in something approximating the race to the sea and the development of trench warfare no matter what the Kaiser's horsemen did or did not do. What is significant is that rethinking the prospects for cavalry's employment proved beyond the collective imagination of the cavalry as well as the high command.

Mechanization was an even more remote concept. As early as 1905, car engineer Paul Daimler demonstrated a surprisingly advanced prototype armoured car at the autumn manoeuvres. It was dismissed as lacking practical utility. In 1914, a couple of improvised armoured trucks were attached to each cavalry division. Equally improvised detachments of machine-gun crews and riflemen in commandeered civilian cars did useful service occupying bridges and road junctions in advance of the horsemen. Only in 1915, however, did the general staff develop specifications for a purpose-built armoured car. The resulting models carried two or three machine guns and were well armoured for the time. One even had a radio. But their bulky shapes and heavy weights rendered them visible on roads and limited their cross-country mobility to virtually zero.[44]

The strategic and tactical circumstances of the developed Western Front reduced German opportunities for employing operational art to another near-zero. Nor did the Russian Front ever quite repay the efforts put into it by the Second Reich. From Tannenberg in 1914 to Riga in 1917, the Russian army acquired an image of being easy to defeat, but hard to finish. The 1915 Battle of Gorlice–Tarnow was archetypical. Pitting comprehensive planning and high-tech heavy artillery and chlorine gas against numbers and inertia, a handful of German divisions tore open the front on a thirty-kilometre sector, captured a third of a million prisoners, and absorbed Russia's available resources in everything from anaesthetics to ammunition. Yet the Russians somehow managed to retreat faster than the Germans could chase them.[45]

Gorlice–Tarnow and its aftermath effectively confirmed pre-war general staff conclusions that the possibilities of decisive military action against Russia were too limited to be worth pursuing in any context. The operational-level successes achieved at Riga were processed as the outcome of tactical victory against an enemy too eroded by defeat, privation, and revolution to serve as a benchmark.[46] Romania in 1916 was similarly written down as a sideshow against a third-rate opponent.[47]

German operational art received a technical window of opportunity when its gunners developed ways of using artillery as a precision instrument of neutralization instead of a blunt tool for blasting ground in the hope of hitting something important.[48] Combined with the storm-troop tactics based on fire and movement by small groups that the infantry had been developing since 1915, they offered the possibility of a tactical breakthrough on a scale that would restore operational mobility and enable strategic objectives.[49] A high command increasingly desperate for an endgame seized the moment.

Erich Ludendorff's often-derided concept of 'punch a hole and see what develops' resembles Erich von Falkenhayn's concept of the 1916 attack on Verdun. Both were ultimately focused on the level of policy: do so much damage that France in one case, the Allies in another, would be impelled to negotiate. When the coalition withstood the shock at policy levels, translating tactical victory to the operational level became decisive. David Zabecki makes a convincing case that German commanders at army-group levels and below did have a reasonable comprehension of the still-emerging principles of operational warfare. From Ludendorff down, however, no one with serious authority had a paradigm, a template, for making that transition.

The system as a whole was focused more on a *Vernichtungsschlacht* than a *Gesamtschlacht*: emphasizing the British army but neglecting the vulnerabilities in the railway network that kept it fed, supplied, and able to move troops. Once the initial attacks failed, objectives shifted almost at random. So did lines of operation. So did coordination among sectors.

Failure to move the offensives to an operational level was tactical as well as conceptual. The artillery system, brutally effective in the initial stages, lacked the organizational flexibility and the tactical mobility to keep pace with changing situations. Too many of its heavy guns were horse-drawn, and too many of the artillery teams had been weakened by hunger. The vaunted storm troopers eventually exhausted first their bag of tactical tricks, then themselves. The storm-troop principle of infiltration, bypassing strong points in the way water seeks the easiest path, generated a downward focus in which there were no objectives—just processes, ultimately leading nowhere in particular. The specially prepared 'attack divisions' were bled white as Allied railroads and trucks reinforced critical sectors before the Germans could advance through them on foot. Their training for offensive operations was, in any case, well below the standard of the storm-troop battalions. Time and again, British and French sources report German follow-up forces moving in what might be called 'columns of flocks': masses bunched formlessly together for emotional closeness and drawing fire like magnets.[50]

By the second day of the offensives, the Germans had torn fifty miles' worth of hole in the British lines. By the end of the next day, they had advanced thirty miles. But, finally, there was no exploitation force able to take the burden from the surviving storm troopers—just more footsloggers. In his memoirs, Ludendorff is mildly critical of the high command's failure to consider the concept. In any case, the tools were lacking. Germany's cavalry on the Western Front had been largely dismounted. German armoured-vehicle designs were primitive, and few in number. They had few tanks, and the best of those were captured, salvaged British models. The army's motor vehicles were mostly heavy trucks, designed to operate on a network of paved streets and roads, within easy reach of maintenance facilities, and correspondingly unsuited to be converted to moving men and weapons forward of a main line of advance, against opposition, over war-ravaged terrain. The result was stalemate, leading first to the kind of drawn-out fighting retreat that German planners and thinkers had predicted meant catastrophe, and then to final visions of an apocalyptic last stand in the Reich itself.[51]

THE RECOVERY: FROM *SITZ* TO *BLITZ*

In 1914 and again in 1918, the Germans were unable to develop their initial advantage in the war's decisive theatre. They could break into Allied defences, and break through them. They could not break out. General Hans von Seeckt began moving the army from Sitz to Blitz. Educated at a civilian grammar school (*Gymnasium*), during the war he had established a reputation as one of the army's most brilliant staff officers and, in March 1920, he became head of the army high command in the newly established Weimar Republic.

Seeckt wore a monocle, but refused to wear blinkers. He disliked slogans. He disliked nostalgia—even the nostalgia surrounding the Great War's 'front experience'. Instead, he called for a return to the principle of pursuing quick, decisive victories. That in turn meant challenging the concept of mass that had permeated military thinking since the Napoleonic Wars. Mass, Seeckt argued, 'becomes immobile. It cannot win victories. It can only crush by sheer weight'.[52]

Seeckt's response was to develop an army capable of 'fighting outnumbered and winning'. The Reichswehr, Seeckt insisted, must dictate the conditions of battle by taking the initiative. Boldness was his first rule; flexibility his second. The manuals issued in the early 1920s emphasized the importance of the offensive.[53] As yet, operational art played no significant role. The underlying principle of Reichswehr planning was less to achieve decisive victory, much less a battle of annihilation, than to buy time for the diplomats to work a miracle.[54]

The Treaty of Versailles had specified the structure of the Reichswehr in detail: a force of 100,000, with enlisted men committed to twelve years of service and officers to twenty-five. It was forbidden tanks, aircraft, and any artillery above three inches in calibre. That Reichswehr faced at least a double, arguably a triple, bind. It could not afford to challenge the Treaty of Versailles openly. It badly needed force multipliers. To seek those multipliers externally, for example by supporting clandestine paramilitary organizations, was to risk destabilizing a state that was Germany's best chance to avoid collapsing into civil war.[55]

Seeckt correspondingly sought internal multipliers. The Treaty of Versailles authorized each Reichswehr division a motor-transport battalion. Some unimaginative officers might agree with the critic who allegedly insisted the trucks were there to haul flour. Seeckt saw motor vehicles as an increasingly valuable supplement to the cavalry that made up almost a quarter of the Reichswehr's front-line strength. German cavalrymen were likely to find motor vehicles appealing precisely because they were deprived of them—a human tendency freeing the Reichswehr from much of the hoof dragging other armies confronted.

In the winter of 1923–4, Reichswehr manoeuvres incorporated cooperation between motorized ground troops and simulated air forces. In 1925, the 1st Division in East Prussia included armoured cars, motorized artillery, and dummy tanks in its manoeuvre orders of battle. Such exercises highlighted the Reichswehr's limited achievements in motorization. They also offered opportunities to consider problems as they arose—and foreign observers noted the Germans seemed well able to correct mistakes involving motor vehicles.[56]

In 1930, the 3rd Motor Battalion was reorganized as a fighting formation including trucks, cars, motorcycles, anti-tank guns—and mock-up tanks. That year the Reichswehr manoeuvres incorporated simulated tank forces. The manoeuvres' emphasis was on challenging 'fog and friction' by speed, manoeuvrability, and flexibility. The fast paces and complex scenarios resulted in high levels of confusion. But the resulting melees, nevertheless, in a sense reflected the outcome sought by a developing German doctrine for combat against superior forces through the use of 'shock and awe' as opposed to mass and firepower.[57]

In 1924, the motor troops were also made responsible for monitoring developments in tank war and preparing appropriate training manuals. 'If tanks were not such a promising weapon', one of their senior officers dryly asserted, the Allies would not have banned them from the Reichswehr.[58] By the mid-1920s, the Reichswehr was moving doctrinally beyond the concept of tanks as primarily infantry-support weapons, and organizationally by considering their use in regimental strength. In November 1926, Wilhelm Heye, Seeckt's successor as chief of the army command, issued a memo asserting that technical developments improving tanks' speed and range had repeatedly shown in foreign manoeuvres the developing potential of mechanization. Operating alone or in combined-arms formations, tanks were becoming capable both of extended manoeuvre against flanks and rear, and of bringing decisive weight to the decisive point of battle, the *Schwerpunkt*.[59]

As early as 1926, however, the Reichswehr was focusing primarily on the use of armoured vehicles as a component of mobile forces separate from the foot-marching infantry.[60] By 1929, theoretical training schedules had been developed for independent tank regiments. Beginning in the early 1930s, the war games, historically central to officer training at all levels, became increasingly theoretical. They dispensed with realistic troop levels and postulated artificial political conditions in order to expand the learning experience of the game situation and enhance the vision and capacity of future field commanders.

This abstraction encouraged wider acceptance of the concept that quality, particularly when enhanced by technology, could overcome numbers. The issues of mobility, surprise, and concentration of force that had initially been keys to tactical survival became the basis of an operational concept depending on the offensive—whose success in turn depended on surprise, deception, and, above all, risk taking.[61]

The Reichswehr did not withdraw to the airy empire of operational dreams. It was still accurate to speak of mobile war developing in a framework of grand tactics as opposed to operational art. Nevertheless, an important aspect of mechanization in Germany is that tanks were added to existing doctrines and embryonic force structures that stressed not only the combination, but also the synergy, of mobility and striking power. The manoeuvres of 1932 featured a defending force with two cavalry divisions and only a single infantry division. Red, the invaders, included an entire cavalry corps, with cyclists and motorcyclists, motorized artillery, and motorized reconnaissance elements. The combat vehicles and the motorized formations were almost all simulated. Results were mixed, particularly when horses and motor vehicles attempted to cooperate directly. But the speed and scope of the exercises impressed all observers. Some motorized units advanced 300 kilometres in three days—a pace unmatched since the Mongol invasions of the Middle Ages.[62]

Myths to the contrary, Adolf Hitler had far less to do with the creation of the German armoured force than the army high command. In 1934, the motor battalions furnished cadres for anti-tank and reconnaissance battalions. The 1st and 2nd Cavalry Divisions took delivery of several hundred motor vehicles. The 3rd traded in its horses altogether and provided the nucleus for the 'experimental armoured division' whose table of organization was issued in October 1934.

Like all of its successors, the 1st Panzer Division was conceptualized as a balanced combined-arms force. Tanks and motorized infantry, motorcyclists and armoured cars, artillery, engineers, and signals would train and fight together at a pace set by the armour. The panzer division was seen as able to break into an enemy position, break through, and break out with its own resources, thereby solving the fundamental German problem of the First World War. But the panzer division was also able to create opportunities on an enemy flank or in his rear areas. It was able to conduct pursuit, and turn pursuit into exploitation. It could discover opportunities with its reconnaissance elements, capture objectives with its tanks, hold them with its infantry, then regroup and repeat the performance 100 kilometres away.[63]

There was nothing unique in the panzer divisions' tables of organization. France had its very similar light mechanized divisions. Polish mobilization plans projected mobile for 'mixed divisions'. In the course of the decade, Austria, Czechoslovakia, Romania, and Bulgaria would collect their respective tank and motorized elements into ad hoc 'fast divisions'.

These reflected available forces rather than any real doctrine. But the German stress on mobility, deep penetration, envelopment, and initiative was original. It institutionalized and reinforced the concept that future campaigns would be decided at neither tactical nor strategic levels, but in the intermediate sphere of operations. In June 1935, Chief of Staff Ludwig Beck concluded a staff ride by asserting that once an enemy front was broken armoured formations could operate effectively, perhaps decisively, on enemy flanks and in the rear areas. The next year, another staff exercise was built around the employment of an entire armoured army. Not only were more panzer divisions organized, but corps headquarters as well—and a separate inspection, or branch, to represent the panzers' interests in the shark tank that was the Third Reich's rearmament programme.[64]

The panzers were neither a direct descendant of Moltke's and Schlieffen's concepts of operational art nor an instrument directly designed to fulfil those concepts. They stemmed, however, from the same matrices: on one hand, policy and strategic imperatives for short, decisive wars, and, on the other, technological factors inhibiting prospects for decision at the tactical level. It was the final element in what Robert Citino calls *Bewegungskrieg*: war of movement, intended to strike rapid, unexpected, decisive blows in the context of a military objective.[65]

The panzers' contribution to the army's operational focus had specific contexts as well. Total war of the kind Hitler seemed willing not merely to risk but to affirm remained, in strategic terms, the wrong kind of war for Germany. And in social and political contexts, a mass war involving the German *Volk* was likely to benefit the Nazis far more than the soldiers.[66] The head-over-heels, improvisational nature of the Third Reich's peacetime mobilization was anything but reassuring. In contrast to the days of Frederick, to 1866, 1870, and 1914, most of the divisions were formed by 'waves' (*Wellen*), each with differing scales of equipment, levels of training, and operational effectiveness. In planning for war, the army was constrained to develop a hierarchy of dependability, with the peacetime divisions of the 'first wave' at its apex—and the mobile divisions at the apex of the first wave.

That situation offered a political and military window of opportunity. The tactical, doctrinal, and institutional concepts refined after 1933 provided the prospect of decisive offensive operations executed by specialized formations within a mass. The high-tech force multipliers, essential for such formations, favoured developing an elite: a functional elite able to employ ways and means of war inapplicable by homogenized mass armies in the pattern of 1914–18. It was an elite that would bring victories despite the institutional weaknesses of the new Wehrmacht—and despite any signs of clay feet or cardboard spine Germany's Führer might show along the way.

PERIHELION

Like the 'German way of war' itself, the panzers were an art form. There was an aesthetic to their concept, their structure, and their employment that continues to defy logical analysis. That same appeal invites confusion and conflation of the panzers' way of war with the concept of operational art. The problem is compounded by the blitzkrieg controversy. Reduced to its essentials, the critique of blitzkrieg is that the German victories of 1939–40 were not consequences of doctrine or planning. They developed from a series of accidents and coincidences reflecting operational improvisations born of the necessity to avoid a drawn-out war of attrition, and responding to strategic imperatives generated by the essentially random nature of the National Socialist regime.[67]

Blitzkrieg was certainly not a structure of concepts like AirLand Battle or counter-insurgency, expressed in manuals, taught in schools, and practised in manoeuvres. The word itself had appeared now and then in German military writing, not in a specific sense, but to refer to the kind of quick, complete victory that was at the heart of the army's operational planning and a central feature of its doctrine and training.[68] To say that blitzkrieg was an *ex post facto* construction, nevertheless, makes as much sense as to collect the components of a watch, shake the pieces in a sack, and expect to pull out a functioning timepiece. Blitzkrieg is a manifestation of the war of movement, that historical focus of Prussian–German planning that Seeckt and his contemporaries sought to restore after the Great War. Blitzkrieg also gives a technologically based literalness to an abstract concept. *Bewegungskrieg* had always been more of an intellectual construction than a physical reality. It involved forcing an enemy off balance through sophisticated planning creatively implemented in a context of forces moving essentially at the same pace. In blitzkrieg, the combination of radios and engines made it possible for an army literally to run rings around its enemy—if, and it was a big if, its moral and intellectual qualities were on par with its material.

The conclusion on 23 August 1939 of the German–Soviet Non-Aggression Pact set a match to long-accumulating tinder. For Hitler, the agreement was a golden opportunity to avert the two-front war of attrition that had brought about Germany's defeat a quarter-century earlier. On 1 September 1939, the German army rolled into Poland: the first stage of a war for global hegemony.

The Polish campaign of 1939 invites comparison with Schlieffen's vision of Cannae on an operational level. One army group with two armies and five mobile divisions drove south-east out of Pomerania and East Prussia; another, with three armies and ten mobile divisions, came north-east out of Silesia. The objective was the Polish army; the plan called for breaking through the Polish frontier positions and creating a double envelopment, the spearheads meeting somewhere east of Warsaw.

Things did not go quite so smoothly on the ground. The envelopment took longer to complete than expected; the Poles proved a less-obliging enemy than hoped. The results were not perfect but better than good enough. Determined resistance could not stop armoured spearheads that took full advantage of an unexpectedly dry summer in a country with few paved roads. The Germans forced small tactical breaches, expanded them into larger ones, and converted them to springboards for exploitation at the operational level. In contrast to virtually every muscle-powered campaign in modern European history, the Germans not only sustained, but also increased, their momentum, throwing the Poles off balance, and keeping them there. Close support by the Luftwaffe enhanced the 'shock-and-awe' effect. An unexpected bonus was the flexibility of the mobile divisions: panzer, light, and motorized. Their ability to change fronts and shift sectors enabled the solving of tactical problems in a matter of days, sometimes hours.[69]

As the Polish army began recovering from the initial shock, Soviet troops crossed its eastern border. *Rotarmisten* shook hands with *Panzermänner* as the extermination squads of their respective governments went to work on 'subversive elements': anyone, Gentile or Jew, who might pose an objective threat to the new orders.

After the fall of Poland, the Third Reich's armoured force was reconfigured. The four light divisions were converted to panzers; the motorized divisions were reduced by a third to facilitate control. The major issue, however, involved armour's use in the coming campaign against the Western Allies. The genesis of the original German plan is familiar. Hitler wanted the Western campaign to begin immediately after the fall of Poland. The high command was reluctant to mount an offensive under any circumstances. Its foot dragging produced no fewer than twenty-nine postponements and a concept that involved sending seventy-five divisions, including most of the army's mobile formations, into the Low Countries to engage the main Anglo-French strength in what was expected to be an encounter battle in central Belgium.

Even before Hitler became directly involved in the planning process, this unpromisingly conventional proposal was generating increasing criticism. It incorporated no proposals for destroying enemy armed forces, speaking rather of creating favourable conditions for future operations. The high command's thinking seemed to go no further than punching a hole and seeing what developed. In that sense, their proposal owed more to Ludendorff's abortive 1918 offensive than the Schlieffen Plan to which it has often been compared.[70]

It required little more than a back-of-the-envelope calculation to determine that the force-to-space ratios imposed by the proposed operation would invite exactly the kind of head-on engagements the army's mechanized elite was ill-configured to fight. Inter-war theorists of independent armoured warfare like J. F. C. Fuller and B. H. Liddell Hart tended to stress disruption, paralysis, as an end in itself. Cut an enemy's nervous system and all that remained was rounding up the demoralized and hungry masses. The Polish campaign had convinced the panzer community that armoured forces were also able to achieve initial breakthroughs even against prepared defences. At a war game held on 7 February, Heinz Guderian, the tankers' horsefly ('gadfly' is too limited to describe Guderian's take-no-prisoners approach), proposed concentrating the armoured forces for a drive across the Meuse River around Sedan, then expanding the bridgehead north-west towards Amiens. The chief of staff insisted on a measured build-up, waiting for the infantry before seeking to exploit the initial success.

A month later, a second war game evaluated the same issue. This time the pressure from on high for using infantry to force the crossing was even stronger. Guderian and the commander of XIV Panzer Corps responded that the proposed conservative employment of the armour was so likely to produce a crisis that they could have no confidence in a high command that ordered it. War games were intended to generate spirited debate with no hard feelings. But when two experienced senior generals flatly declared 'no confidence' in a plan, it was the closest thing possible to saying 'get yourself another boy'.[71]

German doctrine, both generally in the army and specifically in the armoured force, was based on destroying enemy forces by breaking their will and ability to resist. That was also the basis of the alternative concept put forward by Erich von Manstein, then chief of staff to Army Group A. Manstein's proposal was intended as much to provide a central role for his commanding general Gerd von Rundstedt as to furnish a programme for victory. His projected thrust through the Ardennes would transform Rundstedt's army group from a secondary player to the campaign's focal point. Broken terrain made the option a risk—but a calculated risk, taking maximum advantage of the principal German force multipliers: leadership and technology. Hitler, disgruntled with his generals' conventionality and angered by a security breach that put copies of the original plan in Allied hands, took advantage of Manstein's temporary presence in Berlin to discuss his ideas. A few days later, he issued a new operational plan: a 'scythe cut' (*Sichelschnitt*) through northern France.

The 'phoney war', the *Sitzkrieg*, came to a brutal end in the spring of 1940. In February, Hitler, influenced by his admirals' demands for a coastline long enough to provide some operational flexibility, launched an invasion of Denmark and Norway. The Allied response was limited and ineffective. Outnumbered, at the far end of a long supply line, the Wehrmacht, nevertheless, bested the British at their own historic game of power projection—albeit at the cost of most of the ships originally expected to take advantage of the Norwegian bases. Scandinavia, however, became a strategic backwater when, on 10 June, Nazi Germany launched an all-out offensive through Holland, Belgium, and northern France.

The developed German plan used almost a third of the armoured force as bait. One panzer division was part of a 'shock-and-awe' attack on the Netherlands. Two more, plus a motorized division, provided the mobile core of an otherwise foot-powered thrust into Belgium. A chess player might speak of a knight's move, a bullfight aficionado might think of a matador's cape. But the other half of the knight fork, the sword delivering the killing blow, was a 'panzer group' of five armoured and three motorized divisions. Nothing like it had ever existed in the German command structure. Armies and corps, yes, but a 'group' was generally understood as a temporary organization for secondary missions. Rundstedt left no doubt that the concept was on trial by keeping the panzer group organically subordinated to one of his field armies during the campaign. This was anything but a vote of confidence, and proved a constant source of confusion, friction, and bad temper.

Sichelschnitt, on the other hand, benefited from an obliging enemy. An 'obliging enemy' is one that not so much makes mistakes, but behaves as though its orders had been written by the opposition. French generals and staff officers were students and creatures of a doctrine emphasizing the importance of firepower and management. They had no intention of playing to the German army's obvious strength by seeking an encounter battle of the classic sort, as opposed to deploying along a line offering a shorter and stronger position than the one defined by the Franco-Belgian frontier. The Allied high command rushed every available man, gun, and tank into Belgium and Holland. Its goal was to establish a killing ground for the managed battle that would decide the war.[72]

The weight of the German attack, however, was further south, through an Ardennes Forest considered impassable by large motorized forces. Pre-war intelligence reports of German intentions to attack through the Ardennes were processed as referring to no more than a secondary offensive. Initial reports of massive tank columns seemingly everywhere in the forest were dismissed as first-battle jitters. Besides, even if the Germans made it through the trees, they would surely be stopped by the river.

Instead, the Germans fought their way across the Meuse against second-line French troops whose tactics and commanders, rather than their courage, failed them at crucial points.[73] Shrugging off a series of desperate counter-attacks, the panzers swung west, into the Allied rear. On 17 May, the three divisions in Belgium were redeployed south. That put what amounted to Germany's entire mobile force, nine panzer and four motorized divisions and several smaller formations, plus elements of the still-embryonic Waffen SS, under Rundstedt's command for a killing stroke. French commander Maurice Gamelin was asked where were his strategic reserves. He replied laconically '*aucune*' ('there are none'). British and French troops already facing strong German forces to their front did the best they could to cut off the German spearheads. It was not enough.

For tank generals like Guderian and Erwin Rommel, speed was the new mantra; rapidity of movement and thought was the key to modern battle; the panzer force was capable of commanding itself. At 2 a.m. on 21 May, the first German troops reached the coast west of Abbeville. The British Expeditionary Force, most of a French army group, and the entire Belgian army were cut off and hoping for a miracle. Seen on a map, however, the panzer spearheads looked like fingers thrust out from a hand—and correspondingly vulnerable to being seized and broken one by one. Rundstedt advocated a brief halt to allow the infantry to catch up and secure the corridors opened by the tanks. Hitler too sought breathing space to evaluate a situation that had outrun even his imagination. On 24 May, the panzers were shut down. Dunkirk was left to the Luftwaffe.[74]

Did Hitler hold back the armour as a good-will gesture to a Britain he hoped to conciliate? Did cautious senior generals see an unnecessary risk in sending tank armour across broken ground against desperate men in prepared defences? There is no doubt that the tankers were far more comfortable when they turned against France on 5 June. Within days, a new government, headed by Great War hero Marshal Phillippe Petain, was suing for peace while it still had some negotiating room.

What made Case Yellow an exercise in operational art was its geographic scope, its focus on the objective of destroying the enemy forces physically and morally, and its maintenance of momentum while sustaining tactical flexibility. What took it off the board in an operational context was the dithering before Dunkirk: a Führer and a high command equally intimidated by unprecedented success. The German army would conduct only one more operational-level campaign: the overrunning of Greece and Yugoslavia in 1941. Finishing off what remained of the French was a mopping-up exercise. Rommel's triumphs in North Africa, although they represented masterpieces of the operational art, lacked the resources to be translated into strategic achievements, even though his own sense of what they might achieve is often underrated.[75] It was, however, Operation Barbarossa that definitively marked the end of operational art as a factor in German war making.

Five interlocking factors were responsible. No less than the cavalry of 1914, the panzers of 1941 were unsuited for their operational mission. This had little to do with the often-criticized doubling of the panzer divisions' number while halving their tank strength. It reflected an armaments industry with limited production capacity, and policy decisions that spread available resources across the military spectrum. The second factor was a strategic plan that denied any operational element by its lack of focus. In what amounted to an offensive cordon deployment, Germany's three army groups advanced in divergent directions, each led by its own mobile divisions. Military, political, and economic objectives were shifting and conflated—not least because of a belief that the panzers could make good the mind-changes. The war aims of exploitation and extermination meant from the beginning that the Germans were fighting in 360 degrees. Finally, the Germans' logistic weaknesses and the USSR's underdeveloped infrastructure made it impossible to sustain mobility. And underwriting it all was a level of hubris alien to Moltke and Schlieffen, a technocratic arrogance that ignored potential obstacles instead of considering them—or perhaps, seen from another perspective, the solipsism of artists blinded by their inner visions.[76]

Barbarossa's scale exceeded the German grasp of operational art. The successive victories won by the panzers, the huge losses inflicted on men and equipment, the great encirclements of Minsk, Kiev, and Smolensk were essentially exercises in grand tactics, in the context of unravelling strategic objectives that were poorly defined in the first place. Operation Blue of 1942 suffered from the same problems, and thereafter the German army in Russia was impelled into a defensive mode whose paradigm denied any prospects of operational art. Manstein's riposte after Stalingrad, the successes of his backhand, and second-strike counter-attacks in 1943 were virtuoso performances—but again on the level of grand tactics, ultimately no more productive in terms of strategy and policy than the Somme or Passchendaele.[77] They may be constantly described as 'operations', particularly in German technical literature. But words are patient and calling a dog's tail a leg does not make it one.

Operational art is the o-ring between strategy and tactics. By the summer of 1943, the Reich was approaching a dead end in both. Some of the Eastern Front's most experienced armoured commanders were advocating a zone defence: deep and complex, to be sure, but with the panzers being used for immediate intervention to choke off local breakthroughs and mount local counter-attacks, enmeshing the Soviets in a modern version of the Roman arena's *retiarius–secutor* gladiatorial combats. The concept owed more to 1918 than to 1940. Instead of 'punch a hole and see what develops', it was 'plug a hole and hope for the best'. The Soviet experience shows operational art can be defensive as well as offensive. But operational art must serve a strategic objective. Otherwise, it becomes grand tactics. For all its skilful execution, German practice in the war's final months owed more to Wilkins Micawber than to Helmuth von Moltke.[78]

CONCLUSION: FROM WEHRMACHT TO BUNDESWEHR

The steep decline in the fighting power of the army's non-elite elements meant that by 1944 the panzers were being used not only as fire brigades, but also as firewalls. The Ardennes in 1944 and Hungary in 1945 were *Fahrten ins Blaue*, military excursions to nowhere in particular with no serious operational objectives, much less strategic ones.

That pattern was replicated in the rearmed Federal Republic. Institutionally and technologically, the Bundeswehr in its developed form closely replicated panzer formats and experience. Ten of its twelve divisions were armoured or mechanized. Its Leopard tanks were a near-optimal combination of gun power, mobility, and reliability. Its Marder armoured personnel carriers were full-tracked fighting platforms as opposed to the half-track battle taxis of the Second World War.

In general terms, that strength and structure represented to both domestic and foreign analysts a reasonable balance between a meaningful and a non-threatening West German commitment to Atlantic security. During the Cold War, the Bundeswehr evolved along the same lines as the armed forces of Britain and France: stronger than those of the Benelux countries, Denmark, or Norway, better equipped than those of Greece or Turkey, but essentially unable to function independently without the consent of its allies. NATO's Central Front was integrated at the army-corps level; the Bundeswehr's three corps were deployed in separate sectors. With neither a general staff nor any higher commands, the prospects for developing operational art were limited to the point of non-existence.

That was seldom perceived negatively in a Bundeswehr just as committed to a forward defence, as had been its late-war predecessor in Russia. With thirty per cent of the Federal Republic's population and a quarter of its industrial capacity within a hundred miles of the eastern frontier, trading space for time in the Manstein tradition was impossible. Analysis of the defensive operations in Russia between 1943 and 1945, however, strongly suggested that mechanized forces properly trained, equipped, and commanded retained the capacity to check effectively any conventional offensive in Central Europe.

The Bundeswehr doctrine correspondingly called for quick ripostes, trip-hammer blows executed at the lowest possible levels. The Bundeswehr planners increasingly referred to the Eastern Front after 1943, when a few tanks and a handful of men boldly led, committed at the right time, regularly proved worth more than tenfold their number a few hours later. Implemented across the NATO Front, these counter-attacks were expected to stabilize the battle line to a point where nuclear escalation became a calculable option as opposed to a logical development.[79]

The Bundeswehr's approach was never put to the test. It is, nevertheless, significant because it concludes the story of operational art in Prussia and Germany by returning it to its tactical and grand-tactical matrices. German operational art is best understood not as an organic development but as a situational response—arguably a series of responses—to particular circumstances. Beginning in a context of limited wars for limited objectives, it metastasized into a means of conquest and expansion that encouraged and enabled ambitions that ultimately lay outside the capacity, and the will, of society, state, and army alike. That overstretch, in turn, repeatedly impelled regression to grand tactics that could expand and extend wars, but could not win them. War may be an art form, but if one's *métier* is painting miniatures, carving sculptures is likely to be an overstretch.

NOTES

1. Shimon Naveh, *In Pursuit of Military Excellence: The Evolution of Operational Theory* (London: Frank Cass, 1997).
2. Dennis E. Showalter, 'Militärgeschichte als Operationsgeschichte: Deutsche und amerikanische Paradigmen', in *Was ist Militärgeschichte*, eds. T. Kühne and B. Ziemann (Paderborn: Schöningh, 2000), 115–26.
3. Robert M. Citino, *The German Way of War: From the Thirty Years' War to the Third Reich* (Lawrence, KS: University Press of Kansas, 2005). Cf. Dennis E. Showalter, 'German Grand Strategy: A Contradiction in Terms?' *Militärgeschichtliche Mitteilungen*, 48 (1990), 65–102.
4. See C. E. Heller and W. A. Stoft (eds.), *America's First Battles, 1776–1965* (Lawrence, KS: University Press of Kansas, 1986).
5. These points are developed in Dennis E. Showalter, *The Wars of Frederick the Great* (London: Pearson Education, 1996); and in Christopher Duffy, *Frederick the Great: A Military Life* (London: Routledge, 1985).
6. Adelheid Simisch, 'Armee, Wirtschaft, Gesellschaft. Preussens Kampf auf der "inneren Linie"', in *Europa im Zeitalter Friedrichs des Grossen. Wirtschaft, Gesellschaft, Kriege*, ed. B. Kroener (Munich: Oldenbourg, 1986), 41ff.
7. *Tactique et manoeuvres des prussiens. Piece posthume, par M. le D. de G.* (n.p., 1767), is an eyewitness summary of the pre-war manoeuvres.
8. Claus Telp, *The Evolution of Operational Art, 1740–1813: From Frederick the Great to Napoleon* (London: Routledge, 2005), establishes the institutional and conceptual inhibitors of operational thinking in the Frederickian era generally.
9. Franz Szabo, *The Seven Years War in Europe, 1756–1763* (London: Pearson Education, 2007), is perhaps the sternest critic of Frederick since Macaulay.
10. Johannes Kunisch, *Friedrich Der Grosse. Der König und seine Zeit* (Munich: C. H. Beck Verlag, 2004), 503–23, credits Frederick with less success in changing his image. Cf. James M. Sofka, 'The Eighteenth Century International System: Parity or Primacy?' *Review of International Studies*, 27 (2002), 147–63.
11. For the strategic aspects, cf. Frederick R. Kagan's magisterial *The End of the Old Order: Napoleon and Europe, 1801–1805* (New York: First Da Capo Press, 2006), 177 passim; and Frederick Schneid's streamlined *Napoleon's Conquest of Europe: The War of the Third Coalition* (Westport, CT: Praeger, 2005). Brendan Simms, *The Impact of Napoleon: Prussian High Politics, Foreign Policy, and the Crisis of the Executive, 1797–1806* (Cambridge: Cambridge University Press, 1997), presents the politics and diplomacy.
12. Dierk Walter, *Preussische Heeresreformen 1807–1870. Militärische Innovation und der Mythos der 'Roonischen Reform'* (Paderborn: Schöningh, 2003), 143–66, 235–324, is state of the art in scholarship and reasoning on the first Era of Reform.
13. Peter Hofschröer's volumes in the Osprey Campaign series, *Lützen & Bautzen 1813: The Turning Point* (Oxford: Osprey, 2001), and *Leipzig 1813: The Battle of the Nations*

(Oxford: Osprey, 1993), introduce a campaign neglected by military and academic writers for over a century.

14. Gordon A. Craig, 'Problems of Coalition Warfare: The Military Alliance against Napoleon, 1813–1814', in Gordon A. Craig, *War, Politics and Diplomacy: Selected Essays* (New York: Praeger, 1966), 22–45.
15. Peter Hofschröer overstates the case—but not by much—in *1815: The Waterloo Campaign,* 2 vols. (London: Greenhill Books, 1998–9).
16. Dennis E. Showalter, 'The Retaming of Bellona: Prussia and the Institutionalizing of the Napoleonic Legacy, 1815–1876', *Military Affairs*, 44 (1980), 57–63.
17. Naveh, *In Pursuit of Military Excellence*, 40–1.
18. Michael Leggiere, *Napoleon and Berlin: The Franco-Prussian War in North Germany, 1813* (Norman, OK: University of Oklahoma Press, 2002), is an excellent case study in a Prussian context.
19. For this development in context, see Paul Schroeder, *Austria, Great Britain, and the Crimean War: The Destruction of the European Concert* (Ithaca, NY: Cornell University Press, 1972); and Heinrich Lutz, *Zwischen Habsburg und Preussen. Deutschland 1815–1866* (Berlin: Siedler Verlag, 1985).
20. Dierk Walter, 'Roon, the Prussian Landwehr, and the Reorganization of 1860', forthcoming in *War in History*, sarcastically concludes the main result of the new system was renaming the units involved.
21. Eberhard Kessel, *Moltke* (Stuttgart: K. F. Koehler Verlag, 1957), remains the best biography.
22. Cf. 'Bemerkungen vom 12. Juli 1858 über Verändrungen in der Taktik infolge des verbesserten Infanteriegewehrs', and 'Bemerkungen vom April 1861 über den Einfluss der verbesserten Feuerwaffen auf die Taktik', in *Moltkes Militärische Werke*, ed. Grossen Generalstab, Abt. II, 3 vols. (Berlin: Mittler, 1892–1906), II. 71ff.; and Abt. III, 3 vols. (Berlin: Mittler, 1893–1904), III, 29ff.
23. Waldemar Erfurth, *Der Vernichtungssieg. Eine Studie über das Zusammenwirken getrennter Heeresteile* (Berlin: Mittler, 1939), analyses the development of the concept in German military thought.
24. Michael Salewski, 'Moltke, Schlieffen, und der Eisenbahn', in *Generalfeldmarschall von Moltke. Bedeutung und Wirkung*, ed. R. G. Foerster (Munich: Oldenbourg, 1992), 89–102, is a good overview. Cf. Dennis E. Showalter, 'Railroads, the Prussian Army, and the German Way of War in the Nineteenth Century', in *Railways and International Politics: Paths of Empire, 1848–1945*, eds. T. G. Otis and K. Nielsen (London: Routledge, 2006), 21–44.
25. Cf. Kessel, *Moltke*, 444 passim; and Dennis E. Showalter, *The Wars of German Unification* (London: Edward Arnold, 2004), 153 passim.
26. Cf. 'Memoire an seiner Majestät den König vom 25.7.1868 über die bei der Bearbeitung des Feldzuges 1866 hervorgetretene Erfahrungen', and 'Verordnungen für die höheren Truppenführer von 24. Juni 1869', in *Militärische Werke*, Abt. 2, vol. 2, 73ff. passim.
27. Still the best analysis is Rudolf Stadelmann, *Moltke und der Staat* (Krefeld: Scherpe-Verlag, 1950).
28. The most detailed account is Gustav Lehmann, *Die Mobilmachung von 1870* (Berlin: Mittler, 1905); Wolfgang Petter, 'Die Logistik des deutschen Heeres im deutsch-französischen Krieg von 1870–71', in *Die Bedeutung der Logistik für die militärische Führung von der Antike bis in die Neuzeit*, ed. Horst Boog (Herford: Mittler, 1986),

109–33; and Hermann Rahne, *Mobilmachung* (East Berlin: Militärverlag der Deutschen Demokratischen Republik, 1983), 52ff., are good modern overviews.

29. Moltke's campaign plan for 1870 has been the subject of near-theological exegesis. His 'Erste Aufstellung der Armee', begun in the winter of 1868–9 and most recently reworked in July 1870, is in *Militärische Werke*, 1, III, 114ff. Cf. the memo of 6 May 1870 in ibid., 131ff. The quotation is on p. 132. Among the many analyses, Bradley J. Meyer, 'The Operational Art: The Elder Moltke's Campaign Plan for the Franco-Prussian War', in *The Operational Art: Developments in the Theories of War*, ed. B. J. C. McKercher and M. Hennessy (Westport, CT: Greenwood, 1996), 29–49; Kessel, *Moltke*, 538ff., and Arden Bucholz, *Moltke and the German Wars, 1864–1871* (New York: Palgrave, 2001), 155ff., stand out for perception and clarity.
30. Terence Zuber, *The Moltke Myth: German War Planning, 1857–1871* (Lanham, MD: University Press of America, 2008), 209ff.
31. Michael Howard, *The Franco-Prussian War: The German Invasion of France, 1870–1871* (London: Rupert Hart-Davis, 1960), continues to set the standard for the following events. Cf. Showalter, *Wars of German Unification*, 250ff. Geoffrey Wawro, *The Franco-Prussian War* (Cambridge: Cambridge University Press, 2003), has a stronger French perspective.
32. David Ascoli, *A Day of Battle: Mars-la-Tour, 16 August 1870* (London: Harrap, 1987), is a model case study. The still-improvised nature of the concept of *Auftragstaktik* in 1870 is highlighted in Stephan Leistenschneider, *Auftragstaktik im preussisch-deutschen Heer 1871 bis 1914* (Hamburg: Mittler, 2002), 47–55.
33. Kessel, *Moltke*, 562ff.
34. 'Aufsatz vom Jahre 1871 "Über Strategie"', *Militärische Werke*, Abt. 2, vol. 2, 287ff.
35. Michael D. Krause, 'Moltke and the Origins of the Operational Level of War', in *Generalfeldmarschall von Moltke*, 141–64, takes the story forward nicely. Cf. also Carl-Gero von Ilsemann, 'Das operative Denken des Älteren Moltkes', in *Operatives Denken und Handeln in deutschen Streitkräften im 19. und 20. Jahrhundert*, ed. MGFAS (Herford: Mittler, 1988), 17–44; and Stig Förster, 'Facing "People's War": Moltke the Elder and Germany's Military Options after 1871', *Journal of Strategic Studies*, 11 (1988), 209–30.
36. Cf. Antulio Echevarria, *After Clausewitz: German Military Thinkers before the Great War* (Lawrence, KS: University Press of Kansas, 2000), 188–97; and Lothar Burchardt, 'Operatives Denken und Planen von Schlieffen bis zum Beginn des Ersten Weltkrieges', in *Operatives Denken und Handeln*, 45–71.
37. Gregor Schollgen, *Imperialismus und Gleichgewicht. Deutschland, England und der orientalischen Frage, 1871–1914* (Munich: Oldenbourg, 1984); and Peter Winzen, *Bülows Weltmachtkonzept. Untersuchungen zur Frühphase seiner ußenpolitik 1897–1901* (Boppard: Harald Boldt Verlag, 1974).
38. Dennis E. Showalter, *Tannenberg: Clash of Empires* (Hamden, CT: Archon Books, 1991), 30ff.
39. Eric Dorn Brose, *The Kaiser's Army: The Politics of Military Technology during the Machine Age, 1870–1918* (Oxford: Oxford University Press, 2001), 73ff.
40. This seems to be the emerging consensus of years of debate on the major controversy initiated by Terence Zuber, so intense it generated an international conference and a major publication. Cf. Terence Zuber, *Inventing the Schlieffen Plan: German War Planning, 1871–1914* (Oxford: Oxford University Press, 2002); and H. Ehlert, M. Epkenhans and G. Gross (eds.), *Der Schlieffenplan. Analyse und Dokumente* (Pader-

born: Schöningh, 2006), especially Gerhard P. Gross, 'There Was a Schlieffen Plan. Neue Quellen', 117–60.

41. Stig Förster, 'Der deutsche Generalstab und die Illusion des kürzeren Krieges 1871–1914: Meatkritik eines mythos', *Militärgeschichtliche Mitteilungen*, 54 (1995), 61–96.
42. The Hentsch Mission is the primary example. See Bradley J. Meyer, 'Operational Art and the German Command System in World War I', Ph.D. dissertation (Ohio State University, 1988).
43. Dennis E. Showalter, 'Prussian Cavalry, 1806–1871: The Search for Roles', *Militärgeschichtliche Mitteilungen*, 19 (1976), 7–22.
44. Maximilian von Poseck, *The German Cavalry in 1914 in Belgium and France*, ed. J. Howe et al. (Berlin: Mittler, 1923), is a narrative overview; Roman Jarymowycz, *Cavalry from Hoof to Track* (Westport, CT: Praeger Security International, 2008), 130ff., highlights operational shortcomings.
45. These points are developed in R. L. Di Nardo's forthcoming study of Gorlice–Tarnow. I am grateful to the author for making his preliminary chapter drafts available.
46. Laszlo M. Alfoeldi, 'The Huitier Legend', *Parameters*, 5 (1976), 69–74.
47. Ernst Kabisch, *Der Rumänienkrieg 1916* (Berlin: Vorhut Verlag, 1938).
48. David Zabecki, *Steel Wind: Colonel Georg Bruchmüller and the Birth of Modern Artillery* (Westport, CT: Praeger, 1994).
49. Bruce Gudmundsson, *Stormtroop Tactics: Innovation in the German Army, 1914–1918* (Westport, CT: Praeger, 1989).
50. Cf. David Zabecki's conceptually focused *The German 1918 Offensives: A Case Study in the Operational Level of War* (New York: Routledge, 2008) and the general analysis of the campaign and its problems, Martin Kitchen, *The German Offensives of 1918* (Stroud: Tempus, 2001).
51. Michael Geyer, 'Insurrectionary Warfare: The German Debate about a Levee en Masse in 1918', *Journal of Modern History*, 73 (2001), 459–528.
52. Hans von Seeckt, *Thoughts of a Soldier*, trans. G. Waterhouse (London: Ernest Benn, 1930), 55.
53. Robert Citino, *The Path to Blitzkrieg: Doctrine and Training in the German Army, 1920–1939* (Boulder, CO: Lynne Rienner, 1999).
54. Michael Geyer, *Aufrüstung oder Sicherheit? Reichswehr in der Krise der Machtpolitik, 1924–1926* (Wiesbaden: Steiner, 1980).
55. See H. J. Mauch, *Nationalistische Wehrorganisationen in der Weimarer Republik. Zur Entwicklung und Ideologie des 'Paramilitarismus'* (Frankfurt: Peter Lang Verlag, 1982).
56. Cf. Robert Citino, *Quest for Decisive Victory: From Stalemate to Blitzkrieg in Europe, 1899–1940* (Lawrence, KS: University Press of Kansas, 2002), 202; and James Corum, *The Roots of Blitzkrieg* (Lawrence, KS: University Press of Kansas, 1992), 193ff.
57. Corum, *The Roots of Blitzkrieg*; Citino, *Path to Blitzkrieg*; and specifically Robert M. Citino, 'The Weimar Roots of German Military Planning in the 1930s', in *Military Planning and the Origins of the Second World War*, eds. B. J. C. McKercher and R. Legault (Westport, CT: Greenwood, 2001), 59–87.
58. Ernst Volckheim, *Der Kampfwagen in der heutigen Kriegführung* (Berlin: Mittler, 1924).
59. The memo is analyzed and contextualized in Mary R. Habeck, *Storm of Steel: The Development of Armor Doctrine in Germany and the Soviet Union, 1919–1939* (Ithaca, NY: Cornell University Press, 2003), 72ff.
60. This development is contextualized in Azar Gat, *British Armour Theory and the Rise of the Panzer Arm: Revising the Revisionists* (New York: St. Martin's Press, 2000).

61. Karl-Volker Neugebauer, 'Operatives Denken zwischen dem Ersten und Zweiten Weltkrieg', in *Operatives Denken und Handeln*, 97–122.
62. Citino, 'Military Planning', 77ff.
63. Thomas L. Jentz, *Panzer-Truppen*, vol. I (Atglen, PA: Schiffer, 1996), 11ff. The best general analysis is R. L. DiNardo, *Germany's Panzer Arm* (Westport, CT: Praeger, 1997).
64. See generally Wilhelm Deist, *The Wehrmacht and German Rearmament* (London: Macmillan, 1981); and Michael Geyer, 'Rüstungsbeschleunigung und Inflation. Zur Inflationsdenkschrift des Oberkommandos der Wehrmacht von November 1938', *Militärgeschichtliche Mitteilungen*, 30 (1981), 121–86. Beck's position is presented in detail in Klaus-Jürgen Müller, *General Ludwig Beck. Studien und Dokumente zur politisch-militärisch Vorstellungswelt und Tätigkeit des Generalstabchefs des deutschen Heeres* (Boppard: Boldt, 1980).
65. Citino, *German Way of War*, xiii–xiv.
66. Klaus-Jürgen Müller, *Das Heer und Hitler. Armee und nationalsozialistisches Regime 1933–1940* (Stuttgart: Deutsche Verlags-Anstalt, 1969).
67. George Raudzens, 'Blitzkrieg Ambiguities: Doubtful Usage of a Famous Word', *War and Society*, 7 (1988), 77–94.
68. Karl-Heinz Frieser with John T. Greenwood, *Blitzkrieg Legend: The 1940 Campaign in the West* (Annapolis, MD: Naval Institute Press, 2005).
69. The German mobile forces included six panzer, four motorized, and four light divisions, the last of which resembling in structure and intended mission a US Cold War armoured cavalry regiment. Recent operationally focused accounts include Steven J. Zaloga's volume in the Osprey Campaign series, *Poland 1919: The Birth of Blitzkrieg* (Oxford: Osprey, 2002); and Reginald Hargreaves, *Blitzkrieg Unleashed: The German Invasion of Poland, 1939* (Barnsley: Pen & Sword Books, 2008).
70. Still the best for detail is Hans-Adolf Jacobsen, *Fall Gelb: Der Kampf um den Deutschen Operationsplan zur Westoffensive 1940* (Wiesbaden: Steiner, 1957).
71. Heinz Guderian, *Panzer Leader*, trans. C. Fitzgibbon (New York: Dutton, 1952), 90–1. Cf. the notes in C. Burdick and H.-A. Jacobsen (eds.), *The Halder War Diary, 1939–1942* (Novato, CA: Presidio, 1988), 92ff., 98ff.
72. Cf. Bruno Chaix, *En Mai 1940, fallait-il entrer en Belgique? Décisions stratégiques et plans opérationnels de la campagne de France*, 2nd edn. (Paris: Economica, 2005); and D. W. Alexander, 'Repercussions of the Breda Variant', *French Historical Studies*, 8 (1974), 459–88.
73. The contingent nature of the German success in the crucial initial stages is demonstrated by Robert Doughty, *The Breaking Wave: Sedan and the Fall of France, 1940* (Hamden, CT: Shoe String Press, 1990). Cf. Eric Denis, '1940, La Bataille de Stonne. La Resistance heroique de l'armee francaise', *L'Historie Militaire de France, Thematique*, no. 2 (2008).
74. Frieser, *Blitzkrieg Legend*, 291ff., is solid and scathing of the event and its consequences.
75. Dennis E. Showalter, *Patton and Rommel: Men of War in the Twentieth Century* (New York: Berkeley Caliber, 2006), 262 passim.
76. Geoffrey P. Megargee, *War of Annihilation: Combat and Genocide on the Eastern Front* (Lanham, MD: Rowman & Littlefield, 2005), is the best brief overview in English. David Stahel, *Operation Barbarossa and German Military Defeat in the East* (New York: Cambridge University Press, 2009), emphasizes the internal shortcomings of the mobile forces and their consequences for operational art. D. Glantz (ed.), *The Initial*

Period of the War on the Eastern Front, 22 June–August 1941 (London: Frank Cass, 1993), is an anthology with a wealth of detailed unit experiences in the same context. And a suggestive first-hand shopping list of what went wrong from the German military perspective comes from the old *Panzerhase* Hermann Hoth, *Panzer-Operationen. Die Panzergruppe 3 und das operative Gedanke der Deutschen Führung Sommer 1941* (Heidelberg: Kurt Vowinckel Verlag, 1956), 139ff.

77. See particularly the outstanding analysis by Karl-Heinz Frieser, 'Der Rückschlag des Pendels: das Zurückweichen der Ostfront von Sommer 1943 bis Sommer 1944', in *Das Deutsche Reich in der Zweite Weltkrieg*, vol. 8, *Die Ostfront 1943/44*, ed. K.-H. Frieser (Munich: Deutsche Verlags-Anstalt, 2007), 277.
78. The shift is presented and defended by its chief author, Erhard Raus (ed.) and S. Newton (trans.), *Panzer Operations: The Eastern Front Memoir of General Raus, 1941–1945* (Cambridge, MA: Da Capo Press, 2003), 274ff.
79. Cf. generally Bruno Thoss, *Vom Kalten Krieg zur deutschen Einheit. Analysen und Zeitzeugenberichte zur deutschen Militärgeschichte, 1945 bis 1995* (Munich: Oldenbourg, 1995) and Frank Nägler, *Die Bundeswehr 1955–2005. Rückblenden-Einsichten-Perspektiven* (Munich: Oldenbourg, 2007).

3

The Tsarist and Soviet Operational Art, 1853–1991

Jacob W. Kipp

INTRODUCTION

The origins of operational art in Russia are closely connected to the political-military events that shaped the country between the Crimean War and the First World War. Twice, after the Crimean War and after the Russo-Japanese War, military defeat forced the tsarist regime to enact reforms to ensure Russia's social stability, economic modernization, and technological innovation. Both times, Russian officers sought to adapt the military to new organizational requirements, modernize tactics, and obtain modern armaments by domestic production and/or foreign purchase. Thus, war became associated with social crisis, reform, and ultimately revolution.

Defeat by the Anglo-French coalition in the Crimean War set off an era of reform to create a modern economic base for the autocracy, and give it a modern navy, a mass conscript army, a system of military districts to train that army, and a strengthened general staff under the war minister. Military success by this new army during the 1877–8 war with Turkey turned into political defeat when the European powers rejected Russia's *coup de main* and forced it to give up its Balkan gains at the Congress of Berlin. A crisis of autocracy followed, ending with the assassination of Alexander II by terrorists and the assumption of power by his son, Alexander III, who vowed to maintain autocracy, promoted capitalist development, and made the alliance with republican France. The Russo-Japanese War humbled Russian military pride, lost it two fleets, and set in motion a revolution that threatened to sweep away the autocracy, which in its aftermath had grudgingly granted political reforms and created a parliament, the Duma, with limited legislative powers.

Veterans of the Russo-Japanese War undertook reform measures to make the army ready for what they called 'modern war' and began to study the conduct of operations, debate military doctrine, and create the command and control to conduct the operations by fronts controlling multiple armies. In 1914, the autocrat Nicholas II took Russia into another 'popular' war, but after three years of mass industrial war, the monarchy lost its base of support with political revolution bringing an end to the dynasty. Socio-economic collapse followed. This presented the opportunity for a small party of Marxist revolutionaries to seize power in November 1917 with the slogan: 'All power to the Soviets of Workers' and Soldiers' Deputies, bread, land, and peace.'

War and revolution gave birth to the Red Army. 'Operational art' as a recognized term in discussions of military art emerged out of the cauldron of war and revolution that engulfed tsarist Russia and gave birth to Bolshevik Russia. War and preparations for war became a prominent feature of the state that emerged during the Russian Civil War and foreign intervention and throughout the rest of Soviet history.

SVECHIN'S *STRATEGY* AND THE ORIGINS OF OPERATIONAL ART

The first reference to operational art as a concept of military art has been attributed to Aleksandr A. Svechin, tsarist general, officer of the Imperial General Staff, and *voenspets* (military specialist) in the service of the new Bolshevik state. During the First World War, he served at the Stavka (headquarters of the supreme commander), commanded a division, and served as chief of staff first to the 5th Army and then to the Northern Front. Joining the Red Army in March 1918, he organized covering forces at Smolensk during the German advance and then served briefly as chief of the all-Russian main staff.[1] Later he joined the teaching faculty of the Military Academy of the Red Army of Workers and Peasants.

In discussing the education of officers in strategy and operational art, Svechin stressed the utility of deep historical study and observed: 'In essence, all of strategy is basically a contemplation of military history.'[2] Moreover, he informed his readers that to understand his work on strategy, they should read his multi-volume work on the evolution of military art.[3] He addressed the development of military art in its European context and by the juxtaposition of the European and Russian experiences underscored the differences.

According to N. Varfolomeev, the first professor of operational art at the Red Army's military academy, Svechin had first used the term in 1922 in conjunction with his lectures on strategy. At that time, Svechin defined operational art as a critical conceptual linkage between tactics and strategy. In this manner, senior commanders transformed tactical successes into operational 'bounds' to achieve strategic objectives.[4] The time and context of the remarks are particularly important because they point towards the connection of the concept with the post-civil war debates over the interpretation of recent armed conflicts and their implications for the future of the Red Army.

To Svechin, strategy was the pre-eminent part of the art of war but should be seen as one of a number of military disciplines, including tactics and operational art. He specifically called attention to the growing complexity of warfare since the wars of the French Revolution and noted that the conduct of military operations had become 'more complex and profound' and that contemporary commanders could not count on success in any operation, unless they undertook preparations to solve the problems which they would confront in the course of the operation. Strategic foresight (*predvidenie*) was necessary for the conduct of successful operations. Foresight involved a commander's assessment or 'working hypothesis' against which he evaluated the phenomena of war.[5] Under these circumstances, he noted: '. . . we consider the conduct of military operations to be the art of war in the narrow sense of the word.'[6] He defined operational art by referencing its relationship to tactics and strategy. If tactics solve immediate problems and strategy pursues goals defined by the political leadership, then operational art governs tactical creativity and links together tactical actions into a campaign to achieve the strategic goal. 'We call an operation an act of war if the efforts of the troops are directed towards the achievement of a certain intermediary goal in a certain theater of military operations without any interruptions.'[7]

Svechin's starting point was Clausewitz's observation on war as a continuation of politics by other means. Since Napoleon, chancellery war had given way to mass industrial war, driving the evolution of military art. Economic transformations associated with the Industrial Revolution recast the geostrategic balance among states to the advantage of some and the disadvantage of others. Such economic changes also affected class relations within states and internationally. These circumstances dictated specific strategic choices with regard to national preparations for war. They affected the political goals of war, the plans for maintaining domestic stability in time of war, the economic plan of war, diplomacy, and the impact of domestic politics on the conduct of the war. It followed that the conduct of strategy, as the highest level of war, was to be the province not of the military commander but of 'integral military leadership', which would combine the political, military, and economic leadership under the head of state. Coming under strategy, and limited to military problems, was operational art.[8] If tactics solve immediate problems and strategy pursues goals defined by the political leadership, then operational art governs tactical creativity and links together tactical actions into a campaign to achieve the strategic goal;[9] from this, it immediately followed that no amount of operational proficiency could overcome strategic miscalculation regarding the nature of the war embarked upon and the economic and political preparations undertaken.[10]

The core of Svechin's *Strategy* and ultimately its most controversial element to both his contemporaries and present-day analysts was a dualistic strategic paradigm, which he borrowed from Hans Delbrueck, the eminent German military historian and theorist. The poles of this paradigm, attrition (Delbrueck's *Ermattungsstrategie*, or Svechin's *izmor* ['starvation'] in Russian) and destruction (Delbrueck's *Niederwerfungsstrategie*, or Svechin's *sokrushenie* in Russian), were conditioned by the circumstances of war itself. A belligerent power, depending on its war aims, the military potential of its society and economy, and its military capabilities, could employ either model. Like Delbrueck, Svechin thought soldiers were all too eager to take the strategy of destruction as the only appropriate course to seize and exploit the initiative and bring about a decision in a one-sided reading of Clausewitz's assessment of the legacy of Napoleon.[11] The object of destruction was the enemy force in the field. But the transformation of states, societies, and economies in the nineteenth century had created the capacity for mobilization for total war, where the defeated army could be replaced by new levees and new equipment. Svechin warned: 'The task of strategy is greatly simplified if we or the enemy... try to end a war with a destructive strike. Treatises on strategy that have been exclusively concerned with a strategy of destruction in essence turn into tracts on operational art....'[12]

Instead, Svechin offered a strategy of attrition as an alternative to destruction. But, in this case, attrition was a strategy that was not limited to operational art but was politically and economically informed. While destruction is driven by its own logic to seek an immediate decision in a campaign, attrition, depending on the intensity of armed conflict, can range from close to destruction to the absence of combat operations. The level of intensity of combat actions in a given situation depends upon a thorough and careful study of economic and political conditions. 'A very broad range is open for politics, and strategy should be flexible.' A strategy of attrition allows for the shaping of a conflict and for continued political engagement to redefine the conflict to one's advantage in both domestic and international terms.[13] Under such a strategy, the guidance of operations is under the direction of the 'integral military command', and the conduct of operations in a particular theatre depends upon the general staff, which Svechin's colleague and another *voenspets*, Boris Mikhailovich Shaposhnikov, defined as the 'brain of the army'.[14]

Svechin understood military art in the age of imperialism to refer to 'modern war'. It was the war that he had himself fought in Manchuria, on the Eastern Front and during the Russian Civil War. This was war conducted by multiple armies and then by army groups and fronts. In the age of Moltke, the logistical support came from the army's rear. By the First World War, logistics transcended the 'front rear' (*frontovoi tyl*) and became a matter of the state rear (*gosudarstvennyi tyl*). The more developed the capitalist society and state, the stronger this state rear became.[15] This was the fundamental assumption behind his concept of the 'integral military command', which brought the political, military, and economic leadership into a collective body to prepare and conduct warfare. Only in this fashion would the general staff, as the military part of that leadership, be able to understand the political goals and economic constraints to provide sound strategic leadership for the conduct of operations. Conversely, it was failure in this area that had made tsarist Russia vulnerable to economic crisis, social disintegration, and political revolution.

Svechin admitted that when he attended the tsarist General Staff Academy before the Russo-Japanese War, the faculty taught war on the model of Napoleon. Moltke's insights reached Russia only after the Russo-Japanese War, when a younger generation of officers sought to understand the campaigns that they had fought in Manchuria and translated German studies of Moltke's military art into Russian.[16] The First World War had buried Moltke's model of short, decisive wars among major powers. But the Russo-Japanese War had been a harbinger of this trend. In

Manchuria, three Russian armies had faced five Japanese armies with neither side able to achieve decisive results in the field. Russia's 'advanced guard', as he called General Kuropatkin's armies, had lacked an effective system of command and control, never seized the initiative, but had never suffered annihilation. Japanese employment of the strategy of the extended line had forced the Russian armies to withdraw rather than face encirclement as was the case at the last major land engagement of the war at Mukden in February–March 1905. In the end, the war was decided by revolution at home. Russia sued for peace, while the tsarist government sought by a combination of reform and repression to stem the tide.

Following that war, Russian military reformers, including Svechin, had sought to understand modern war and to develop a military doctrine that would respond to its demands. Fronts appeared as the higher headquarters to exercise command and control of multiple armies under the overall direction of the Stavka. Svechin was one of the reformers to call into question the strategic obligations that Russia assumed in its alliance with France, criticizing the commitment to an initial offensive against East Prussia before Russia could complete its mobilization and deployment of forces, and proposing that France assume the defence against the initial German offensive. His fears were dismissed in higher political and military circles of the old regime. No one in St. Petersburg dared to antagonize the French after the disaster of the Russo-Japanese War. On reviewing the Great Military Programme of 1909, Svechin understood that, while tsarist Russia had increased its mobilization potential by raising reserve forces from deep within the empire, it had not fundamentally changed the pace of the deployment of those forces to the threatened fronts. Russia's railroad system could not make its supposed 'steamroller' move any faster.

As the leading Soviet expert on the lessons of the First World War, Svechin appreciated the difference between the wars fought on the Western Front with its immobile trench lines and the *Gummikrieg* (rubber war) on the Eastern Front, where advances were possible but decision elusive. He was well aware of the success which General Aleksei Brusilov had achieved on the Austrian Front in the summer of 1916 and noted operational and tactical innovations (broad-front attack, extensive preparation of the assault troops, short and precise artillery preparation, and small-unit infiltration of the Austro-Hungarian trenches) that contributed to both the breakthrough and exploitation of the initial success. But he questioned the logic of continuing such operations to support Allied efforts on the Somme, when a German counter-offensive was imminent. The debacle in Romania, after it entered the war, unhinged the Russian line and undercut any further major offensive operations until the ill-starred Kerensky Offensive of 1917.

Unlike the young Red commanders, who saw class warfare as the dominant form of future conflict, Svechin did not see the victories against the Whites as harbingers of future war. Instead, wars between nation states posed the greatest threat to the Soviet Union as an international pariah. To his eye, the case worth study and consideration was the failed Soviet offensive against Pilsudski's Poland. Here, he saw multiple operational problems, from ineffective command and control to operational overreach beyond culmination exposing the Red Army to a devastating Polish counter-offensive. Ideological enthusiasm had blinded the military and political leadership to operational limits of the force committed. Poland was likely to be the launching point of an operation against the Soviet Union, and so the study of that campaign became a persistent theme in his writing.

The Soviet Union should be prepared for a long war with maximum mobilization of society and economy. Defence industries should be moved deep within Soviet territory to avoid their loss in the initial enemy offensive. Soviet forces would rely upon mass mobilization of men, material, and technology to defeat the enemy. To harass the enemy's rear while it conducted an active defence and counter-attacks, the Soviet Union would embrace 'people's war'. The final defeat of the enemy would come about through the organization of limited operations by particular fronts and groups of fronts. Coordinating them was the province of operational art and should be carried out by the Stavka.

Given his vision of the probable opponent, Svechin expected that Soviet forces would have to conduct breakthrough operations on the model of Brusilov and would need to find the appropriate instrument to exploit success. The practical depth of penetration that would be achieved in these operations depended heavily upon the logistical support which the attacking forces would enjoy. In a memo to Boris Shaposhnikov, chief of the Red Army's Main Staff (RKKA), Svechin said that since Soviet industry remained undeveloped, it was doubtful whether the Soviet Union was able to achieve qualitative or quantitative parity with the advanced capitalist powers. He was even more worried about the young Red commanders' enthusiasm for revolutionary warfare and preventive war.[17]

In Stalin's Soviet Union, expressing one's view was never without danger to life and limb. In the spring of 1930, a dispute over the primary direction of the enemy threat emerged, pitting Svechin against two of those commanders, Mikhail Tukhachevsky and V. K. Triandafillov. Svechin pointed to south and south-western borders and the risk of Anglo-French support for Romania. Tukhachevsky and Triandafillov for their part looked to the threat from Poland. Shaposhnikov sided with the two Red commanders and also rejected Svechin's concerns about the ability of the USSR to create a modern military force on a par with those of the encircling capitalist powers.[18] In late September 1930, Shaposhnikov, *voenspets* and graduate of the tsarist General Staff Academy, put in his request to join the Communist Party. By that time, other *voenspetsy*, including Svechin, were already under arrest by the Unified State Political Administration (OGPU).

TUKHACHEVSKY, MECHANIZATION, DEEP OPERATIONS, AND THE BATTLE OF ANNIHILATION

Within the RKKA Military Academy, the Faculty of Operational Art, which was established in 1924, steadily developed its curriculum and engaged in research relating to the form and content of operational art. N. Varfolomeev pioneered the study of shock armies in breakthrough operations during the German and Allied campaigns of 1918. Triandafillov studied the problem of command and control of fronts and armies and explored the problem of logistical support for deep operations by modern armies.

It was in this context that Mikhail Tukhachevsky, who was then chief of the RKKA Military Staff (1925–8), emerged as the chief promoter of both mechanization and deep operations. During the civil war, Tukhachevsky, former Guard officer in the Tsarist Army, escaped prisoner of war, and war hero, had championed class politics as the means to bring the revolution from without. He even took part in the suppression of the Kronstadt naval revolt. When that technique failed to bring victory during the Polish campaign of 1920, of which he had been the commander, he started seeking other means to achieve such shock. For inspiration, he looked to the civil war. Specifically, in August–September 1919, General K. K. Mamontov's IV Don Cavalry Corps had attacked the Bolshevik Southern Front. Using air reconnaissance to find a gap in the Red Army's lines, Mamontov moved deep into the enemy's rear, wrecking rail lines, destroying military stores, and creating panic across six *gubernias* (districts).

At the time, Lenin and the Bolsheviks took the threat seriously enough to create an Internal Front under M. M. Lashevich to restore order and engage Mamontov's forces on their return to Denikin's lines. Assessing this successful use of cavalry, the Revolutionary Military Council authorized the creation of the First Cavalry Army (*Konarmiia*) under the command of S. M. Budennyi and tasked it with a raiding function analogous to that of Mamontov's corps. In this case, *Konarmiia* included cavalry divisions, an armoured-car battalion, mounted infantry, cart-mounted machine guns, air reconnaissance assets, and an armoured train. From this point on, Budennyi's *Konarmiia* served as shock troops for the Red Army and was assigned to various fronts to conduct deep raids into the enemy's rear. After the war, its operations remained the subject of a military debate.

Following Lenin's proclamation of the New Economic Policy (NEP) in 1923, demobilization got under way. Senior Red Army commanders might warn of the need to prepare the Soviet defence industry for fighting the encircling capitalist powers. However, the reality of the NEP demanded a small standing army, foreign procurement of technology, and modest investments in domestic production. Not everybody accepted these ideas; in the discussions of the Five-Year Plan, Tukhachevsky had emerged as an outspoken champion of the militarization of the Soviet economy as a first step towards the creation of a mass mechanized army with large-scale armoured forces and long-range aviation. His initial proposals to the Central Committee of the Party were rejected by Stalin who labelled them as 'Red militarism'.[19] In 1928, Tukhachevsky was moved out of the Red Army Staff to command the Leningrad Military District. There he remained until 1931, finding both a major concentration of military units and leading enterprises of the defence industry. He was thus able to continue his own study of and agitation for the development of 'deep battle' and its transformation into deep operations leading to the annihilation of the enemy throughout the depth of his defences. This would be achieved by organizational innovations and be based on the large-scale mechanization of the Red Army.

The issuance of new field regulations, the drafting of which he had played a leading role while in the Red Army Staff, in 1929, provided Tukhachevsky with an opportunity to recast training in the Leningrad Military District to reflect not only the new regulations, but also his attempt to articulate his own concepts in summer manoeuvres of the troops under his command. He also engaged the Soviet military press to present his views to the army and party. In 1929, the Red Army got its first mechanized regiment, and Tukhachevsky continued to agitate for the creation of mechanized corps.[20] In 1930, the People's Commissariat of Defence (NARKOMO) authorized the creation of the first experimental airborne detachment composed of three rifle companies in the Red Army. Tukhachevsky, who had advocated such a force, used the experiment to integrate airborne assault (*vozdushnyi desant*) into deep operations by experimenting with parachute landings and the introduction of mechanized capabilities into the detachment, including the air landing of light trucks, motorcycles with sidecars, and tankettes.[21] Aviation, armour, and airborne forces would make possible the conduct of deep operations to achieve decisive success in the initial period of war.

While Tukhachevsky in Leningrad perfected the deep operation concept, the political-ideological climate in the Soviet Union underwent profound changes. Bolshevik ideology had by the 1920s embraced the technological transformation of state, society, and economy as a defence of the revolutionary gamble of 1917. Bolshevik élan, Marxist-Leninist ideology, and mass industrial production would create a socialist order and protect the regime from both foreign and domestic threats to its existence. The first Five-Year Plan of 1929 called for mass domestic production of aircraft and armour, with production targets in the next four years of 3,500 aircraft and 5,000 tanks. Stalin's slogan, 'socialism in one country', which had been originally articulated in 1924 under the NEP, now began to take on the form of a command economy. Military requirements, derived from threat analysis, would drive subsequent central planning ventures towards high annual productions of tanks and aircraft at the expense of investment in infrastructure.

Tukhachevsky became the central link between the emerging total war economy and operational art. Championing the militarization of the Five-Year Plan, he linked increased armaments production with the restructuring of the Red Army to 'new forms of operational art'.[22] His vision was of a mass mechanized army, composed of 260 infantry and cavalry divisions, 40,000 aircraft, and 50,000 tanks.[23] He went ahead in spreading his own version of large-scale mechanization, deep operations, and the battle of annihilation. He put forward his case in an introduction he wrote for the Russian edition of J. F. C. Fuller's *The Reformation of War.* Rejecting Fuller's concept of a small professional mechanized force, he posed a hypothetical case of war between two opposing forces organized along the lines advocated by Fuller and one reflecting his own vision:

We imagine a war of Great Britain against the USA, a war, for instance, which breaks out on the Canadian border. Both armies are mechanized, but the English have let's say Fuller's cadres of 18 divisions but the US Army has 180 divisions; the first has 5,000 tanks and 3,000 aircraft, and the second has 50,000 tanks and 30,000 aircraft. The small English Army would simply be crushed. It is clear that discussions about small, but mobile and mechanized armies in major wars are a cock-and-bull story, and only frivolous people can take them seriously.[24]

Such a mass mechanized force was precisely what the Soviet Union now set out to create. Tukhachevsky himself played the leading role, first through his post as director of armaments for the Red Army, which he held from 1931 to the mid-1930s, and then as first deputy commissar for defence when he assumed responsibility for training the Red Army.[25] Much of this was driven by his commitment to the concept of deep operations and its linkage to a strategy of annihilation. No aspect of the technology associated with the conduct of deep operations—armour, mechanized infantry, aviation, artillery and rockets, engineers, and radio communications—escaped his attention. These were the means needed to execute his version of operational art, deep operations, as the decisive form of combat for the Red Army.

During this period, Tukhachevsky played a leading role in creating mass mechanized forces for the Soviet Union. Under his leadership, the Red Army also conducted large-scale manoeuvres involving the execution of deep operations against 'opposing forces' in 1935 and 1936.[26] He belonged to that group of young Red commanders which embraced the idea that the Red Army could be transformed into such an instrument so that it could carry war into the territory of any enemy that attacked the USSR and inflict upon that enemy a decisive defeat. The only strategy for the Soviet Union was one of annihilation achieved through the conduct of deep operations.

Such views might make some sense in the face of the threat of Poland and Romania in the 1920s.[27] By the mid-1930s, they did not. As early as 1934, Narkomo Voroshilov spoke of the growing threat from Germany and Poland and the possible cooperation of Japan in a general war against the Soviet Union.[28] The new international environment demanded the precise correlation of international policy, military strategy, and operational art with the first shaping the latter two. At the precise movement of the emergence of this threat, Stalin chose effectively to decapitate the Red Army.

FROM THE GREAT PURGE TO THE GREAT PATRIOTIC WAR

By the mid-1930s, Stalin had emerged as the sole heir to Lenin and the leader of the Soviet Union. For two decades, he had been involved in the senior leadership of the Bolshevik Party and the Soviet state, and in that capacity he had been involved in every aspect of foreign, defence, and internal policy. In military affairs, he had been actively involved in prosecuting the civil war, and many of his military associations formed during that era influenced his assumptions about the conduct of war. He had played a leading role in directing Soviet foreign policy during the decades of its isolation as a pariah state, a revolutionary bastion of socialism surrounded by hostile capitalist powers. In internal policy, he had carried out a revolution from above that consolidated a totalitarian state bent upon rapid industrialization and the forced collectivization of agriculture. This revolution had laid the basis for the militarization of the Soviet economy and maximized the capacity of the state to mobilize the society. He had done all this by terrorizing class enemies, national minorities, and even his own party elite.

In 1936, the Red Army received the Temporary Field Regulation-36 (*PU*-36). Soviet deep-operations theory, as presented in *PU*-36, emphasized a *troika* of surprise, deception, and secrecy to create the operational preconditions for success. *PU*-36 called for a succession of combined-arms blows, led by mechanized formations and supported by tactical aviation and airborne troops, to break through the enemy's defences through their entire depth and create conditions for exploitation and destruction of the enemy by means of manoeuvre and shock.[29] Meeting engagements in which the second echelon would encounter and destroy the enemy's reserves as they moved up to join the battle were to lead to encirclements.[30] However, within a year of the publication of *PU*-36, many of those who had championed and promoted its concepts were dead, victims of a sweeping purge of the Red Army's leadership. Among them were Tukhachevsky, the real dynamo behind the changes of the period 1931–5, as well as Svechin. Once the terror instrument was turned loose upon the Red Army, it devastated the greater part of the military elite, including 3 of 5 marshals, 13 of 15 army commanders, 50 of 57 corps commanders, and 154 out of 186 division commanders. This created many opportunities for the rapid advancement of junior commanders, but it also meant that many rose too rapidly and lacked both the experience and the education for the ranks they assumed. Moreover, the survivors could not be sure that the same terror might not be used against them.

STRATEGY AND OPERATIONAL ART IN THE SOVIET–FINNISH WAR, 1939–40

In October and November 1939, the Soviet government put pressure on Finland to conclude a treaty of friendship and mutual assistance that included demands for the transfer of Finnish territory—the Karelian Isthmus, the Hango Peninsula, and the Rybachi and Srednyi Peninsulas in the north—to the Soviet Union. The Finns refused to negotiate their own destruction—giving up the fortified positions on the Karelian Isthmus would have left Finland effectively defenceless—and prepared to fight. They mobilized their forces in mid-October; the war itself began on 30 November.

Stalin and his commissar for defence, Klenemtii Voroshilov, believed that the war would be short and decisive. In June 1939, during the crucial period when the

Soviet Union still faced the threat of war with Germany and Japan, Stalin asked Marshal Shaposhnikov to present the general staff's views on plans for war with Finland. Shaposhnikov noted the difficulties involved in penetrating the deeply echeloned defences of the Mannerheim Line on the isthmus and proposed the concentration of significant forces and means in the theatre and specific training and preparations for assaults on fortified positions before launching operations. He stated that the campaign itself would involve several months of heavy fighting. Stalin accused Shaposhnikov of being over-cautious and rejected his recommendations. Instead, he ordered General Meretskov, commander of the Leningrad Military District, to prepare his own war plan for Finland, giving him three weeks to accomplish the task.[31] In his memoirs, Meretskov does not discuss the details of these plans, confining his remarks to cryptic comments about Shaposhnikov's plan and its wisdom. In July, when he presented his own plan to Stalin and Voroshilov, they approved it and said that the war should be 'short and swift'. When Meretskov objected, they promised the full resources of the Soviet Union to achieve rapid victory.[32]

The Leningrad Military District was transformed into the North-Western Front and the Baltic and Northern Fleets were subordinated to that front. The command arrangements took no account of the vastness of the theatre or the problems of exercising strategic-operational command of control over diverse forces operating on distant axes. The North-Western Front under General Meretskov sent four armies—the 7th, 8th, 9th, and 14th—into the attack. The 7th Army, which was under Meretskov's direct command, represented the primary effort. It was to advance up the Karelian Isthmus, penetrate the Mannerheim Line, and, with the 8th Army advancing around the western and northern shore of Lake Ladoga, surround the Finnish defenders and then advance on Helsinki. The 9th Army was supposed to advance across central Finland to the Swedish border and cut northern Finland off from the south. The 14th Army, with the assistance of the Northern Fleet, was to advance and take the Finnish port of Petsamo and cut northern Finland off from foreign assistance. This was to be a preventive war with the outcome being the removal of the current Finnish government and its replacement by a pro-Communist one, which would make the territorial concessions Moscow had demanded and be a dependable ally in the future.[33]

Soviet accounts of the Winter War divide the conflict into two periods. The first, which was noteworthy for Soviet maximalist war aims, including the creation of a Finnish People's Republic under Soviet sponsorship to govern post-war Finland, can rightly be called a series of tactical defeats adding up to operational failure that lasted from December to early February 1940. The 7th Army, with an overwhelming superiority in men, tanks, and artillery, mounted a broad advance up the isthmus. Its initial attacks did not focus on one sector of its frontage and did not create a solid concentration of forces against any one point. In two weeks of fighting, it failed to penetrate the Mannerheim Line and suffered heavy losses. Soviet troops went forward without good intelligence and ran into barbed-wire entanglements, tank traps, and dense minefields which inflicted serious losses and stopped the attack until mine-detection devices could be deployed and the fields cleared. Finnish pillboxes and bunkers proved resistant to indirect fire. Finnish guns had excellent fields of fire against the advancing troops. Progress was measured in hundreds of metres and thousands of killed and wounded. No major breakthrough could be achieved and a stalemate ensued.[34]

The attack around Lake Ladoga by the 8th Army turned into battles of annihilation against isolated road-bound Red Army columns of mounted infantry and tanks. They were cut off by Finnish ski troops attacking in small units from the surrounding forests. The Finns were equally successful in stopping the attack of the 9th Army in Central Finland where Red Army units found themselves encircled by numerically inferior Finnish forces.

By late December, the Soviet political and military leadership were embarrassed by the initial failures and increasingly nervous about the growing prospects for foreign intervention by Anglo-French forces. Stalin responded to the initial failures by asking the general staff to assess the situation and recommend measures to ensure victory.[35] Speaking to the military council, Shaposhnikov presented the same recommendations the general staff had offered a month before. Stalin had responded to the crisis by shaking up the command structure, sacking corps and division commanders. Now he asked the council who should replace Meretskov as front commander. Semen Konstantinovich Timoshenko, then the commander of the Ukrainian Military District, responded by saying he would accept the post on condition that the measures recommended by Shaposhnikov were adopted.[36]

On 7 January 1940, Stalin officially replaced Meretskov as commander of the North-Western Front, leaving him as commander of the 7th Army, and appointed Timoshenko to command that front, which now consisted of the 7th and 8th Armies. Timoshenko spent a month preparing his forces for the offensive, which began on 11 February and continued into early March. This time, the Soviet 7th Army focused its assault forces on specific strong points, brought combined arms into play, and broke through the final defensive positions of the Mannerheim Line by using heavy artillery in direct fire on pillboxes and bunkers. It then took Vyborg and was poised to advance on Helsinki itself. Soviet losses in men and material were still heavy, but the momentum of the attack convinced Mannerheim that the time had come to end hostilities. In the end, the Finns agreed to new terms and an armistice was signed on 13 March 1940. Finland had to give up more territory with over a tenth of its population fleeing areas now under Soviet control.

As Carl Van Dyke has pointed out, the Soviet–Finnish War was followed by a vigorous programme of military reforms aimed at improving the tactical and operational capabilities of the Red Army. These reforms had not yet transformed the Red Army when the Wehrmacht struck in June 1941, but they did lay the foundation for the recovery of the forces in the course of that war.[37]

But interested outside observers drew their own conclusions about the Red Army's combat capabilities. On 1 January 1941, as plans for the German invasion of the USSR were proceeding, Fremde Heere Ost of the German general staff offered an assessment of the morale and combat power of the Red Army. It stated that on the basis of its poor performance in Finland, the Red Army was undergoing reforms to strengthen its discipline and troop training and this was expected to take years, even up to a decade. Senior commanders of large formations were unequal to conducting large-scale operations and individual soldiers lacked the initiative to operate effectively on the modern battlefield.[38] The war with Finland had exposed Soviet military weaknesses the Wehrmacht could exploit in the coming war.

A TALE OF TWO OPERATIONS: URANUS AND MARS

One of the more controversial issues associated with the Zhukov–Vasilevsky team and their mastery of operational art concerns their roles as Stavka representatives coordinating two nearly simultaneous multi-front operations in the autumn and winter of 1942: Operations Uranus and Mars. Operation Uranus, the Soviet counter-offensive at Stalingrad, was launched on 19 November 1942 and involved the South-Western, Don, and Stalingrad Fronts. Its objective was the encirclement and the destruction of the German 6th Army. Operation Mars, the Soviet offensive conducted by the Kalinin and Western Fronts, had as its objective the reduction the Rzhev salient defended by General Walter Model's 9th Army. It was launched on 24–5 November 1942.

Along with the near-simultaneous Battle of El Alamein, Operation Uranus has been hailed as a turning point in the Second World War. The scale of these two operations says much about the nature of operational art as practised by the Western Allies and the Soviet Union. At El Alamein, Montgomery directed an army of 230,000 troops, 1,440 tanks, 2,310 tubes, and 1,300 aircraft against Erwin Rommel's Army Africa, a German–Italian force of 80,000 men, 540 tanks, 1,300 tubes, and 350 aircraft.[39] In the Stalingrad counter-offensive, the Stavka committed a Soviet force of 1.1 million men, 1,460 tanks, 15,300 tubes, and 1,350 aircraft against a German–Romanian force of 1 million men, 675 tanks, 10,300 tubes, and 1,220 aircraft.[40]

The end of the summer fighting had put the German 6th Army and 4th Tank Army into Stalingrad and some of the most intense and bloody urban combat of the war. Hitler was fixated on taking the city and most German senior officers considered the Red Army to be quite weak and incapable of large-scale offensive operations. Fremde Heere Ost was predicting a Soviet blow on the Moscow axis for the early autumn. Soviet counter-attacks in the immediate vicinity of Stalingrad had not broken the dogged German drive towards the bank of the Volga, and the Oberkommando des Heeres (OKH) assumed that there was no immediate Soviet operational threat to Army Group B.

In this context, Zhukov and Vasilevsky met with Stalin in September and proposed a more sweeping solution to the crisis at Stalingrad. Noting the fact that the flanks of the 6th and 4th Panzer Army to the north and south of Stalingrad were held by the 3rd and 4th Romanian Armies and that neither of these armies possessed significant mobile reserves, they proposed a deep envelopment of Stalingrad using the forces of the three fronts, augmented by new forces from the Stavka reserve. The South-Western Front would jump off from the bridgeheads it already held on the south side of the Don River. These forces would strike the flanking Romanian armies, break through, and complete the encirclement of 6th Army and 4th Panzer Army. While mobile forces advanced to the west and south-west on the external front of the envelopment, other troops comprising the inner envelopment would isolate the Stalingrad force and destroy the pocket. At first, Stalin expressed fears that the plan was too ambitious and proposed to move the flank attacks closer to Stalingrad. But Zhukov and Vasilevsky stated their opposition and stressed the vulnerability of the Romanian armies. Finally, Stalin agreed. Both men then went to Stalingrad to begin preparations.

The most difficult role in the period of preparations fell to Vasilii Chuikov who assumed command of the 62nd Army in Stalingrad that September. When asked by his front commander, Colonel-General Andrei Eremenko, and Nikita Khrushchev, senior party representative to the front, if he understood his mission, he replied: 'We will defend the city or die in the attempt.'[41] The men of the 62nd Army did both over the next two months, albeit at the cost of monumental losses. The deeper the German forces were drawn into the urban fighting, the more likely the success of the flank offensives by the South-Western and Don Fronts.

The Stavka spent two months preparing for Uranus. Fresh forces were deployed and concealed from German observation. Generals Vatutin and Rokossovsky were appointed commanders of the South-Western and Don Fronts on Zhukov's recommendation. Soviet rear services expedited rail movement of Stavka reserves to the attacking fronts' assembly areas. As he had done at KhalKhin-Gol in 1939, Zhukov ordered the troops to build defensive positions to make the enemy believe that the Red Army was going over to the defence in preparation for winter. Meanwhile, Soviet intelligence started delivering more information on the status of the Romanian units targeted for attack.[42]

On 19 November, the Soviet forces struck the Romanian lines, achieving complete surprise. Massed artillery fire announced the beginning of the offensive. Advancing infantry, supported by tanks, penetrated the Romanian forward defences and created openings for the commitment of tank and cavalry formations to mount the deep attack with the objective of the South-Western and Stalingrad Fronts meeting to encircle the 6th Army and elements of the 4th Panzer Army. The link-up at Kalach took place on 21 November. Inside the pocket, 290,000 German and Allied troops were trapped.

Hitler refused to abandon Stalingrad, and Goering pledged that the Luftwaffe would supply the besieged army by air. In December, Field Marshal Erich von Manstein's attempt to break the encirclement failed. Soviet forces followed Uranus with Operation Little Saturn to expand the external front, striking towards Rostov on the Don to cut off Army Group A in the Caucasus and to clear the lower Don region. While failing to reach Rostov, the attack did push back the German forces and captured a number of airfields used by the Luftwaffe in its attempt to resupply Stalingrad.

Initially, the Stavka itself was surprised by the number of troops, roughly 290,000, that had been encircled at Stalingrad. Accordingly, it re-enforced the encircling forces and, on 10 January 1943, it mounted Operation Ring to reduce the pocket. In almost a month of bloody fighting, the Soviet forces cut the encircled German forces into parts and forced a final surrender of Field Marshal von Paulus on 2 February. About 90,000 men marched into captivity. By winning a decisive victory, Zhukov and Vasilevky had demonstrated the Red Army's mastery of operational art.

Whereas Operation Uranus was a great success, the almost simultaneous Operation Mars is usually considered a failure and has been labelled Zhukov's 'greatest defeat'.[43] The objective was to dislodge the Germans from the Rzhev salient west of Moscow, known as 'the Rzhev meat grinder' owing to the heavy casualties inflicted on attacking Soviet forces. Initially timed to precede Operation Uranus, Operation Mars was delayed because of heavy rains and muddy conditions. When the heavy frost came and the ground hardened, the Stavka rescheduled to start on 25 November. Then nothing went right. Fog and snow reduced the effectiveness of the initial artillery preparation. The attacking forces made progress on only one axis, and Model's counter-attacks with available armour first contained the initial penetrations and then surrounded elements of a mechanized corps and rifle corps. The Soviets suffered heavy casualties and made only very limited gains; they did not succeed in removing the threat to Moscow once and for all. Possibly, in order to save Zhukov's reputation, some Soviet–Russian critics have claimed that Operation Mars has been misinterpreted. In reality, they claim, it was a relatively minor undertaking aimed at drawing attention away from the Stalingrad Front.[44]

KURSK: THE PREMEDITATED DEFENSIVE OPERATION

The strategic-operational success at Stalingrad did not mean the German army had forever lost the initiative on the Eastern Front. In February–March 1943, Field Marshal von Manstein conducted a brilliant counter-blow against the offensive of the South-Western Front towards Kharkov. Vasilevsky, who observed this operation from the Stavka, noted that Vatutin incorrectly assumed that German defences were weak and that his forces had an opportunity to drive on towards Kharkov and beyond to the Dnieper. Stalin approved the advance towards Kharkov, and, when that city fell, he approved the continuation of the offensive. In fact, Manstein had rallied his new command, Army Group Don, and received serious re-enforcements from the west, including SS Panzer units now operating as an SS Panzer Corps. Manstein achieved a brilliant success. The local commanders and the Stavka had underestimated the recovery power of the Wehrmacht and the operational skills of Field Marshal von Manstein.[45] Stalin sent Zhukov to the threatened sector and released sufficient Stavka reserves (the 64th Army, the 1st Tank Army, and the 21st Army) to change the correlation of forces and stop the advance of Manstein's armour, but these forces could not liberate Belgorod.[46]

As winter operations gave way to the spring *razputista*, the Germans had retaken Kharkov and advanced to Belgorod. To the north, following Operation Mars, Army Group Centre had conducted a staged withdrawal under Soviet pressure to positions in front of Smolensk and Orel. Between these two positions, the Soviet forces held a bulge in the line with the city of Kursk in its centre. Both the OKH and the Stavka recognized the importance of the Kursk bulge and after the heavy fighting in the winter of 1942–3 were aware that operational objectives for the summer campaign of 1943 would have to be more limited.[47] For the Germans, the OKH had to take into consideration not only the losses sustained at Stalingrad, but also developments outside of the Eastern Front, particularly the fact that the Panzer Army Africa was trapped in Tunisia and being smashed to pieces by joint US and British forces.

With limited assets, the German high command needed a victory in the east to rob the Red Army of the initiative before the Allied forces assembled in North Africa could regroup and mount follow-on operations somewhere in the Mediterranean. Even a cursory look at the map of the Eastern Front led to the conclusion that the Kursk bulge offered operational advantages. Striking from Orel and Belgorod, the forces of Army Group Centre under von Kluge and Army Group South under von Manstein could cut off the salient and trap the Soviet forces with the pocket. Hitler approved Operation Citadel, but then delayed its execution in May in order to permit the rearming of the German Panzer forces with new technology.

During the same period, Vasilevsky ordered the main intelligence directorate (GRU) of the general staff to assess the enemy situation in the sector of the front covered by the Central, Voronezh, and South-Western Fronts. On 8 April, Zhukov, basing himself on the initial intelligence assessment, identified the Kursk bulge as the likely target for the Wehrmacht's summer offensive. Addressing Soviet operational goals for the summer of 1943, he proposed to Stalin that the Red Army not launch its own summer offensive, but engage in the construction of a deeply echeloned defence of the bulge and accept the German blow. Zhukov proposed to bleed German armour in a battle with this premeditated and deeply echeloned defence at Kursk and then mount offensive operations north and south of the bulge.[48]

The scale of forces deployed at Kursk suggests the magnitude of the struggle. The OKH practically stripped the rest of the Eastern Front to get the mass of armour and aviation deployed there. The Stavka released its reserves to the fronts. While the Germans managed to come close to the Soviets in armour with somewhat over 3,000 tanks, assault guns, and self-propelled artillery, in the air they were at a slight disadvantage in aircraft with the Soviets massing 2,900 planes against about 2,050 for the Luftwaffe. But in manpower and artillery, the Soviets achieved an overwhelming superiority of 1.1 million versus 430,000 men and 25,000 versus about 10,000 barrels.[49]

On 5 July, General Model and Field Marshal von Manstein unleashed their offensives against the northern and southern bases of the salient with the intention of cutting off all Soviet forces within it. Kursk has been presented as the greatest tank battle of the Eastern Front, but it was as much a combined-arms fight. Soviet infantry, anti-tank guns, and artillery inflicted losses on the attackers and limited the manoeuvre of German armour. Soviet engineers had mined the area, created anti-tank obstacles, and constructed bunkers and command posts to manage the fight. Both sides employed massed aviation in support of the tactical fight, and the intensive struggle for command of the air began in May and continued up to the beginning of the operation. On the morning of 5 July, the Soviet air force struck German airfields at dawn but did not inflict serious damage. Air power on both sides now shifted its emphasis to direct combat support. Given the growing threat to the Reich from Allied bombers, this was the last time the Luftwaffe would be able to mass fighter aviation in the east.

In the north, Model, who attacked with armour and infantry, found his forces coming under heavy artillery fire before they could jump off. This created some confusion, and caused his forces, which were only making slow progress, to become tied down in the Central Front's defences. At this juncture, on 12 July, Zhukov authorized Popov's Bryansk Front to initiate Operation Kutuzov and attack with its 4th Tank Army and 61st Army with the objective of cutting off Model's forces at Orel. Only the intervention of the Luftwaffe reduced Soviet armour and permitted the 9th Army to retreat.

In the south, Manstein struck with Hoth's 4th Panzer Army and Army Detachment Kempf and managed to break through two lines of tactical defences, causing Zhukov to order elements of the Steppe Front to advance and take on the German armour in a series of meeting engagements. The commitment of Rotmistrov's 5th Guards Tank Army at Prokhorovka against the II SS Panzer Corps on 12 July produced a major tank fight and resulted in what was probably a Soviet tactical draw and operational success.[50] Manstein had assumed that a breakthrough by the II SS Panzer Corps would put his forces beyond the Soviet tactical defences and into open country. In fact, Prokhorovka was at the third, but not the last, Soviet defensive belt. His flank units were still hemmed in by Soviet infantry and artillery, and his troops were approaching exhaustion as new Soviet units joined the fight.[51]

On 13 July, following the news of the Allies landing in Sicily, Hitler called his commanders back to East Prussia for consultation. Hitler proposed a temporary pause in Operation Citadel and the dispatch of some armour units to Italy to bolster its defence in case of Sicily's fall. Manstein asked that the operation continue in order to destroy more Soviet armour and delay a follow-on Soviet offensive. Hitler agreed to a short continuation. On 16 July, the 4th Panzer Army's units returned to their jump-off points. The myth of Blitzkrieg was dispelled in those deeply echeloned and prepared defences at Kursk. In the absence of surprise, tactical competence and advanced technology would not overcome a well-prepared and well-conducted defence. For Vasilevsky, the defensive success set the stage for broad offensive possibilities against the Wehrmacht, which Soviet forces were now in a position to exploit.[52] Russian military commentators today still find Kursk to be worthy of study as the classic example of a successful premeditated defence.[53] Andrei Kokoshin, former first deputy minister of Russia and a leading scholar of Soviet and Russian military history, has called Kursk 'the greatest event in world history because it was the point when Germany finally lost the strategic-operational initiative'.[54]

Manstein had inflicted some damage on the Red Army. A major regrouping of forces went forward in the Voronezh and Steppe Fronts with replacements of men and equipment going to those units that had suffered losses at Kursk. Operation Polkovodets Rumiantsev was not launched until 3 August. But its initial success, which liberated Belgorod and opened the door to Kharkov, demonstrated that the battle of attrition at Kursk had bled the Wehrmacht much more than the Red Army. By 23 August, Kharkov was in the hands of the Red Army and German forces were falling back towards the Dnieper.

BAGRATION AND LVOV–SANDOMIERZ: OPERATIONAL ART MATURED

Undoubtedly, the most outstanding example of Soviet operational art during this period involves the linked operations Bagration and Lvov–Sandomierz in the summer of 1944. The geostrategic situation confronting Hitler's Germany was dire. The Wehrmacht's losses on all fronts in 1943 had been severe. Moreover, US and British bombers were now attacking the Reich's cities day and night. Allied forces had just landed at Normandy and secured and expanded their beachhead and were gathering strength for their breakout. In Italy, Rome had fallen on 5 June. In the east, the Soviets had lifted the Blockade of Leningrad, swept across the Dnieper, and liberated Odessa and Sevastopol. The German position was vulnerable. Army Group North still held a line from the Gulf of Finland and through Narva, Pskov, and Nevel covering the Baltic states, Army Group Centre held the Belorussian 'balcony', with Vitebsk, Bobruysk on the Berezina River, and Mogilev on the Dnieper River serving as strong points, down to the Pripiat Marshes. Army Group North Ukraine held the German line from the Pripiat Marshes south to the Carpathian Mountains with Lvov close behind its forward positions. The major Soviet summer offensive was expected here and German armour had shifted to this sector of the front.[55] Army Group South Ukraine held the line from the Carpathian Mountains to the Black Sea coast with its southern sector anchored on the Dniester and covering Bessarabia and the coastal approach to the Romanian capital and the oilfields at Ploesti. The demands of a two-front war meant that the German defenders were spread thin. Mobile formations, that is, Panzer Corps, could not provide significant mass against all possible axes the Soviets might use. This was the strategic situation on the eve of Operation Bagration.

The Soviet general staff had begun planning its major summer offensive during the winter. It had requested and received the arms, men, and logistical support it required from the State Defence Committee. Soviet industry and Lend Lease were now capable of supplying the Red Army with the weapons and means to conduct manoeuvre warfare on a new scale and to supply sufficient stocks so that follow-on offensive operations could be prepared as others were executed. In practising operational art, Soviet commanders could afford to be more innovative. The echelonment of attacking forces was the rule and not the exception. Air superiority was a given in any major operation.

Though the Soviet spring offensive against Jassy–Kishenev having failed, the Stavka used it to keep German attention focused on Army Group North Ukraine. It also ordered the Karelian Front to attack the isthmus defences and Petrozavodsk, drawing attention away from Belorussia. Taking into account the many streams and rivers in the Belorussian theatre, the Stavka augmented the attacking units with additional engineering troops and bridging assets. For operational security, radio communications were kept to a bare minimum with the headquarters relying on landlines. Zhukov and Vasilevsky were designated as Stavka representatives for Bagration, with Zhukov overseeing the 2nd and 3rd Belorussian Fronts, and Vasilevsky overseeing the 1st Baltic and the 1st Belorussian. The plans as developed involved a first blow by these four fronts, which would strike from the Pripiat Marshes to Nevel with the intent of encircling and destroying the 3rd Panzer Army, the 4th Army, and the 9th Army and culminate in the encirclement of Minsk. Zhukov worked closely with Rokossovsky in developing a more sophisticated scheme for his initial attack, which would involve two breakthroughs by the 1st Belorussian Front. To accomplish this, the front's boundaries were expanded to permit the envelopment of Bobruisk by its forces, the 61st Army and the 48th Army, while the 65th Army and the 3rd Army served as the exterior armies for exploitation with the 65th enveloping Minsk from the south and the 3rd advancing on Minsk from the east.[56] Follow-on objectives for these fronts took the form of advances into Lithuania and Latvia towards the Baltic coast south of Riga and within striking distance of East Prussia.

In the follow-up blow, Operation Lvov–Sandomierz, Konev's 1st Ukrainian Front, supported by the 1st Belorussian Front, would strike south of the Pripiat along the Lvov and Lublin–Brest axes. Successes in this operation led the Stavka to set deeper operational objectives for both fronts. The 1st Ukrainian was ordered to advance and seize a bridgehead across the Vistula at Sandomierz and the 1st Belorussian Front was ordered to clear the east bank of the Vistula and seize bridgeheads across the Vistula at Pulawy and Demblin. The greatest weight of the armour and mechanized forces was deployed with Konev's front. Before the launching of Bagration, the Stavka directed the main staff of the partisan movement to organize attacks on German rail movement and communications. On 19 June, partisan detachments struck with enough effect to disrupt rail movement for a day. Air support for Operation Bagration came from the 3rd, 1st, 4th, and 16th Air Armies, as well as Long-Range Aviation and Air Defence Forces (PVO) with a total air strength of 5,300 aircraft. The Soviet air force, which enjoyed a seven to one advantage over the Luftwaffe during Bagration, began the campaign with powerful fighter sweeps to disrupt German air intelligence. As the ground operation began, Soviet bombers from Long-Range Aviation started their own attacks on German troop concentrations and artillery positions. Ground-attack aviation worked in direct support of Soviet armoured formations.

Operation Bagration began on 22 June 1944, the third anniversary of the German attack. The initial assaults were tactical probes to determine the exact character of the German defence. On 23 June, the full weight of the offensive was unleashed. The 1st Baltic Front, under General O. Kh. Bagramian, attacked with the 4th Shock Army towards Nevel in the north at the seam between Army Group North and Army Group Centre with the task of preventing the movement of reinforcements from the north, and used the 43rd Army to seize Polotsk and mount the northern envelopment of Vitebsk. The 2nd Guards and 51st Armies, which formed the second echelon of the front, developed the attack, advancing on the Western Dvina and seizing Dvinsk. General Ivan Cherniakovsky's 3rd Belorussian Front sent the 39th Army to envelop Vitebsk from the south to ensure the encirclement of the city and its garrison. Once the 11th Guards Army had broken through the tactical defences north of Smolensk, Rotmistrov's 5th Guards Tank Army advanced and took Orsha and enveloped Minsk from the north. Georgiy Zakharov's 2nd Belorussian Front, the weakest of the attacking fronts, had the task of taking Mogilev and crossing the Dnieper and advancing towards Minsk. Rokossovsky's 1st Belorussian Front, by far the strongest operational formation in Operation Bagration, sent its 3rd and 48th Armies to encircle the German 9th Army from the north and put pressure on Minsk. The 65th Army struck just north of the Pripiat Marshes and enveloped the 9th Army from the south and sent forward detachments to envelop Minsk from the south.

Rokossovsky committed four armies (the 2nd Tank Army and the 8th Guards, the 61st and 47th Armies) and General Pliev's cavalry-mechanized group to advance through the 'impassable' Pripiat Marshes and strike the Germans further west in the direction of Brest and Lublin. Lublin fell to Soviet forces on 24 July, and, on 25–6 July, they seized bridgeheads across the Vistula at Pulawy and Demblin. Heavy fighting around Brest continued to slow the progress of the 47th Army.

During this period, General Radzievsky's 2nd Tank Army advanced towards Warsaw with the intent of cutting off German forces east of Vistula and then developing a turning movement across the Bug to threaten the envelopment of Warsaw from the north. However, he ran into the Herman Goering Division and the 19th Panzer Division. Between 30 July and 3 August, new SS Panzer divisions, brought up to bolster the 9th Army before Warsaw, joined the fight. The Soviet 2nd Tank Army was badly mauled, suffering such losses that it had to be withdrawn when the 47th Army arrived. It should be noted that the Stavka had committed no additional tank or mechanized forces on the Warsaw axis. And no Stavka reserves were released to support operations by Rokossovsky's 1st Belorussian Front during August and September 1944. Not until early September did Rokossovsky take up positions in the suburb of Praga on the eastern bank of the Vistula, opposite Warsaw.[57]

The commander of Army Group Centre, Field Marshal Ernst Busch, watched the speed and power of the Soviet offensive develop into an operational crisis for his army group as the encirclements closed on his forward echelon, and he had no reserves to stop the attack towards Minsk. On 28 June, Field Marshal Model replaced the unlucky Busch. Panzer units were moved from Army Group North and Army Group North Ukraine's forces to try to close the developing gap in Army Group Centre's lines. By 4 July, Minsk was encircled. Model's attempt to create a stable defensive line failed, and the Soviets moved forward in pursuit and deep exploitation. By mid-July, Bagration had achieved its objectives and effectively destroyed Army Group Centre. Pursuit would continue into August with Vilnius, Kaunas, Grodno, and Bailystok in Soviet hands. By that point, Soviet forces had outrun their own logistics and had to pause to regroup and resupply and await the movement of their railheads forward to the fronts' immediate rear.

German losses have been estimated, with the casualties totalling 300,000 dead, 250,000 wounded, and about 120,000 captured.[58] Gerd Niepold, who served as the G3 of the 12th Panzer Division and took part in the fighting, estimated that Army Group Centre had twenty-eight divisions destroyed and that Bagration had brought about 'the destruction of Army Group Centre'.[59] General Makhmut Gareev in looking at the lessons and conclusions from Bagration drew attention to the heavy losses suffered by Soviet forces—765,813 killed, wounded, missing in action, or ill of which 178,507 died.[60] What Gareev saw as new in the area of operational art was the very scale of the operation. It involved four fronts and the well-developed echelonment of forces, which allowed for mechanized units to conduct deep exploitation after breakthroughs. Reserve formations were available to harass retreating German units trapped in large encirclements. Trying to escape, they disintegrated as combat units. As Gareev points out, Soviet operational and tactical commanders now possessed a sound common understanding of their craft and could make use of opportunities as they developed in battle.[61]

In May, Konev, who had been in command of the 2nd Ukrainian Front, was posted to command the 1st Ukrainian Front. He was told to begin preparations for an offensive operation to destroy Army Group North Ukraine, complete the liberation of the Soviet Ukraine, that is, the territories of eastern Poland occupied by the Red Army in 1939, and begin the liberation of Poland, that is, those territories which the Soviet government considered to be Polish territory.[62] Zhukov assumed the role of Stavka representative to the 1st Ukrainian Front. Konev's operational design involved elements of the 1st Ukrainian Front advancing on two diverging axes towards Lvov–Przemysl–Sandomierz and Lublin, where they would then support the 1st Belorussian Front in an advance on Pulawy–Demblin with the objective of seizing bridgeheads across the Vistula. His proposal for two major axes met with resistance from Stalin who saw it as too ambitious. He, however, justified his course of action and Stalin agreed but put the responsibility on Konev's shoulders if his innovation did not work. To ensure it did, Konev devised a robust deception plan to demonstrate a major concentration of armour on the front's left flank while he concealed the movement of tank and mechanized forces to the centre and right flanks from which they could advance against Lvov and Rava-Ruska.[63] The deception worked and German intelligence kept its focus on what Konev showed and did not find what he concealed, thereby achieving operational surprise.

On 13 July, the Stavka unleashed Konev's 1st Ukrainian Front in the Lvov–Sandomierz operation with the objective of defeating and destroying Army Group North Ukraine, now under the command of Colonel-General Josef Harpe. Harpe had at his disposal the 4th Panzer Army, the 1st Panzer Army, and the 1st Hungarian Army, which was under the operational control of Colonel-General Gottard Heinrici's 1st Panzer Army because the Hungarians were no longer considered reliable allies. He had Panzer armies in name only with a total armour strength of 420 tanks, assault guns, and other armour vehicles. He had about 370,000 men and could call upon air support from two air fleets with about 1,000 aircraft. Against this force, Konev could deploy seven armies and an air army with roughly 1.2 million troops, 2,050 tanks and self-propelled artillery, 16,000 tubes, and 3,250 aircraft.

Konev's plan envisioned penetrations of the German tactical defences at several points and the introduction of second-echelon mechanized forces to complete encirclements and form the external exploitation force, striking into the enemy's operational depths. He held General Aleksei Zhadov's 5th Guards Army as a front reserve. He kept his tank armies for deep exploitation, but increased the density of armoured forces with his combined-arms armies to ensure their ability to penetrate the tactical defences.[64] He achieved overwhelming favourable correlations of forces in manpower, armour, artillery, and aviation on the axes of attack.[65] The 3rd Guards, the 1st Tank, and the 13th Armies were to advance on the axis Rava-Ruska, and the 60th, 38th, 3rd Guards Tank, and the 4th Tank Armies were to advance on the Lvov axis.[66] Once through the enemy's tactical depths, their pincers were to encircle and destroy the German XIII Corps.

Konev began his offensive with a tactical reconnaissance of the German frontlines on the evening of 13 July. It revealed that the main enemy forces were falling back on their second line of positions behind a weak rearguard in order to escape the effects of the Soviet artillery preparation. With this information, he authorized the 3rd Guards and 13th Armies to advance without artillery preparation and rely upon tactical aviation to strike the enemy's tactical strong points.[67] The Soviet attack swept aside the rearguard and pre-empted the establishment of a stable defence on the second line of trenches. The 3rd Guards Army opened a breach on the Rava-Ruska axis and the 1st Guards Tank Army was sent to exploit, seizing a bridgehead across the Bug River and advancing on Lublin. A counter-attack by the grossly understrength 16th and 17th Panzer Divisions of the 1st Panzer Army failed. The 13th Army turned south to become the right arm of an envelopment of the German XIII Corps at Brody.[68]

While the northern attack enjoyed success from the beginning, the southern attack towards Lvov, which began on 14 July, ran into stiff resistance. The initial penetration by the 60th Army of the tactical defence was only 3–4 km and German re-enforcement sought to blunt the Soviet offensive. The 60th Army managed to create a narrow corridor through the German tactical defences at Koltov and found itself engaged with German forces seeking to close the corridor.

On 16 July, Konev gambled and sent the 3rd Guards Tank Army through that gap to close the pocket on the German XIII Corps.[69] The XIII Corps's attempt to disengage and escape encirclement failed, and on 18 July the pincers closed around the corps and other elements of the 4th Panzer Army. The 3rd and 4th Guards Tank Armies continued their advance deep into the enemies' rear. To the south, the 4th Tank Army was ordered to envelop Lvov from the south, cutting the city off from re-enforcement.

At this juncture, General Baranov's cavalry-mechanized group was ordered to attack towards the Vistula in cooperation with the 8th Guards Army of the 1st Belorussian Front. Instead, it found itself engaging enemy defences at Zholkev. Konev ordered the commander to fix the defenders and continue manoeuvring west to make contact with Rybalko's 3rd Guards Tank Army, thus permitting that force to envelop Lvov from the north. By this point, Lvov, whose defences were originally weak, had been re-enforced. Konev ordered his tank armies to bypass the city and cut it off by deep envelopment and leave the follow-on infantry units to reduce the city. Facing encirclement, the defenders of Lvov stood their ground, and Konev found his forces involved in brief but intensive street fighting until the city was liberated on the morning of 27 July.[70] Finding his front with a 200-km gap, Harpe authorized the withdrawal of the 4th Panzer Army on the Vistula, while the 1st Panzer and 1st Hungarian Armies fell back on the Carpathian Mountains.

On 28 July, the Stavka, assessing these developments, authorized the 1st Ukrainian Front to continue its operations and seize a bridgehead across the Vistula in the Sandomierz area. Regrouping his forces, Konev, on 29 July, mounted the next phase of the operation to seize the bridgehead. Against light German resistance, the 3rd Guards Army seized the bridgehead. Both the Stavka and the OKH recognized the importance of the bridgehead. Konev moved the 13th Army and the 3rd Guards Tank Army to support the bridgehead and brought up additional anti-tank assets to blunt the anticipated German effort to reduce the bridgehead. The OKH also recognized the danger posed by this bridgehead and rushed reserves from Army Group South Ukraine, including Panzer and Panzer Grenadier divisions, to assist Harpe in reducing the bridgehead. In heavy fighting, Soviet forces held the bridgehead. Konev committed his front reserve, General Zhadov's 5th Guards Army, into the bridgehead. He moved artillery assets into the fight to beat off German Panzer attacks and sent General Leliushenko's 4th Tank Army into the fight. The German forces broke off their attacks to eliminate the bridgehead. He again regrouped his forces and committed the 13th Army, the 1st Guards Tank Army, and part of the 3rd Guards Tank Army against the German XLII Corps to expand the bridgehead and take Sandomierz, which fell on 18 August.[71]

In a little over a month's fighting, the 1st Ukrainian Front had advanced over 250 km and inflicted serious damage upon Army Group North Ukraine. The OKH had restabilized the situation on the Vistula by drawing forces from Army Group South Ukraine and thereby making it vulnerable to the next multi-front operation which the Stavka had planned at Jassy–Kishinev, which began on 20 August 1944. The advance into the Balkans continued into late 1944, when the Red Army was stopped before Budapest. The Soviet offensive to remove the

Germans from Poland began in January 1945 and carried the front from the Vistula to the Oder and the approach to Berlin. In the south, the Red Army seized Budapest and Vienna and was advancing towards Prague. The final operation of the Eastern Front was the capture of Berlin during which Stalin had Konev and Zhukov racing against each other to secure the German capital before the western Allies might arrive. Eisenhower, judging Berlin as a political and not a military objective, never approved any race. In the end, Soviet operational art with considerable costs in men and materials put Soviet power in control of the ancient capitals of Central and Eastern Europe and thereby set the stage for both the Iron Curtain and the East–West military confrontation along the inner-German border. The last execution of Soviet operational art came with the surprise entry of the USSR into the war against Japan and took the form of a lightning operation 'to break the spine of Japan', in the words of Stalin, that is, the Kwantung Army, in Manchuria as part of a negotiated intervention by the United States, Britain, and the Soviet Union. That event took place in the context of Truman's decision to use the atomic bomb against Japan, and the twin blows of 6 and 9 August brought to an end that war and set the stage for post-war tensions in the Far East. The emergence of nuclear weapons had a profound impact on Soviet operational art in the post-war period—during the US nuclear monopoly and after the USSR acquired atomic and then nuclear weapons.

OPERATIONAL ART FROM 1945 TO 2003

When contemporary Russian students of operational art seek to provide a periodization of the development of Soviet/Russian operational art, they start with the decade before the war. It was during this period that the foundations for the concept were laid and the tank and mechanized armies capable of putting it into practice were built up. The next period covers the years of the Great Patriotic War and the immediate post-war period through to 1953, when Stalin died.[72] The discussion of operational art stresses the lessons learnt during the war and the development of a truly mechanized force to conduct combined-arms warfare on a multi-front scale.

General-Major Kopytko, the former deputy chief of the chair of operational art at the Academy of the General Staff, treats the entire period from 1954 to 1985 as a single whole dominated by the appearance of nuclear weapons and ballistic missiles. By the late 1950s, under the leadership of Nikita Khrushchev, the Soviet Union embarked upon the military-technical revolution in which nuclear weapons and ballistic missiles were seen as the new definition of national power. Since the Soviet Union was undergoing a demographic crisis because of a low birth rate during the war, this revolution was supposed to provide security while the ground, air, and naval forces were cut. The strategic concept for such a military posture was laid out in the three editions of Marshal V. D. Sokolovsky's *Military Strategy* between 1962 and 1968 and focused upon nuclear war fighting as the dominant characteristic of modern war.[73]

Operational art during this period made its reappearance as a relevant part of military art during the initial period of war. However, it was still nuclear-armed missile forces that fundamentally shaped the nature of future war and expanded the effects that could be achieved. The deployment of forces under the conditions of the possible employment of nuclear weapons demanded greater mobility and a protective system against radiation for armour combat systems. The forces developed for this operational environment were designed to conduct operations for which there was no practical experience. Troops could exercise the doctrine and operations research professionals might find ways to simulate the conduct of operations, but there was no way to estimate the actual impact of nuclear weapons on the conduct of operations. Modelling a NATO–WTO conflict, including the prospect of the linkage of conventional, theatre-nuclear, and strategic forces, posed a profoundly difficult problem.

In the 1970s, Soviet military specialists, led by Colonel-General Andrian Danilevich, senior special assistant to the chief of the operations directorate of the Soviet general staff, began to examine the possibility of an extended conventional phase of a NATO–WTO war.[74] This was undertaken in the context of strategic nuclear parity and modernized theatre-nuclear arsenals, particularly the solid-fuel SS-20 IRBM. By the end of the decade, instead of estimating that 5–6 days would pass before the conflict became nuclear, the Soviets assumed that conventional operations would last long enough to carry their forces all the way to France. They believed that the use of nuclear weapons would be catastrophic and operationally counter-productive.[75] They used, as their model, the Manchurian strategic offensive of 1945. In other words, in the case of a NATO–WTO war, a theatre-strategic offensive, based upon a modernized concept of deep operations, aimed at encircling and annihilating large portions of NATO forces and advancing to the Rhine. Crossing the river, the Soviets believed, would trigger NATO tactical nuclear use.[76]

From 1979 onwards, the general staff also began to examine the possibility of escalation control after nuclear use and addressed the idea of intra-war termination of nuclear use. To be decisive, the Soviet conventional strategic operation depended upon quantitative advantages in men and material. As Danilevich admitted, 'the Soviets did not win the Great Patriotic War because Soviet generalship and fighting skills were superior to those of the Germans. The Soviet armed forces simply overwhelmed the Germans with superior numbers of airplanes, men, tanks, and artillery'.[77] In a general conventional offensive, Soviet forces might commit 40,000 tanks in multiple echelons and end the war with just 5,000 left.

By the early 1980s, the GRU was aware of qualitative improvements in US theatre-nuclear forces (ground-launched cruise missiles [GLCMs] and Pershing IIs). It also recognized emerging enhanced conventional capabilities associated with better command and control and precision strike, by which the United States was seeking to counter Soviet quantity with qualitatively superior conventional weapons systems. What was re-emerging was the necessity for reflection (*razmyshlenie*) upon strategic choices based on an assessment of the probable war confronting the state and the economic means available to prepare for and conduct such a war. The chief of the general staff, Marshal Ogarkov, cast an unblinking look at the future evolution of warfare. He began to call attention to an emerging 'revolution in military affairs' that affected conventional forces through automated command and control, informatization, precision, and weapons based on new physical principles.[78] He championed the professionalization of the military, greater control by the general staff over weapons development, and force structure changes, including the abolition of National Air Defence Forces (*PVO Strany*).

To counter NATO's emerging theatre-nuclear and conventional capabilities, Ogarkov embraced a new organizational concept proposed by Colonel-General Gareev. It focused on the Operational Manoeuvre Group as a counter-measure to NATO's emerging capabilities. Specially designed, highly manoeuvrable brigades would permit penetration and raiding on an operational scale, making enemy counter-strikes more difficult.[79]

These trends posed a profound challenge to the dominant concept regarding the desirability and even necessity of seizing the strategic initiative and mounting offensive operations early in the war. Orgakov's call for a 'revolution in military affairs' that would lead to a profound transformation of the Soviet military because of the appearance of new weapon systems based on automated command and control, electronic warfare, and 'weapons based on new physical principles, which was reshaping conventional warfare' was not favourably received by Dimitry Ustinov, minister of defence and representative of the arms industry. In the end, it was Ustinov who, as a member of the Politburo, won the struggle; Orgakov was fired, and the dominance of strategy over operational art, which he had sought to endow with some degree of independence, reaffirmed.

At this time, Soviet analysts, including those in the GRU, were trying to assess the implications of a profound shift in the articulated strategy of the United States. The Reagan administration had begun to speak of an 'early victory in a protracted conventional war'. This was to be achieved by a shift away from the mass production of conventional weapon systems, that is, artillery and tanks, towards 'precision-strike systems'. Masses of precision-strike weapons might destroy forward-deployed conventional forces and disrupt their operations in the initial period of war. They thus called into question the mobilization for mass industrial war, which the Soviet Union had built in the 1930s, perfected during the Great Patriotic War, and sustained throughout the Cold War, even when nuclear weapons had become the core of both nations' strategic postures.[80]

As part of that debate, General-Major V. V. Larionov and A. A. Kokoshin championed a doctrine of sufficient defence. They used the Battle of Kursk to support the possibility of an asymmetric response to the threat of an opponent's offensive operations. At Kursk, the Soviet Stavka had made a conscious choice to stand on the defence to meet and defeat the German summer offensive against the Kursk bulge in order to drain German mechanized forces, set conditions for a Soviet offensive towards Belgorod–Kharkov, and prepare for the liberation of the Ukraine to the Dnieper River.[81]

Meanwhile, within the Soviet Union, glasnost was making it possible to address the 'blank pages' of Soviet history in a more systemic fashion. This included discussing the costs of the Soviet victory in the Great Patriotic War and calling into question the rationality of offensive war fighting based upon mass industrial war in the context of nuclear parity and the emerging revolution in conventional capabilities. Such criticism undermined the legitimacy of the Soviet armed forces by bringing into question the ideology, the institutions, and the values of the Soviet system. The outcome was the collapse of the Soviet military and, ultimately, the Soviet system.[82]

Soviet operational art, which emerged out of the Stalinist system designed to fight and win a total war, collapsed in the face of a qualitative shift in the nature of future war from an industrial model to one based on information and control. That shift posed a problem for party control that Leonid Brezhnev had been unwilling and unable to address. As Vitaly Shlykov observed, 'Stalin created a unique system for the preparation of the economy to mobilize for war . . .'.[83] It was a system that would finally break the Soviet Union, not in war but under the burden of perpetual preparation for war on all fronts and by all means.[84]

The command system which had worked during the Stalin industrialization, the Great Patriotic War, and even the nuclear and space challenges was unable to meet this new challenge.[85] Cybernetics and the inability to create an information society posed problems that the Stalinist model in even a less repressive form could not answer. Mass was no longer sufficient to win wars or to guide a society and economy.

With the end of the Soviet Union in 1991, the mobilization base for mass industrial war disappeared in Russia. The general staff continues to study the evolution of military art and speculate on the nature of future war. Much of that speculation concerns the definitions of the threats to Russia and the capacity of the national economy to adapt to the informatization of warfare.[86]

CONCLUSION: REFLECTIONS ON THEORY AND PRACTICE

Under the Soviet system, the general staff and the Stavka framed the conduct of operations, mobilized new formations, and controlled the reserves of the high command. These reserves were the paints that operational artists would apply on the broad canvas of the Eastern Front. Initially, they did so in defensive operations under desperate conditions of the initial surprise attack; then during the counter-offensives at Moscow, Stalingrad, and Kursk; and, finally, during the great offensive operations that liberated Soviet territory and carried the war into Eastern Europe and to Berlin, Hitler's capital.

In the difficult environment created by Stalin's paranoia and the cult of his genius, Shaposhnikov and his school had focused their considerable intellectual and organizational skill on the role of the general staff in modern war. The objective was to offer effective strategic guidance by anchoring the conduct of operations in a specific political-strategic situation. To that end, Shaposhnikov had even recommended Svechin's *Strategy* to Stalin during the first difficult year of the war.[87] As the Soviets recovered from the initial surprise and forged the instruments to execute deep operations with increased sophistication and greater means, their skill at applying operational art grew.

Whereas Stalin by his forced industrialization of the Soviet Union had provided the resources with which to wage total war, the detailed design came from Svechin (albeit that he ended up being shot). Svechin provided the political-strategic concept of war, formulated the system of command and control, and recommended the strategy finally adopted out of necessity. Strategy would guide operational art. The brush strokes that Soviet commanders applied were the gift of Tukhachevsky: deep operations of multiple fronts deeply echeloned with tank armies providing the means for shock and deep manoeuvre. If Western operational art was like the work of individual great masters, Soviet operational art was more like that of the studio art of Peter Paul Rubens—prolific but under the control of one master. In major operations, Stalin and the Stavka provided immediate direction; in secondary operations, they only controlled the most critical details, and in some other operations they provided models but left the local commanders to execute the work after providing the instruments.[88] This helped to ensure that the Red Army would be a learning organization and incorporate that learning in subsequent operations. The strategic operational creations that emerged out of 'the Great Patriotic War' became the most important source of legitimacy for the regime. They enabled it to survive in an ossifying form until it finally collapsed under the weight of its own all-consuming military preparations for the war that did not come. The regime refused until Gorbachev's glasnost and perestroika to ever acknowledge in detail the costs that victory in the Great Patriotic War had imposed on Soviet society. In continuing to prepare for total war in both its conventional and nuclear manifestations and in the context of strategic isolation, when the regime faced not only the United States and its allies, but also a hostile People's Republic of China, the USSR clung to an operational art that did not fit the conflicts which it faced, especially in Afghanistan, and finally found its forces in Eastern Europe reduced to an unwanted army of occupation. The Russian armed forces have been made to give up any hope of conventional parity, and since 1999 have conducted military exercises involving explicit nuclear first use to counter-acknowledge operational superiorities of potential adversaries employing precision-strike systems in a form of non-contact war on the model of NATO's air campaign against Yugoslavia. The poor performance of the Russian army in Yeltsin's Chechen War did lead to reforms, but as was demonstrated in the Russian intervention against Georgia over the independence of South Ossetia, the Russian army still relies on the instrument of mass industrial war and has not achieved the 'informatization' of its own armed forces.

NOTES

1. Viktor Khudoleev, 'Ofitser, myslitel', patriot', *Krasnaia zvezda*, 29 August 2008, 1. On Svechin's writing on these conflicts, see A. A. Svechin, *Voina v gorakh: Takticheskoe issledovanie po opytu russko-iaponskoi voiny*, 2 vols. (St. Petersburg: Tipografiia V. A. Berezovskogo, 1907); A. A. Svechin, *V vostochnom otriade: Ot Liaoiana k Tiuenchenu i obratno—Marshi, vstrechi, boi nabliudeniia* (Warsaw, 1908); A. A. Svechin and Iu.

D. Romanovskii, *Russko-Iaponskaia voina* (Oranienbaum: Izdanie Ofitserskoi Strelkovoi Shkoly, 1910); A. A. Svechin, *Takticheskie uroki russko-iaponskoi voiny* (St. Petersburg: Izdanie Ofitserskoi Strelkovoi Shkoly, 1912); A. A. Svechin, editor-in-chief, *Voenno-istoricheskii sbornik: Trudy Komissii po issledovaniiu opyta voiny 1914–1918*, 3 vols. in 4 books (Moscow: Tipografiia I. D. Sytina, 1919–21).

2. Aleksandr A. Svechin, *Strategy*, trans. and ed. Kent D. Lee (Minneapolis, MN: Eastview Press, 1992), 77. See also A. A. Svechin, 'Izuchenie voennoi istorii', *Voina i revoliutsiia*, no. 4 (April 1927), 49–66.
3. A. A. Svechin, *Istoriia voennogo iskusstva*, 3 vols. (Moscow: Vyshei voennyi redatsionnyi sovet, 1922).
4. N. Varfolomeev, 'Stategiya v akademicheskoy postanovke', *Voina i revoliutsiia*, November 1928, 84.
5. Svechin, *Strategy*, 70–4.
6. Ibid., 67.
7. Ibid., 69.
8. Ibid., 67.
9. Ibid., 69.
10. Ibid., 81–163.
11. Ibid., 65–6. On this one-sided reading, see Jon Tetsuro Sumida, *Decoding Clausewitz: A New Approach to 'On War'* (Lawrence, KS: University Press of Kansas, 2008), 179–80.
12. Ibid., 240. Svechin noted that 'the study of Napoleon's campaigns was reduced to the study of operational rather than the strategic art'.
13. Svechin. *Strategy*, 246–7.
14. B. M. Shaposhnikov, *Mozg armii*, vol. 1 (Moscow: Voennyi vestnik, 1927), 110–12.
15. A. A. Svechin, 'Gosudarstvennyi i frontovoi tyl', *Voina i revoliutsiia*, no. 11 (November 1928), 94–108.
16. Bruce W. Menning, 'Ni Mol'tke, ni Mekhen: Strategiia v Russko-Iaponskoi voine', in O. P. Airapetov (ed.), *Russko-Iaponskaia voina, 1904–1905: Vzgliad cherez stoletie* (Moscow: Modest Kolerov i Izdael'stvo 'Tri Kvadrata', 2004), 15–37.
17. Lennart Samuelson, *Plans for Stalin's War Machine: Tukhachevskii and Military-Economic Planning, 1925–1941* (Basingstoke: Macmillan, 2000), 100–2.
18. A. M. Vasilevskii and M. V. Zakharov, 'Predislovie', in B. M. Shaposhnikov, *Vospominaniia – voenno-nauchnye trudy* (Moscow: Voenizdat, 1974), 13–14.
19. V. M. Ivanov, *Marshal M. N. Tukhachevskii* (Moscow: Voenizdat, 1990), 234–6.
20. Ibid., 237–40.
21. Ibid., 241–2.
22. Lennart Samuelson, *Soviet Defence Industry Planning: Tukhachevskii and Military-Industrial Mobilization, 1926–1937* (Stockholm, Sweden: Stockholm Institute of East European Economies, 1996), 118.
23. Ibid., 124.
24. M. N. Tukhachevsky, 'Predislovie k knige Dhz. Fullera "Reformatsiia voiny"', in M. N. Tukhachevsky, *Izbrannye proizvedeniia*, II, 152.
25. Sally W. Stoecker, *Forging Stalin's Army: Marshal Tukhachevsky and the Politics of Military Innovation* (Boulder, CO: Westview Press, 1998), 135–69.
26. Ivanov, *Marshal M. N. Tukhachevskii*, 269–72, and M. A. Gareev, *Obshchie-voiskovye ucheniia* (Moscow: Voenizdat, 1983), 93–9.
27. In 1928, the main intelligence directorate of the Red Army Staff completed a major study on the prospects of future war with Poland and Romania as the main opponents supported by the British and French. Svechin and Tukhachevsky both took an active

part in this study. See USSR, RKKA, IV Upravlenie Shtaba, *Budushchaia voina* (Moscow, 1928).

28. A. A. Kol'tiukov, 'Vooruzhennyi konflikt u ozera Khasan: Vzgliad iz XXI veka', in V. N. Kuzvelen'kov (ed.), *Voennyi konflikt v raione ozera Khasan: Vzgliad cherez shest' desiatiletii* (Sbornik dokladov, soobshchenii i dokumental'nykh materialov) (Moscow: Redaktsionno-izdatel'skii tsentr general'nogo shtaba vooruzhennykh sil RF, 2003), 9.
29. *Vremennyi polevoi ustav RKKA (1936)*, 9–20.
30. Ibid., 82–95. See also G. Isserson, 'Vstrechnoe srazhenie budushchego', *Voennaia mysl'*, no. 7 (July 1938), 10–26.
31. Ibid., 8.
32. Kirill Meretskov, *Serving the People* (Moscow: Progress, 1971), 104–5.
33. Carl Van Dyke, *The Soviet Invasion of Finland, 1939–1940* (London: Frank Cass, 1997), 27.
34. Ibid., 35–102.
35. Ibid., 103–25.
36. K. M. Simonov, 'Glazami cheloveka moego pokolenniia: Besedy s Marshalom Sovetskogo Soiuza A. M. Vasilevskim', *Znamia*, May 1988, 79–80.
37. Van Dyke, *The Soviet Invasion of Finland, 1939–1940*, 222–4.
38. V. I. Dasgichev, *Bankrotstvo strategii germanskogo fashizma: isoricheskie ocherki, doukmenty i materially: Agressiia protiv SSSR, padanie 'Tret'ei imperii', 1941–1945*, vol. II (Moscow: Nauka, 1973), 90–1.
39. Fred Majdalany, *The Battle of El Alamein: Fortress in the Sand* (Philadelphia, PA: University of Pennsylvania Press, 2003), 155–6.
40. Ministerstvo Oborony SSSR, Institut voennoi istorii, *Sovetskaia voennaia entsiklopediia*, vol. 7 (Moscow: Voenizdat, 1979), 517–21.
41. Antony Beevor, *Stalingrad: The Fateful Siege, 1942–1943* (New York: Viking Books, 1998), 127.
42. Ibid., 220–35.
43. David M. Glantz, *Zhukov's Greatest Defeat: The Red Army's Epic Disaster in Operation Mars, 1942* (Lawrence, KS: University Press of Kansas, 1999), 319.
44. Tennant H. Bayley, *Spy Wars: Moles, Mysteries and Deadly Games* (New Haven, CT: Yale University Press, 2007), 117; Pavel Sudoplatov et al., *Special Tasks* (New York: Little, Brown and Company, 1994), 158–9; M. A. Gareev, 'Operatsiia "Mars" I sovremennye "Marsiane"', *Voenno-istoricheskii zhurnal*, no. 10 (October 2003), 18.
45. Vasilevsky, *Delo vsei zhizni*, 283–4.
46. Zhukov, *Vospominaniia i razmyshleniia*, vol. 3, 10–11.
47. David M. Glantz and Jonathan House, *When Titans Clashed: How the Red Army Stopped Hitler* (Lawrence, KS: University Press of Kansas, 1995), 160.
48. Ibid., 13–15.
49. Ibid., 165; M. N. Kozhevnikov, *Komandovanie i shtab VVS Sovetskoi Armii v Velikoi Otechstennoi voine, 1941–1945 gg.* (Moscow: Izdatel'stvo 'Nauka', 1977), 141–2.
50. Niklas Zetterling and Anders Frankson, *Kursk 1943: A Statistical Analysis* (London: Frank Cass, 2005), 101–10.
51. Erich von Manstein, *Lost Victories* (Chicago, IL: Regnery, 1958), 448–9; Friedrich W. Mellenthin, *Panzer Battles* (Norman, OK: University of Oklahoma Press, 1956), 229–30.
52. Vasilevsky, *Delo vsei zhizni*, 203–4.
53. V. Shemetov, 'Kurskaia bitva: Istoriia, znachenie, uroki, krakh "Tsitadeli" i Pantery', *Krasnyi voin*, no. 37 (May 2003), 3; N. V. Kormil'tsev, 'Krakh nastupatel'noi strategii vermakhta', *Voenno-istoricheskii zhurnal*, no. 7 (July 2003), 2–9.

54. Andrei Kokoshin, 'Kurrskaia bitva: Velichaishee sobytie mirovoi istorii', *Krasnaia zvezda*, 5 July 2003, 1; also, re. the debate over the Battle of Kursk, A. Kokoshin and V. Larionov, 'Kurskaia bitva v svete sovremennoi obrononitel'noi doktriny', *Mirovaia ekonomika i mezhdunarodnye otnosheniia*, no. 8 (August 1987), 32–40; Viktor Miasnikov, 'Kak kovalas' asimmetrichnost'', *Nezavisimoe voennoe obozrenie*, 17 October 2008, 15.
55. Gerd Niepold, *Battle for White Russia: The Destruction of Army Group Centre, June 1944* (London: Brassey's, 1987), 15–16.
56. Konstantin Rokossovskii, *Soldstkii dolg* (Moscow: Voenizdat, 1972), 247–59.
57. For a biography of Konstantin K. Rokossovsky, see 'Marshal Sovetskogo Soiuza Konstantin Konstantinovich Rokossovskii: Biografiia', <http://www.rokossowski.com/bio.htm>, accessed 22 June 2009; ibid., 3.
58. Steven J. Zaloga, *Bagration, 1944: The Destruction of Army Group Centre* (Oxford: Osprey, 1996), 71.
59. Niepold, *Battle for White Russia*, xi.
60. Makhmut Gareev, 'Operatsiia 'Bagration: Uroki i vyvody', *Krasnaia zvezda*, 22 June 2004.
61. Ibid.
62. Konev, *Zapiski komandyiushchego frontom*, 201–2.
63. Richard N. Armstrong, *Soviet Operational Deception: The Red Cloak* (Ft. Leavenworth, KS: Combat Studies Institute, 1988), <http://carl.army.mil/resources/csi/Armstrong/ARMSTRONG.asp>, accessed 10 June 2009.
64. Konev, *Zapiski komandyiushchego frontom*, 216.
65. Ibid., 217–19.
66. Ibid., 207.
67. Ibid., 226.
68. Ibid., 226–8.
69. Ibid.
70. Ibid., 235–7.
71. Ibid., 247–50.
72. V. K. Kopytko, 'Evoliutsiia operativnogo iskusstva', *Voennaia mysl'*, no. 12 (December 2007), 63.
73. V. D. Sokolovskii (ed.), *Voennaia strategiia* (Moscow: Voenizdat, 1962).
74. Ibid., 19–20.
75. John C. Hines, Ellis M. Mishulovich, and John F. Shull, *Soviet Intentions, 1965–1985: Soviet Post-Cold War Testimonial Evidence* (McLean, VA: BDM Corporation, 1995), 23.
76. Ibid., 24.
77. Ibid., 25.
78. Jacob W. Kipp, 'The Labor of Sisyphus: Forecasting the Revolution in Military Affairs during Russia's Time of Troubles', in Thierry Gongora and Harold von Riekhoff (eds.), *Toward a Revolution in Military Affairs?* (Westport, CT: Greenwood Press, 2000), 87–104.
79. Hines, Mishulovich, and Shull, *Soviet Intentions, 1965–1985*, 72–3.
80. Vitaly Shlykov, 'Chto pogubilo Sovetskii Soiuz? Genshtab i ekonomika', *Voennyi Vestnik*, no. 9 (September 2002), 64–93. See also Jacob W. Kipp, 'The Changing Soviet Strategic Environment: Soviet Military Doctrine, Conventional Military Forces, and the Scientific-Technical Revolution in Military Affairs', in Carl Jacobsen et al. (eds.), *Strategic Power: USA/USSR* (London: Macmillan, 1990), 435–56.
81. A. Kokoshin and V. Larionov, 'Kurskaia bitva v svete sovremennoi obrononitel'noi doktriny', *Mirovaia ekonomika i mezhdunarodnye otnosheniia*, no. 8 (August 1987),

32–40. See also Viktor Miasnikov, 'Kak kovalas' asimmetrichnost'', *Nezavisimoe voennoe obozrenie*, 17 October 2008, 15.

82. William E. Odom, *The Collapse of the Soviet Military* (New Haven, CT: Yale University Press, 1998), 118ff.
83. Vitaly Shlykov, 'Fatal Mistakes of the U.S. and Soviet Intelligence: Part One', *International Affairs*, XLII, nos. 5–6 (1996), 158–77.
84. Ibid.
85. N. N. Moiseev, *Sotsializm i informatika* (Moscow: Izdatel'stvo politicheskoy literatury, 1988), 62ff.
86. Makhmut A. Gareev and Vladimir Slipchenko, *Budushchaia voina* (Moscow: OGI, 2005).
87. Roi Medvedev, *Chto chital Stalin: Liudi i kniga v totalitarnom obshchestve* (Moscow: Izdatel'stvo 'Prava Cheloveka', 2005), 63.
88. The most important documents for the guidance of operations came in the form of lessons learnt from other operations and collected by the directorate for the utilization of war experience of the general staff, which were published periodically between 1942 and 1947. See USSR, Upravlenie po ispolzovaniiu opyta voiny, General'nogo Shtaba Krasnoi Armii, *Sbornik materialov po izucheniiu opyta voiny*, 26 vols. (Moscow: Voennoe izdatel'stvo Narodnogo Kmoddariata Oborony, 1942–7).

4

Operational Art and Britain, 1909–2009

Hew Strachan

DOCTRINE AND OPERATIONAL ART

In 1982, two former officers of the Royal Artillery, Shelford Bidwell and Dominick Graham, published the first serious study of how the British army had both waged and thought about war in the first half of the twentieth century. Bidwell, a brigadier who had been commissioned in 1933 and had served in North Africa and Italy in the Second World War, edited the *Journal of the Royal United Services Institute* between 1971 and 1975. Graham, who also served in the Second World War, but in Norway and North-West Europe as well as in North Africa, had become professor of military history at the University of New Brunswick. They, therefore, knew of what they spoke. Titled *Fire-Power: British Army Weapons and Theories of War 1904–1945*, their book blazed a trail so developed and widened by subsequent historians in the following quarter-century that it can be easy to forget the intellectual vacuum that preceded its appearance.

Three transformations have occurred since 1982. First, our knowledge of the tactical and operational thought of the British army for the First World War in particular (Graham's special area of expertise) is now more complete than that for any other major European army. Second, the British army has since acquired a reputation for operational excellence which, even if somewhat tarnished since 2003, would have amazed both Bidwell and Graham, both of them witnesses to the succession of reverses and humiliations undergone by the same army between 1940 and 1942. Third, much of that success has been predicated on the development of doctrine, at least since 1989.

Bidwell and Graham began their study with an identification of the principal deficiency in the British army of 1906. It lacked 'what military men called "doctrine": the definition of the aim of military operations; the study of weapons and other resources and the lessons of history, leading to the deductions of the correct strategic and tactical principles on which to base both training and the conduct of war'.[1] Not much had changed in their professional lifetimes. Writing the epilogue to their book in 1981, they concluded that, 'despite its achievements since 1906, the Army remains what it was then, *sans* doctrine and an unprofessional coalition of arms and services'.[2]

Bidwell's and Graham's definition of doctrine linked it directly to operational art. Like doctrine, operational art looks both ways, to tactics and to strategy; like doctrine, operational art aspires to harmonize the two. But the complexions of both doctrine and operational art are dependent on which direction they are pointed towards at any one time. In 1909, the year in which *Field Service Regulations Part I: Operations* was first published by the general staff, much doctrine was rooted in tactics. For Bidwell and Graham, writing about the two world wars, doctrine was a professional matter, divorced from its political context, and, therefore, located more at the interface between operations and tactics than between operations and strategy.[3] Since the end of the Cold War, doctrine has shaped strategy more than tactics. During the 1990s, according to Markus Mäder, British doctrine focused on the 'military-strategic level', which is 'the bridge that links policy objectives with operational effect'.[4] By 2009, with doctrine focused on irregular war as much as regular, its aspirations to be apolitical could not be sustained against the weight of strategic expectation which it had to carry.

It follows that doctrine is not the same as operational art. Indeed Graham, in an essay published in the same year as *Fire-Power*, specifically associated doctrine with tactics, rather than with the operational level of war.[5] In this, he was in good company: tactics, Clausewitz concluded, 'is that part of war in which theory can develop most fully into positive doctrine'.[6] Troops in combat need routines, common practices, both to create cohesion and to provide instinctive responses when the confusion and chaos of battle are unleashed.[7] Doctrine at this level comes closer to dogma: in the nineteenth century, it could be reflected in the orders of non-commissioned officers on the drill square more than in the directives issued by generals. Doctrine today, as it approaches the strategic levels of war, is less happy with dogma: the current catchphrase is that doctrine informs soldiers how to think, not what to think. NATO's 2003 definition of doctrine reflects this ambiguity: 'it is authoritative, but requires judgement in it application'. The tactics, techniques, and procedures (TTPs) of the British army in 2009 were the products of doctrine (although rarely recognized as such), but they were not manifestations of operational art. Operational art, therefore, does not have to be predicated on doctrine. If this were not the case, the British history of operational art would be very short. The first formal British doctrine, identified as such, *Design for Military Operations—the British Military Doctrine*, was not published until 1989; by then, official publications of the British army had been using the word 'operations' for eighty years, and individual British soldiers had been employing it in unofficial publications for twice as long.

This is not just a matter of the relationship between the so-called levels of war: tactics, operations, strategy, and policy; it is also a reflection on the nature of generalship. Operational art is practised by generals. Most commanders have a secure grasp of tactical procedures and the majority are then inclined to see the operational level of war in comparable terms: for them, the purpose of doctrine is to create common standards and routines. The intention is to make a large organization function along similar lines and pull towards common goals. But there is not much art in that. The exceptional commander rises above doctrine, and, indeed, many commanders of armies, from Alexander the Great to Gustavus Adolphus, have never been 'indoctrinated'. Those possessed of military genius may or may not know the rules, but more importantly they have the imagination to know when to waive them, disregard them, or reinterpret them. The progenitor of what we now call operational art, Napoleon, did not employ the term and was not the product of doctrine in the sense in which it is understood today. He only rarely used the word strategy, perhaps the nearest synonym for operational art in most nineteenth-century military minds. For Napoleon, war was a matter of tactics, grand tactics, and, above them both, policy. His successors, anxious to rationalize what he had done into procedures, to change it from an art to a science, and to make it into doctrine, began to formulate a theory of operations. And so there is a further distinction between operational art and doctrine: the former can be an individual matter, whereas the latter is collective.

EUROPEAN INFLUENCES AND BRITISH STRATEGY

Clausewitz eschewed the word 'operations' in *On War*; the regular appearance of it or its derivatives in the 1976 English translation by Michael Howard and Peter Paret is a concession to the debates and proclivities of their era, not those of the original author. Although centrally concerned with the interaction between strategy and tactics, he maintained a clear conceptual division between the two.[8] The German word in *On War* most frequently rendered as 'operations' by Howard and Paret is *Handeln*, the 'business' of war. This is in itself a salutary reminder for historian and theorist alike: neither should necessarily attribute to a word used 100 or 200 years ago either the same meaning or the same precision applied to it today.

So where does that leave Jomini? His reputation as the principal interpreter of the Napoleonic era and the most influential strategic theorist of the entire nineteenth century was founded on his *Traité des grandes opérations militaires*. At one level, Jomini was using *opérations* not as armies do today but as Clausewitz was using *Handeln*. Jomini's fundamental principle, 'to operate, with the largest number of forces, in a combined effort on the decisive point', used 'operate' in a sense from which Clausewitz would not have dissented.[9] He meant no more than the business of conducting war: most of the *Traité* is a history, a comparative account of the wars waged by Frederick the Great, the armies of the French Revolution, and Napoleon, and the title pages of its volumes say as much. But superimposed on *l'histoire critique* was a grander design, represented by the overarching title of the book and explained by Jomini in his preface. Earlier attempts to write didactic books on war had, in his view, lost their way in details, neglecting 'the important combinations of military science'. He exempted from this charge two writers on the Seven Years War, Henry Lloyd and Georg von Tempelhoff, and credited Lloyd in particular with presenting 'some profound ideas on the lines of operations, on strategic manoeuvres [*les mouvements stratégiques*], and principally on the systems of battle'. Lloyd convinced Jomini of something he had not previously appreciated: 'he demonstrated to me that the operations of war were able to be reduced to simple and definitive principles'.[10]

The effect of simplicity and definition was to endow 'operations' with a pregnancy rejected by Clausewitz (who, it must be remembered, wrote *On War* after Jomini had published the *Traité*, even if the latter's *Précis de l'art de la guerre* (1838) was then able to respond to Clausewitz after the Prussian's death in 1831). Jomini's chapter defining 'lines of operations when considered as manoeuvre' furnished the launching pad for something much more ambitious. He provided a classification of the lines of operations—simple, double, and multiple, interior and exterior; he distinguished between lines of operations on an extended front and deep lines of operations, between concentric and eccentric (or divergent) lines of operations, and between secondary and accidental lines of operations.[11]

Jomini's *Traité*, and its successor volumes, both *Tableau analytique des principales combinaisons de la guerre, et de leurs rapports avec la polititique des états* (1830) and *Précis de l'art de la guerre*, which were designed to encapsulate the essence of the original argument by reversing the structure (i.e. by putting the theoretical conclusions first, and then using history solely as an exemplary illustration), were the founding documents of 'operational art' as understood by the armies of Europe in the nineteenth and even twentieth centuries. And yet at one level they were not, because Jomini saw his subject not as an art but as a science; he preferred the word 'dogma', not doctrine.[12]

That certainty, the reduction of the conduct of operations to maxims and principles, ensured him an audience which broke the bounds of language (if writing in French in the early nineteenth century was any obstacle to universal comprehension) and even of strategic culture. Britain may have been primarily a naval power, secure or relatively so in its island status, but that did not prevent British soldiers from internalizing Jominian precepts. The first great British military historian, General Sir William Napier, himself a veteran of the Napoleonic Wars, reviewed the *Traité* in generous terms for the *Edinburgh Review* in 1821 and referred to it in his *magnum opus*, the *History of the War in the Peninsula and the South of France*.[13]

Napier's own interests and focus were predominantly tactical, and in this he was representative of most of the British army up to the Crimean War and even thereafter. The *Aide-Mémoire to the Military Sciences*, published by a committee of officers from the Royal Engineers in three bulky volumes between 1846 and 1852, contained no entry under 'strategy' or—for that matter—'operations', but cited Jomini extensively in its article on the 'tactics of the three arms'. However, the first volume began with an introductory essay to the whole entitled 'Sketch of the Science and Art of War', by Lieutenant Colonel C. Hamilton Smith. Drawing heavily on Jomini, Hamilton Smith divided his subject matter into 'strategics' and 'tactics', and under the former heading dealt with 'offensive operations' (at length) and 'defensive operations' (more briefly). His categorization of lines of operations was that presented by Jomini in the *Traité*, but Hamilton Smith anticipated a problem which would grow in significance for British military thinkers the more they addressed issues of operational art and tried then to render them into doctrine. 'A British military writer', he opined, 'may view the questions involved in the term "great operations" ("grande tactique" of the French) either as they are based on the general principles of the science, in the light they are viewed by continental strategists, or, narrowing the subject, take it up on the insular position of the empire and the local conditions which result from it'.[14]

Thus, three embryonic points can be made about British military thought by the mid-nineteenth century. First, the word 'operations' in the precise sense used by Jomini had acquired currency: Lieutenant Jervis W. Jervis even published *A Manual of Field Operations* in 1852. Second, operations occupied a position that related to both strategy and tactics: Hamilton Smith subsumed most of his discussion of operations under strategy, but he still associated them with grand tactics, and that point could be made with even more force about Jervis. Third, but less certainly, the distinction between what was required of a European Continental army and what would be required of a British army—what today's analysts would call 'strategic culture'—was beginning to impinge. As Hamilton Smith recognized, in strategic terms the British army was always likely to be operating offensively as it would form an expeditionary force to land in Europe or elsewhere, and it was precisely for that reason that his discussion privileged offensive operations before defensive. The defence of the British Isles, defensive operations in a strategic context, was the navy's job, not the army's.

HAMLEY AND HENDERSON

For most of Hamilton Smith's contemporaries, the specifically national variables of 'strategic culture' did not mean that 'operational art' as it was understood in Britain should differ from 'operational art' as it was interpreted in France or Prussia. His own wholesale lifting from Jomini undermines any claim that here in prototype was 'a British way in war'. Because strategy was believed to be a science, determined by the application of principles, it had a universal quality, capable of rising above the specifics of geographical position just as it surmounted change over time. E. B. Hamley's *The Operations of War*, first published in 1866 and last reprinted and updated in 1922, depended on just such assumptions for its success.

Hamley, another Royal Artillery officer, thought Jomini the 'prince of strategists'.[15] Appointed the first professor of military history when the Staff College was established at Camberley in 1857, he quickly realized that the study of military history by the average officer was unlikely to prove productive, unless that officer possessed a theoretical framework which enabled him to interpret the wars about which he was reading. The inspiration behind *The Operations of War* was firmly didactic and positivist. Like Jomini, Hamley believed that there were constant principles to be applied in war, and that operations were a matter of planning and logistics, of choosing one's own line of operations, and mastering those of the enemy. 'Strategic culture' played no part in his understanding of war: neither colonial warfare nor the role of sea power figured. His case studies were Napoleonic, supplemented by illustrations from the American Civil War and, in the second and later editions, from the Wars of German Unification. Hamley came close to using 'operations' as Clausewitz had used *Handeln.* Although the title of his book made the military use of the word 'operation' current, he did not define 'operational art'. Moreover, he saw operations as belonging in that purely professional sphere to which Bidwell and Graham would also in due course allocate them. 'The Theatre of War is the province of Strategy—the Field of Battle is the province of Tactics', Hamley laid down. 'All operations must ultimately rely for success upon power of fighting; for it is of no avail to conduct an army into situations which it cannot maintain in battle. It is the object of Strategy so to direct the movements of an army, that when decisive collisions occur it shall encounter the enemy with increased relative advantage.'[16]

Hamley's understanding of operations was, therefore, less developed than that of Jomini, and his book was both mired in the tactical past and limited in conception. But he was enormously influential, enjoying a prestige unequalled by any other 'English military writer in the nineteenth century' and producing 'one of the most significant books ever written by a British soldier'.[17] Although *The Operations of War* was dropped as the only text specified for the Staff College entrance examinations in 1894, it remained on most reading lists up to the First World War; it was updated before that conflict by Sir Lancelot Kiggell, who was to be Haig's chief of staff in 1916 and 1917, and after it by Sir George Aston. According to Aston, Hamley's book had influenced Sir John French in his decisions in the retreat from Mons in 1914.[18]

The Operations of War was the most obvious British precursor of *Field Service Regulations Part I: Operations.* Hamley saw operations as the link between tactics and strategy, even if he did not say so in so many words. His most important successors as British military writers, John Frederick Maurice and G. F. R Henderson, did not. Maurice, the professor of military art and history at the Staff College between 1885 and 1892, wrote an essay on war for the *Encyclopaedia Britannica,* which was separately published in 1891. It divided war into strategy and tactics, without reference to operations at all. Henderson, who succeeded Maurice at the Staff College, in 1902 penned a piece on strategy for the same publication which used the word 'operation' sparingly, and then solely in the more general sense of Clausewitz, not in the specific and scientific framework of Jomini.[19] Significantly, Henderson, although writing at the beginning of the twentieth century, used phrases for operational art that had been favoured by Napoleon 100 years earlier: he spoke of 'grand tactics' and 'the tactics of the three arms combined'.[20]

However, this does not mean that either Maurice or Henderson was unpersuaded of the value of lines of operations or of the roles of planning and supply; what their approaches reveal is a much more general point. For all nineteenth-century analysts, Clausewitz and Jomini, Hamley and Henderson, strategy and operations were closely aligned. Even if operational art came close to conceptual birth in the hands of Jomini and Hamley, neither would have been entirely happy with a hierarchy of warlike activities which both separated out operations from strategy, and then subordinated the former to the latter. In the *Précis*, Jomini said that war consisted of five parts: strategy, grand tactics, logistics, tactics of the different arms, and the art of the engineer; operations, his discussion of which was subsumed under strategy, was not one of them.[21] Hamley represented an advance only in that he did not define strategy or tactics, and eschewed all such categorization. Maurice focused on tactics, and saw them as changing. This was the principal reason for his dissatisfaction with Hamley, not his aspiration to address the operational level of war, and Maurice went on to ask whether changes in tactics had also altered strategy. His answer was affirmative but precisely because his understanding of strategy lay not at the interface of military and political activity, but was set by what today would be called operational considerations: 'The campaign, the large field of war which concerns the marches and movements of armies striving against one another to obtain positions of vantage for the actual combat, is the province of strategy'.[22]

It is, therefore, not quite true to say that the British army did not consider the operational level of war in the nineteenth century. It did, but mostly, when it did so, it called it strategy. Strategy was the business of the general, not the politician; the distinction between it and operational art was moot. In this, Britain was fully in accord with more general European practice. Clausewitz defined strategy as the use of the battle for the purposes of the war. He saw much of the tactical activity of his own day as indecisive, and went on to argue that it was the aftermath of battle, the pursuit, that determined its wider outcome. His successors, particularly in France and Germany after the Franco-Prussian War, mostly inverted the relationship. Henderson assumed that the battle itself, not its exploitation, would be decisive. 'Strategy', he wrote, 'is the art of bringing the enemy to battle', and 'the end of strategy is the pitched battle'.[23] Crucially, however, for both sets of interpretations, the relationship between tactics and strategy was the central issue in war.

Definitions of strategy which were limited, professional, and Continentalist were not just responses to the dominance of French and German role models, like Napoleon or Moltke, or of French and German literature (although they were certainly both those things). They were also an acknowledgement that a British national strategy would, because of Britain's status as an island and as an empire, look very different from a French or German one. For mainland European armies after 1871, the slide from strategy in the sense of operational art to strategy as a system of national defence was logical: the likely theatres of campaign and the best methods of operating within them were clear enough. Alsace and Lorraine, the Ardennes, and the Vosges were probable battlegrounds and their armies would be their principal instruments in war. The problem for Britain was that there was no such easy transition from Continental modes of operating to likely scenarios for actual war. If Britain fought any one of France, Germany, or Russia, its primary weapon would be the Royal Navy, and decisive battles seemed more likely to be fought at sea than on land. Hamley may have suppressed the peculiarities of strategic culture, which Hamilton Smith had highlighted in 1846, but Henderson knew that he could not. Although Henderson defined strategy in terms that belong on the operational spectrum, he was well aware of 'the importance of the close concert between strategy and diplomacy', and was cognizant of the challenges created 'when the ocean intervenes between two hostile states'.[24] So the intellectuals of the British army had to face two ways—towards Europe for its military thought, and towards the British Empire for its national strategy.

In December 1905, just over two years after Henderson's death in March 1903, Jackie Fisher, who had become First Sea Lord the previous year, called for reductions in the army's budget, arguing that 'our national life depends absolutely and solely on the Navy' and that 'the Army was no use without it to save the Empire from ruin'.[25] Henderson had already responded to the case of the so-called blue-water school by asserting that 'A state . . . which should rely on naval strength alone could look forward to no other than a protracted war, and a protracted war between two great Powers is antagonistic to the interests of the civilised world'. He believed that, in the event of European war, Britain would have to have the capacity to intervene, to adopt the offensive, and to mount amphibious operations: 'An army supported by an invincible navy possesses a strength out of all proportion to its size'. The British army's role was, therefore, an expeditionary one. 'The military operations of a maritime state' involved not only the capture of 'colonies, naval arsenals and coaling-stations', but also 'timely diversions, by attracting a large portion of the enemy's fighting strength on the mainland' to aid 'the armies of an ally'.[26]

This was what Liddell Hart after the First World War would call the British way in warfare. Nor was Henderson a lone voice in British military circles. Charles Callwell published *The Effect of Maritime Command on Land Campaigns since Waterloo* in 1897 and he reworked it as *Military Operations and Maritime Preponderance* in 1905. Others would follow—most famously Julian Corbett, whose *Some Principles of Maritime Strategy* was published in 1911, and George Aston, a Royal Marine, whose books included *Letters on Amphibious Wars* (1910) and *Sea, Land, and Air Strategy* (1914). But there was a further complication, which Liddell Hart would overlook when he formulated the British way in warfare, but which neither Henderson nor Callwell did. The British army might be called upon to mount an amphibious landing in the event of war with a European power, but it also faced the daily certainty of colonial garrisoning against a bewilderingly different array of opponents in radically diverse climates and geographies. The army could not know whom it would fight next or where it would do so.[27] Strategy at the level of national policy created uncertainty for military thought; it demanded flexibility and adaptability. British military thinkers wrote more about tactics than strategy for a number of pragmatic reasons. The first was no doubt to do with comfort zones; they felt at ease with the level of war at which they had begun their careers as subalterns. The second was also a reflection of modernity; technological and industrial change, the railway and the rifle, meant that the conduct of war was being changed from the bottom up. The third was that tactics could be made into doctrine, but for Britain neither operations nor strategy could.

Doctrine at the strategic level implied that the theatre of war—or of operations—could be anticipated in advance. Henderson, therefore, rejected doctrine, and the Jominian legacy, as inappropriate for the British army. 'War is assuredly no mechanical art', he wrote. 'Broadly speaking, it is a war between the brains and grit of the two commanders, in which each strives to outwit and outlast the other; a conflict in which accident plays so prominent a part that mistakes, in one form or another, are absolutely unavoidable'.[28] Instead of doctrine, Henderson looked to principles, and even here he was at pains to stress that some principles conflicted with each other, and that, therefore, 'strategical principles are neither to be rigidly applied nor over-scrupulously respected. They are to be obeyed rather in the spirit than in the letter; and the strategist, to be successful, must know exactly how far he can go in disregarding them or in modifying them'.[29]

Henderson was a profoundly influential figure in the British army before 1914, the posthumous edition of his writings would be reprinted after the First World War, and his principal historical study, *Stonewall Jackson and the American Civil War*, would be studied at the Staff College long after that. Sir William Robertson, who was at the Staff College in 1897–8, alongside Douglas Haig and many others who would achieve fame in the First World War, wrote in his memoirs that, 'Of the different causes which are alleged to have given us the victory over Germany, not one should be assigned a more prominent place than the influence and teaching of Henderson at the Staff College'.[30]

Robertson's tribute is significant in view of his subsequent reputation. Henderson expected the British army to be used in conformity with the expectations created by its imperial commitments and by British sea power; Robertson, who was Chief of the Imperial General Staff between late 1915 and early 1918, would become—in the eyes of Liddell Hart and others who fell under his sway—the arch-Continentalist, the man who used the creation of a British general staff to subvert British generalship and to convert the British army into a mass army on European lines. In 1902, the British army was uncertain of its role in national policy, and the case for doctrine was accordingly easy to dismiss. In 1914–18, its role would be clear enough: the issue, as it adapted, and as its colonial roles became subordinated to Continental priorities, was whether it now needed doctrine the better to wage European war. The debate was also a product of increasing army size. The bigger the army and the more it depended on short-term citizen soldiers, the greater the case for a doctrine that was committed to paper rather than thinking that was informally transmitted. Moreover, size created a wider gap between tactics and strategy: a command level emerged that inserted itself between the tactical competence of the battalion and the strategic role of the army. The corps practised the 'tactics of the three arms combined', to use Henderson's phrase, but it did more than that: it had to accommodate not just field but also heavy artillery, not just cavalry but also aircraft and, in due course, tanks. If operational art had an institutional home, it would be the corps, a self-contained formation capable of independent operations and the innovation which had enabled Napoleon to fuse manoeuvre with battle.

THE GENERAL STAFF AND THE CREATION OF DOCTRINE

Bidwell and Graham presumably chose 1904–6 as their departure dates as these were the years when Britain finally created a general staff. Many Liberals feared that such a body would inevitably make European war the focus of its planning activities and that such plans would themselves limit the strategic flexibility both required by Britain's imperial commitments and vouchsafed by British sea power. From the vantage point of 1918 and afterwards, their fears looked justified. The British army did refashion itself on European lines between 1904 and 1916, and some would argue that the British general staff did indeed hijack British national strategy. But such interpretations both over-privilege hindsight and underestimate the intelligence of the officers of the general staff; they also neglect the legacy of Henderson.

From the outset, the general staff orientated itself around its worst-case scenario, war in Europe, but it did not as a result neglect its colonial commitments. It developed plans for many areas of operations other than support for France or Belgium, including the defence of India, Egypt, and even Canada.[31] The British army remained organized along lines adapted for imperial garrisoning, and Britain rejected European models of conscription. Henderson's challenge, therefore, remained: how was the army to develop doctrine for one sort of war which did not make it unfit for all the other eventualities it was expected to confront?

The general staff's answer was *Field Service Regulations Part I: Operations*, and like many answers to difficult questions it rested on compromise. The preparation of both it and its companion volume, *Field Service Regulations Part II: Organization and Administration*, was in the hands of Douglas Haig, director of staff duties between 1907 and 1909. At a conference of general staff officers held at the Staff College in January 1908 the draft *Field Service Regulations* was debated, and Haig referred 'to a note at the top of the first page, which said that these Regulations were not intended for small campaigns'. No such note appeared in the published version. He went on to cite the example of the South African War, 'where three entirely different systems were adapted by three different headquarters'. The new regulations would replace diversity with uniformity; they were to be 'the law' for officers and their amendment was to be the product of collective discussion and centralized decision making: 'unanimity', he declared, 'is an essential condition of collective action'.

Haig wanted the general staff to replace the regiment as the fountainhead of the army's education, and to produce a doctrine for war on the continent of Europe. Those more loyal to Henderson's precepts were deeply concerned about the implications for the conduct of small wars, and the need for flexibility and adaptability in all wars. Robertson had begun the proceedings by arguing that the job of a general staff was to lay down general principles.[32] Although as persuaded as Haig of the need for the general staff to be the central intellectual organ of the army, and equally determined that 'any scheme for the creation of a National Army should be based on European and not Asiatic conditions',[33] he was less dirigiste. He wrote, when commandant of the Staff College in 1912, in a paper summarizing his reactions to a battlefield tour, that the aim of the regulations was 'to train the judgment of all officers so that when left to themselves they may do the right thing; to make the best use of the ground; to avoid normal formations and hard and fast rules; and to train the individual'.[34] Haig took great pride in the *Field Service Regulations*, for whose publication he had to fight,[35] but their content reflected Robertson's philosophy more than his own. 'They lay down certain principles', Robertson wrote in 1912, 'but they do not pretend to show how those principles must be treated or modified under conditions which are so infinitely diversified'.[36]

Like the teaching of Henderson whom Robertson so much admired, the published version of *Field Service Regulations Part I* rested on the assumption of expeditionary warfare, and the consequent reliance of the army on the Royal Navy. This was a 'joint' document *avant la lettre.* Chapter III, headed 'Movements by Land and Sea', began with a paragraph on 'strategical concentration', which put at least as much, if not more, weight on movement by water as by land, and contained an independent section on 'movements by sea'. The latter stated that overseas expeditions would be undertaken for three possible reasons—to establish a base for operations against the enemy's field army, or against a coastal fortress; to create 'a flying naval base'; or to conduct raids against shipping and lines of communication. *Field Service Regulations* accepted that 'the success of such operations demands as a first postulate the command of the sea'; that it would be the navy's decision as to when that state had been reached; and that the navy must be free to act to preserve command of the sea on its own terms, 'having in view the general strategical situation afloat'. It was to be understood, the manual went on, 'that each service is working for a common object, and will render the other all assistance that lies in its power'.[37] And just to make sure that the army, at any rate, could understand the navy, appendix II of the publication was composed of definitions of naval terms and orders.

Chapter X of *Field Service Regulations* covered 'Warfare Against an Uncivilized Enemy', and divided its subject matter according to geography, one section covering mountain warfare and the other bush fighting. It began, as did every chapter, with a statement of general principles concerning the chapter's particular topic. The opening premise of chapter X was that, 'in campaigns against savages, the armament, tactics, and characteristics of the enemy, and the nature of the theatre of operations demand that the principles of regular warfare be somewhat modified'.[38] The next paragraph went on to stress the need for flexibility and adaptability, the capacity to be able to meet unexpected conditions and to be able to beat 'the enemy at his own tactics'. But the important point to note was the emphasis on *modifying*, not on replacing, the principles of warfare. Regular and irregular wars were subsumed within the same general framework. At its most basic level, this was shown by the incorporation of 'small wars' within the same operational publication as that devoted to 'big wars'. At the conceptual level, it was reflected in the relationship between strategy and tactics. The cardinal principle in wars against an uncivilized enemy was that his susceptibility 'to moral influences is a most important factor in the campaign', and that, therefore, 'a vigorous offensive, strategical as well as tactical, is always the safest method of conducting operations'.[39] Similarly, the second paragraph of the opening chapter of the text as a whole asserted that 'success in war depends more on moral than physical qualities', and the chapter on battle began with the statement that 'decisive success in battle can be gained only by a vigorous offensive'.[40] Any distinction between colonial conflicts and wars against European opponents lay in the application of the principles, not in the principles themselves. *Field Service Regulations Part II: Organization and Administration*, published at the same time as part I, made this point crystal clear:

> Although the strength and composition of the forces in the field must vary according to the enemy to be encountered, and the nature of the prospective theatre of operations, yet the general principles which govern their organization remain practically the same whether operations are conducted under civilized or uncivilized conditions, and whether a small force or a large one is employed. It is only the application of principles in detail which vary, and once the principles themselves are clearly understood, it is comparatively simple to adjust such details to any given case.[41]

Field Service Regulations followed a sequence from strategy to tactics, the purpose of strategy being the tactical pay-off, to bring the enemy to battle, the decisive act in wars of any and all types. This relationship between tactics and strategy was the same as that which Henderson had spelt out in 1902, but it should not necessarily be regarded as Henderson's last word on the subject. The sixth edition of 'Notes on strategy by Colonel Henderson compiled for the use of students at the Staff College', dated 1912 and to be found in William Robertson's papers, set out a more Clausewitzian relationship between strategy and tactics, as well as between strategy and policy. Addressing the latter point first, Henderson stated that strategy and policy must be in harmony. What followed then switched to a more Jominian tack, stressing the choice of objectives in war, the need to adopt a line of march which both covered one's own communications and threatened the enemy's, and the primacy of concentrating superior force on the decisive point. The fourteenth and fifteenth headings stressed that tactics could be a departure point, rather than a terminus, for strategy: victory in battle created a new strategic situation, and strategic pursuit—not battle—was dubbed 'the decisive operation in war'. Henderson still did not address 'operational art' as a distinct topic, but his principles included ideas which would be subsumed by that heading. His sixteenth principle was that 'the strategic counterstroke is the best weapon of the defence' and his eighteenth that 'MANOEUVRE IS THE ANTIDOTE OF INTRENCHMENTS'.[42]

These principles, even if they were the basis for instruction at the Staff College, were not reflected in the *Field Service Regulations*. The official publication eschewed 'operational art', did not discuss Jominian lines of operation, and, although it boasted 'operations' in its title, contained no definition of that word (or of strategy or tactics, for that matter). Its focus, like Henderson's published work, was on the 'tactics of the three arms'. 'The full power of an army', it stressed, 'can be exerted only when all its parts act in close combination'. In a typically Hendersonian turn of phrase, it declared that 'the fundamental principles of war are neither very numerous nor in themselves very abstruse, but the application of them is difficult and cannot be made subject to rules'.[43] However, it did not then set out what the fundamental principles of war were. Neither concentration of force on the decisive point (the ninth principle in Henderson's notes on strategy) nor economy of force, both of them perennials in most lists of the principles of war, figures in the index. Surprise does, but not as a general principle of war; instead, it was important in siege operations, necessary in night operations, and to be guarded against by the principle of protection. The regulations were full of 'general principles' for application within specific topics, but totally lacking in general principles per se.

In other words, although the *Field Service Regulations* was designed to prepare a British Expeditionary Force for war in general, either in Europe or in the empire, it was not, despite Haig's best endeavours, designed to be a doctrine for a specific sort of war. In April 1911, Major L. H. R. Pope-Hennessy, an infantryman then engaged in translating *Les transformations de la guerre*, the work of the French general Jean Colin, into English, published anonymously a review of the *Field Service Regulations*, together with other works on contemporary warfare, in the *Edinburgh Review*. 'It is among the first duties of the General Staff of a great modern national army', he declared, 'to indoctrinate it with a clear conception of the basic principles of war, and of the method on which it intends to apply those principles to the conduct of national war'. Pope-Hennessy believed that all that the British general staff had done so far was to produce a 'method of action':

> It is a matter of moment for us to follow the process by which the thinking organ of an army, the General Staff, extracts from the records of the past and the wars of the present the principles which have governed the success and failure of great commanders; to learn how from those principles it forms a conception of war adapted to the circumstances and characteristics of the nation and army it serves; and then to note how, transmitting the conception into doctrine permeating the whole body of the army, it leads that army to seek for victory along certain definite lines, to follow which has become instinctive to leaders and subordinates alike.[44]

The issue was not just whether Britain should have a doctrine at all, given its Continentalist associations, but also whether that doctrine should be modelled on Germany's or France's. The former aimed at applying superior force through envelopment: there was none of this in the *Field Service Regulations*. By contrast, whole chapters were devoted to protection, embracing flank guards, rear guards, and so on, and to information, a section which discussed such topics as the role of advance guards in detecting the enemy's line of advance and in screening one's own. These were the key themes of French doctrine, which aimed to retain freedom of movement and to observe the principle of economy of force, so that fresh troops could intervene at the right time. In this respect, at least there was more doctrine in the *Field Service Regulations* than Pope-Hennessy cared to admit. Both the *Field Service Regulations* (at least between the lines) and Pope-Hennessy (more explicitly) were acknowledging that doctrine could be the framework for the development of operational art. The trouble was that many officers of the British army went further than a simple neglect of doctrine; they rejected it. Another literate infantry officer, J. F. C. Fuller, spoke for many when he declared at the Royal United Services Institute in 1914 that, 'I have no doctrine, for I believe in none. Every concrete case demands its own particular solution.... If there is doctrine at all then it is common sense, that is action adapted to circumstances'.[45]

In 1912, Pope-Hennessy returned to the charge with a second article which pointed out that the principles of command, in other words the exercise of operational art, rested on the commander's ability to control his forces, and, therefore, on a general who knew how he intended to use his army and an army who understood that intention. He used the word 'operations' when describing how Napoleon had harmonized his principles of command. Following his own reading of the recently published French literature, not just that by Colin, but also by Hubert Camon, he attributed Napoleon's defeat in 1813–15 to the failure of his subordinate commanders to follow the workings of their commander's mind. By contrast, the success of the elder Moltke in the Wars of German Unification was to be attributed to harmony between his intentions and the actions of his subordinate commanders, a 'unity of thought which is the fruit of common adherence to a common doctrine'. For Pope-Hennessy, the choice was stark—intellectual order or intellectual anarchy.

He dismissed the argument that doctrine would be 'bad for an army, which may be called up to operate against a great variety of enemies in various totally dissimilar theatres of war'. The 'doctrine of no doctrine', resting on what he called an empirical conception of war, could not be defended by reference to the 'infinite variety of situations ranging from war against Afghans in Afghanistan to war against Germany in Belgium'. Major war should be given priority over small wars. Defeat in Afghanistan could be rectified, but 'if the British Army is beaten by a Continental Army in Europe, be it in Belgium or in Norfolk, the defeat will be decisive'.[46]

THE FIRST WORLD WAR

At the end of August 1914, the British Expeditionary Force was defeated in Belgium by a Continental army. Whether that defeat was due to the lack of doctrine or a lack of skill in the exercise of operational art was not much debated at the time. Instead, the focus lay in creating an army that in terms of both size and organization was better fitted for European war than the exiguous force dispatched to France on the outbreak of war. But the emulation of the major European armies in itself created the need to engage with the operational level of war. Specifically, it elevated the command level at which the tactics of all arms were combined to the corps.

The *Field Service Regulations* had laid down in 1909 that the basis for the organization of the field army was the division, 'a self-contained formation, comprising all arms and services in due proportion, complete in itself with every requisite for independent action'.[47] However, European armies regarded the corps, the next formation up in the hierarchy of army organization, as the basis of army organization. Britain's rejection of the Continental model was a reflection of both the small size of its army and its need to retain an organization adaptable to small wars as well as big ones. But the British Expeditionary Force was planned to be six divisions strong, and Haig was of the view that such a span of command was beyond the powers of one general.[48] The *Field Service Regulations* therefore went on to allow for the formation of corps, each composed of two or more divisions, when several divisions were mobilized. In August 1914, the British Expeditionary Force was accordingly divided into two corps, and so went to war with a command structure in which nobody was trained and for which no staff establishment had been laid down.

At one level, the onset of trench warfare vindicated the British decision to make the division the key building block of its army. The divisions, whose full wartime establishment in 1914 was about 18,000 men, achieved steady identities, determined by the units serving within them, as well as by regional affiliations and their organizational origins. Moreover, the character of the war pushed the weight towards the tactical end of the operational spectrum. The coordination of the three arms—or four with the addition of air power—became the key to operational success, and this was manifested at the tactical level as armies struggled to break through. The chances of strategic exploitation of battlefield victory depended on tactical solutions, and the sheer difficulty of its achievement in the intensely competitive environment of the Western Front meant that strategy as traditionally defined played second fiddle for much of the war. All the pre-war doctrinal debates in European armies about envelopments, advance guards, and lines of operations appeared increasingly recondite and even irrelevant.

Nonetheless, the tactical constraints of trench warfare also elevated the corps level of command. The key to unlocking trench systems was heavy artillery, a commodity in very short supply in 1914–16, and even when available in greater numbers still treated as a corps asset. Nor did divisions have an artillery staff large enough to produce the sort of sophisticated fire plans necessary by 1916 and after. The demand was tactical, to generate firepower, but the command level was operational, and the art was in the coordination of the other arms, particularly infantry, with what the artillery could do.[49]

Trench warfare may, ironically enough, have opened up the operational level of command in an institutional sense, but it did not seem to do much for 'operational art' in a creative sense. Corps headquarters focused on planning before action rather than command during it. The systems were scientific, depending on early forms of operational research to analyse effects and to suggest changes, and the essence in a mass army was on management not inspiration. The progressive loosening of trench warfare in 1918 had a reverse effect. Institutionally, the need for mobility meant that the corps had to decentralize command once more, giving divisions greater freedom, and allowing them more control of their own firepower. But, in terms of strategy, words which had seemed lost in 1915–17 re-entered the considerations of planners. The biggest constraints on the Allied advances in 1918 were logistic: a form of war which assumed fixed lines of operations was replaced by one where the possibility of threatening those of the enemy gave meaning to operational art once more.

Douglas Haig's response to all this was to stress the continuing validity of the *Field Service Regulations* of 1909. On 22 August 1918, his headquarters issued guidance for the conduct of future attacks which referred to *Part I: Operations*, left to subordinate commanders' decisions about how to attack, and sought to reunite tactics and strategy. Advance guards were to identify enemy defences, and thereafter 'units and formations should be directed on *points* of strategic and tactical importance some distance ahead . . . and they should not be ordered to move on objective lines'.[50] Haig argued that the flexibility and adaptability of the *Field Service Regulations*, their adherence to principles not doctrine, had been vindicated by the outcome of the war. When he penned his final dispatch on 21 March 1919, he concluded that the First World War possessed 'the same general features and the same necessary stages which between forces of approximately equal strength have marked all the conclusive battles of history'. He went on to refer to the 'accepted principles of war', to the 'axiom that decisive success in battle can be gained only by a vigorous offensive', and to the 'close and complete co-operation between all arms and services'.[51]

THE LESSONS OF THE FIRST WORLD WAR

Haig recognized changes but subsumed them within an overall framework of continuity; others saw just change. Strategy in particular no longer meant what it had meant to Jomini, and even to Clausewitz. The war had been won by alliances and by the mobilization of national resources. J. F. C. Fuller and—in due course—Basil Liddell Hart added the adjective 'grand' to the noun 'strategy' to describe something more akin to policy than to what armies did within theatres of war. The effect was to open out the possibilities for operational art more explicitly to describe how armies were commanded. And Haig's critics were increasingly persuaded that it was to this level, that of army command, that the principal traumas of the First World War could be attributed. The mass army was ponderous, the staff system had generated predictability not imagination, and the emphasis on firepower had worked against manoeuvre. 'Armies, through their own lack of foresight, were reduced to the position of human cattle', Fuller fulminated in *The Reformation of War*, published in 1923; 'they browsed behind their fences, and on occasion snorted and bellowed at each other'. Fuller dubbed this 'the last lap of the physical epoch'. He called the plans for 1919, to which he himself had contributed but which were never implemented because of the suddenness of the German collapse, 'the first lap of the moral epoch'. Fuller imagined masses of fast tanks driving deep towards the enemy's command headquarters and railheads, 'which for slaughter substituted nervous shock, aiming a mortal blow at the brain in place of a physical blow at the body of the enemy's army'.[52] For Fuller, war at its most elemental was a matter of science, as its theory depended on scientific method and its practice was shaped by technology. But its application required art. Mobility was the key to putting art into operations.

The chapter in *The Reformation of War* devoted to 'the science and art of war' is, above all, a discussion of the principles of war. Fuller castigated the 1909 *Field Service Regulations* for their failure to spell out what the principles of war were, but somewhat disingenuously failed to mention that the first post-war revision of *Field Service Regulations, Volume II: Operations: Provisional*, published in 1920, had remedied the deficiency.[53] Moreover, those principles were to all intents and purposes identical to those listed by Fuller in *The Reformation of War*—maintenance of the objective, the superiority of the offensive, the effect of surprise, the concentration of forces in time and space, economy in the use of force, the priority of security, the value of mobility in conferring flexibility and achieving surprise, and the need for cooperation. Fuller's principles claimed 'greater universality' than anything Jomini had written, but did so 'at the price of greater abstraction from any concrete reality'.[54] Between 1920 and 1935, *Field Service Regulations* passed through four editions, and, although the specific principles were changed and adapted, the principle of having principles remained.[55]

Four revisions to *Field Service Regulations* in fifteen years give the lie to the argument that the army failed to address the lessons of the First World War. By 1916, Robertson himself had moved away from the Hendersonian position he had espoused before the war, just as Haig was moving in the opposite direction: 'each war has its own peculiarities, but one would think that no war was ever so peculiar as the present one, and Field Service Regulations will require a tremendous amount of revising when we have finished with the Boche', he wrote to Henry Rawlinson, then commanding the 4th Army in the Battle of the Somme. He went on, 'Principles, as we used to call them, are good and cannot be disregarded, but their application is a very difficult business, and I think that we still take these principles too literally'.[56] After the war was over, the general staff did not turn its back on war in Europe in its rush to embrace the familiarity of imperial commitments. Lord Cavan, the chief of the Imperial General Staff, said in 1922 that 'the present policy is to train for a small war against an enemy whose armament is on an equality with our own'.[57] Nor was it quite so content as it had been before the war to use a generalized vision of war to cover all wars. The chapter in the 1920 *Field Service Regulations* on 'Warfare against an Uncivilized

Enemy' said that in such operations 'the normal application of the principles of regular warfare' should be '*considerably* modified',[58] and the 1935 edition began a chapter now called 'Special Types of Warfare' with the statement that 'In the preceding chapters warfare in a highly developed country against a civilized enemy had been the type mainly considered'.[59]

Freeing operational thought from its need to embrace all types of war enabled it to focus on major war: it seemed as though Henderson was out, and Haig (at least in this respect) was in. Doctrine, and with it operational art, should have grown on the back of such assumptions. But it did not. The 1935 *Field Service Regulations* was divided into three, not two, volumes, the third called *Operations—Higher Formations*. Whereas part II treated 'the tactical employment of all arms in co-operation', part III covered 'the principles governing the employment of all armed forces in war'. But it promised more than it delivered. The third volume was still focused on 'the tactical employment of larger formations'. Operations remained a dirty word in the sense of a level of war between tactics and strategy. And so too did doctrine—still typecast as Teutonic and dogmatic, the enemy of flexibility. Hence the continued stress on the principles of war: they underpinned the commitment to adaptability rather than to convergent ways of thinking.

For all its readiness to take war against 'first-class' enemies as its benchmark, the general staff was reluctant to impose too much shape on how it envisaged the fighting which would result. In 1929, Major General Sir Frederick Maurice, the son of J. F. Maurice and a former director of military operations at the War Office, published a book called *British Strategy: A Study of the Application of the Principles of War*. Strategy was defined by Maurice in traditional terms, as 'the leading of troops up to the time of contact with the enemy', and tactics as 'the methods of employing troops in contact with the enemy'. Based on the principles of war as enumerated in *Field Service Regulations*, *British Strategy* carried the imprimatur of the chief of the Imperial General Staff, Field Marshal Sir George Milne. Milne drew particular attention to chapter IX, that on the principle of mobility. 'Mobility', the chapter began, 'is one of the chief means of manoeuvre, which is in turn the means of engaging in battle to advantage'.[60]

Maurice's book was in direct descent from Henderson in two respects. The first was its title: the epithet 'British' was deliberate, a contrast to (in the words of Milne's introduction) 'the ideas of continental strategists, generally expressed in terms untuned to British ears and dealing with situations likely to affect continental powers more than the British empire'.[61] The second lay in Maurice's emphasis on the principles of war, derived from a study of military history, 'fundamental truths which . . . remain immutable, just as do the mechanical principles which govern the art of architecture, whether the materials used are wood, stone, iron or reinforced concrete, just as the principles of harmony, which govern the art of music'. However, according to Maurice the principles of war were not, strictly speaking, principles at all, but methods, guides to action, 'by which certain results can be obtained'. As Maurice confessed, 'a mere knowledge of the principles of war . . . will not help a soldier to solve a problem of war any more than a knowledge of the principles of painting will, without steady practice and natural aptitude, enable an artist to paint a picture'.[62] Milne had told the annual general staff conference in 1927 that 'the interpretation [of *Field Service Regulations*] as you get on in the service, especially as regards senior officers of the General Staff, must be left to you to a great extent'.[63]

Fuller, on the other hand, distanced himself from Henderson's legacy.[64] He was not satisfied with an approach to the study of war which depended so much on history to the exclusion of the future, and which stressed the art involved in the application of the principles rather than the science on which those principles rested. In 1926, *The Foundations of the Science of War*, the most ambitious of all his books, aimed to marry the wisdom of the past to the speculations surrounding the future by the use of scientific methods, not least because, 'as regards war, . . . everything is changing. We are faced by air warfare, and mechanical warfare on land, and submarine warfare at sea, and chemical warfare everywhere'.[65] The book rested on a system of principles and on Fuller's belief in war's threefold order. Both ideas were developed in more pragmatic and less abstruse fashion in 1931 in *Lectures on F. S. R. II*, Fuller's commentary on *Field Service Regulations*. Its introduction said that *Field Service Regulations* was 'pre-eminently a guide to action, in which a common doctrine is laid down that in no way should be considered a rigid dogma'. Doctrine was a word whose use Fuller had repudiated in 1914, but he now employed it in a way that was both flexible (so meeting its standard criticisms in British circles) and modern. Moreover, Fuller divided 'the controlling objects in war' into a threefold hierarchy, political or 'grand strategical', 'strategical', and tactical. His definitions of tactics and strategy were fairly traditional. The latter was 'the art of moving armies towards the battlefield in such a way that when the battle takes place it will be fought at the greatest advantage; consequently strategy is the foundation of planning, which is the main duty of the general'.[66] However, when such a definition was put alongside that of grand strategy, which used not only military force, but also economic pressure, financial disorganization, and propaganda, Fuller was effectively associating strategy with operational art.

This point became even clearer in the following year, when Fuller's *Lectures on F. S. R. III (Operations Between Mechanized Forces)* tackled the issue of future warfare. He juxtaposed a revolution in land warfare created by new technologies and the unchanging principles of war to argue that the sum total would be evolutionary, 'not a new type of war, a war totally unrelated to the present type, but a new form of war, a form arising out of the petrol engine which has greatly accelerated movement and enhanced carrying power'. His definition of strategy reflected the transitional quality of his thought. Now it said nothing about battle, pointing no longer to strategy's tactical pay-off, but to its political outcome: 'The aim of strategy is to clinch a political argument by means of force in place of words'. Into the gap which he had thus opened between strategy and tactics, he put operational art. Thanks to the advent of more mobile and flexible forces, 'generalship can be developed into a high art, and battles into works of art and not merely daubs of blood'. In formulating his plan, the general of the future would have to embrace the high tempo of the action, and would have to realize that 'the idea of the plan must be flexible, that it must embrace a number of alternative actions'. And to tempo and unpredictability, he added depth. The formal methods of attack and defence would be abandoned, as attacks would need to threaten the defence from all directions and the defence would have to respond accordingly. 'The reason for all this', Fuller concluded, 'is that battles in the future are likely to become more and more area operations and not merely positional ones'.[67]

Fuller went on to use the word operations in conjunction with manoeuvre, reverted to the phrase 'tactical operations' a few pages further on, and fell back on 'grand tactical problems in mechanized wars' in his discussion of the defence.[68] But the point is clear enough. Fuller was groping towards an articulation of what later generations would call operational art, was putting it in the context of war as a whole, not of a 'British way', and was ready to see this as a basis for doctrine. Nor was he alone. Basil Liddell Hart's *The Decisive Wars of History: A Study in History* had been published in 1929. This was the book which in its later editions would be called *Strategy: The Indirect Approach*, a reading of the history of land warfare which, as Liddell Hart himself put it when describing Epaminondas's victory at Mantinea in 362 BC, lay 'on the borderline between strategy and tactics' but in which an 'arbitrary division is false'. Liddell Hart described 'pure strategy', which he distinguished from grand strategy and its relation to policy, in terms which stressed movement and surprise, and which sought strategic dislocation through the mystification of the enemy.[69] Both of them eschewed the word 'operations', but Fuller with his interest in 'grand tactics' and Liddell Hart with his in 'field strategy' or manoeuvre were converging on the same issue from different perspectives.[70]

THE SECOND WORLD WAR

Both Fuller and Liddell Hart enjoyed close connections with senior officers in the British army, and both were able to exercise considerable influence on its thinking—to a much greater extent than either of them was prepared to acknowledge. This leverage was increased by the army's lack of doctrine, which meant that those who thought about their profession were naturally drawn to both Fuller's and Liddell Hart's writings.[71] And yet the British army of the Second World War is widely, and probably rightly, criticized for failing—not only in the battles of 1940–2, but also in those of 1944–5—in the exercise of operational art. Why was that the case?

The first answer is the intemperate nature of Fuller's own advocacy, his damning of those who disagreed with him as stupid and ignorant, and his determination to write in prose that seemed pretentious and obscure. Although *British Strategy* can be read as a counter to *The Foundations of the Science of War*, the point should not be laboured. Maurice's book did not attack Fuller by name, and, after all, in December 1926 Milne gave Fuller charge of the Experimental Mechanised Force created precisely to test his theories. But in 1927 Maurice wrote the foreword to a blistering rebuttal of Fuller by V. W. Germains, in which he rejected the notion that the tank had revolutionized warfare and criticized 'those who are attempting to create what they call a Science of War, and are launching their theories, in accordance with modern tactical methods, under a smoke cloud of verbiage'.[72]

Maurice's foreword was not a rejection of the tank, but a plea for balance in adopting it, for the pre-eminence of combined-arms warfare, and also for the recognition that a small professional mechanized force in the event of major war could be no more than the 'advanced guard of our national army'.[73] Inter-war advocates of the tank everywhere, not just in Britain, faced two fundamental problems. One was how to mechanize the whole of a mass army, given its cost. Britain's answer was to mechanize on a broad front but to keep the army small; when conscription was reintroduced in 1939 and the army expanded, it had no quick answer to procurement. The other general problem was the challenge which fast tanks posed to the rest of the army if the infantry was not mechanized, since the latter could not keep pace with the former. Britain's answer in 1931–2 was to divide cruiser tanks which were lightly armoured from heavily armoured infantry tanks that were slow; it then abandoned the development of medium tanks altogether. Dividing up the battlefield in this way meant that tactical solutions replaced operational thought.

Combined-arms warfare, like balance more generally defined, was the casualty of a debate polarized and politicized by Fuller in the 1920s and by Basil Liddell Hart in the 1930s. Its outcome was an exaggerated view of the independent capabilities of armour, sustained by a selective reading of the German invasion of France in 1940 and fomented that winter by Lieutenant General Richard O'Connor's defeat of the Italian 10th Army in Libya in a genuinely lightning campaign. The ease of this initial victory in North Africa encouraged the 'Desert Rats', as the British 7th Armoured Division was dubbed, to neglect artillery–armour cooperation, and to eschew the concentration of fire in favour of dispersal, with disastrous consequences against the integrated tactics practised by the Afrika Korps in North Africa. The failures of British armour in the battles of 1941 and 1942 were in part due to poor decisions with regard to tank design, but they were also a reflection of a wider intellectual and institutional failing. The general staff had not managed to exploit the victories of the last 'hundred days' of 1918 to impose itself on an army which had a strong tradition of independence among subordinate commands. An inheritance of the regimental system, it left divisions in the 1930s and into the early years of the Second World War free to train and prepare for battle according to the ideas of their own commanders, and not according to a common body of thinking developed and sustained by the general staff.[74]

The British army lacked a doctrine. So much was design. Such an approach should have accorded with the emphasis on the principles of war, the determination to avoid dogma, and the need for flexibility and adaptability demanded of an army with colonial responsibilities. Paradoxically, however, it competed with a top-down approach to command which served all too often to stifle such initiative and inhibited the exploitation of success. The army preached decentralization but practised control. Defeat at Dunkirk was attributed to insufficiently specific and detailed instructions. As a corps commander in the home forces in June 1941, Montgomery told his subordinates that close-order drill was an aid to operational discipline.[75] His subsequent success with the 8th Army in North Africa rested on his ability to plan at the tactical level, to resurrect the principles of infantry and artillery cooperation so painfully learnt by the British army by 1918, and to inculcate those tactical methods by thorough training. What he could not do was to rely on mission command, a readiness to use directives, while leaving the details of their execution to subordinates. As the army had no doctrine, it had no general body of ideas within which subordinate commanders could be free to exercise their own judgement, and without that its understanding of the operational level of war also remained limited.[76] As in the First World War, firepower became the means to open up the opportunity for manoeuvre, but in the process the means threatened also to become the ends. The approach worked well enough at El Alamein, and it was consolidated by the outcome, the only independent victory won by a British army against German troops in the whole war. Better communications, real-time intelligence, and the virtuous circle between the two, meant that the army of 1944–5 possessed the tools to practise operational art, if not the nous. But the better they did these things, the less the pressure to address the conceptual dimension.[77]

THE BRITISH ARMY OF THE RHINE

The post-war British army was shaped in Montgomery's image; he was, after all, chief of the Imperial General Staff between 1946 and 1948, and a powerful self-propagandist until his death in 1976. This meant that subordinates conformed to the 'master plan', as indeed the circumstances of the Cold War obliged them to do. If flexibility and decentralization of command found a home in the army, it was in the practice of counter-insurgency in the withdrawal from empire; the more independent-minded officer established his niche in special forces, in contracts with and attachments to other armies, especially in the Middle East, but not in the British Army of the Rhine. Moreover, this was a separation of roles which reopened divisions between the combat arms: irregular warfare was, above all, a job for the infantry, while heavy tanks took up permanent home in north Germany. The mental world of the latter became that of the 'retired officer', more anxious to extend his appointment and its tax-free benefits than to widen his thinking about war; 'the only thing joint' about the joint headquarters of the Rhine army and the Royal Air Force (RAF) 'was that we were in the same place'.[78]

In 1985, a lengthy and exhaustive study of British military thought since 1945 observed that studies of 'military art' tended to be subsumed within discussion of military policy, and that 'civilian strategists' focused on nuclear deterrence.[79] It made no mention of operational art, and nor, two years later, did *Warfare as a Whole*, the work of General Sir Frank Kitson, who had just finished his career as commander-in-chief, United Kingdom Land Forces. Having published *Low Intensity Operations: Subversion, Insurgency and Peacekeeping* in 1971, the distillation of lessons learnt over the two decades of colonial withdrawal, Kitson was one of the army's most distinguished commentators on counter-insurgency. But Kitson's use of the word 'operations' in his title had been Clausewitzian, not Jominian, and, although some of those campaigns had been characterized by joint political and military planning at the theatre level, most famously and successfully in Malaya, Kitson had not equated the resulting strategy with operational art. Even he saw the extensive campaigning outside Europe as separate from, and at a subordinate level to, the possible war within Europe. *Warfare as a Whole* bemoaned the army's lack of doctrine, but its focus on tactics and training suggested that Kitson understood doctrine as Clausewitz had, not as a source of inspiration for commanders.[80]

The central concepts underpinning NATO war games designed to prepare for the defence of Western Europe against a Soviet invasion were also tactical, emphasizing firepower at the expense of manoeuvre. Committed to the forward defence of the inner German border, commanders could not trade space for time because that would involve the sacrifice of the very territory which they were seeking to protect. Soviet conventional superiority meant that such exercises almost invariably concluded with the use of nuclear weapons, so rendering the operational level of war entirely redundant. But by the early 1980s, the revival of the Campaign for Nuclear Disarmament, sustained in part by the debate surrounding the basing and deployment of cruise missiles, made the early use of nuclear weapons increasingly unacceptable to politicians, some of whom advocated a declaration of no first use by NATO, a principle which struck at the roots of nuclear deterrence strategy. At the same time, the missile technologies appropriate to lower-yield nuclear warheads could also deliver conventional munitions with increasing accuracy. This created the possibility of striking Soviet second echelon forces deep inside Warsaw Pact territory, so disrupting their capacity to sustain a conventional armoured breakthrough. The urgency of looking at conventional options which gave depth rather than linearity to the shape of the battlefield was heightened by the recognition that, under the leadership of Marshal N. V. Ogarkov as chief of the general staff, the Soviet army had developed a new doctrine, designed, in the words of Christopher Donnelly, the director of the Soviet Studies Research Centre at the Royal Military Academy Sandhurst, to 'present NATO with a problem *at precisely that level with which it is at present least well organized to cope—the operational level*'.[81] Accepting the Soviet policy of no first use of nuclear weapons, it seemed to make inoperable the early use of even limited nuclear options. 'Operational manoeuvre groups' would engage NATO forces so intimately, to such a depth, and with such suddenness that any nuclear munitions would inflict massive casualties on NATO's own forces, as well as on those of the enemy.[82]

BAGNALL AND BRITISH MILITARY DOCTRINE

The external pressures forcing the British Army of the Rhine to think about the operational level of war were political and strategic, and rested, above all, on the nature of the Soviet threat and the eroding acceptability of an early recourse to nuclear weapons. But there were also internal and independent drivers. Nigel Bagnall, the commander of 1 (British) Corps between 1981 and 1983, had begun his service as an infantry officer with the Green Howards, serving in Malaya, Cyprus, and Borneo, but he had commanded an armoured regiment, the 4th/7th Dragoon Guards. His career thereafter was focused more on the threat of major war in Europe than on withdrawal from empire. Like Kitson, he had also had an opportunity to reflect on his experiences as a Defence Fellow at Oxford University. His studies of the German army's defensive battles on the Eastern Front in the Second World War suggested that inferior NATO conventional forces could check superior Soviet forces with armoured counter-strokes, using manoeuvre to trade space for time, and so achieving the offensive at the operational level while implementing a strategic defence. He knew too that 1 (British) Corps' battle would have to be coordinated with that of its neighbour, 1 (German) Corps, a task made easier in 1985 when he took over command of Northern Army Group (NORTHAG), a joint command of which the Belgians and the Dutch were also part but in which the British and the Germans were the leading players.[83]

Bagnall now embraced and preached the operational level of war, and his intellectual inspiration for this was the German army. To that extent, the British army mirrored, but was independent of, comparable trends in the army of the United States. The Americans, smarting from their defeat in Vietnam, had resolved not to learn from it but to turn their backs on irregular warfare and counter-insurgency. Focusing on major war in Europe, they used doctrine as one means to re-establish their sense of professional self-worth, and in the 1982 edition of *Field Manual 100–5: Operations* had endorsed the use of manoeuvre in preference to attrition, stressing the operational level of war more than the tactical. For the Americans, too, the Germans were the models, although they—like Bagnall—failed to notice that the Wehrmacht's successes in 1940–1 were less the reflection of doctrine than of improvisation.[84] *Blitzkrieg* as an operational method was a product of the defeat of France in 1940, not a cause; moreover, in 1941–2, once Germans became wedded to it as a system, it failed them in the Soviet Union.[85] Operational art had not made good the inadequacies of bad strategy for Germany, but the lack of a clear distinction between operational art and strategy in the military thought of the time—and in the period immediately after the war—obscured that. The essence of German staff training had revolved around the application of solutions to practical problems. Helmuth von Moltke the Elder and Alfred von Schlieffen, the dominant Prussian chiefs of staff between the end of the Franco-Prussian War and the outbreak of the First World War, had taught operational skills through war games, staff rides, and map exercises which rested on the specific conundrums posed by the defence of Germany's frontiers.

This too was what gave unity to NATO thinking in the 1980s. The enemy could be clearly identified, his own methods of fighting were the subject of constant monitoring by the intelligence services, and the geography of the potential battle zone was known and familiar. Bagnall stressed the need for flexibility within doctrine but he could do so within the certainties provided by fixed parameters.

Bagnall completed his career as chief of the general staff in 1985–8, and left a legacy that was both personal and institutional. The 'Ginge' group (so called in reference to the colour of Bagnall's hair, but never so called to his face) was an informal gathering that cut across rank, but whose ways of thinking were embraced by his successors, including Martin Farndale, who followed him as the corps commander and at NORTHAG, and Peter Inge, his successor but one as chief of the general staff who then went on to become chief of the defence staff. The 'Ginge' group was duly succeeded by the 'Pinge' group. Institutionally, in 1988 Bagnall set up the Higher Command and Staff Course within the army's Staff College, and tasked it specifically with teaching the operational level of war to the next generation of senior officers.

The Higher Command and Staff Course was unlike anything else seen by the British army in the twentieth century, except possibly the annual conferences held before the First World War in the immediate aftermath of the general staff's establishment. At its heart was syndicate discussion, the trusted tool of the Staff College, applied here not only to explore concepts, but also to shape them. Precisely because both operational art and manoeuvre were to all intents and purposes new to British officers, their contours were unclear and the students who studied them were pioneers: questions were as important as answers. The debate itself produced a generation of officers for whom the operational-level war became not just a means to promotion within their profession, but also an embedded part of their mental processes. Between 1988 and 1991, these officers—from an army which had not necessarily seen publication as a passport to advancement—published thirty-two papers.[86] Military history itself acquired a legitimacy it had struggled to possess in military education over the preceding twenty years, the Staff College even appointing a resident historian, Brian Holden Reid, to teach on the Higher Command and Staff Course, and the intellectual mavericks of the past, J. F. C. Fuller and Basil Liddell Hart, whose work had anticipated the evolution of operational art, being reinstated on reading lists. Figures from the margins of military life entered the mainstream, most notably Brigadier Richard Simpkin, a product of the Royal Tank Regiment who had been retired for nearly twenty years and a student of the army which had done most to develop operational thought, that of the Soviet Union.[87] Simpkin's *Race to the Swift: Thoughts on Twenty-First Century Warfare*, published in 1985, contrasted attrition theory, which he characterized as focused on the seizure of ground and the inflicting of casualties through fighting, with manoeuvre theory, which 'regards fighting as only one way of applying military force to the attainment of a politico-economic aim—and a rather inelegant last resort at that'. Whereas attrition, according to Simpkin, used 'the same basic techniques . . . on a larger scale up through the levels', manoeuvre acquired special significance at the operational level of war, because it had its own mission; it is 'a dynamic, closed-loop system, characterised by speed and appropriateness of response', and it is 'synergetic—that is, its whole must have an effect greater than the sum of its parts'.[88] Manoeuvre now clearly meant much more than mobility; indeed, it defined the thinking commander, determined to set the tempo of operations and to use pre-emption and surprise to seize the initiative. When Peter Inge said of Bagnall's contribution, that doctrine was not what to think but how to think, he was not being platitudinous.[89]

The same message was reiterated in 1989 in *Design for Military Operations—the British Military Doctrine*, the first military doctrine described as such ever published by the British army. The 1988 *Statement on the Defence Estimates* observed that 'we have not . . . developed any universally applicable theoretical structure for the organized study of war', and it went on to contrast what were at best 'tactical principles and regulations' with the 'systematic and markedly more comprehensive' Soviet concept of doctrine.[90] Bagnall realized that a stated doctrine was the corollary of the Higher Command and Staff Course, and in a very real sense *Design for Military Operations* was its product, written at a whirlwind pace by Lieutenant Colonel Timothy Granville-Chapman in a room in the Staff College, adjacent to the course and influenced directly by its debates. The doctrine divided wars into three sorts: general war, limited war, and low-intensity conflict, and divided war itself into four levels: grand strategic, military-strategic, operational, and tactical. Operational art, it said, was the vital link between military-strategic objectives and the tactical employment of forces: it 'embraces both decisions taken at the operational level and the outcome of those decisions, often tactical activity but bearing on the strategic level'. Although the manual was wary about being too precise on the nature of operational art, beyond the observation that it was the business of generalship, its characteristics included freedom of action through the exercise of initiative, joint activity (particularly air–land cooperation), scale, concentration of force, and 'total effect'. 'Without the operational level military strategy cannot be implemented in the most effective way', because without it resources 'may be squandered in tactical battles fought in the wrong place and at the wrong time': the 'Power of the whole—the operation—is greater than the sum of its parts—the battles'. The principal means by which these principles would be applied was manoeuvre, which 'seeks to inflict losses indirectly by envelopment, encirclement and disruption, while minimising the need to engage in frontal attrition'.[91]

AFTER THE COLD WAR

By 1989, therefore, the British army had, almost in one fell swoop, embraced both doctrine and operational art. However, their adoption had been predicated on the need to get away from the legacy of, in Bagnall's own words, 'the bush fire emergencies of the Empire', and to focus on NATO, its deterrence strategy, 'the conventional capability to make it credible', and 'a visible capacity to wage war if it fails'.[92] The end of the Cold War confronted the operational level of war with two challenges. First, did it embrace an approach that possessed universal applicability, that was relevant not just to a coalition conflict in Europe, but also to other forms of war elsewhere in the world? In other words, were the principles of manoeuvre warfare comparable with the principles of war espoused by the *Field Service Regulations* and so transferable to all forms of war? Or had the army, in pursuing Continentalism, in measuring itself against a 'first-class enemy', disqualified itself from meeting other sorts of enemy in different environments? And, secondly, was the operational level of war, which stressed scale and took the corps as its basic formation, going to be able to survive the cuts in defence expenditure, the 'peace dividend' of the Cold War's end and already inaugurated by the 1991 defence review 'Options for Change'?

The first question seemed to be convincingly answered while the review was in train. The British Army of the Rhine's 1st Armoured Division was transferred, effectively lock, stock, and barrel, to the Gulf to fight in the coalition war against Iraq. It did so under the command of Rupert Smith, who had been an inspirational director of studies on the Higher Command and Staff Course, and Patrick Cordingley, a student on the first course, commanded one of the division's two brigades. The course of the land war in 1991 vindicated both the operational level of war and its emphasis on manoeuvre. What had been designed to check a Soviet conventional drive across the urban sprawl of north-west Europe proved as applicable to the invasion of an Arab state in desert conditions. The lessons of the Gulf War, therefore, seemed to point unequivocally forwards, not backwards.[93] And, if there had been doubters in the British defence community, they would not have been heard. The most important consideration for the British armed services was the need to be able to operate alongside the Americans, and where they went Britain—like the other NATO allies—had little choice but to follow. Some of the paths down which the Americans then led—the 'revolution in military affairs', 'effects-based warfare', and network-centric operations—became overstated in their presentation, and promised technologies which the British would be hard pushed to afford, but doctrine was king, and American doctrine was—albeit largely unobserved—becoming dogmatic. American doctrine in the 1980s had been developed in crisis—against the background of defeat in Vietnam, with an awareness of Soviet numerical strength, and conscious of the need for better conceptual drivers as a means to compensate for both. By the end of the 1990s, it was posited on the basis of superiority, not inferiority, and rested not on questioning and doubt but on increasing certainty and self-confidence. Although it still paid due deference to manoeuvre, the United States's ability to mass fire effects gave attrition readmission by the back door, and could be justified by the trite but true observation that manoeuvre and attrition were not alternatives but two sides of the same coin. Armies manoeuvred to bring fire to bear, and then used fire to be able to manoeuvre. Developed outside the pragmatic context of imminent threats comparable with those faced by Germany before 1914 or NATO in the 1980s, American doctrine became self-referential, a basis for orders not for discussion. Led by technology rather than debate, its view of war neglected the social and political conditions which could shape war's conduct, as opposed to its causation. With no peer in sight, the United States was thinking about war without an effective enemy, and so was losing contact with the essence of war itself, its clash of wills.

The answer to the first question, that on doctrine's universal applicability, also helped resolve the second, that on the survival of the operational level of war. If the operational level provided answers that were applicable to all wars, then the British armed forces had to embrace its imperatives. With the end of the Cold War, NATO created the Ace Rapid Reaction Corps (ARRC). The British army fought hard to be given control of the ARRC headquarters, so that it could keep intact its planning skills and the capacity for corps command. In 1992, it was rewarded by the appointment of Jeremy Mackenzie, deputy commandant and then commandant of the Staff College in the early days of the Higher Command and Staff Course, to be the ARRC's first commander. Successive chiefs of the general staff, despite the deployment of the British army to Northern Ireland and to the Balkans, maintained that the capacity to fight a major war was the benchmark for all other activity; low-intensity operations, counter-insurgency, and peacekeeping would be accommodated within the envelope of war fighting. 'We must not settle back to thinking small, no matter how reduced our army is to become', the inspector general of doctrine and training, Lieutenant General Sir Garry Johnson, told the Royal United Services Institute in 1991: 'We must continue to think and teach at the operational level and across the spectrum of warfare from high to low-intensity, and if at all possible to maintain forces capable of operating without reinforcement at this level'.[94] The vocabulary of the Central Front was shoehorned into the new circumstances.

Some of this transfer was sensible and pragmatic: to argue that the operational level of war was not just applicable to large-scale armoured conflicts, and that it applied not just to the corps level of command, as did another alumnus of the Higher Command and Staff Course, Alistair Irwin, was fair enough.[95] Operational art was now linked to campaign planning, whatever the unit level at which theatre command was exercised, because that was the point at which military and political effects interfaced. Thus, in 2000, a brigadier, David Richards, commanded the UK Joint Task Force in Sierra Leone. Furthermore, manoeuvre now became the way of looking at all sorts of wars, just as applicable in 'operations other than war' as in the large conventional battles for which it was developed.[96] Before the First World War, Henderson, Haig, and Robertson, when faced with not dissimilar dilemmas, adopted a comparable approach, a generic view of war, resting on principles applicable across all wars, but adaptable to each. The army's response in the 1990s was 'balance' across 'the spectrum of warfare' (as Johnson had called it but which came to be called 'the spectrum of conflict'). In practice, this meant that, although the army was committed to the equivalent of wars against uncivilized enemies, it was structured and equipped—and even more importantly intellectually prepared for—war against a 'first-class enemy'.

It seemed to work. The army established a reputation for excellence which appeared to have a historical pedigree but which was at odds with its perceived record after the Crimean War or the First World War, and was not really backed by its achievements in the Second World War, at least in 1940–2. In the past, if it had been deemed to have been any good at anything, it was the 'small wars which allow scope for the man and his Regiment to shine', but these were now seen by Johnson and others as a 'trap' to be avoided.[97] Second, the government was persuaded. Constraints on the defence budget did not prevent the continuing procurement of equipment designed to implement the manoeuvrist vision.

JOINT WARFARE

The success which doctrine had produced convinced the other services to imitate the army's example. The trouble was that the army's departure point for doctrine, the operational level of war, had less conceptual resonance in the air or at sea, than it did on land. In one respect, at least from the army's viewpoint, the RAF had nothing to lose by following its lead. *Design for Military Operations* rested on the idea of the 'air–land' battle, of fighting on NATO's Central Front in three dimensions. Group Captain Peter Millar, the RAF officer on the army's first Higher Command and Staff Course, dutifully concluded his course essay by writing:

> The case is clear that the worst possible threat to the Central Region [of NATO] requires the full use of air power to help counter it, that air power should be controlled by the corps, and that many other advantages accrue to the corps in having the ability to use air power beyond the FEBA [forward edge of the battle area] as much as possible.[98]

No soldier was going to dissent from that, but many airmen did—particularly in the aftermath of Operation Desert Storm in the first Gulf War. In 1991, driven by its awareness of the need to make a wider political statement about the utility of air power against the background of 'Options for Change', the RAF produced *Air Power Doctrine.* In 1993, the revised edition of *Air Power Doctrine* stressed not the air–land battle but the strategic air offensive, arguing for the relevance of the independent use of air power in the post-Cold War world. Although it paid ritual obeisance to the notion of jointness, it made no mention of 'manoeuvrism', and its preferred adjective was 'strategic' not 'operational'.[99]

The navy's response, *The Fundamentals of British Maritime Doctrine*, though delayed until 1995 and even then reluctant, similarly made a statement about national strategy more than about operational methods or effects. As its use of the descriptor 'maritime' rather than 'naval' suggested, its focus was on sea control, sea denial, and maritime power projection, rather than on war. The First Sea Lord, Sir Jock Slater, referred in his foreword to 'an evolving set of principles, procedures and practices' that was more redolent of the tone of the 1909 *Field Service Regulations* than it was of the army's more recent publications (although, unlike the 1909 *Field Service Regulations*, *The Fundamentals of British Maritime*

Doctrine listed the principles of war in an appendix).[100] Its discussion of the operational level of war was bracketed with the strategic in a brief section pregnantly headed 'the significance of land warfare concepts for maritime doctrine'.[101] Naval commanders in battles at sea reckoned to find themselves in situations where the tactical and the strategic collapsed in on each other. In 1914, at the outset of the First World War, John Jellicoe, on his appointment to command the British Grand Fleet, had issued Grand Fleet Battle Orders, which were essentially tactical instructions. On 31 May 1916, at the Battle of Jutland, his decisions, however tactically determined, could have decided the course of the war. Shortly after 6.15 p.m., Jellicoe had crossed the 'T', putting the Grand Fleet at right angles to the German High Seas Fleet, which was still in line ahead, thus bringing overwhelming firepower to bear through manoeuvre. Despite holding the tactical advantage, Jellicoe had then turned away because of the dangers to Britain's long-term control of the North Sea's exits if the fleet had suffered heavy losses to torpedoes. The operational level of war had little explanatory value, except as a term to explain the mix of both tactics and strategy that shaped Jellicoe's decisions.

Nor was the antithesis between attrition and manoeuvre of any meaning. 'Historically and from the standpoint of modern doctrine, a navy does not have a choice between manoeuvre and other styles of warfare', *The Fundamentals of British Maritime Doctrine* stated: 'Manoeuvre warfare theory is the intelligent use of force and is a logical development of the "principles of war"'.[102] Ships, like aeroplanes, manoeuvre in order to bring fire to bear, the one depending on the other. In his discussion of war on land, Simpkin had acknowledged that the antithesis between attrition and manoeuvre was only theoretical, that 'once fighting starts, the two theories become complementary'.[103] But the army, its thinking shaped by its need to escape the dilemmas of relative weakness if faced by the Warsaw Pact, increasingly saw attrition, whose use rested on superior resources, as vicious, and manoeuvre, where wit might compensate for brawn, as virtuous. And the other two services denied their own best instincts to follow the army's lead. The first edition of the joint defence doctrine, published in 1997, embodied this polarization, defining manoeuvre warfare as a 'warfighting philosophy that seeks to defeat the enemy by shattering his moral and physical cohesion—his ability to fight as an effective, coordinated whole—rather than by destroying him physically through incremental attrition'.[104]

In the same year, the three services' Staff Colleges were united to form the Joint Services Command and Staff College, located first at Bracknell (where its commandant was Timothy Granville-Chapman) and then at Shrivenham. The Higher Command and Staff Course could no longer focus on the corps counter-stroke on the central European front, not least because for many of those now on the course such issues would have been irrelevant, even if the Cold War had still been in full swing. But the search for common denominators meant that the cutting edge created by conceptual difference disappeared from the debate. Manoeuvre, a word with clear connotations in land warfare, associated with mobility and with lines of operations, and manoeuvre warfare, which was itself now described as 'invariably joint', were subsumed by the 'manoeuvrist approach', a term coined in 1994 and adopted by *British Defence Doctrine* in 1996. The latter was 'attractive to a numerically inferior side, or to a stronger side which wishes to minimise the resources committed'; it was a synonym for flexibility, for the use of surprise, for the exercise of initiative, and stressed tempo and the need to get inside the enemy's decision-making cycle.[105] Such ideas were similar to Fuller's 'moral epoch' and Liddell Hart's 'indirect approach', the latter a phrase which *British Defence Doctrine* specifically employed. As many critics of the 'indirect approach' have argued, catchy labels are unhelpful if their use removes the need for genuine thought or for the exposure of genuine differences; glibness can become an obstacle to reflection. Moreover, in the joint environment, and even more in an allied context, words that pretend to have precision but do not can create an impression of mutual understanding that is false. The 'manoeuvrist approach' itself raised questions, and was designed to do so: it had become the overarching framework within which all types of military activity from peacekeeping to stabilization could nestle, and its purpose was to instil an attitude of mind, a way of thinking, a readiness to recognize and exploit the enemy's weaknesses. Manoeuvre itself, the way of operating, was being lost sight of, not least because of the ambiguity created by the use of terms which were derivatives of manoeuvre but which carried very different meanings.

Even before the creation of the Joint Services Command and Staff College, the army had separated the development of doctrine from the Higher Command and Staff Course. In 1994, it established a directorate for doctrine and concepts. At one level, this was a positive and beneficial step, no more than a reflection of the subject's importance. Its more malign side effects would not become evident until 1999, when the Joint Doctrine and Concepts Centre was created alongside, but independent of, the Joint Services Command and Staff College. Two consequences followed. First, because the development and delivery of education and doctrine were now under the chief of the defence staff, they were separated from the services that used them. Second, because the two institutions were separate—even if co-located—commands, the link between the development of ideas from bottom up and the dissemination of doctrine from top down was broken. As the operational experience of comparatively junior officers, gained in Iraq and Afghanistan, grew from 2003 onwards, the effects of the division became more evident. No mechanism existed for capturing their experience or for putting those experiences against the broader context derived from wider study. Moreover, the very tempo of operations became an excuse for not allowing time to reflect on and learn from what was taught. The opportunities for wider study, free from the imperatives of career progression, such as the Defence Fellowships enjoyed by Kitson and Bagnall, became less frequent, and rarely taken up by officers on an upwardly mobile trajectory. By the beginning of 2009, six years on from the original invasion of Iraq, the British armed forces had yet to write their account of subsequent events or of their lessons. Even more seriously, the army had not revised its counter-insurgency doctrine since 2000, and the efforts of the Development, Concepts and Doctrine Centre (as the Joint Doctrine and

Concepts Centre became in 2006) to address the topic were limited to what was called a 'Joint Doctrine Note', published in March 2007. *Countering Irregular Activity within a Comprehensive Approach* failed to capture the imagination of many soldiers. Despite the fact that the author of the *Design for Military Operations*, Timothy Granville-Chapman, now had overall responsibility for doctrine as vice-chief of the defence staff, doctrine development failed to respond to the changes in war's character. Such successes that were to be gleaned from Iraq and Afghanistan seemed to be gained in spite of doctrine, not because of it. Returning commanders rarely couched what they had been doing in terms of 'manoeuvrism' or the 'manoeuvrist approach', even though such terms remained the core of command philosophy and as such staple fodder both in the Staff College and in the Development, Concepts and Doctrine Centre.

THE LOSS OF OPERATIONAL ART?

Operational art, having been subsumed in campaign planning in the 1990s, lacked an institutional home. British troops in Iraq and Afghanistan did not operate under a single, national theatre headquarters. As a junior partner in an American-led coalition, Britain's own operational methods became dependent on the United States's. First, the British stress on 'manoeuvrism' suffered from America's propensity for attrition; then, America's energetic espousal of counter-insurgency in December 2006 made Britain's seem leaden footed. More immediately the United Kingdom's Permanent Joint Headquarters at Northwood, just outside London, took over campaign planning at the national level, but distance robbed it of the immediate contact with the battlefield on which the 'manoeuvrist approach' depended. Nor was the situation clarified by the fact that the Ministry of Defence in Whitehall, which housed both the minister and the chiefs of staff, also had a command function.

Despite the fact that operational art at the theatre level was forfeit, or perhaps precisely because it was, doctrine continued to have a dominant role in the debate. The pressures of current operations meant that neither the Permanent Joint Headquarters nor the Ministry of Defence had much time for longer-term thinking, and so both increasingly looked to the Development, Concepts and Doctrine Centre to do this for them. Doctrine in 1989 was focused at the operational level, even though *Design for Military Operations* specifically declared that it was a document designed to be above the operational level, which it defined as applicable to particular theatres of war.[106] When *British Defence Doctrine* was first published in 1996 as the coping stone to the edifice of doctrinal publications, it declared itself to be 'concerned chiefly with the strategic level' and 'the linkages between national policy and military operations'; operational doctrine itself now nestled underneath it.[107] Moreover, although directly reflective of defence policy in a broader sense, and focused on expeditionary and joint warfare conducted to tackle risks at their point of origin, its appearance preceded—rather than followed—the Strategic Defence Review, published in 1998.

In other words, by the late 1990s doctrine's focus on the operational level of war had enabled it to move from a concentration on the equivalent of 'grand tactics' to strategy; and in the absence of clear policy it increasingly acquired the capacity to become the master, not the servant, of strategy. In 1988, the strategic context had been set by the Soviet threat and the need to meet it with a conventional capability. After 1991 scenario-driven defence thinking was replaced by the acquisition of capabilities, although less was said about how those capabilities (especially those designed for 'high-end warfighting') would be employed. The attractions of operational art to NATO armies rested precisely on this ability to trump the vagaries of policy. It became, in the words of two commentators writing in 1996, 'a vehicle for military leaders to tie the hands of those they are supposedly serving', since 'the new doctrine provides a ready-mixed solution that defense intellectuals, diplomats and politicians would find far harder to disassemble'.[108] As the assumptions of the Strategic Defence Review found themselves at variance with realities on the ground, and especially so after 2003, defence operating assumptions ceased to relate to current commitments. The latter were met by 'urgent operational requirements', which left the long-term strategy nominally in place but rendered it increasingly unsustainable. The government's half-hearted response to this deficit, the National Security Strategy, published in March 2008, defined its goals in terms which were so broad and aspirational that they bore little relationship to deliverable outputs. It spurned hard choices and specific goals, and so failed to fill the strategic vacuum into which doctrine was stepping.

Doctrine did this in two ways. First, the understanding of the operational level of war, where doctrine had its birth in 1988–9, acquired an increasingly strategic complexion. The changes effected in the Staff College's organization and curriculum at its lower rungs edged the content of the Higher Command and Staff Course away from the interface between operations and tactics to that between operations and strategy (with knock-on effects for the Royal College of Defence Studies, which sat above it in the hierarchy). Second, doctrine became a means of public communication, a means of explaining what the armed forces do and how they do it. The successor publications to the original *Field Service Regulations* had become 'restricted', not for wider dissemination, but *Design for Military Operations, Air Power Doctrine, The Fundamentals of British Maritime Doctrine*, and *British Defence Doctrine* were all made commercially available. Just as the enemy could now read how the British armed forces were thinking about war, so could their own public. For over a decade after the appearance of the Strategic Defence Review in 1998, nothing comparable was published by the government of the day in terms of strategic guidance.

Thus, doctrine had the capacity to fill the need for an explicatory narrative. The example of the US army's *Field Manual 3–24*, that on counter-insurgency, completed in December 2006, was instructive; downloadable online, it was also published commercially by the University of Chicago Press. The sequence of overlapping British doctrines being prepared in 2009 to deal with stabilization operations (the responsibility of the Development, Concepts and Doctrine Centre) and counter-insurgency (carried out by the Army's Land Warfare Centre) was also—like *Field Manual 3–24*—intended for publication. The armed forces' own statements of intent provided the strategic narrative for the understanding of how defence policy was to be implemented, and became the basis for policy itself. The adoption of the so-called comprehensive approach, a term coined within the Ministry of Defence in response to operational realities in Iraq and Afghanistan, was a case in point. Designed to deal with situations on the ground in the most effective manner possible, its implications reached into the relationships between the Ministry of Defence on the one hand and the Foreign and Commonwealth Office and the Department for International Development on the other. For the latter two, 'the comprehensive approach', for all its apparent inclusiveness, was stamped 'made in the Ministry of Defence', just as the 'manoeuvrist approach' had been 'made in the army'. An operational concept appropriate to the armed forces proved to be at odds with the wider philosophies that underpinned the missions of their departments.[109]

In 1993, Alistair Irwin, whose career was shaped by the campaign in Northern Ireland and was to become its general officer commanding in 2000, stressed that it was at the operational level that the politician 'will legitimately have an effect on what is being done'.[110] His point was largely overlooked, and so too was its corollary. Generals, charged with stabilization operations in a multinational environment and in somebody else's country, need to be able to operate (and the word is used advisedly) at the political level. The wars in Iraq and Afghanistan demanded a different understanding of operations from the scenarios which confronted Bagnall and the 'Ginge' group. Clearly, the exercise of operational art has always required an appreciation of the strategic effects of the use of military force, but its primary field for creativity—its 'art'—lay in its intimate understanding of the tactics and capacities of armed forces and their relationship to the principles of war. The creativity of the commander in Iraq and Afghanistan was applied more in the political realm, in dealing with allies and political masters. Much of the rest was tactics.

In becoming joint, and in being applied to war in all its forms, doctrine also lost its meaning. Since it had to command consent across the armed forces, across departments, and across allies, so it lost the spark which came from debate. It became ossified. The army might try to develop counter-insurgency doctrine from the bottom up through the directorate of land warfare, the residual legacy of its directorate of doctrine and concepts, but its product had to mesh with the joint doctrine on stabilization operations, and both then had to command consent in the wider security community. Moreover, single-service doctrine had no obvious forum in which it could be taught when the ownership of professional education was itself joint. Operational art had become stove-piped, a process, and even a science. In continuing to stress the 'manoeuvrist approach', while simultaneously embracing stabilization operations, doctrine did more than match words that have competing meanings. It also created conceptual confusion. From 2006 onwards, the tempo of the enemy in Afghanistan proved faster, since he possessed both the initiative and the greater capacity for surprise. The advantages of the British (and the American) armed forces proved to be (in the parlance of the 1990s) attritional, the application of superior firepower in order to destroy the enemy. The deployment of insufficient troops into theatres of war, a shockingly inadequate force-to-space ratio, encouraged a resort not to manoeuvre but to overwhelming firepower. In the conclusion to his book on the fighting in Afghanistan in 2006, the writer, James Fergusson, speculated whether his use of the title 'A Million Bullets' was hyperbole; it was not. Over a twelve-month period, British troops in southern Afghanistan fired over three times that number of bullets; *pro rata* that was roughly twice the British army's consumption in 1916, at the height of the First World War.[111] The use of fortified positions, so-called platoon houses, and the creation of a garrison at Camp Bastion could not any longer be sensibly construed within a framework derived from the military philosophy of the 1990s.

These may or may not be the ways to prevail in counter-insurgency campaigning (the consensus would say they are not), but that is also precisely the sort of question which doctrine should ask, and which operational art should help to answer. A clutch of scholars, significantly none of them British, has looked at the twentieth-century British army and expressed surprise that an institution which so doggedly refused to embrace doctrine until 1989 managed, nonetheless, to be successful. An Australian, Alberto Palazzo, concluded that this was a deliberate choice, a product of its 'institutional ethos'.[112] Two Americans, Deborah Avant and John Nagl, comparing what they saw as relative British success in the Malayan campaign of 1948–60 with American failure in Vietnam, came to compatible conclusions. All three of them relied on the image of the British army as an adaptive organization, able to learn and respond, and better than the United States at meeting the changing characters of the wars that it had confronted in the twentieth century. The image was perhaps too rose-tinted for most of the army's historians and probably not even familiar to those who have served and loved it. The army had not proved fleet of foot before 1989: it took the first year of the South African War, the first two years of the First World War, the first three years of the Second World War, and the first four years of the Malayan 'emergency' before it shaped itself and its way of thinking to the war in hand. Its character traits had been less open to improvisation than the idealized version of its history suggested. Indeed, its slowness to adapt to the wars in Iraq and Afghanistan should have been a source of surprise and disappointment only to those, like Palazzo, Nagl, and Avant, who had been bewitched by the notion that the British army has had some ability to be more adaptive in the past.

In fact, the British army itself was surprised by the failings which the conflict in Iraq and Afghanistan exposed.[113] Bagnall's legacy was felt to have survived less in the ability to wage the corps battle, the 'intellectual flame' of high-intensity warfare which had in reality been all but extinguished, than in its offshoot, the 'manoeuvrist approach'. The diffusion and division of campaign planning, and its implications for the exercise of operational art, were meant to be offset by the fact that the mental agility which 'manoeuvrism' contained could be exercised down to brigade level. Frequently, it had not been, often because brigadiers were not clear whether they did have the authority so to act, but sometimes because that flexibility of thought had also been lost. When the single service staff colleges were amalgamated, the word 'command' was inserted in the new collective title, the Joint Services Command and Staff College. But can a college do both at the same time, and can the same campus also deliver 'defence management', while keeping the 'manoeuvrist approach' alive within operational art?

The interpretations of the Australian and American scholars mentioned above, even if questionable as history, can however help the armed forces of Britain answer these questions as they confront the future. Doctrine, Palazzo argued, 'is a construct of a particular time, a response to a particular strategic situation, and a solution to a set of particular operational problems'.[114] But if the fear prevails that doctrine will become dogma, located in the last war not in the current one or the coming one, an army is left without any intellectual purchase on the challenges of armed conflict. Palazzo was, of course, right about the problems of doctrine, but the answer is not that embraced by the British army until 1989: to neglect doctrine. Instead, doctrine has to be constantly re-examined, so that its intellectual, theoretical, and more abstract qualities are tied to realities in a continuous and iterative process. To do that well, the army has to be what John Nagl called a learning institution.[115] Learning is not simply absorbing instruction and completing courses; that is training, and, although the army has frequently confused the two, they are not the same. Learning involves debate and dispute, so that teaching and enquiry are linked, doctrine is internalized, and its implications understood and 'owned' by those who have to practise it. Finally, the fact that operational art in wars of intervention and stabilization flourishes more at the political than at the tactical end of the operational spectrum requires an integration of civil and military authority which trumps the norms of conventional civil–military relations in democratic states. This was Deborah Avant's point in relation to Malaya.[116] To produce British armed forces that are comfortable as learning organizations and aware of their political roles may not be easy, but they are the essential ingredients in the generation of operational art in the early twenty-first century.

NOTES

1. Shelford Bidwell and Dominick Graham, *Fire-Power: British Army Weapons and the Theories of War, 1904–1945* (London: Allen and Unwin, 1982), 2. I am very grateful to Lieutenant General Sir John Kiszely and Colonel Richard Iron for reading and commenting on this piece, even if they do not agree with everything in it. I have also benefited from conversations over many years with Lieutenant General Sir Alistair Irwin and Major General Jonathan Bailey.
2. Ibid, 295.
3. Ibid, 294.

4. Markus Mäder, *In Pursuit of Conceptual Excellence: The Evolution of British Military-Strategic Doctrine in the Post–Cold War Era, 1989–2002* (Bern: Peter Lang, 2004), 23.
5. Dominick Graham, '"Sans Doctrine": British Army Tactics in the First World War', in Timothy Travers and Christon Archer (eds.), *Men at War: Politics, Technology and Innovation in the Twentieth Century* (Chicago, IL: Transaction, 1982).
6. Carl von Clausewitz, *On War*, edited and translated by Michael Howard and Peter Paret (Princeton, NJ: Princeton University Press, 1976), book 2, chapter 4, 152; it should be pointed out that the German word used here by Clausewitz, as so often, is not *Doktrin*, as the translation suggests, but *Lehre*, or lessons.
7. On which see S. L. A. Marshall, *Men against Fire: The Problem of Battle Command in Future War* (3rd edn., New York: Wm Morrow, 1966), 17, 22, 26–40, 49, 116, 133–5, 170, 181.
8. On Clausewitz's use of the word 'operations', see Hew Strachan, *Carl von Clausewitz's On War: A Biography* (London: Atlantic Books, 2007), 87, 109–10, 120; Hew Strachan, 'Clausewitz en anglais: la césure de 1976', in Laure Bardiès and Martin Motte (eds.), *De la guerre? Clausewitz et la pensée stratégique contemporaine* (Paris: Economica, 2008), 112–13.
9. Antoine Henri Jomini, *Traité des grandes operations militaires, contenant l'histoire critique des campagnes de Frédéric II, compares à celles de l'Empereur Napoléon; avec un recueil des principes généraux de l'art de la guerre*, 5 vols. (2nd edn., Paris: Chez Magimel, 1811), vol. IV, 275.
10. Ibid., vol. I, ii.
11. Ibid., vol. II, 272–3.
12. Ibid., vol. I, i; vol. IV, 284–6.
13. Jay Luvaas, *The Education of an Army: British Military Thought, 1815–1940* (London: Cassell, 1965), 10–12, 18–19; see also Hew Strachan, *From Waterloo to Balaclava: Tactics, Technology and the British Army, 1815–1854* (Cambridge: Cambridge University Press, 1985), 2–8.
14. *Aide-Mémoire to the Military Sciences*, 3 vols. (2nd edn., London: John Weale, 1853), vol. i, 2.
15. Edward Bruce Hamley, 'Lessons from the War', *Blackwood's Magazine*, vol. 79 (1856), 236–9, quoted in Luvaas, *Education of an Army*, 135.
16. Edward Bruce Hamley, *The Operations of War Explained and Illustrated* (Edinburgh: Blackwood, 1866), 55.
17. Luvaas, *Education of an Army*, 164–5.
18. Hamley, *Operations of War* (7th edn., Edinburgh: Blackwood, 1922), v.
19. G. F. R. Henderson, *The Science of War: A Collection of Essays and Lectures, 1891–1903* (1st edn., 1906; London: Longmans, Green, 1919), 39–50.
20. Ibid., 70–86.
21. Antoine Henri Jomini, *The Art of War*, translated by G. H. Mendell and W. P. Craighill (Philadelphia, PA: Lippincott, 1862), 66.
22. [John] Frederick Maurice, *War* (London: Macmillan, 1891), 8.
23. Henderson, *Science of War*, 39; see also 11, 70.
24. Ibid., 16.
25. Fisher to Lord Tweedmouth, 23 December 1905, in Arthur J. Marder (ed.), *Fear God and Dread Nought: The Correspondence of Admiral of the Fleet Lord Fisher of Kilverstone*, 3 vols. (London: Cape, 1952–9), vol. II, 66.
26. Henderson, *Science of War*, 26, 29–30.
27. See Henderson on this, in Luvaas, *Education of an Army*, 244.

28. Henderson, *Science of War*, 45.
29. Ibid., 42.
30. William Robertson, *From Private to Field Marshal* (London: Constable, 1921), 83; see also Brian Bond, *The Victorian Army and the Staff College, 1854–1914* (London: Eyre Methuen, 1972), 159.
31. John Gooch, *Plans of War: The General Staff and British Military Strategy, c.1900–1916* (London: Routledge, 1974).
32. Report on a conference of general staff officers at the Staff College, 7–10 January 1908, held under the direction of the chief of the general staff, Haig papers, National Library of Scotland Acc. 3155/81, 3, 27, 46, 48; see also Gooch, *Plans of War*, 113–15.
33. 'The true standard of our military needs', *c.*1906, Robertson papers, Liddell Hart Centre for Military Archives, 1/2/9, 11.
34. 'Remarks on a visit to battlefields', 1912, Robertson papers, 1/2/12.
35. J. P. Harris, *Douglas Haig and the First World War* (Cambridge: Cambridge University Press, 2008), 45–6.
36. 'Remarks on a visit to battlefields', 1912, Robertson papers, 1/2/12.
37. General Staff, War Office, *Field Service Regulations Part I: Operations*, 1909 (London: HMSO, 1914; reprinted with amendments), 46, 67–9.
38. Ibid., 196.
39. Ibid., 197. The last point is in bold in the original.
40. Ibid., 13, 131. Again, the last point is in bold in the original.
41. General Staff, War Office, *Field Service Regulations Part II: Organization and Administration* (London: HMSO, 1909; reprinted with amendments to October 1914), 24.
42. Notes on strategy by Colonel Henderson compiled for use of students at the Staff College (6th edn., March 1912), Robertson papers, Liddell Hart Centre for Military Archives, 1/2/10 (capitals in original).
43. *Field Service Regulations Part I: Operations*, 14. Here, the first quotation is in bold in the original.
44. [L. H. R. Pope-Hennessy], 'The British Army and Modern Conceptions of War', *Edinburgh Review*, vol. 213, no. 436 (April 1911), 321–46; here 324, 326, 346.
45. Quoted in Albert Palazzo, *Seeking Victory on the Western Front: The British Army and Chemical Warfare in World War I* (Lincoln: University of Nebraska Press, 2000), 12.
46. [L. H. R. Pope-Hennessy], 'The Place of Doctrine in War', *Edinburgh Review*, vol. 215, no. 439 (January 1912), 1–30; here 18, 21, 28.
47. *Field Service Regulations Part II*, 25.
48. Report on conference of general staff officers, 1908, Haig papers, National Library of Scotland Acc. 3155/81, 17, 25.
49. On the corps on the Western Front, see Andrew Simpson, 'The Operational Role of British Corps Command on the Western Front, 1914–18', Ph.D. thesis (University of London, 2001); Andy Simpson, 'British Corps Command on the Western Front, 1914–1918', in Gary Sheffield and Dan Todman (eds.), *Command and Control on the Western Front: The British Army's Experience, 1914–18* (Staplehurst: Spellmount, 2004). See also Jonathan Bailey, *The First World War and the Birth of the Modern Style of Warfare* (Strategic and Combat Studies Institute: The Occasional, no. 22, 1996).
50. Quoted in Simpson, 'Operational Role of British Corps', 194.
51. J. H. Boraston (ed.), *Sir Douglas Haig's Despatches (December 1915–April 1919)*, 2 vols. (London: Dent, 1919), vol. i, 319–20, 321, 325, 330.
52. J. F. C. Fuller, *The Reformation of War* (London: Hutchinson, 1923), 86–7, 119.

53. J. F. C. Fuller, *The Foundations of the Science of War* (London: Hutchinson, 1926), 14, claims that Fuller himself was the author of the principles contained in the 1920 *Field Service Regulations.*
54. Azar Gat, *Fascist and Liberal Visions of War: Fuller, Liddell Hart, Douhet, and Other Modernists* (Oxford: Oxford University Press, 1998), 25.
55. The others were 1924 and 1929; see David French, *Raising Churchill's Army: The British Army and the War against Germany, 1919–1945* (Oxford: Oxford University Press, 2000), 13–34.
56. Quoted in David French, 'Doctrine and Organization in the British Army, 1919–1932', *Historical Journal*, XLIV (2001), 500.
57. Ibid., 503–4.
58. General Staff, War Office, *Field Service Regulations, Vol. II: Operations. 1920. Provisional* (London: HMSO, 1920), 261. Emphasis added.
59. General Staff, War Office, *Field Service Regulations, Vol. II: Operations—General. 1935* (London: HMSO, 1935), 176.
60. Frederick Maurice, *British Strategy: A Study of the Applications of the Principles of War* (London: Constable, 1929), 51, 168.
61. Ibid., xv.
62. Ibid., 3, 24, 27.
63. Quoted in French, *Raising Churchill's Army*, 22.
64. Brian Holden Reid, *J. F. C. Fuller: Military Thinker* (Basingstoke: Macmillan, 1987), 111.
65. Fuller, *Foundations of the Science of War*, 17.
66. J. F. C. Fuller, *Lectures on F.S.R. II* (London: Sifton Praed, 1931), xii, 1, 8; see also 34.
67. J. F. C. Fuller, *Lectures on F.S.R. III (Operations between Mechanized Forces)* (London: Sifton Praed, 1932), 11, 37, 44.
68. Ibid., 84, 89, 131.
69. B. H. Liddell Hart, *The Decisive Wars of History: A Study in Strategy* (London: Bell, 1929), 19, 147–58.
70. Brian Holden Reid, *Studies in British Military Thought: Debates with Fuller and Liddell Hart* (Lincoln: University of Nebraska Press, 1999), 15–17; see also 74–90, 177–8, 182.
71. Ibid., 1.
72. Victor Wallace Germains, *The 'Mechanization' of War* (London: Sifton Praed, 1927), xi.
73. Ibid., xiv.
74. J. P. Harris, *Men, Ideas and Tanks: British Military Thought and Armoured Forces, 1903–1939* (Manchester: Manchester University Press, 1995), is the best guide on these issues, and see esp. 278, 316–19.
75. French, *Raising Churchill's Army*, 193–4.
76. On the lack of doctrine especially early in the war, but even in 1944–5, see Timothy Harrison Place, *Military Training in the British Army, 1940–1944* (London: Frank Cass, 2000), 9–16, 122–3, 137–51, 165–6, 169.
77. For criticism of Montgomery as an operational-level commander, see Williamson Murray and Allan R. Millett, *A War to Be Won: Fighting the Second World War* (Cambridge, MA: Belknap, 2000), 443, 456–7, 483.
78. Antony Beevor, *Inside the British Army* (London: Chatto and Windus, 1990), 161.
79. Julian Lider, *British Military Thought after World War II* (Aldershot: Gower, 1985), 180; see also Dierk Walter, *Zwischen Dschungelkrieg und Atombombe. Britische Visionen vom Krieg der Zukunft 1945–1971* (Hamburg: Hamburger Edition, 2009).

80. Frank Kitson, *Warfare as a Whole* (London: Faber, 1987), 153–4.
81. Christopher N. Donnelly, 'Soviet Operational Concepts in the 1980s', in the report of the European Security Study, *Strengthening Conventional Deterrence in Europe: Proposals for the 1980s* (London: Macmillan, 1983), 133 (italics in the original).
82. The report of the European Security Study, *Strengthening Conventional Deterrence in Europe*, was the key public document in launching this debate; John J. Mearsheimer, *Conventional Deterrence* (Ithaca, NY: Cornell University Press, 1983), set the intellectual contours, and Hew Strachan, 'Conventional Defence in Europe', *International Affairs*, LXI (1984), 27–43, summarizes its development.
83. Bagnall's contribution is still in need of a full study, but Colin McInnes, *Hot War, Cold War: The British Army's Way in Warfare, 1945–95* (London: Brassey's, 1996), 54–75, covers the main points, and see also John Kiszely, *The British Army and Approaches to Warfare since 1945* (Strategic and Combat Studies Institute: The Occasional, no. 26, 1997), reprinted in Brian Holden Reid (ed.), *Military Power: Land Warfare in Theory and Practice* (London: Cass, 1997).
84. Richard Hooker, Jr (ed.), *Maneuver Warfare: An Anthology* (Novato, CA: Presidio, 1993), contains many of the most important texts for Americans, and makes clear how important the German, rather than the Russian, model was.
85. Karl-Heinz Frieser, *Blitzkrieg-Legende. Der Westfeldzug 1940* (Munich: Oldenbourg, 1995) is the best exposition of these points; for a classic but self-serving misinterpretation of history designed to suit the British army's agenda, see Garry Johnson, 'An Option for Change without Decay', *Journal of the Royal United Services Institute for Defence Studies*, CXXXVI, no. 3 (Autumn 1991), 12.
86. Mäder, *In Pursuit of Conceptual Excellence*, 99; these papers appeared in the publications of the Strategic and Combat Studies Institute, and also in J. J. G. Mackenzie and Brian Holden Reid (eds.), *The British Army and the Operational Level of War* (London: Tri-Service Press, 1989).
87. The key text here is Shimon Naveh, *In Pursuit of Military Excellence: The Evolution of Operational Theory* (London: Frank Cass, 1997); Naveh's book is dedicated to the memory of Simpkin.
88. Richard Simpkin, *Race to the Swift: Thoughts on Twenty-First Century Warfare* (London: Brassey's, 1985), 24.
89. Mäder, *In Pursuit of Conceptual Excellence*, 89.
90. Michael Yardley and Dennis Sewell, *A New Model Army* (London: W. H. Allen, 1989), 89.
91. *Design for Military Operations—The British Military Doctrine*, prepared under the direction of the chief of the general staff (London: HMSO, 1989), 39–47.
92. Nigel Bagnall, 'Foreword', in Mackenzie and Reid (eds.), *British Army and the Operational Level of War*, vii.
93. Colin McInnes, 'The Gulf War, 1990–1', in Hew Strachan (ed.), *Big Wars and Small Wars: The British Army and the Lessons of War in the 20th Century* (London: Routledge, 2006), 162–79.
94. Johnson, 'An Option for Change without Decay', 13.
95. A. S. H. Irwin, *The Levels of War: Operational Art and Campaign Planning* (Strategic and Combat Studies Institute: The Occasional, no. 5, 1993), 3.
96. J. J. A. Wallace, 'Manoeuvre Theory in Operations Other Than War', in Reid (ed.), *Military Power*, 207–26.
97. Johnson, 'An Option for Change without Decay', 13.

98. Peter Millar, 'The Central Region Layer Cake', in Mackenzie and Reid (eds.), *The British Army and the Operational Level of War*, 31.
99. Mäder, *In Pursuit of Conceptual Excellence*, 104–28, makes the key points.
100. *The Fundamentals of British Maritime Doctrine. BR 1806* (London: HMSO, 1995), 5.
101. Ibid., 71.
102. Ibid., 73.
103. Simpkin, *Race to the Swift*, 23.
104. *UK Glossary of Joint and Multinational Terms and Definitions (JWP 0–01.1)*, M-3, quoted in Mäder, *In Pursuit of Conceptual Excellence*, 89; see also Kiszely, *The British Army and Approaches to Warfare since 1945*; and Charles Grant, 'The Use of History in the Development of Contemporary Doctrine', in John Gooch (ed.), *The Origins of Contemporary Doctrine* (Strategic and Combat Studies Institute: The Occasional, no. 30, 1997), 10–11.
105. *British Defence Doctrine: Joint Warfare Publication (JWP) 0–01* (London: Ministry of Defence, 1996), 4.8–9.
106. *Design for Military Operations*, 3.
107. *British Defence Doctrine*, 1.4.
108. B. J. C. McKercher and Michael A. Hennessy (eds.), *The Operational Art: Developments in the Theories of War* (Westport, CT: Praeger, 1996), 4.
109. Andrea Barbara Baumann, 'Clash of Organisational Cultures? The Challenge of Integrating Civilian and Military Efforts in Stabilisation Operations', *Journal of the Royal United Services Institute*, CLIII, no. 6 (December 2008), 70–3.
110. Irwin, *The Levels of War*, 8.
111. James Fergusson, *A Million Bullets: The Real Story of the British Army in Afghanistan* (London: Transworld, 2006), 324; the figures for the First World War are derived from a daily output of roughly 15,000 rounds per day in 1916 for an army of 200,000 men.
112. Alberto Palazzo, *Moltke to Bin Laden: The Relevance of Doctrine in the Contemporary Military Environment* (Canberra: Land Warfare Studies Centre, September 2008), 2.
113. Broadly speaking, it welcomed the criticisms contained in 'Losing their way? The British army suffers from lack of soldiers, lack of money and lack of conviction', *Economist*, 29 January 2009. See also Warren Chin, 'Why did it all go wrong? Reassessing British Counterinsurgency in Iraq', *Strategic Studies Quarterly* (Winter 2008), 119–35; David Betz and Anthony Cormack, 'Iraq, Afghanistan and British Strategy', *Orbis*, LIII (2009), 319–36; Michel Goya, 'La frustration britannique', chapter 14 of *Irak: les armées de chaos* (Paris, 2008).
114. Alberto Palazzo, *Moltke to Bin Laden*, 1.
115. John Nagl, *Learning to Eat Soup with a Knife: Counterinsurgency Lessons from Malaya and Vietnam* (Chicago, IL: University of Chicago Press, 2002).
116. Deborah Avant, *Political Institutions and Military Change: Lessons from Peripheral Wars* (Ithaca, NY: Cornell University Press, 1994), 103–26.

5

American Operational Art, 1917–2008

Antulio J. Echevarria II

INTRODUCTION

This chapter traces the evolution of American operational art since the early twentieth century. It argues that the US military brought war's 'first grammar', meaning the principles and procedures related to overthrowing an opponent by armed force, to near perfection as evidenced by Desert Storm in 1991, Afghanistan in 2001–2, and the initial invasion of Iraq in 2003. Since the beginning of the twentieth century, American operational art has centred on defeating an adversary either by annihilation or by attrition. This art has not been restricted to land operations, and is clearly evident in the history of US naval and air campaigns, even if those services initially regarded it as unnecessary due to their perceived ability to exert 'direct strategic influence'.[1] The recent move towards fully integrated joint operations has virtually reified both the art and the level, while, at the same time, accelerating efforts to perfect war's first grammar.

In the summer of 2003, however, US operational art encountered, or rather re-encountered, a 'second grammar' of war, known variously (and rather loosely) as insurgency, guerrilla warfare, or irregular warfare. While not entirely new, the principles and procedures relevant to this grammar posed significant challenges to a military organization reared on battle-centric concepts and in the process of transforming into a leaner, faster, knowledge-based combat force. Although significant progress has been made in countering this approach in recent years, both in theory and in practice, it is not yet clear whether American operational artists can become as proficient at war's second grammar as they have at its first.

As Clausewitz wrote, 'war has its own grammar, but not its own logic'.[2] Although his concern was to describe the relationship between war and policy, the focus, here, is on the term grammar because of its unique ability to capture the collective concepts, principles, and procedures germane to the conduct of war. As such, it accords well with the classic conception of operational art, which is the design of battles or operations as well as the conceptual and practical linking of them into coherent campaigns to achieve victory.[3] Just as gifted writers, such as William Shakespeare or Thomas Carlyle, could create literary classics using English grammar, so too a competent operational artist can achieve success while employing war's grammar. The key, of course, is to know which grammar to apply, and when, because both of the writers mentioned above dared to violate the rules on occasion. Indeed, it is not likely their achievements would have been as brilliant otherwise.

Since the early 1980s when the US army officially embraced the operational level of war, American doctrine has distinguished the art from the level; unfortunately, much confusion still surrounds the terms. The former is officially defined as 'the application of creative imagination by commanders and staffs – supported by their skill, knowledge, and experience – to design strategies, campaigns, and major operations and organize and employ military forces'.[4] The definition makes rather too much of 'creative imagination', whereas 'design' is what should be stressed. Achieving success is ultimately what matters, whether done creatively or not.

The operational level, in contrast, is defined as the command echelon at which the design of operations takes place. That echelon has traditionally been located at corps and higher formations, since the resources necessary for campaign planning and coordination were not to be found in division headquarters.[5] The explicit purpose behind institutionalizing the operational level of war was to establish 'a level of activity that would connect tactical actions and strategic purposes'.[6] While the level undoubtedly did that, it also insulated the study of tactics from political interference, thus facilitating the perfection of war's first grammar. In fact, some have justly argued that operational-level processes tend to take strategic planning out of the hands of policy makers.[7] Still, the American military is hardly unique in gravitating towards the study of tactics, which are as concrete as they are essential. It is also not surprising that the creation of an operational level, quite distinct from the art, would encourage this inclination.

Operational art is the principal element in any party's art of war. An art of war includes not only operational art, but also military strategy. Operational art is, in a word, the 'way' that is used to move military means in the direction of achieving strategic aims. It is tempting to consider operational art in isolation of both the aims it is supposed to serve as well as the means it has at hand: it thus takes on an abstract and wholly theoretical quality. To prevent that, the following discussion will occasionally touch upon the strategic aims at stake in each of the conflicts as well as the quantities and types of forces available. To underscore the point by means of analogy, a fencer ought to know not only the art of fencing in a theoretical sense (the different capabilities and limitations of the epee and the sabre, for instance), but also whether the blade one plans to use is appropriate to the aim we wish to achieve, and reliable in combat. Even exquisite knowledge of the art of fencing would avail little if we arrived at the contest with a ceremonial dagger while our opponent came armed with real sword.

Until the second half of the twentieth century, US operational art rarely differed in concept from its European counterparts. In practice, however, it was uniquely complicated by the fact that, each time a war broke out, it was necessary to mobilize, train, equip, and deploy large numbers of men and material across vast oceans. These circumstances contributed to inconsistent operational performance, and high casualties, in many of America's first battles. American officers were typically forced to learn quickly, while, at the same time, attempting to earn the respect of more experienced allies and foes. A central planning body was only established after the Spanish–American War (1898); modelled along the lines of the German general staff, its purpose was to conduct contingency planning.[8]

Since the middle of the nineteenth century, American operational doctrine called for conducting offensive operations aimed at defeating an opponent's main force. It was a doctrine that pitted strength against strength, and it was considered valid for land operations as well as those at sea. Operational art was referred to as the 'operations of war' and was defined as the 'means and methods' for achieving victory. Terms, such as plan of campaign, theatre of operations, and lines of operations, were in common use.[9] None of the US military's experience before the Great War—a major civil war, campaigns against Native Americans, and several small wars—had contradicted the doctrine.

The expansion and modernization of the US navy were also under way, partly in response to the rapid economic growth of American industry and commerce in the closing decades of the nineteenth century. Captain Alfred Thayer Mahan's theories of sea power provided a rationale for establishing a 'blue-water' navy, while also reinforcing the offensive doctrine of pitting strength against strength. Although Mahan's ideas were fairly complex and evolved over time, they rest upon four fundamental assumptions: (*a*) competition, if not conflict, among nations was perpetual; (*b*) the chief arena for that competition in the modern era was the seas; (*c*) a large navy of capital ships was the best tool for securing sea lines of communication; and (*d*) diplomacy worked best when it followed a successful decision at sea.[10] Mahan's theories were essentially battle-centric, aimed at achieving a decision at sea by a clash of arms. This was the doctrine with which the US navy went to war in 1917.

THE GREAT WAR

Even after more than a decade of reforms, the US military was hardly ready for a mass, industrial-age conflict in Europe. The US army was a mere constabulary force of 100,000 officers and men with some experience fighting rebels in the Philippines and bandits in Mexico; the US navy had 64,000 officers and men and 300 ships, with an operational emphasis on battleships.[11] War was declared in April 1917, but mobilization was fraught with friction at every level; Allied and German strategic estimates appeared correct in not expecting the United States to contribute significantly to the war until 1919.[12] Although mobilization, overseas deployment, and logistical support are not strictly part of the operational art, they clearly influence what that art can achieve in practice. If the American Expeditionary Force (AEF) of two million soldiers could not be assembled, deployed 3,000 miles, and supported, then any operational doctrine calling for massing combat power would have been useless.

Despite the strategic forecasts and repeated efforts by Allied commanders to feed American soldiers into the French and British armies as replacements, the

AEF was deployed intact as a separate field army, and was ready for combat operations by August of 1918. Some US formations fought successful tactical actions against the Germans earlier during the Battles of Cantigny (May) and Chateau-Thierry and Belleau Wood (June). However, it was not until the St. Mihiel and Meuse–Argonne offensives in September 1918 that Americans actually put their operational doctrine into practice on the battlefield.[13]

The St. Mihiel offensive began on 12 September; nine US divisions and five French divisions attacked after a four-hour artillery barrage, supported by 3,000 guns, 267 tanks, and 1,500 aircraft.[14] The attack met with little resistance as the Germans had already begun to withdraw, leaving only outposts in the forward lines; some 15,000 German prisoners were captured at a cost of 7,000 Allied casualties. The Meuse–Argonne offensive began on 26 September, with fifty-two American divisions (1,250,000 men) participating, though ten of those served in French and British armies. The operation was supported by over 1,000 planes, 2,700 guns, and nearly 200 tanks, while the infantry enjoyed an 8:1 numerical superiority.[15] The attack had to cross very difficult terrain in the Argonne Forest and to penetrate three lines of German defences. Progress was painfully slow for the first few days, but did cause the Germans to send a cable to President Wilson requesting a peace settlement based on his Fourteen Points. However, the Allies continued to push the offensive. By the armistice, the AEF had about 1,250,000 troops engaged in the offensive, and it suffered about 120,000 casualties of all types (about ten per cent of its fighting strength), of whom about 25,000 were killed; for that price, it had advanced some thirty-four miles and occupied 580 square miles of territory.[16] (American casualties overall by the time of the armistice were about 320,710.)[17]

Overall, the operations were successful. Still, the operational performance of the AEF left quite a bit of room for improvement. It is worth pointing out, however, that the command had only three months of experience at practising the operational art before the armistice ended hostilities on 11 November 1918. Not surprisingly, the lack of practical operational experience among senior commanders and staffs was a significant problem. It was particularly evident in the amount of time higher command echelons took to develop and issue orders; they were also slow to perceive and respond to changes in the situation. They 'fought the plan, rather than the enemy', as the expression goes, meaning they adhered rather too rigidly to the scheme of manoeuvre instead of exploiting whatever opportunities presented themselves. American pre-war doctrine had been written in a vacuum, and was developed for a generic foe, rather than for the fighting habits and style of the German army.

The chief tactical-operational problem facing the US army, as with all armies at this time, was the coordination of fire and movement of large numbers of troops over vast expanses of space, particularly in the rough terrain of the Argonne, and in the face of stiffening German resistance. Although American officers spent considerable time in the pre-war years debating issues, such as how to balance border protection and coastal defence, tasks which seemed rather remote in 1918, a number of them had followed tactical and technological developments in

Europe and were quite familiar with the principal ideas underpinning industrial-age warfare. The exigencies of modern warfare were thus not entirely a surprise, except with regard to logistics. American ground operational doctrine, which stressed conducting offensive operations and massing overwhelming combat power at the decisive point, was not inconsistent with the attrition-based strategy of the Allies, and it did accord with the strategic and political objectives of the United States.[18] However, the operational doctrine was not adequately supported by the AEF's logistical system. As a result, several logistical and communication problems were evident from the AEF's first operation to its last: transportation of troops, materiel, and casualties between and among command echelons; delivery of orders; and coordination with adjacent units and higher headquarters.[19] These were shortcomings that experienced armies tend to work out over time; but the war would end before the US army had time to identify and correct them.

The US navy found that the doctrines of Mahan were not entirely sufficient for the operational tasks it had to perform during the war. It had been built and trained, and had developed an operational art, for the mission of defeating another navy. Instead, it found itself cooperating with the Royal Navy to hunt down and destroy German submarines. This required mental reorientation on the part of US naval officers, as well as the construction of many more destroyers. When the US navy entered the war, it had 70 destroyers, only 44 of which were modern, with which to execute its anti-submarine mission; by war's end, it had 248 destroyers, 60 large subchasers, and 116 small ones built or being built.[20] Within eighteen months, the US navy had essentially changed the entire balance of its force structure from one designed to defeat a surface enemy to one capable of neutralizing a sub-surface threat. A substantial, if temporary, intellectual reorientation was necessary, and it had to be accomplished without a corpus of theory, such as that offered by Mahan, to pave the way.

THE INTER-WAR PERIOD

The US armed forces were rapidly demobilized after the Great War. During the 1920s and 1930s, the active-duty strength of the army—once well over two million officers and men—rarely numbered more than 135,000. The navy was also reduced in size, and even the Washington (1922) and London (1930) Agreements, which allowed it to maintain a force equal in strength to that of the British Royal Navy in terms of capital ships and cruisers, did not seem to help. No new battleships were built until 1937, but Congress did authorize the construction of sixteen armoured cruisers, and the conversion of two older battleships into aircraft carriers. The Japanese imperial navy did pose a credible threat, and that clearly slowed the demobilization of the US navy. Like the army, the navy was not sufficient to carry out the contingency plans developed during the inter-war period.[21] The Great Depression also contributed to the severity of fiscal constraints, slowing the development and adoption of new technologies, and forcing already conservative bureaucracies to become almost miserly in terms of the number and types of programmes they would fund.

A great deal of effort went into extracting lessons from the AEF's experiences in 1918, which were discussed and debated and eventually incorporated into the military education programmes at the staff and war colleges. However, the shift to a national policy of isolation negatively influenced the development of the US army's operational doctrine by depriving it of a strategic logic. In a word, the army's doctrine became schizophrenic, caught between two opposing tendencies. On the one hand, the 1923 version of the *Field Service Regulations* emphasized the use of offensive operations to achieve military objectives. On the other hand, the *Manual for Commanders of Large Units* (1930), which was intended to supplement the *Field Service Regulations* and fill a doctrinal gap by providing some much-needed guidance for higher commanders, reflected what, for some, was the war's most important lesson—the power of the defensive—and infantry–artillery cooperation. It advocated a defensive doctrine similar to the approach found in the French army's *Instruction provisoire du 6 Octobre 1921 sur l'emploi tactique des grandes unites* [Provisional Instruction on the Tactical Employment of Large Units] (1921); indeed, as the commandant of the US Army War College noted in 1938, the *Manual for Commanders of Large Units* was essentially a translation of that manual.[22] As one officer noted, the publication of the *Manual for Commanders of Large Units* would leave the US army with a 'hybridized tactical doctrine which would produce the utmost confusion'.[23] Nonetheless, the manual was published.

The utility of the *Manual for Commanders of Large Units* was also questionable, given the publication in 1926 of the US army's manual for *General Tactical Functions of Larger Units*. The *General Tactical Functions of Larger Units*, which provided a framework of sorts to enable commanders to link tactical actions together, clearly showed that operational planning was being further developed. Among other things, this publication identified five main components or phases of plans of operations: 'mobilization, concentration, advance, occupation of positions, and combat'.[24] It is clear that mobilization was considered one of the principal components of American operational art.

The *General Tactical Functions of Larger Units* also reaffirmed the primacy of tactics in war's first grammar: 'Where tactical and strategic considerations conflict, tactical considerations must govern. The gaining of decision in combat is of primary importance'.[25] The idea of placing tactical considerations above strategic ones is not unusual in military thinking. In the face of seemingly vague or contradictory policy guidance or strategic objectives, it is natural to default to grammar. However, this gave commanders tacit approval to ignore strategic considerations. In short, the *General Tactical Functions of Larger Units* also shows that, even early on, the *raison d'être* of operational art was tactical success.

Notwithstanding its earlier schizophrenia, by the late 1930s American operational art remained centred on the idea of applying as much combat power as possible to achieve a decision on the battlefield. In fact, the US army's *Principles of Strategy* (1936) stressed, in bold letters, that the first law of strategy was 'BE

STRONGER AT THE DECISIVE POINT'.[26] During the 1920s and 1930s, concepts, such as centre of gravity and culmination point, saw greater prominence in US military theory and doctrine.[27] The centre of gravity was defined as the enemy's main fighting force. The culminating point was defined essentially as a point which, brought about by the 'inevitable process of weakening', '... does not assure any future success' for the attacker.[28] That these concepts were drawn from Clausewitz's theories is obvious. They joined many Jominian concepts, such as lines of operation and decisive points, which had long been in use.

American military theory was also influenced by European debates on the potential and preferred use of mechanized formations, particularly with respect to the use of the 'wide envelopment' and the 'penetration and encirclement' of enemy forces as a prelude to achieving a battle of annihilation. In these ways, American doctrine differed little from its European counterparts. Armoured vehicles were in short supply, however, and while much is made of the German use of cardboard tanks to compensate for the lack of real ones, such measures do not reveal logistical and maintenance requirements, which are essential to understanding operational limitations. The major doctrinal differences were more evident in that Americans put more emphasis on phased operations, and coordination between land and naval forces, and the air elements of both. Joint planning and training for staff officers and commanders also improved throughout all branches of the American military, with multi-service war games and training exercises taking place on a more regular basis.

Historians have recently challenged the popular image that air power advocates were struggling to advance new ideas against service parochialism and resistance to change. Considerable evidence, in fact, suggests that the key leaders in the US army, such as George C. Marshall, and in the US navy, such as William A. Moffett, were receptive to exploring the capabilities of air power, and they clearly recognized it would have an essential role in future warfare.[29] That is not to say there was not prejudice against the new arm, particularly in an era in which budgets were exceedingly small. In addition, the rapid development of civil aviation within the United States, especially after 1930, helped create an environment conducive to conceptual and technological innovation. There was, however, a tendency on the part of air power enthusiasts to make bold claims with respect to the anticipated accuracy and efficacy of long-range bombing, which was advanced as one sure way to avoid repeating the stalemate and high casualties of trench warfare. These claims worked as a double-edged sword, creating expectations that would be impossible to meet and adding an air of unreality to the body of theory as a whole.

The First World War revealed three key lessons: air superiority had to be established before other air operations could take place, long-range bombing held promise but was not particularly accurate, and aircraft had vital reconnaissance and close air support roles to play in surface operations.[30] Each of these evolved into major roles and missions, which, in turn, pointed to the need for different aircraft designs: pursuit, bombardment, and attack in the form of close air support, respectively. American *air* operational art during the inter-war years was, in many respects, an effort to prioritize these roles and missions and to fashion them into a coherent grammar.

It is an oversimplification to see inter-war air power theories as a running debate between two major schools of thought: the ground-support advocates and the long-range bombing enthusiasts. As historians now make clear, the thinking in the Air Corps Tactical School (ACTS) evolved during the inter-war years: from an initial emphasis on achieving air superiority; to providing close air support to ground operations, that is acting as 'flying artillery'; to the use of precision daylight bombing to destroy a country's vital production and distribution areas, and presumably breaking its will to fight in the process.[31] By the late 1930s, bombing enthusiasts dominated American air power theory, with ACTS doctrine even going so far as suggesting that in the majority of cases the modern bomber would be able to fight its way through enemy air defences and arrive on target and deliver its payload. Similarly, US military observers who witnessed the Battle of Britain in 1940 pointed out that, while British and German bombers proved susceptible to fighters, American bombers were much better armed, and would be flying at a higher altitude, and thus the lessons of that battle did not pertain.[32] By the attack on Pearl Harbor, American operational art in the air had settled on a grammar of war that rested on a number of nested, and vulnerable, assumptions: that a nation's vital areas could be identified, and hit from high altitude; that once hit, they could be destroyed; and that, if destroyed, the result would be the collapse of the enemy's will to resist; and that fighters need not escort long-range, high-altitude bombers.[33] This grammar would encounter much need for refinement during the war, but would not receive it.[34]

Despite the US navy's experience with submarine chasing in the Great War, it reaffirmed the validity of Mahan's basic concept that the primary objective of operations at sea was the 'destruction of the enemy's main force'.[35] The operational value of the submarine was not lost on the Americans. However, ethical, legal, and technical issues slowed its integration. The submarine was considered by many to be unethical for a variety of reasons, not least of which was that submarines were too small to take on crews and passengers of the vessels they sunk; nor were their own crews large enough to take control of vessels willing to surrender as an alternative to being sunk. War on commerce, sinking merchant vessels, was not lawful. Technological issues with range, depth, speed, and torpedo development also had to be resolved, but fiscal restraints essentially slowed technological progress. These issues notwithstanding, American political and military leaders did not want to give up on the submarine, particularly as long as the Japanese continued to add them to their own inventory. Still, the constraints were such that US operational planners considered submarines suitable for two missions only: coastal protection and fleet operations (attacks against warships); submarines were to attack only heavy warships, such as battleships and aircraft carriers.[36]

The US navy did anticipate the operational need for aircraft carriers: early on, it realized it would have to take its air support with it in the vast expanses of the Pacific Ocean, and it would need to bring enough of it to fight an enemy's sea- and land-based planes; otherwise, the US fleets would become dependent on land bases. However, Americans did not fully appreciate the operational potential of that particular technology—and how it could prove decisive in a theatre—until the United States was well into the war.[37] The battleship remained the fleets' capital ship going into the war. Yet, the US navy's pre-conflict war games revealed key differences in the dynamics of engagements between battleships and aircraft carriers; in the former, fire occurred in streams which could be adjusted as the battle progressed, while, in the latter, firepower was delivered in pulses, as aircraft needed time to return to ship, rearm, refuel, and relaunch. This difference was key information for operational planners, who had to plan for enough carriers to be present in any major operation so that a defensive canopy of air protection was always present. The games also showed, beyond question, that an opponent's aircraft carriers must always be the first target in any strike, and must be rendered combat ineffective as soon as possible in order to establish air superiority.[38] The newer battleships were now several orders of magnitude faster and more powerful than their predecessors were in the Great War, and operational artists still referred to battleships as capital ships. However, in operational planning and execution, aircraft carriers had become the real gauge of a fleet's power.

American operational art at sea also took on an added dimension with amphibious operations; but only marginally so, when one considers how important they would become in the war. American experience with amphibious operations began well before the Great War, with landings at Santiago, Cuba, and Manila serving as examples. The doctrinal publication for such operations, *Tentative Manual for Landing Operations*, was completed in 1934; it was made authoritative the following year.[39] Like most countries, the United States had few fiscal resources available in the inter-war years to put into defence spending in general; so amphibious concepts and technologies received little attention.

THE SECOND WORLD WAR

If American mobilization for the First World War was a rough start which grew more efficient as time went on, that for the Second World War was similar, even if it was unprecedented in size and, more importantly, completely exceeded the estimates and capacities of the three Axis powers combined. By 1943, American production figures alone greatly surpassed those of the Axis: 47,000 US planes to 27,000 Axis aircraft; 24,000 American tanks to 11,000 Axis; six US heavy guns for every one produced by the Axis. By war's end, the United States was producing sixteen warships for every one built by Japan.[40] Certainly, the disparity between Allied (particularly American) and Axis production figures and population bases meant that the latter could not afford to suffer severe losses. Thus, while the war might have seemed to have been a series of manoeuvre battles on one level, on another it was simply a matter of grinding Axis strength down through a number of heavy blows; it is not entirely clear, therefore, how often operational art actually equates to art, rather than something more akin to elementary math.

Fortunately, the sheer weight of this amount of material production, combined with war stuffs produced by the Soviet Union, made it possible for the Allies—of which the American formations provided an ever-increasing percentage—to engage and destroy large portions of Axis forces in major land, sea, and air battles. However, pre-war planning and training exercises had not prepared commanders and staffs to handle such large numbers of personnel under arms. As one historian explained, 'by 1939, the Army had virtually forgotten how to conduct training on a broad scale. Very few officers could handle organizations larger than a battalion'.[41] In other words, when the war began, American operational art existed more in theory than in practice.

The ability to mobilize and deploy vast resources helped compensate for early operational blunders and setbacks. The first such setback was the Japanese dual attack on Pearl Harbor and the Philippines on 7 December 1941; American forces lost 8 battleships sunk or badly damaged, and over 300 aircraft were destroyed or damaged, crippling the striking power of the US Pacific Fleet and the US Far East Air Force.[42] This audacious attack left US territorial possessions in the Pacific isolated, and they fell in rapid succession to Japanese assaults. These were focused assaults, concentrating combat power on the capture of key airfields, road junctions, and the neutralization of critical fighting formations. Japanese operational art was thus an application of modern manoeuvre principles in a theatre that was characterized by vast expanses of water and scattered island groupings, rather than European road and rail networks. American operational art would learn from and copy this approach, and turn it against the Japanese. It was not until the Battle of Midway in June 1942, however, that the Japanese advance would be decisively halted, losing four of their six carriers and hundreds of trained pilots and air crewmen; in a single day, the Japanese navy lost more experienced men than she could generate in a year. Although the Japanese would continue to advance in other areas, they had lost the initiative, and began to consider transitioning to a strategy of attrition with the aim of achieving a negotiated settlement. The outcome of the battle enabled the Allies to launch a tentative counter-offensive against the Solomon Islands and Guadalcanal two months later.

At the outbreak of the war, the United States had some seventeen army divisions rated as combat ready, along with another twenty or so in various states of mobilization; however, as noted above, the commanders and staffs lacked the training necessary to employ these combat-ready divisions as corps and armies.[43] As tautological as it may sound, operational art is nothing without operational capability. The lack of operational-level experience was a significant shortcoming that plagued US forces for the first few years of the war. There were also critical shortages in ammunition and other supplies and a tendency to send forces overseas in an ad hoc, stopgap manner to respond to crises, all of which greatly hampered the coherent articulation of US operational grammar.

A notable setback took place at Kasserine Pass in February 1943, where the US 2nd Corps clashed with a portion of Rommel's Panzer Army Africa. American forces were inexperienced and overly aggressive, falling for the German tactic of baiting-and-running, inviting opposing armour to pursue into a screen of anti-tank guns. The 2nd Corps attempted several counter-attacks with the 1st Armored Division, but they were uncoordinated and too slow in unfolding. American forces were driven back some fifty miles, and lost about 200 tanks; 3,000 men killed and wounded; and 3,700 prisoners.[44] However, conflicting priorities within the Axis command prevented Rommel from exploiting the victory by continuing his advance north-west to the supply bases at Tebessa, and attempting to drive a wedge between Allied forces in Tunisia.

The encounter at Kasserine revealed that American operational art needed to reform its grammar from the ground up. The US army assessed that its 'basic principles' were sound, but that better all-arms cooperation was needed in practice.[45] Among other things, the practice of 'pooling' tank, tank destroyer, and anti-aircraft battalions at division level hindered the development of 'coordinated teamplay' (cohesion and efficiency), which, in turn, limited American operational effectiveness.[46] Communication problems also plagued coordination between ground forces and aircraft, a combat-critical skill that was not given sufficient attention during the inter-war years. In addition, the Americans allowed the Luftwaffe to gain air superiority over the battle area, which in modern warfare is unacceptable.

General George S. Patton III is credited with turning the performance of the US 2nd Corps around in a few short weeks, which he did, in part, by relieving incompetent commanders, instilling discipline, and insisting on better planning and coordination from his staff. He launched a successful counter-attack on 16–17 March against the rear of the Mareth Line, defeating several German counter-attacks in the process; this success enabled Montgomery's 8th Army to sweep the Mareth Line from the east, dislodging the south-eastern flank of German and Italian forces. The Allies pressed home their advantage, and the campaign culminated two months later with Axis forces hemmed into a small pocket in northern Tunisia, cut off from resupply, and deprived of air cover; some 275,000 German and Italian troops surrendered in a major victory for the Allies.

Patton achieved headline-grabbing victories in the Sicilian campaign a few months later. His 7th Army was ordered to land along the Licata–Ragusa shoreline, and drive north-west towards Palermo, shielding the right flank of Montgomery's 8th Army from counter-attack. He did that and more. Within a fortnight of landing, Patton had taken Palermo and swung east to advance on Messina, entering the city on 16 August, a day ahead of Montgomery. He had tried two minor amphibious assaults to outflank German positions, each of which met with limited success. They would, however, become part of Allied modus operandi in the campaign on the peninsula.

Despite the relatively rapid advances of the Americans and British, the Germans fell back in relatively good order, completing a complicated withdrawal from Sicily to the Italian mainland across the Strait of Messina under cover of darkness. By now, the commanders and staffs of the 7th Army had gained valuable combat experience, at both amphibious operations and offensive manoeuvre. Air–ground cooperation still required work, but the victories in Tunisia and Sicily had given the Americans much-needed confidence in their leadership, methods, and weapons, among which was the new Sherman tank.

On 3 September, the Allies crossed the Strait of Messina onto the Italian mainland. The US 5th Army, under Lieutenant General Mark Clark, landed at Salerno on 9 September, and was to drive towards Rome along the peninsula's west coast. Montgomery's 8th Army landed at Reggio and Catanzaro, and was to push northward to link up with Clark, then advance along the west coast. The campaign's scheme of manoeuvre thus consisted of two parallel drives up the eastern and western coastlines of the peninsula. Amphibious 'hooks' would be used to outflank any serious German resistance along with close air support and naval gunfire. A fierce German counter-attack at Salerno, for instance, was defeated, in part, by superior firepower in the form of naval gunfire and close air support. The battle also illustrated how fire and movement were more than a tactical technique: it was now also operational in nature, requiring planning and coordination at corps headquarters and higher.

As a further example, the sites for the amphibious 'hooks' were, in part, limited by the operational range of air cover, which was initially based in Sicily. As the Allied advance progressed, its air cover would leapfrog forward to ensure coverage for the next series of operations. This task was, of course, made easier by the fact that more of the Luftwaffe's planes were being diverted to defend the German homeland from Allied bombing offensives. However, the point is that the forward movement of ground forces was often driven by the need to capture another airfield so that air cover could be extended; thus, fire and movement, always mutually reinforcing on a tactical level, had become mutually dependent on an operational one.

The terrain on the Italian mainland favoured the defence, and the Germans were able to establish four successive defensive lines across the peninsula, each of which slowed the Allied advance considerably and inflicted heavy losses. Inclement weather and the eventual relocation of substantial Allied combat power for the invasion of France also contributed. The Allies achieved a number of breakthroughs of these defensive lines, but no real breakout and exploitation. This became a campaign of attrition, but it did tie down German forces that might have been available for the Eastern Front, or used to strengthen defences along the north-western and southern coastlines of France. However, the Allies paid a high price, losing about 320,000 casualties (114,000 US) by the end of the war.[47]

Mark Clark's style contrasted sharply with Patton's, so much so that the former has been accused of incompetence. These accusations have some merit. The most glaring example came after the fall of Monte Cassino and the penetration of the Winter Line. Instead of attacking and cutting off the German 10th Army, he turned his forces towards Rome, occupying it on 4 June 1944. Clark had disobeyed the direct orders of his superior, General Harold Alexander, and enabled substantial German forces to escape and establish a new defensive line north of Rome.

The invasion of Normandy on 6 June 1944 showed marked improvement in the US operational art, with better cooperation among Allied air, sea, and ground forces. Some 4,000 ships and landing vessels transported nearly 176,000 troops and materiel across the English Channel to breach Hitler's Atlantic Wall; 600 Allied warships, 2,500 heavy bombers, and 7,000 fighters were in support. By the conclusion of the first day, five divisions were ashore in addition to three airborne divisions, which had been dropped further inland; these numbers included the 4th US Infantry Division on Utah Beach, and the 1st US Infantry and 29th US Infantry Divisions on Omaha Beach, as well as the 82nd and 101st US Airborne Divisions. Within a month, the total number of troops ashore had grown to one million, with 150,000 vehicles.[48] The Normandy countryside favoured the defence, however, and the advance only crawled forward, enabling considerable German formations to reinforce the sector, despite steady Allied air interdiction along the main routes.

Although Patton was already a controversial figure, his reputation for aggressiveness made him the perfect choice to 'command' the notional 1st US Army Group, as part of Operation Fortitude, the deception plan to make the Germans believe that the invasion of France would occur at Pas de Calais. He was subsequently put in command of the US 3rd Army, which made a historic contribution to American operational art with the breakout from Normandy in August 1944. Typically, infantry units, supported by air bombardment, armour, and artillery, would achieve a local penetration, which would then be exploited by armour and other mechanized formations with air elements providing flank security and forward reconnaissance. The culmination of the breakout was the encirclement and destruction of the German 7th Army and 5th Panzer Army (10,000 dead and 50,000 prisoners) as cohesive fighting formations in and around the Falaise–Argentan gap; this operation, though not a complete success, opened the way to rapid exploitation and pursuit by several Allied mechanized formations across northern France.[49]

The advance of Allied forces wound down due to the length of their logistical tails and lines of communication, which had to move from the Cherbourg Peninsula and north-west coastlines to the borders of north-eastern France. Several other campaigns followed, notably the Lorraine and Rhine campaigns, which took American forces into Germany; however, the pattern was generally the same: an infantry or armour assault and penetration with an abundance of air power to protect the flanks and disrupt the movements of enemy reinforcements.

In the Pacific, Allied campaign strategy eventually settled on a two-pronged advance, crossing 14,200 miles of archipelagos and major islands. The series of island-hopping campaigns carried out by the United States and the other Allied powers could not have been successful without the cooperation—which was hardly without friction—that developed between air, naval, and ground forces. The Japanese could not make up the losses they suffered at Midway, in the Philippines, Leyte Gulf, and elsewhere, while also prosecuting a vast land war within China. The US submarine force succeeded in severely constricting the flow of Japanese shipping: some 300 submarines sank 4,779,902 tons of merchant shipping as well as 540,192 tons of warships during the war, 54.6 per cent of all Japanese tonnage.[50] The island-hopping campaigns (1943–5) of General Douglas

MacArthur and Admiral Chester Nimitz continued to close the ring around Japan, bypassing a number of the strategically insignificant islands; MacArthur advanced from the south and south-west towards the Philippines, while Nimitz pushed from Hawaii across the Central Pacific. Despite suffering horrific casualties and fighting hopelessly outnumbered, the Japanese continued to resist; it took the dropping of two atomic bombs, one on Hiroshima and one on Nagasaki, inflicting some 220,000 casualties in a span of three days, to convince Tokyo to surrender in August 1945.

Although the ability to bring to bear superior numbers over vast distances was clearly a major factor in the success of American operational art, numbers never tell the whole story. The long-range bombing campaigns, which clearly involved a form of calculus, were also an effort, pushed energetically by air power theorists, to break the will of the Axis populace—to strike directly at what some call an opponent's psychological centre of gravity. Before the war, a fair amount of optimism prevailed among these theorists about how effective such an air campaign could be; however, actual results fell far short of expectations. Although considerable debate still surrounds the issue, it seems clear that the bombing of major cities and industrial centres alone was not sufficient for victory, but might well have been necessary.

Indeed, the destructive power of modern, heavy bombers was unparalleled. The bombing of Hamburg in 1943, for example, generated 90,000 casualties over the course of four months. The controversial bombing of Dresden in 1945 resulted in 80,000 casualties in the space of three months, while the most devastating of the Tokyo raids caused 125,000 casualties during the month of May 1945.[51] Yet, rather than forcing their governments to surrender, civilian populations tended to become inured to the destruction, desiring not to capitulate, but to strike back. Arguably, their will to fight was strengthened rather than weakened.[52] It is difficult to know the true extent to which Axis production figures were diminished by Allied bombing; after all, German production figures actually increased during the period of the bombing; part of that can be explained by the fact that Germany shifted to a full wartime economy only after 1943. However, it seems clear that the Allied bombing effort, while not sufficient for success, was certainly necessary. Resources pulled to defend the German heartland from attack were not available to make a difference on either the Eastern or Western Fronts. What these events reveal is just how interconnected operations in the air, on land, and at sea had become. Operational success or failure in one dimension influenced operations in the others. In a manner of speaking, the separate dimensions were becoming more interdependent.

THE KOREAN CONFLICT

American operational art changed little between 1945 and 1950. Much of the equipment from the Second World War remained in service, though there were improved tank, artillery, and aircraft models, particularly jet aircraft. The US army demobilized from eight million men and eighty-nine divisions to less than 600,000 and ten under-strength divisions; most units were only manned at two-thirds their authorized strengths, and many lacked organic armour.[53] Although a number of the Second World War veterans remained in service, training was not as intense as it had been in the years before 1945, and overall the level of combat readiness was low.

Thus, when North Korean forces began their offensive on 25 June 1950, military units of the United States and the Republic of Korea performed poorly. Casualties were high, as UN forces fell back all the way to the Pusan Perimeter.[54] On 15 September 1950, UN forces, under the command of General Douglas MacArthur, successfully counter-attacked at Inchon with a surprise amphibious operation, which some historians have called 'Pattonesque', that required immense cooperation among all three services. By 22 September, the operation had succeeded in capturing Seoul and cutting most of the major north–south transportation routes; the North Koreans fell back with heavy losses, while UN forces advanced rapidly north to the Manchurian border.

UN intelligence failures, combined with extraordinary efforts at concealment by the Chinese, contributed to a successful counter-offensive by Communist forces, which drove UN forces back with heavy losses. Nearly 200,000 Chinese troops had moved into staging areas undetected. Once their offensive began in late October 1950, it gained ground rapidly and changed the complexion of the war. Chinese intervention eventually forced an alteration in US policy: the Truman administration was now prepared to accept limited objectives, namely restoring the political autonomy of the Republic of Korea, in order to avoid a general war and potential nuclear escalation.[55]

However, MacArthur remained fixed on achieving military victory, stressing the likely necessity of crossing the Yalu River and taking the war into Manchuria. The Chinese counter-offensive eventually stalled as the flow of logistics, though but a fraction of that required by UN forces, was continually disrupted by air attacks, and because the Chinese practice of living off the land had run its course. Thereafter, a series of smaller offensives and counter-offensives, driving back and forth across the 38th parallel, characterized the remainder of the war until an armistice was signed on 27 July 1953. Truman's war for limited objectives had finally come to an end, at the cost of some 139,000 American casualties (34,000 dead), 50,000 South Korean deaths, and nearly a million and a half North Korean and Chinese casualties.

MacArthur was relieved in April 1951 for his repeated and public disagreements with Washington's policies.[56] Ironically, MacArthur's approach has been described by some historians as representative of the American way of war; that is, the 'habit of thinking of war in terms of annihilative victories'.[57] It is actually more accurate to say that this operational approach was simply the further refinement of war's first grammar, which—notwithstanding the US Marine Corps' *Small Wars* manual (1940)—formed the primary focus of American operational art. It was partly the legacy of the Second World War that war was considered to have only one proper grammar.

Contrary to the popular view, the US military did give considerable attention to studying war's second grammar in the form of a Maoist-style people's war. The US army, for instance, produced several doctrinal publications in the early 1950s, at the height of the Korean conflict: FM 31-20 *Operations against Guerilla Forces* (February 1951), FM 31-21 *Organization and Conduct of Guerilla Warfare* (October 1951; updated 1955 and 1958), and FM 31-15 *Operations against Airborne Attack, Guerilla Action, and Infiltration* (January 1953). In addition, articles began to appear more frequently in professional journals regarding guerrilla warfare and how to counter it. Clearly, fighting the Chinese People's Liberation Army had raised interest in the potential existence of a second grammar of war. The doctrine was revised and updated throughout the Vietnam conflict, particularly as the US special forces expanded: FM 31-15 *Irregular Forces* (May 1961), FM 31-16 *Counterguerilla Operations* (February 1963; updated March 1967), FM 31-22 *U.S. Army Counterinsurgency Forces* (November 1963), FM 31-73 *Advisor Handbook for Counterinsurgencies* (April 1965), and *Advisor Handbook for Stability Operations* (October 1967). To be sure, some of the methods outlined in this growing body of doctrine could be described as heavy-handed, to say the least.[58] Still, the problem was not that a knowledge base did not exist, or was not being cultivated; rather, it was that the knowledge was considered exclusive, applicable only to those with specialized training; that is, not to general-purpose forces.

THE VIETNAM CONFLICT

The use of overwhelming combat power, which, as we have seen, had long been central to American operational art, was severely challenged during the Vietnam conflict. With the expansion of nuclear arsenals after the Korean War, realization set in that the United States would not have time to mobilize to the extent it had hitherto in the event of a major war. Mobilization locations and supply depots would provide lucrative targets for nuclear strikes. A strategic reserve was constituted and a system of reserve call-up implemented and reformed, but their timely arrival in the event of a general conflict was considered unlikely. Instead of a system of prolonged mobilization and deployment designed to crush an opponent with mass, war stocks had to be compiled and positioned in advance at strategic locations, and units stationed in Europe and Korea had to be prepared to fight with what they could carry, or could obtain through local means. Operational theory and doctrine, while still centred on the idea of concentrating overwhelming combat power at the decisive point, also began to consider the idea of fighting outnumbered and winning. The concept of active defence was one expression of that.

Meanwhile, US policy gradually shifted from massive retaliation to flexible response. As this shift occurred, the US military was expanded so that it could respond better to limited wars, such as the Korean conflict, and insurgencies, what Secretary of Defense Robert McNamara referred to as Third World 'brush-fire wars'.[59] Military doctrine retained many of the concepts used in the Second World War and the Korean conflict. The key addition was the concept of air mobility, particularly with the use of helicopters, which added greater opportunities for vertical envelopment. The destructiveness of modern firepower technology raised awareness of the power of the defence, particularly when combined with air mobility which enabled rapid concentration and dispersal of forces. The emphasis on the defence and on destroying enemy forces, rather than clearing and holding terrain, was almost a necessity given the challenges NATO forces faced in Europe; this thinking was directly applied to the situation in South-East Asia.[60]

From 1965 to 1968, US military involvement in Vietnam escalated steadily from 6,000 to 536,000 personnel; some 800,000 South Vietnamese troops were also engaged, as well as 68,000 soldiers from other countries.[61] Initially, US strategy sought to use a combination of strategic bombing and 'search and destroy' missions to inflict losses heavy enough to convince the Hanoi government to relent in its efforts to take control of South Vietnam. Unfortunately, early tactical victories by US forces, such as in the Ia Drang Valley in 1965, might have induced American leadership to adhere too long to this approach, which placed a greater premium on destroying the enemy than on protecting the civilian populace.[62] Although it was a force-oriented strategy, military actions were generally tightly controlled and limited so as to avoid provoking intervention by the People's Republic of China or the Soviet Union.

As the bombing increased—from 63,000 tons in 1963 to 226,000 tons four years later—and search and destroy efforts intensified, the enemy became frustratingly difficult to find. Manufacturing facilities were dismantled and moved, and resupply lines from China and elsewhere were easily concealed in the triple-canopy forests and hills. Hanoi's tactics changed on 31 January 1968, when it launched the Tet Offensive. Although the offensive failed militarily at the cost of tens of thousands of casualties, it did undermine the credibility of the Pentagon and the White House, both of which had been claiming steady progress militarily and politically. Public opinion turned even more sharply against the war after the My Lai massacre became public knowledge in the autumn of 1969, and the shooting incidents at Kent State University and Jackson State University in 1970, where several students lost their lives.[63]

US President Johnson's policy of gradual escalation was then abandoned by the Nixon administration, which in 1969 expanded the war into Cambodia to attack enemy bases. This effort was conducted in conjunction with attempts to implement 'Vietnamization' programmes designed to replace US military forces with South Vietnamese ones. However, the shift came too late, and widespread corruption within the Saigon government undermined most of the Vietnamization and re-building programmes almost from the start. By late 1970, American strategic goals had thus shifted decidedly to 'Peace with Honor', which meant that everything that could have been done to save an ally had been done, and military withdrawal would now commence. Nonetheless, it was not until 27 January 1973, after an intensive 'Christmas bombing offensive' of North Vietnam by B-52s, that the Paris Peace Accords were signed by both sides, thereby enabling the US withdrawal.

Although the US military encountered a second grammar of war during this conflict, it left that grammar behind, eagerly turning it over to special forces which were intentionally designed for that purpose. In the meantime, conventional operational doctrine turned its attention to the Herculean task of defeating Warsaw Pact forces in Europe.

LIMITED WAR, NUCLEAR WAR, AND THE CRISIS FOR OPERATIONAL ART

The advent of nuclear weapons gave rise to an important debate within American defence circles, one that would also have crucial implications for operational art. The issue was the continued utility of war in the rapidly unfolding atomic age or, more precisely, whether and how armed conflict could be used if escalation was not desired. To many scholars and defence intellectuals, it appeared that conventional warfare had become obsolete. As Bernard Brodie argued, atomic weapons seemed to have created a new strategic environment in which armed conflict had to be either avoided or contained.[64] Other influential scholars, such as Robert E. Osgood, the leading proponent of limited-war theory, and Thomas C. Schelling, the principal advocate of coercive diplomacy, agreed. Osgood maintained that in any war, an array of acceptable outcomes existed short of total military victory.[65] Schelling went so far as to suggest that the application of military force could be adjusted like a rheostat, increasing or decreasing the level of pain for an opponent until concessions were extracted.[66] In other words, they appeared to say that war's grammar needed to become as flexible as its logic.

Whereas Brodie, Osgood, and Schelling put a premium on limiting violence to avoid escalation, other notable theorists, such as Herman Kahn, gave considerable thought to 'thinking the unthinkable', namely how to fight and possibly win a nuclear war.[67] Kahn did not eschew escalation, but rather assumed it would happen; he analysed hypothetical cases in detail, finally creating an escalation ladder that both anticipated responses and prescribed them. This approach to war did not entirely eliminate operational art, but did change it into something military professionals found disagreeable; the kind of grammar Kahn envisioned did not need artists, only technicians.

As a result of this debate, American operational artists found that the very grammar they had refined over the course of three major wars was now suddenly too risky to employ.[68] They were, in a manner of speaking, caught on the horns of a dilemma. If they countered the limited-war school of thought, as many did, on the basis that it violated critical principles of war's first grammar, they ran the risk of moving towards Kahn's school of thought, which would ultimately make them irrelevant.[69] Yet, by defining themselves against Kahn's clinical, technician-like approach, they moved in the direction of admitting that war's first grammar was not sacrosanct.

In fact, there was a real possibility that weapons of mass destruction might be used in the next war; so both civilian schools of thought made some valid points. During the 1960s and 1970s, it became clear that Soviet operational thinking did not eschew the use of such weapons, and, instead, had thoroughly integrated them into its doctrine. Military training in the United States and across NATO thus had little choice but to include instruction in how to react to and fight in biological, chemical, and nuclear environments. In important respects, then, arguments for a more flexible grammar could not be ignored.

American operational art delivered a dual response. The first response was to continue to refine the art itself from a largely conventional standpoint, integrating air, ground, and naval power, into a more sophisticated first grammar. At times, the admonitions of nuclear theorists were set aside completely, as with the debates between 'manoeuvrists' and 'attritionists' in the 1970s and 1980s, which blissfully proceeded as if a confrontation with the Warsaw Pact would remain conventional; the debates did yield interesting insights, nonetheless.[70] This response formed part of the intellectual background behind the 1982 version of the US army's operations manual, FM 100-5, which introduced the AirLand Battle concept. The manual did not overlook the role of weapons of mass destruction, but it did reinforce the importance of war's first grammar to American operational art with statements such as 'the object of all operations is to destroy the opposing force'.[71] That emphasis was even stronger in the 1986 edition of FM 100-5, which declared that the 'essence of operational art' was 'the identification of the enemy's operational centre of gravity and the concentration of superior combat power against that point to achieve decisive success'.[72] It also stressed the synchronization of mobility and firepower, not only across the forward line of friendly troops, as the active defence concept of the 1976 version of FM 100-5 did, but also throughout the depth of the battle area. The idea of the 'deep attack' was clearly not new, as it had existed in Soviet doctrine for some time. However, what was new for the American operational art, and what some have called revolutionary, was the idea of conceiving the entire depth of an opponent's attacking formations as one 'integrated' battle.[73]

The institutionalization of the operational level of war by the United States and other NATO members also came, in part, as a response to the organizational and doctrinal challenges posed by the Warsaw Pact. The operational level of war provided a way to integrate the various national doctrines and command and control structures of NATO members into something resembling a coherent effort.

The second response involved moving towards an alternate grammar of war with a body of doctrine referred to as military operations other than war (MOOTW), with missions ranging from show of force to humanitarian assistance.[74] The number of such operations rose dramatically after the Cold War. In 1990, the United Nations had five peacekeeping operations under way, excluding those on the Korean Peninsula, involving about 10,000 troops; whereas, in 2006, it listed eighteen such operations employing nearly 73,000 troops, while the costs of such operations had risen from $800 million in 1990 to $41 billion in 2006.[75] It is hardly surprising that such operations, whether called MOOTW or something else, received little attention during the Cold War, since they would have taken valuable training time and other resources away from preparing for combat with the Warsaw Pact.

THE FIRST PERSIAN GULF WAR, 1990–1

Even though the first Gulf War was fought largely according to the principles of AirLand Battle doctrine, a portion of the campaign was shaped by the ideas of a new generation of air power theorists, of whom US Air Force Colonel John A. Warden III was perhaps the most famous.[76] In 1988, Warden published a text outlining how long-range precision-strike technology could be used to target a foe's leadership and will to fight, while avoiding not only costly ground campaigns, but also the extensive destruction traditionally associated with strategic bombing.[77] The central concept was that an adversary's leaders could be 'decapitated', paralysed, or neutralized, by striking certain communications and infrastructural (and even cultural) targets simultaneously. Although Warden's ideas had begun to circulate within the air force, they were by no means mainstream. Nonetheless, the Gulf War provided an opportunity to put the theory to the test, at least partially, particularly as Warden was put in charge of the planning cell within the Pentagon responsible for developing targeting options.[78]

The Gulf War was divided into two phases: Desert Shield, which was defensive in nature, designed to deter further Iraqi aggression, in particular an invasion into Saudi Arabia; and Desert Storm, which was a combined and joint counter-offensive aimed at expelling Iraqi forces from Kuwait, unless they withdrew by 15 January 1991, in accordance with the UN Security Council Resolution. In a style reminiscent of AirLand Battle doctrine, the United States and its coalition partners marshalled some 680,000 troops, 3,000 tanks, 2,000 aircraft, and 100 warships for the counter-offensive, while Saddam Hussein had at his disposal some 336,000 troops and 9,000 tanks.[79]

The counter-offensive consisted of two phases: an air phase and a ground phase. The air phase began on 17 January 1991, with most Iraqi command and control facilities and anti-aircraft defences being knocked out within hours. A key feature of this phase was the use of Tomahawk cruise missiles and F-117 stealth fighters. Once air superiority was established, the air campaign shifted to knocking out Iraqi armour and artillery pieces; it was estimated that nearly a third of Iraqi combat capability was destroyed during this phase.

The land phase of the counter-offensive opened on 24 February 1991, and lasted barely 100 hours. Coalition mechanized forces swiftly executed an enveloping movement around the Iraqi right flank, cutting off large numbers of fighting formations. Iraqi units deserted wholesale or were quickly smashed by the superior firepower of coalition forces. Images of the 'Highway of Death' filled television screens and the covers of popular magazines. In anticipation that such images might generate a popular backlash against further prosecution of the war,

General Colin Powell recommended halting the advance, and President Bush agreed. A peace agreement was signed, but—in an oversight that was to be much criticized later—it left Saddam Hussein in power. Iraqi forces were estimated to have suffered 25,000–65,000 casualties, while the coalition lost less than 200 personnel.[80]

The conflict did raise the question as to whether war's first grammar might be prosecuted more cleanly and from a distance with long-range precision targeting, coupled with a small ground presence in the form of special-operations troops and indigenous forces. Some pundits called this the 'new' American way of war, even though precision munitions made up only a small percentage of the ordinance used.[81] Others declared that air power was 'America's Asymmetric Advantage', and that it had the potential to revolutionize operational practice.[82] Dissenting voices, mostly from army and marine officers, argued that a well-trained ground force was still needed to compel an adversary to accept terms.

The 1993 edition of FM 100-5 continued to emphasize the importance of war's first grammar and 'decisive victory', even though it acknowledged that the Cold War had ended and the nature of the threat had changed.[83] It went on to say that the principal role of the US army in the post-Cold War era was deterrence and the ability to project power anywhere; however, it also stated that 'the objective of the military in war is victory over the opposing military force'.[84] *Joint Vision 2010* (1996) and *Joint Vision 2020* (2000) were intended to lay out a joint concept for US military forces in response to force-sizing pressures and the anticipated demands of the future security environment.[85] They described four concepts which were to set a course for the further modernization of US forces: dominant manoeuvre, precision engagement, focused logistics, and full-dimensional protection, all of which were to lead to the objective of full-spectrum dominance.

In contrast to this emphasis, the principal challenge for operational art in the Bosnian and Kosovo conflicts, which came a few years later, was to roll back aggressive parties and to provide security or safe zones so that political and economic stability could be achieved. Once rollback was achieved, it was not clear to what extent, if any, operational art remained relevant.

In keeping with the promise that information technologies would bring about a general 'revolution in military affairs' (RMA), the US military began to explore ways to transform war's first grammar. Information was hailed as the key to lifting the 'fog of war'.[86] A number of new (and old) theories were advanced, such as network-centric warfare (NCW) and effects-based operations (EBO). NCW was the idea of linking all military platforms and command structures together through an information infrastructure, or 'infostructure', which would permit rapid information sharing and greater efficiency and flexibility in mission execution.[87] EBO was, ostensibly, a process for obtaining a desired strategic outcome or 'effects' by applying the 'full range of military and other national capabilities at the tactical, operational, and strategic levels'.[88] EBO made rapid headway in defence circles. Even though it had not been approved as official doctrine, it began to appear in doctrinal publications and was being taught at defence colleges. Finally, the commander of US Joint Forces Command killed the concept in August 2008, arguing, rightly, that it ran counter to the history of warfare.[89]

AFGHANISTAN AND THE SECOND GULF WAR

American operational art was never closer to perfecting war's first grammar than during the initial operations in Afghanistan in 2001–2 and Iraq in 2003. The quick collapse of the Taliban in Afghanistan and the dramatic successes in the initial phases of Operation Iraqi Freedom, which featured the fall of Baghdad in record time and with remarkably low casualties on both sides, seemed like the realization of perfection. In short, results were fairly close to what was desired, at least with respect to combat. It is evident now that the political aims were not achieved in either of the initial campaigns.

Yet, from an operational perspective, it seemed evident that a number of improvements had been made, such as overall coordination between the two vital combat functions of fire and movement. Some analysts saw these results as evidence of at least a partial success for NCW: 'What we're seeing is essentially net-centric warfare for the joint task force commander. The next step is network-centric warfare for the warfighter—reflecting increased "jointness" at the tactical level of war'.[90] To be sure, the cooperation between ground and air forces, between manoeuvre elements—whether small groups of special-operations forces or larger mechanized formations—and elements capable of delivering direct and indirect fires was never perfect. Yet, it was more exquisite than any level of cooperation realized hitherto.

However, appearances were deceptive in a number of ways: the causes of success were not always related to the principles of speed, knowledge, and precision.[91] Moreover, as events revealed, American operational art had become exquisite at winning battles; that is, at war's first grammar; but it had not prepared enough for the possibility that competence in a second grammar would be needed. That is not to say that processes and protocols were not in place for establishing peace or, more precisely, for transitioning from decisive military operations to security operations and political and economic reconstruction, referred to in joint operational doctrine at the time as phase IV.[92] What is clear is that not enough forces were in place to provide security in the event that a civil war broke out, and that a great many hasty assumptions were made about how the transition to a post-conflict environment would flow.

When the complex (or informal) insurgency began to emerge in the late spring and early summer of 2003, the United States and its coalition partners were not prepared. The insurgency itself—the term is not entirely adequate to describe the phenomenon—evolved from a largely sporadic and inchoate resistance to a loose, if violent and volatile, alignment of anti-American interests in the form of sectarian militias, foreign jihadists, and Sunni-Arab insurgent groups. By late summer of 2003, the basic symptoms were essentially recognized by American leaders, though not uniformly.

Still, the US military's overall doctrine, training, and techniques were not geared to conducting counter-insurgency operations, which had largely been abandoned after El Salvador. The US military's joint operations manual, JP 3-0, and its manual for planning joint operations, JP 5-0, both describe the 'essence of the operational art' as being able 'to produce the right combination of effects in time, space, and purpose relative to a [center of gravity] to neutralize, weaken, defeat, or destroy it'.[93] In other words, a fundamental transition, or relearning, had to occur, but the initial approach, as doctrine indicated, was to treat counter-insurgency as simply combat against irregular forces, which exacerbated the problem.[94]

The search for appropriate methods eventually led to the rediscovery of classic insurgency doctrine along the Maoist model. The result was FM 3-24 *Counterinsurgency*, produced jointly by the US army and US marine corps (MCWP 3-33.5), which appeared in final form at the end of 2006.[95] The volume—which set counter-insurgency operations within the framework of offensive, defensive, stability, and support operations as established by FM 3.0 (2001)—has been much criticized for addressing only the Maoist model, which it does, and for not providing specific guidelines for how to win in Iraq, which clearly it does not. Its principal writer claimed that the manual does not 'de-emphasize combat operations', but rather that it stresses the importance of achieving legitimacy, which requires the ability to accomplish 'non-military operations, such as repairing broken sewer lines and building relationships with the local people'.[96] Establishing legitimacy is part of the classic formula for defeating insurgencies; however, legitimacy is culturally constructed, and thus achieved in different ways. What seems to have worked in Iraq thus far—in conjunction with the Surge, which more than anything demonstrated commitment—is that coalition forces have encouraged some militias and insurgent groups to align themselves against others, such as al-Qaeda. However, as always, such alignments remain tentative. All political relationships are tentative.

American operational art continues to develop war's second grammar with energy. Its progress has been rapid, if uneven. British scholars and military professionals were once critical of the heavy-handed approach American military commanders took to counter-insurgency. Recent observations suggest that the situation has reversed.[97] Still, operational doctrine is only a set of guidelines; it cannot cover every situation. It may prove its worth simply by not getting in the way of efforts to establish the kinds of political relationships necessary to secure peace.

CONCLUSION

Over the last century, American operational art has continuously improved the concepts and methods by which it fights battles. In so doing, it assumed, as many militaries have, that winning battles would lead, ultimately, to winning wars.

America's experience in the Vietnam conflict called that assumption into question. Although it won many battles, almost all of them in fact, in the end those victories were not enough.[98] Still, it would be inaccurate to argue that the winning (or losing) of battles is irrelevant. Plenty of belligerents have surrendered after losing major battles. Nonetheless, the Vietnam conflict brought home the point that war had at least two kinds of grammar; that point was not new, but it was also not widely understood.

For most of the twentieth century, American operational practice could count on having time to mobilize and deploy large military forces. The numerical superiority of those forces typically compensated for lack of training and experience. The US military could afford to learn on the job, as it were. It is still doing that, though one has to wonder whether the campaigns in Iraq and Afghanistan would have been as protracted had its doctrine and institutional learning been more complete.

American operational art also confronted a dual crisis in the middle of the twentieth century with the advent of nuclear weapons. The strategic environment called for the ability to adjust the application of military power gradually, as one adjusts a rheostat, to coerce an opponent into compliance, while, at the same time, avoiding escalation. This way of thinking ran counter to the training and experience of military professionals, for whom the object of war was to overwhelm one's foe as quickly as possible, and to remove the physical and psychological means to resist.

The response of American operational art was to reaffirm the importance of battle, and of war's first grammar. The value of manoeuvre, for instance, was reasserted, regardless of the likelihood that the next conflict might involve weapons of mass destruction, which would surely render the principles underpinning manoeuvre irrelevant. That reaffirmation proved prescient, however, as many of the manoeuvre precepts of AirLand Battle doctrine were also validated in Desert Storm. The US military also published doctrine covering counterinsurgency operations and military operations other than war; however, these missions were intended to be dealt with by forces specially trained for the purpose, or as lower priority missions. In addition, it embraced the operational level of war, which not only offered practical organizational structures that facilitated multinational planning, but also established a conceptual space in which military professionals could develop and discuss tactical concepts and capabilities without the interference of non-professionals.

The RMA that the first Gulf War seemed to have ushered in took American operational theory to lofty heights. Precision-strike capabilities and information technologies combined to inspire new (and old), if unidimensional, attempts to perfect war's first grammar. The need for sustained counter-insurgency operations in Afghanistan and Iraq exposed the limitations inherent in focusing on one grammar. Yet, it remains to be seen just how far the US will allow itself to develop war's second grammar.

To define operational art in terms of 'creative imagination', as the official definition did, is problematic. Creativity, like beauty, is highly subjective, and has little to do with effectiveness. Art is, by definition, creative; but appreciating it is merely a matter of taste. For parts of the twentieth century, American operational art was little more than the relentless application of superior force; but it proved effective. In contrast, American operations in Afghanistan in 2001–2 and Iraq in 2003 amounted to an exquisite application of force in terms of speed, knowledge, and precision; however, these principles failed to produce an overall victory. US operational planning and execution focused too much on war's first grammar, which is why the classic definition of operational art is also problematic. It is not enough merely to 'design' and 'link' operations, as the classic definition holds, with only one grammar in mind. Contemporary operational art requires mastering two grammars.

NOTES

1. Daniel Moran, 'Operational Level of War', in Richard Holmes (ed.), *Oxford Companion to Military History* (Oxford: Oxford University Press, 2001), is an excellent summary.
2. Carl von Clausewitz, *Vom Kriege*, Book VIII, ch. 6B, 991.
3. Brig. Justin Kelly and Michael James Brennan, *Alien: How Operational Art Devoured Strategy* (Carlisle, PA: US Army War College, 2009), offer the classic definition: the 'skillful design and execution of operations', with operations confined within the context of the campaign plan. Cf. John English, 'The Operational Art: Developments in the Theories of War', in B. J. C. McKercher and Michael A. Hennessy (eds.), *The Operational Art: Developments in the Theories of War* (Westport, CT: Praeger, 1996), 7–28, which suggests 'if *strategy* is the art of war and *tactics* the art of battle, then *operations* is the art of campaigning'.
4. <http://www.dtic.mil/doctrine/jel/doddict/data/o/index.html>, accessed October 2009.
5. Whether that remains true is another matter; some argue that operational art must now be developed at battalion headquarters. Huba Wass de Czege, 'Systemic Operational Design: Learning and Adapting in Complex Missions', *Military Review*, vol. 89, no. 1 (January–February 2009), 2–12.
6. Richard M. Swain, 'Filling the Void: The Operational Art and the U.S. Army', in *Operational Art*, 147–72.
7. Kelly and Brennan, *Alien*.
8. *American Military History* (Washington, DC: Center of Military History, 1989), 343–57; James E. Hewes, Jr., *From Root to McNamara: Army Organization and Administration, 1900–1963* (Washington, DC: GPO, 1975).
9. William A. Kobbe, *Notes on Strategy and Logistics* (Ft. Monroe, VA: Artillery School Press, 1896), 17; Henry L. Scott, *Military Dictionary* (New York: D. Van Nostrand, 1864), 574; cf. BG (ret.) Harold Nelson, 'The Origins of Operational Art', in Michael D. Krause and R. Cody Phillips (eds.), *Historical Perspectives of the Operational Art* (Washington, DC: Center of Military History, 2005), 333–48.
10. Philip A. Crowl, 'Alfred Thayer Mahan: The Naval Historian', in Peter Paret (ed.), *Makers of Modern Strategy from Machiavelli to the Nuclear Age* (Princeton, NJ: Princeton University Press, 1986).

11. Timothy K. Nenninger, 'American Military Effectiveness in the First World War', in Allan R. Millet and Williamson Murray (eds.), *Military Effectiveness: Volume I: The First World War* (Boston, MA: Unwin Hyman, 1987), 129–30.
12. David Trask, 'The Entry of the USA into the War and its Effects', in Hew Strachan (ed.), *World War I: A History* (Oxford: Oxford University Press, 1998), 239–52.
13. Allan R. Millett, 'Cantigny, 28–31 May 1918', in Charles E. Heller and William A. Stofft (eds.), *America's First Battles, 1776–1965* (Lawrence, KS: University Press of Kansas, 1986), 149–85.
14. *American Military History*, 398.
15. Ibid., 399.
16. Trask, 'Entry of USA into the War', 43.
17. *American Military History*, 403.
18. Nenninger, 'American Military Effectiveness', 141.
19. Millett, 'Cantigny', 180–1.
20. Nenninger, 'American Military Effectiveness', 129.
21. Ronal Spector, 'The Military Effectiveness of the U.S. Armed Forces, 1919–1939', in Allan R. Millet and Williamson Murray (eds.), *Military Effectiveness: Volume II: The Interwar Period* (Boston, MA: Unwin Hyman, 1990), 72.
22. William O. Odom, *After the Trenches: The Transformation of the U.S. Army, 1918–1939* (College Station, TX: Texas A&M University Press, 1999).
23. Ibid., 121.
24. General Service Schools, *General Tactical Functions of Larger Units* (Ft. Leavenworth, KS: General Service Schools, 1926), 1–2; cf. Nelson, 'Origins of Operational Art', 340.
25. *General Tactical Functions*, 3; cf. Nelson, 'Origins of Operational Art', 340.
26. *The Principles of Strategy for an Independent Corps or Army in a Theater of Operations* (Ft. Leavenworth, KS: Command and General Staff College, 1936), 37.
27. William K. Naylor, *The Principles of Strategy* (Ft. Leavenworth, KS: General Service Schools, 1920); cf. Col. (ret.) Michael R. Matheny, 'The Roots of American Operational Art' (unpublished paper).
28. Naylor, *Principles*, 49, 106.
29. Williamson Murray, 'Strategic Bombing: The British, American, and German Experiences', in *Military Innovation*, 107.
30. Ibid., 115.
31. Ibid., 123–5; Phillip S. Meilinger, *Paths of Heaven: The Evolution of Airpower Theory* (Maxwell AFB, AL: Air University Press, 1997).
32. Murray, 'Strategic Bombing', 126; and Richard R. Muller, 'Close Air Support: The German, British, and American Experiences, 1918–1941', in *Military Innovation*, 144–90.
33. Murray, 'Strategic Bombing', 127.
34. Tami Davis Biddle, *Rhetoric and Reality in Air Warfare: The Evolution of British and American Ideas about Strategic Bombing, 1914–1945* (Princeton, NJ: Princeton University Press, 2002).
35. Holger H. Herwig, 'Innovation Ignored: The Submarine Problem—Germany, Britain, and the United States, 1919–1939', in *Military Innovation*, 154.
36. Ibid., 255–6.
37. Geoffrey Till, 'Adopting the Aircraft Carrier: The British, American, and Japanese Case Studies', in *Military Innovation*, 191–226.
38. Barry Watts and Williamson Murray, 'Military Innovation in Peacetime', in *Military Innovation*, 399–400.

39. Alan R. Millet, 'Assault from the Sea: The Development of Amphibious Warfare between the Wars', in *Military Innovation*, 50–95.
40. J. Garry Clifford, 'World War II: Military and Diplomatic Course', in Paul S. Boyer (ed.), *Oxford Companion to United States History* (Oxford: Oxford University Press, 2001), 846.
41. Martin Blumenson, 'Kasserine Pass, 30 January–22 February 1943', in *First Battles*, 226–65, here 229.
42. *American Military History*, 423–4.
43. Ibid., 435.
44. Martin Blumenson, *Patton: The Man behind the Legend, 1885–1945* (New York: Morrow, 1985), 181.
45. War Department, 'Training Lessons from the Tunisian Campaign', reprint of Training Memorandum 44, 4 August 1943, in *Kasserine Pass Battles: Doctrines and Lessons Learned*, vol. II, part 3 (Washington, DC: Center of Military History, 1993), 1.
46. Major General E. N. Harmon, Cdr. 2nd Armored Division, 'Notes on Combat Experience during the Tunisian and African Campaigns <1943>', in ibid., 3; see also Russell A. Hart, *How the Allies Won in Normandy* (Norman, OK: University of Oklahoma Press, 2004), 281.
47. George F. Botjer, *Sideshow War: The Italian Campaign, 1943–45* (College Station, TX: Texas A&M University Press, 1996); Dominick Graham, *Tug of War: The Battle for Italy, 1943–1945* (New York: St. Martin's Press, 1986).
48. John Keegan, *Six Armies in Normandy: From D-Day to the Liberation of Paris* (New York: Penguin, 1994).
49. Russell F. Weigley, 'Normandy to Falaise: A Critique of Allied Operational Planning in 1944', in *Historical Perspectives*, 393–414.
50. Herwig, 'Innovation Ignored', 253.
51. Richard J. Overy, *The Air War, 1939–1945* (Washington, DC: Potomac, 2005); *Why the Allies Won* (New York: Norton, 1997).
52. United States Strategic Bombing Survey, *Summary Report (European War)*, 30 September 1945; *Summary Report (Pacific War)*, 1 July 1946.
53. *American Military History*, 540–2.
54. Roy K. Flint, 'Task Force Smith and the 24th Division: Delay and Withdrawal, 5–19 July 1950', in *First Battles*, 265–99.
55. Col. (ret.) Stanlis D. Milkowski, 'After Inch'on: MacArthur's 1950 Campaign in North Korea', in *Historical Perspectives*, 415–38.
56. D. Clayton James and Anne Sharp Wells, *Refighting the Last War: Command and Crisis in Korea, 1950–1953* (New York: Free Press, 1993).
57. Russell F. Weigley, *The American Way of War: A History of United States Military Strategy and Policy* (Bloomington, IN: Indiana University Press, 1977), 382.
58. Andrew Krepenevich, Jr., *The Army and Vietnam* (Baltimore, MD: Johns Hopkins University Press, 1986).
59. 'Armed Forces; Fighting Brush Fires,' *Time*, 29 September, 1961; <http://www.time.com> (accessed 21 November 21 2009).
60. George C. Herring, 'Vietnam War', in *United States History*, 807.
61. George C. Herring, *America's Longest War: The United States and Vietnam, 1950–1975* (New York: Alfred A. Knopf, 1979).
62. George C. Herring, 'The 1st Cavalry and the Ia Drang Valley, 18 October–24 November 1965', in *First Battles*, 300–26.
63. Herring, *America's Longest War*.

64. Bernard Brodie, *The Absolute Weapon* (New York: Harcourt Brace, 1946).
65. Robert E. Osgood, *Limited War: The Challenge to American Strategy* (Chicago, IL: University of Chicago Press, 1957).
66. Thomas C. Schelling, *Arms and Influence* (New Haven, CT: Yale University Press, 1966).
67. Herman Kahn, *On Thermonuclear War* (Princeton, NJ: Princeton University Press, 1960); *On Escalation: Metaphors and Scenarios* (New York: Praeger, 1965).
68. I. D. Holder, 'A New Day for Operational Art', in R. L. Allen (ed.), *Operational Level of War—Its Art* (Carlisle, PA: US Army War College, 1985), 4–1, 4–2, underscores the 'belief that nuclear weapons meant the end of conventional warfare'.
69. Harry G. Summers, Jr., *On Strategy: A Critical Analysis of the Vietnam War* (Novato, CA: Presidio, 1982).
70. Shimon Naveh, *In Pursuit of Military Excellence: The Evolution of Operational Theory* (London: Frank Cass, 1997), 263, describes it as 'the longest, most intoxicating and creative professional debate which ever occurred in the history of American military thought'.
71. Department of the Army, *FM 100-5 Operations*, 20 August 1982 (Washington, DC: GPO, 1982), 2–1, 2–2; Swain, 'Filling the Void', 159; Allan English, 'The Operational Art', in Allan English, Daniel Gosselin, Howard Coombs, and Laurence M. Hickey (eds.), *The Operational Art: Canadian Perspectives, Context and Concepts* (Kingston, ON: Canadian Defence Academy, 2005), 16.
72. English, 'Operational Art', 16.
73. Naveh, *Pursuit of Military Excellence*, 292–5.
74. Joint Publication, *JP 3-07. Joint Doctrine for Military Operations Other Than War* (Washington, DC: 16 June 1995).
75. Cf. United Nations Peacekeeping Operations, Background Note, dated 28 February 2006, <http://www.un.org/depts/dpko/dpko/bnote.htm>, accessed October 2009.
76. John Andreas Olsen, *John Warden and the Renaissance of American Air Power* (Washington, DC: Potomac, 2007).
77. In brief, Warden maintained that strategic paralysis or psychological collapse would result by attacking critical points in each of five 'rings' simultaneously: leadership, organic or system essentials, infrastructure, population, and fielded military forces. John A. Warden III, 'The Enemy as a System', *Airpower Journal*, vol. 9, no. 1 (Spring 1995), 40–5.
78. Lawrence Freedman and Efraim Karsh, *The Gulf Conflict, 1990–1991: Diplomacy and War in the New World Order* (Princeton, NJ: Princeton University Press, 1991), 316–17.
79. Brigadier General John S. Brown, 'The Maturation of Operational Art: Operations Desert Shield and Desert Storm', in *Historical Perspectives*, 439–82.
80. Anthony H. Cordesman, 'Persian Gulf War (1991)', ibid., 588.
81. General Ronald Fogelman, USAF, 'Airpower and the American Way of War', speech presented at the Air Force Association's Air Warfare Symposium, Orlando, Florida, 15 February 1996; cf. Grant T. Hammond, 'The U.S. Air Force and the American Way of War', in Anthony D. McIvor (ed.), *Rethinking the Principles of War* (Annapolis, MD: Naval Institute Press, 2005), 109–25.
82. Michael Ignatieff, *Virtual War: Kosovo and Beyond* (New York: Metropolitan, 2000).
83. Department of the Army, *FM 100-5 Operations*, 14 June 1993 (Washington, DC: GPO, 1993), 1–3.
84. Ibid., 1–4.

85. US Joint Chiefs of Staff, *Joint Vision 2010* (Washington, DC: GPO, 1996); *Joint Vision 2020* (Washington, DC: GPO, 2000).
86. Admiral Bill Owens, *Lifting the Fog of War* (New York: Farrar, Strauss, and Giroux, 2000).
87. Arthur K. Cebrowski, 'Network-Centric Warfare: An Emerging Military Response to the Information Age', presented at the 1999 Command and Control Research and Technology Symposium, 29 June 1999; see also David S. Alberts, John J. Gartska, and Frederick P. Stein, *Network Centric Warfare: Developing and Leveraging Information Superiority* (Washington, DC: C4ISR Cooperative Research Program, 1999), 2.
88. Rapid Decisive Operations White Paper, January 2002, 20.
89. General J. N. Mattis, USMC, Commander US Joint Forces Command, 'USJFCOM Commander's Guidance for Effects-Based Operations', *Parameters*, vol. 38, no. 3 (August 2008), 18–25.
90. John Ferris, 'A New American Way of War? C4ISR in Operation Iraqi Freedom: A Provisional Assessment', in John Ferris (ed.), *Calgary Papers in Military and Strategic Studies* (Calgary: University of Calgary, 2008), 156.
91. Stephen Biddle, *Afghanistan and the Future of Warfare: Implications for Army and Defense Policy* (Carlisle, PA: US Army War College, 2002); 'Speed Kills? Reassessing the Role of Speed, Precision, and Situation Awareness in the Fall of Saddam', *Journal of Strategic Studies*, vol. 30, no. 1 (February 2007), 3–46.
92. Joint Publication, *JP 3-0. Joint Operations* (Washington, DC: GPO, 2001); Joint Publication, *5-0. Joint Operation Planning* (Washington, DC: GPO, 1995).
93. Joint Publication, *JP 3-0. Joint Operations* (Washington, DC: GPO, 2006), iv–12; Joint Publication, *5-0. Joint Operation Planning* (Washington, DC: GPO, 2006), iv–9.
94. Steven Metz, *Learning from Iraq: Counterinsurgency in Iraq* (Carlisle, PA: US Army War College, 2007).
95. Department of the Army, *FM 3-24 Counterinsurgency*, 15 December 2006 (Washington, DC: GPO, 2006).
96. Michelle Gordon, 'Army, Marine Corps Unveil Counterinsurgency Field Manual', *Army News Service*, 15 December 2006.
97. David Betz and Anthony Cormack, 'Iraq, Afghanistan, and British Strategy', *Orbis* (Spring 2009), 312–36.
98. Harry G. Summers, Jr., *On Strategy: A Critical Analysis of the Vietnam War* (Navato, CA: Presidio, 1995).

6

The Rise and Fall of Israeli Operational Art, 1948–2008

Avi Kober

INTRODUCTION

Although the Israel Defense Forces (IDF) demonstrated operational-art skills as early as the state's War of Independence, it took its first steps towards formal operational-art thinking only in the mid-1990s, when the Operational Theory Research Institute (OTRI) was established. Israeli commanders educated at the OTRI started referring to themselves as 'operators', or 'shapers' of operations, internalizing imported concepts, such as 'extended battlefield', 'deep operations', 'synchronization', and so on. The OTRI team believed that, alongside the adoption of a relatively solid, though imitated, ready, off-the-shelf, Soviet-inspired American operational thinking, delving into non-military, postmodern philosophy would equip senior officers with the tools necessary for dealing with the complex and changing realities of war. Classical military thinkers became no more than names whose sayings were occasionally cited but whose writings were not read or studied in depth.[1]

Throughout its lifetime, from its establishment in 1995 to its closure in 2005, the institute failed to offer written materials on operational art in general and Israeli operational art in particular. Given the neglect of classical military theory by the IDF's education system and the OTRI's focus on the writings of postmodern architects and philosophers, only a handful of IDF commanders were intellectually and professionally competent to criticize the OTRI's ideas, whereas many others just adopted its pompous language. The Winograd Commission called the OTRI's language a 'tower of Babel', pointing to it as an impediment to the creation of a common language and mutual understanding between commanders at the operational and tactical level during the Second Lebanon War.[2] This language was considered by many IDF commanders obscure, unclear, confusing, and empty, and the combination of problematic operational concepts and an unclear language for orders had a detrimental effect.[3]

In a paper published in 2007 for the US Department of Defense's director of the Net Assessment Office, titled 'Operational Art and the IDF: A Critical Study of a Command Culture',[4] author Shimon Naveh attributed the IDF's poor operational art to a combination of addiction to tactics and its failure to become a learning institution. Three 'waves' of operational art are described in the paper: in the late 1940s, between the mid-1950s and 1967, and between 1995 and 2005. These waves are attributed, respectively, to the revolutionary spirit of the Haganah's striking force (Palmach), Chief of Staff Moshe Dayan's offensive approach and sophistication, and the establishment of the OTRI. On the other hand, the period between the late 1940s and the early 1950s is portrayed as the first negative period in Israeli operational art, resulting from the disbandment of the Palmach by Prime Minister David Ben-Gurion during wartime. The paper refers to the Palmach's disbandment as a 'coup',[5] although the fact is that Ben-Gurion dissolved it into three IDF brigades in order to ensure the unity of command, and that Palmach members would form the backbone of the IDF's high command for many years to come. The post-1967 so-called 'long dark age' is explained by the myth of Israeli-armoured invincibility, the deterioration of operational art into a mere set of technical rules, and the detachment of the Israeli 'paradigm of offensive preemption' from the new strategic reality. The current poor condition of Israeli operational art is attributed to the OTRI's disbandment and the 'purge' undertaken by ex-Chief of Staff Dan Halutz of the institute's adherents among the senior IDF commanders, many of whom were 'Paras' (paratroopers) and former members of the special forces, mainly for 'political' reasons.[6] According to the paper's author, had the OTRI managed to spread its ideas among a greater number of commanders, the Second Lebanon War might well have looked differently, perhaps like a replica of Operation Defensive Shield. Throughout the paper, the author expresses regret that the institute invested in middle-rank commanders, many of whom left military service after a few years.

The poor state of the IDF's intellectualism is no novelty.[7] The explanation this paper offers for it, however, suffers from two major weaknesses. First, it has a strong personal and political bent. Israeli operational art is described as a struggle between the 'good guys', that is, the Palmach 'revolutionaries', Dayan, and the 'Paras', and the OTRI's team and supporters, on the one hand, and the 'bad guys', that is, Ben-Gurion, the square-headed, tank-centric school, and Chief of Staff Dan Halutz's general staff on the other. Second, it does not offer any clear sense of what should be considered good or bad operational art.

This chapter's focus is operational art and the IDF's assessment. It undertakes to analyse critically the reasons for both the rise and fall of Israeli operational art. The key to the issue, in a nutshell, is that, until the early 1970s, the dominance of high-intensity conflicts (HICs), the existence of clear objectives, and favourable conditions for manoeuvre on the battlefield enabled operational art to blossom. Since the early 1970s, however, new conditions have affected Israeli operational art negatively: the prevalence and dominance of low-intensity conflicts (LICs), the central role played by the tactical and grand-strategic levels of war at the expense of the operational and strategic levels, the ascendancy of firepower over manoeuvre, the cult of technology, and post-heroic tendencies. Both the previous rise and subsequent fall of operational art as a result of this change in conditions are reflected in the relative importance and role played by force multipliers employed by the IDF during its wars to compensate for its inferiority in the force ratios and cope with other strategic and operational constraints. The IDF's command system and its commanders' generalship were reflective of the above conditions and served as a facilitating or debilitating factor affecting the employment of the force multipliers.

The choice to focus here on force multipliers and the IDF's command system and its commanders' generalship stems from the fact that the concept of operational art has broadened so much that it has almost lost its coherence. By discussing it from a force multiplier point of view, one can relate, in a more concise and tangible way, to many of the issues often considered parts of operational art, such as the tension between strategic, operational, and tactical logic, objectives, and constraints; the tension between disrupting the enemy's effort and destroying its force; the tension between top-down and bottom-up effects; dilemmas concerning the preferred centres of gravity; the dilemma between decentralized and centralized command systems; inter-arm and inter-corps cooperation and jointness; the dynamic relationship between firepower and manoeuvre; and so on. As force multipliers have probably been the most typical Israeli way of compensating for its strategic vulnerabilities, they also seem to be tailor-made for the analysis of the unique characteristics of Israeli operational art.

THE RISE OF ISRAELI OPERATIONAL ART

The period up to the early 1970s was Israeli operational art's golden age. The principal security threat then was clearly and simply defined as one emanating from a 'conventional' attack by a coalition of Arab armies. The likelihood of quantitative inferiority in case of war against a coalition of enemies was great, creating the 'few-against-the-many' logic and ethos (which did not always match reality, as will be shown below) that propelled Israeli operational art to adopt and develop a series of force multipliers that would compensate for it. As the lack of strategic depth made the absorption of Arab attacks on Israeli territory intolerable, Israeli operational art opted for offence and first strike not only as force multipliers, but also as a means of creating artificial depth. Although Arab–Israeli inter-state military confrontations only rarely involved Israeli society directly, the belief that Israeli society and economy could not withstand protracted conflicts of an attritional nature moved towards blitzkrieg. Other reasons for blitzkrieg were the need to pre-empt superpower involvement or intervention during the war and the arrival of Arab expeditionary forces at the battlefronts. Israeli HICs were waged across the entire spectrum of the levels of war, with the operational level playing a central role. LICs were considered minor challenges, located on the geographical periphery; that is, the frontier areas.

Operational art demonstrated by the IDF during Israel's early wars would not have been imaginable without the existence of battlefield conditions favourable for manoeuvre. IDF commanders acted upon good intuition and rich experience gained throughout a number of HICs. Operations, particularly those carried out on the ground, were often characterized by non-linear thinking and abundant creativity, imagination, and audacity. A decentralized command system simultaneously reflected and encouraged these skills. A gap, however, existed between the great importance of the operational level, on the one hand, and the almost non-existent formal military thinking invested in it on the other.

The following sections present in more detail the conditions under which Israeli operational art developed from the late 1940s to the early 1970s, and the way it was applied.

Conditions

The challenge of general quantitative inferiority

Although Israel was surrounded by enemies from three directions, and despite the consequent worst-case-scenario assumption adopted by its war planners regarding a simultaneous multi-front and multi-enemy confrontation, in 1948–9, 1956, 1982, and 2006, the IDF did not suffer from quantitative inferiority on the battlefield. The following section refers to the early wars.

When the War of Independence broke out, the IDF did not yet exist as a regular army; it was gradually built during the fighting. Knowing how inferior the new state would be vis-à-vis the Arab world both demographically and militarily, the Israeli political leadership took a great risk by declaring independence when only a thread seemed to separate success from another tragedy for the Jewish people. The calculated risk succeeded, though, thanks not only to the wise military conduct of the war on the Israeli side and the quick shift from a militia force to a regular army, but also to the insufficient forces dispatched by the Arab states to the battlefield due to complacency regarding the chances of defeating the emerging IDF quickly, Jordan's defection from the Arab war coalition,[8] and the negative impact that the embargo declared and imposed by the great powers had on Jordan's and Egypt's war effort.[9] On the Israeli side, the embargo was bypassed thanks to a supply of weapons from Czechoslovakia—a Soviet satellite—and via illegal purchases in the United States. Israel was gradually able to balance Arab weapon-systems superiority, and the IDF even achieved air superiority in the later stages of the war.[10]

In 1956, Egypt fought alone against Israel, after its Arab allies—Syria and Jordan—preferred evasion to cooperation.[11] Thus, it was only in 1967 that the IDF found itself, for the first time, in a position of real quantitative inferiority (1:2.5), coping with it successfully thanks to two main factors. First, again, was the division within the Arab war coalition. Second was the application of force multipliers, which was feasible thanks to the ascendancy of manoeuvre over firepower on the battlefield, discussed in greater detail below.

The need for artificial strategic or operational depth

The fact that Israel lacked strategic or operational depth made it believe that it had to create such depth artificially by transferring the fighting onto the enemy's territory. After the Israeli withdrawal from the Sinai Desert in 1957, Israel enjoyed the benefit of strategic or, at least, operational depth on the Egyptian Front for the first time, as there was no significant Egyptian military presence in the Sinai thanks to Egypt's voluntary demilitarization of the peninsula. Had the Egyptians decided to initiate an attack on Israel, they would have been forced to cross hundreds of kilometres of desert on their way to the international border, allowing fresh Israeli forces time to mobilize, deploy, and counter-attack, taking advantage of the diminishing power of the Egyptian attack. The demilitarization of the Sinai was eventually violated by the Egyptians in May 1967.

The 1967 war started exactly from the classical situation that was considered *casus belli* for Israel and created an intolerable situation for the absorption of the enemy attack. The Egyptian and Israeli armies were both deployed along the international border, Egypt had already blocked the Straits of Tiran and formed an alliance with other Arab states, and Israel felt it had no choice but to make sure that the war was not waged on its own territory or began with an Arab first strike.

Favourable conditions for manoeuvre

Israeli operational art during the early HICs owed much of its good performance to the ascendancy of manoeuvre over firepower. The relatively convenient force-to-space ratio, coupled with the dominance of weapon systems capable of manoeuvring on the battlefield, particularly the tank, enabled the IDF to fight short and relatively cheap wars in 1956 and 1967, in which it launched the first strike and brought about the enemy's quick collapse, psychologically and/or physically.

In 1948–9, the number of Arab and Israeli brigades together deployed on the battlefronts was between twenty-five during most stages of the war and thirty at its final stage. Not only was that number far from creating density on the battlefield, the adversaries' forces were dispersed along four fronts. In 1956, Egyptian and Israeli forces deployed in the Sinai Peninsula did not exceed twenty brigades—again constituting a small number relative to the empty spaces of the desert, although the dunes sometimes limited mobility and manoeuvrability. In 1967, for the first time, the force-to-space ratio grew significantly—on the Sinai Front alone the number of brigades almost tripled, reaching fifty-five formations—but manoeuvrability was, nonetheless, retained.

Manoeuvrability depends, in part, on the nature of the dominant arm or the 'dominant weapon system', to use J. F. C. Fuller's terminology.[12] In 1948–9, infantry was still the dominant factor on the Arab–Israeli battlefield. The War of Independence's most important operations, such as Operation Danny on the Jordanian Front, Operation Hiram on the Lebanese Front, or Operations Yoav and Horev on the Egyptian Front, were all carried out primarily by infantry.

As a result of the huge psychological effect the Israeli armour had on the Arab forces in the Sinai in 1956, thanks to its mobility, firepower, and protection, the debate that took place prior to the war between the infantry school, headed by Chief of Staff Moshe Dayan, and the armour school, led by Generals Haim Laskov and Meir Zorea, was decided in favour of the latter. The armour became the dominant weapon system, constituting the backbone of Israeli manoeuvre, offence, and battlefield decision, although it needed the support of other arms and corps, particularly air power.

The 1967 Six Day War found the infantry's relative share in the ground forces' structure in considerable decline. The diminishing importance of the infantry was reflected in the infantry/armour quantitative ratio, which, by 1956, changed from 10:1 in the infantry's favour to 3:1, and, by 1967, was only 2:1.[13] During the 1967 war, spearhead tank battalions advanced continuously in the enemy's territory, sustained by the supply units that followed in their wake as part of what Edward Luttwak and Dan Horowitz called a 'linear integration' system, which was both crucial for and typical of blitzkrieg.[14]

Manoeuvre-enabled operational art

Quantitative inferiority—real or perceived, actual or potential—has always existed in the back of Israeli war planners' minds, dictating operational art that focused on compensating for such inferiority via a series of force multipliers. The most important force multiplier was offence, which constituted a form of war, campaign, or battle that was crucial for achieving a battlefield decision.

Offence

Despite their admiration for Clausewitz's teachings in general and his preference for defence, which he saw as the stronger form of war, in particular Moltke and Schlieffen became advocates of offence and indirect approach after having intellectually analysed the changes that took place on the battlefield as a result of the military-technological developments that followed the Industrial Revolution, as well as Germany's strategic circumstances. By contrast, IDF commanders have been completely unaware of the spectrum of opinions presented by military thinkers on the question of which form of war was stronger: offence or defence.[15] Their common sense and good intuition, however, guided them to prefer offence, based on the belief that it was perfectly suited to compensating for Israeli quantitative inferiority, because of the attacker's ability to choose the time and place where the confrontation would take place and concentrate forces at that point. Thanks to offence, Israel could also transfer the war to the enemy's territory so as to avoid the need to absorb an enemy attack on Israeli soil. As a battlefield decision could only be achieved via offence, manoeuvrability, which was a condition for a ground offence, served as an enabling factor. And, indeed, although, in principle, operational art is not confined to offence but is equally relevant to defence, since the War of Independence's first truce in the summer of 1948 Israel has opted for offence as its preferred form of war and campaign, not only in HICs, but also in low-intensity operations—a tradition that started with the pre-1956 reprisals carried out by Unit 101 and the paratroopers.

Indirect approach

Completely avoiding direct confrontation between enemies has always been wishful thinking, even in the eyes of thinkers, such as Sun Tzu or Liddell Hart, who saw a decision without battle as the ultimate military achievement one could imagine.[16] What the indirect approach can offer is a way of creating optimal conditions for encountering the enemy by upsetting its equilibrium before engaging it physically, and of minimizing the scope, intensity, duration, and casualties during military encounters. As such, it constitutes an important aspect of operational art. It is no wonder, therefore, that the IDF adopted it even without learning it from books.

Liddell Hart's biographer, who, like the great thinker himself, presented the IDF as one of his best pupils, cited Yitzhak Rabin's admission that the implementation of the indirect approach during the War of Independence had 'largely coincided with Israel's choice of methods designed to overcome her inferiority in arms and numbers and the vulnerability of her people and territory'.[17] Although IDF commanders were hardly exposed to Liddell Hart's writings,[18] here too they applied the indirect approach based on common sense and good intuition.

Three resounding failures of direct attacks on Latrun during the War of Independence, intended to open the way to the besieged Jerusalem, only heightened the awareness among Israeli commanders of the need for an indirect approach. And, indeed, most of the important successes of the indirect approach at the operational level during that war can be attributed to ground manoeuvres aimed at encircling or enveloping enemy troops: for example, the capture of the Arab towns of Lydda and Ramla during Operation Danny in the summer of 1948 following a pincer attack, the envelopment of Kaukji's liberation army during Operation Hiram in the autumn of that year, and the encirclement of the Egyptian forces during Operation Horev in December 1948–January 1949. During Operation Yoav on the Egyptian Front in the autumn of 1948, the indirect approach also took on other forms. For the first time, it was carried out via an air attack, with the bombing by the Israeli Air Force (IAF) of Gaza airport, which inflicted damage on Egyptian aircraft. On the ground, IDF troops managed to sever Egyptian transportation lines from Gaza to Rafah and from Iraq-al-Manshiya to Beit Jubrin, and to block the retreat lines of Egypt's main effort forces.

In 1956, IDF units were advancing quickly westward, deviating from Chief of Staff Moshe Dayan's instructions to avoid direct confrontation with the Egyptian strongholds by bypassing them. Two main Egyptian strongholds—Abu Agheila and Rafah—were captured, the former partially, on 31 October, in an indirect approach, and the latter completely, during the night of 31 October–1 November, in a direct approach. More typical of the indirect approach, however, was the 9th Brigade's advance along the eastern shore of the Gulf of Eilat, along an axis considered by the Egyptians impassable, culminating in a combined pincer attack on Sharm el-Sheikh by the 9th Brigade and the paratrooper brigade, after the latter arrived from the Mitla Pass.

In yet another aspect of the indirect approach, the IDF had left the capture of most of the Gaza Strip to the later stages of the war—2–3 November—until the Egyptian dispositions in the rear of the city of Gaza and Han Yunes fell into Israeli hands. In 1967, Egypt was expecting an attack at the central axis of the Sinai, as had occurred in 1956. The Israeli ground forces' main effort, however, was focused at the northern axis. Between the morning of 5 June and the morning of 6 June, the 7th Armoured Brigade manoeuvred in the direction of Rafah and el-Arish, penetrating between the 20th and 7th Egyptian Brigades. At the same time, paratroopers encircled Rafah from the south, attacking it from the supposedly impassable dunes. On 6 June, Tal's forces continued advancing westward towards el-Arish and the Suez Canal.

On the central axis, on 5 June, Abraham Yoffe's division moved towards Bir-Lakhfan. In a manoeuvre very similar to the one carried out by the IDF during Operation Horev in 1948–9, on 6 June, a brigade from Yoffe's division, led by Colonel Yishka Shadmi, penetrated between the Egyptian strongholds at the northern axis (where Israel Tal's division was fighting), and the central axis (where Sharon's division was advancing), heading to Bir Lakhfan, encountering only one Egyptian company on its way. Shadmi's brigade arrived at the Egyptian rear, blocking the reinforcement lines at Jebel Libni, thereby easing Tal's operational effort. On 7 June, tanks from Shadmi's brigade moved more than 150 kilometres among Egyptian forces in the direction of the Mitla and Gidi Passes, reaching them despite the difficulties. They blocked both passes with only nine tanks, keeping them closed until the retreating Egyptian forces were destroyed.

On the southern axis, late at night on 5 June, the Um Katef stronghold was attacked by Ariel Sharon's division, which followed in the footsteps of its reconnaissance unit that had moved along the northern flank of the stronghold in ostensibly impassable dunes. One paratrooper force waited for nightfall in order to land troops from helicopters in the Egyptian artillery's rear, managing to neutralize it. Having broken through the thin flank of the Egyptian trenches and having taken the northern segment of the trench system during the night, a path was opened in the morning of 6 June for Israeli tanks to engage the Egyptian armour in the perimeter.

The most notable expression of the indirect approach on the Jordanian Front was the envelopment carried out by combined forces from the central and northern commands. The attack was launched from the south (the Jerusalem area) and north (the Jenin area) along the mountainous terrain of East Samaria, forcing the Jordanians to retreat eastward. The fall of the Samaria region into Israeli hands triggered the collapse of the Judea region almost without a fight.

Concentration of forces

The IDF concentrated forces against the Arab war coalitions of 1948 and 1967 according to 'the logic of the few', determining in advance where the main effort would be built in order to amass sufficient forces at that point for achieving a battlefield decision. Further concentrations of forces were to follow sequentially on the other fronts or battle zones. A few examples will demonstrate the effect that a concentration of forces had on the force ratios at the operational level.

In the War of Independence, during Operation Yoav in the autumn of 1948 and the decisive Operation Horev in December 1948–January 1949, both against Egypt—the strongest link in the Arab coalition—the force ratios were 1:1 thanks to the concentration of forces, while in Operation Hiram in the autumn of 1948, on the weaker Lebanese Front, IDF forces enjoyed a quantitative edge of 1.3:1 over Kaukji's liberation army, again thanks to a concentration of forces.

In the Six Day War, which was also waged against an Arab coalition, the IDF compensated for its general quantitative inferiority by a sequential concentration of forces. On the Egyptian Front, the inferiority of 1:2.3 was balanced by air superiority, whereas on the remaining fronts the IDF enjoyed a quantitative equality, after having shifted forces from one front to another. In a calculated risk, which proved to be one of the principal reasons for its success in the 1967 war, Israel concentrated all of its combat-aircraft power during the initial stages of the war on the Egyptian Front for the aerial first strike, leaving almost no aircraft for the protection of the Israeli rear and the other fronts. The subsequent destruction of Arab air power served the war effort on the ground, making manoeuvre, offence, and blitzkrieg possible.

Against a single enemy and a single front, which was the case in 1956 thanks to Jordan's and Syria's defection from their coalition with Egypt,[19] the IDF enjoyed a superiority in force ratios, allowing itself initially to disperse its forces with the aim of concentrating them later on, once the weaker points in the enemy deployment had been identified. The deliberate dispersion of forces as a temporary step in order to force the enemy to disperse as well, since it cannot be certain where the adversary's main effort will be made, is compatible with the spirit of the indirect approach and can be found in both Jomini's and Liddell Hart's recipes.[20] It is true, however, that such a modus operandi is often a luxury reserved for those enjoying quantitative superiority and is typical of mountainous-terrain warfare, which Israel employed in 1967 on the Northern Front (see below).

Interestingly, at the strategic level, the IDF tended to adopt a Clausewitzian logic, whereby it is only the defeat of the stronger link in the enemy's chain that could ensure its defeat in the entire war. Such logic was implemented by the IDF in 1948–9, when Prime Minister David Ben-Gurion instructed the concentration of as many forces as possible on the Egyptian Front during Operations Yoav and Horev, standing firm against objections by senior commanders, such as the chief of operations and acting chief of staff Yigael Yadin, who were reluctant to leave only a small force on the Jordanian Front lest the Jordanians and the Iraqis should decide to attack Israel while most of its forces were assembled against the Egyptians.[21]

In 1967, Egypt was chosen to be the first target for attack, as the Israeli high command believed that defeating it would significantly weaken the Arab war coalition and bring about its collapse. A concentration of forces was also implemented on each of the battlefronts. On the Egyptian Front, the main effort was built at the northern axis of the Sinai Peninsula, and on the Jordanian Front it was built in Samaria. On the Northern Front, where the IDF had to overcome Syrian fortifications located in steep mountainous terrain, Israel started its offensive with a broad-front attack—advancing along five different axes simultaneously—which is compatible with the 'logic of the many' and mountainous-terrain warfare. Having identified two weak points in the Syrian deployment—at the northern and central axes—the IDF concentrated its force against them. Attacking sequentially was possible in 1967 thanks to the IDF's blitzkrieg capabilities, which quickly enabled a battlefield decision on each front, and the concentration of air power.

Another difference between concentrating forces against a coalition as opposed to a single enemy in the Israeli case pertained to the force-concentration aspect of operating on interior or exterior lines. When fighting against a single enemy at the strategic level, the IDF preferred operating on exterior lines, as evidenced in 1956 and partly in 1982. Multi-enemy and multi-front conditions, on the other hand, imposed fighting on interior lines strategically, but allowed operating on exterior lines at the lower operational and tactical levels, as was demonstrated in 1948–9, for example, in Operations Hiram and Horev, and in 1967.

If, until the Six Day War, Israel's interior lines were short and as such could contribute to the quick transfer of forces from one front to another, after having captured the territories Israeli interior lines became much longer, negatively affecting the IDF's ability to enjoy its advantages, as was proved in the 1973 October War.

First strike

The idea of a first strike shares the same spirit as Sun Tzu's notion of attacking the enemy's war plans or strategy as a centre of gravity,[22] except that Sun Tzu thought of disrupting the enemy's war effort by non-military actions, whereas, in the Israeli case, disruption was to be achieved via actual use of force, preferably by launching a first strike in the form of either prevention (as in 1956) or preemption (1967). Although delivering a first strike has never been an explicit principle in Israeli war doctrine, Israelis have always believed that striking first, if only possible with the backing of a great power or a superpower, might have an irreversible effect on the enemy. And, indeed, both in 1956 and in 1967, the first strike had a considerable negative effect on the Arab war effort.

In 1956, the initial stages of the Israeli ground first strike were disguised as a reprisal operation, in order to enable the withdrawal from the Sinai without losing face should France and Britain fail to live up to their commitment to join the war. But once they did join, their aerial first strike on Egypt had a great impact on Israeli ground operations, creating favourable conditions for achieving a quick battlefield decision on the ground. In 1967, the IAF's first strike (code-named Operation Moked) destroyed the Arab air forces on the ground. Some 450 aircraft were destroyed within hours. The Israeli attack was launched in the morning, at a perfect time—when the commander of the Egyptian army, Field Marshall Abd al-Hakim Amer, and other senior Egyptian commanders were on their way to visit an airbase in the Sinai, and when the Egyptian troops were occupied with routine preparations for a new day. The attack resulted in Israeli air supremacy, which contributed heavily to the ground effort.

Blitzkrieg

Putting aside the question of whether blitzkrieg is a strategy or a tactic, a doctrine or warfare,[23] it was one of Israel's best expressions of operational art. It brought about the enemy's psychological collapse, shortened the war's duration, and achieved a battlefield decision before the superpowers or a significant number of Arab expeditionary forces had the chance to intervene. Blitzkrieg was first applied in 1956 but reached its peak in 1967 thanks to the fast advance of Israeli tanks into enemy territory, which was effectively supported by a decentralized logistical system and aerial protection and enabled by a mission-oriented command and control system and the high quality of field commanders (see below).

The operational plan prepared by Chief of Staff Moshe Dayan prior to the 1956 war constituted, perhaps for the first time in Israel, a clear blitzkrieg orientation. Dayan's instructions to the forces were to advance as quickly as possible in the Sinai while bypassing the enemy's main strongholds and avoiding frontal engagements. The main idea of the deep penetration was to arrive in the Suez Canal area as soon as possible, serving as a pretext for the great powers to issue an ultimatum to both Israel and Egypt to withdraw from the canal zone; otherwise, they would have to intervene. Egypt's expected refusal to comply would then serve as the trigger for such intervention. In practice, though, neither the IDF's attack on Abu Agheila nor the one on Rafah was indirect. The IDF troops faced great difficulties in capturing the strongholds, but that became considerably easier following the Egyptian high command's retreat order that had been issued on 1 November after the great powers' attack in the canal zone.

Ironically, the seeds of Israeli tank-based blitzkrieg were sown in the Sinai War as a result of an unauthorized movement of the 7th Armoured Brigade. The commanding officer of the Southern Command, Colonel Assaf Simhonni, violated Dayan's explicit instruction to refrain from using armour during the initial stages of the war in order to lower the profile of the Israeli operations in the Sinai until the great powers joined the war. Once they were given the order to move, Israeli tanks took part in the fighting at the northern and central axes, advancing long distances each day without major technical problems. Had it not been for a fledgling logistical system (which was not yet sufficiently adjusted to support the blitzkrieg); the limited mobility of the infantry, the artillery, and the engineering corps; and the direct confrontations with Egyptian strongholds, the IDF might have completed its missions even faster.

During the mid-1960s, the IDF underwent major logistical reform. From then on, divisions or brigades were directly in charge of 'pushing' supplies to their own forces along the lines of operation.[24] The motivation to do so was high, the communication lines were relatively short, and personal acquaintances between the providers of supplies and the fighting forces made the mission simpler.

Experience-based generalship and a decentralized command system

Faithful to the IDF's traditional performance-oriented approach, common sense, and improvisation skills, most IDF commanders would enthusiastically agree with the editor of this volume that carrying out operations is something commanders must have at their fingertips, which both contemporary and classical military thinkers have referred to as creativity, *coup d'œil*, or genius.[25] The fact that, during Israel's early wars, up until the late 1960s/early 1970s, IDF commanders often demonstrated exceptional skills in operational art cannot be ignored. Being 'practical soldiers',[26] however, they put their faith in experience and experience-based intuition rather than any intellectually acquired knowledge,[27] taking advantage of battlefield conditions that were favourable to manoeuvre in order to carry out a series of manoeuvre-based force multipliers. The IDF also proved that compensating for quantitative inferiority is not confined to the operational level, but rather can and should take place at every level of war, including tactical-level confrontations, which are often referred to by operational-art adherents as 'attrition'.[28]

During Israel's early decades, the IDF developed a decentralized mission-oriented command system without explicit reference to foreign models. According to Israeli military historian Martin van Creveld, even if it had been inspired by the German *Auftragstaktik*, this could not be acknowledged due to the sensitivities entailed in referring to any German system.[29] Two dominant figures were the command system's spiritual fathers—Chief of Staff Dayan in the mid-1950s and Chief of Staff Yitzhak Rabin in the pre-1967 years.[30]

Since in 1956 it was imperative that the IDF reached the Suez Canal zone as quickly as possible, Dayan shaped the operational efforts as separate campaigns, trusting field commanders at all levels that they would understand what had to be done and how and when to do it, in order to achieve the strategic and operational objectives without further instructions. Commanders were allotted free rein in making their own operational and tactical decisions with maximum flexibility, as long as they adhered to the assigned objectives and missions,[31] and maintained the unity of command. Indeed, Dayan preferred commanders who pushed forward, even if this sometimes entailed unauthorized actions, such as the advance of the 7th Armoured Brigade or the advance of paratroopers led by Ariel Sharon into the Mitla Pass, both in 1956, or the advance of forces from Israel Tal's division to the Suez Canal in 1967 despite an explicit order by Defence Minister Dayan to stop a few kilometres away from the canal. Likewise, the 1967 blitzkrieg would not have been possible had each operational effort been closely controlled from above and constrained by advanced planning.

THE FALL OF ISRAELI OPERATIONAL ART

Affected by the 'aura of prestige' that surrounded the IDF after the 1967 war, the Israeli sense of severe threat was replaced by complacency to the point of hubris. As a result of the 1973 October War, the IDF undertook a major quantitative increase in the hope of neutralizing its dependence on sequential concentrations of forces. In the wake of the peace with Egypt and Jordan and the stable disengagement agreement with Syria—which, virtually isolated, was left behind—the Israeli siege mentality started to diminish.

On the other hand, the relatively convenient enemies of the past, who, time and again, had demonstrated a lack of sophistication, imagination, boldness, and cohesion, became much more sophisticated, both operationally and technologically. Egyptian post-1967 strategy was tailor-made for its real military capabilities. The Palestinians have demonstrated flexibility in challenging Israel by alternately using guerrilla tactics, terror, and civil disobedience, and Hezbollah's fighters have been highly motivated, well trained and equipped, and have used simple but effective technology and psychological warfare, which no revolution in military affairs (RMA)-inspired doctrine can cope with effectively.[32]

Israeli fortifications along the Suez Canal after 1967 and its settlements along and within the new post-1967 borders created a territorial reality that denied strategic or operational depth. Only in the wake of the peace process with Egypt did the Sinai again become a buffer zone, as it had been during the period 1957–67. Waves of Palestinian terror within the territories and the Green Line have been another manifestation of the futility of Israeli dreams of strategic or operational depth in the West Bank. Furthermore, transferring the war to the enemy's territory—as Israel did in 1956, 1967, and 1973—became almost irrelevant and even too risky in an LIC-dominated reality.

A combination of developments has taken the sting out of the IDF's operational art. Influential, in particular, have been the LIC and the attritional nature of the conflicts that have engaged Israel, the ascendancy of firepower over manoeuvre, the cult of technology, post-heroic norms, the strengthening of linear thinking, and commanders' lack of real combat experience. These new conditions and their impact on Israeli operational art will be elaborated below.

Conditions

The transition from HICs to LICs

The 1973 October War was the last purely HIC confrontation. Once Egypt opted for peace, the likelihood of Arab–Israeli HICs decreased considerably. With the growing terror challenges in the 1980s, LIC challenges have started being referred to as a strategic threat to Israel, and Israeli military operations have been conducted against non-state players (the limited confrontation with Syrian troops in Lebanon in 1982 excluded). Paradoxically, the shift from HICs to LICs constituted a deterioration in the challenges confronting the IDF. In LICs, the manoeuvre, which is usually necessary for an operational and strategic decision, loses much of its importance. The fear that capturing territory in future wars might lead to another protracted war of attrition of an LIC nature channelled the IDF to adopt an operational conception that focused on firepower rather than ground manoeuvre, which was supposed to apply to LIC too,[33] something that augurs badly for operational art.

Years of policing missions in the territories have weakened the IDF's operational skills against regular and semi-regular/hybrid challenges even further. Many of the IDF's weaknesses that were exposed during the Second Lebanon War derived from the nature of the IDF's activities in the territories. This should not have come as a surprise. In the late 1980s, Martin van Creveld started talking and writing about what policing missions would do to the IDF. In 1998, more than a decade after the outbreak of the first intifada, he warned that 'ten years of trying to deal with the intifada have sapped the IDF's strength by causing troops and commanders to adapt to the enemy. The troops now look at mostly empty-handed Palestinian men, women, and children as if they were in fact a serious military threat'.[34] As if predicting the IDF's poor performance during the Second Lebanon War, van Creveld added: 'Among the commanders, the great majority can barely remember when they trained for and engaged in anything more dangerous than police-type operation; in the entire IDF there is now hardly any officer left who has commanded so much as a brigade in real war'.[35] Before the war, at least two general staff members, Generals Yishai Boer and Yiftah Ron-Tal, warned of the negative implications of the preoccupation with policing missions in the territories, claiming that the IDF was losing its manoeuvrability and conventional fighting capability.[36]

If until May 2000 the IDF had gained some operational experience from fighting against Hezbollah in southern Lebanon, following its withdrawal to the international border in mid-2000, fighting terrorists and suicide bombers became the IDF's almost sole source of combat experience. Israeli troops became used to confronting a numerically inferior and poorly trained and equipped opponent, enjoying excellent tactical and operational intelligence provided by military intelligence and the General Security Service (GSS), massive logistical and technical support, and a familiarity with the combat zones in which they had been fighting for many years.

None of these advantages that the IDF enjoyed in the territories were present during the war in the summer of 2006. Hezbollah's fighters were highly motivated, and well trained and equipped. The tactical intelligence—if any—that was provided to the ground troops by military intelligence was of low quality, compared to the high-quality intelligence provided by the GSS on the territories and on southern Lebanon prior to the 2000 withdrawal. Commanders lacked experience in operating large formations in general and armoured formations in particular. Logistical support was rather ineffective, and some of the fighting took place in unfamiliar terrain.

The decline of the strategic and operational levels of war

Whereas 'regular' war is usually waged across the entire range of the levels-of-war pyramid, in wars of attrition in general and LICs in particular military encounters often take place at the tactical level, usually limited in terms of forces, time, or place. On the other hand, the objectives of those engaged in such conflicts and sometimes also the targets they choose to hit are beyond the direct battlefield at the grand-strategic level; that is, the enemy's society and economy. Tactical achievements or failures are often directly translated into achievements or failures at the grand-strategic level. This happens because the weaker side seeks to bypass confrontation at the strategic and operational levels of war because it acknowledges the stronger side's edge at these levels. Israel has been experiencing this reality since the late 1970s/early 1980s, both in the territories and from southern Lebanon. Egypt started the 1969–70 War of Attrition based on the same logic, except that, instead of attacking Israeli civilians directly, it assumed that the war along the canal would indirectly weaken Israeli society and the economy, as a result of the casualties and the economic price inflicted.

For their part, state players engaged in LICs or wars of attrition are sometimes tempted to take advantage of their operational and strategic superiority for initiating large-scale operations in order to put an end to the weaker side's modus operandi. And indeed, after becoming easily frustrated by the elusiveness of guerrillas and terrorists, Israel's response to Palestinian terror from Lebanon in the late 1970s/early 1980s included two large-scale operations—Operation Litani (1978) and Peace for the Galilee ([1982], which later escalated into a war). In 2002, during the second intifada, Israel launched Operation Defensive Shield, a large-scale operation in the West Bank. Against Hezbollah, the IDF launched three large-scale operations—Accountability (1993), Grapes of Wrath (1996), and Changing Direction ((2006), which later became the Second Lebanon War). The effectiveness of these operations varied; some, for example Defensive Shield and Changing Direction, had longer-term effectiveness, while the effect of other operations proved to be limited or temporary.[37]

The voices calling for crushing terror notwithstanding, both the IDF and the political echelon eventually understood that, for coping with national uprisings and terror, purely military skills would be insufficient. Instead, a multidimensional approach must be adopted that combines military and non-military means. And, indeed, unlike most of its previous LICs, when it had merely been using force, during the intifadas closures, sieges, and other measures aimed at the enemy's society and economy became part of the IDF's modus operandi, proving to be no less effective. For a military whose expertise was the employment of violent means, this was a sobering experience.

This does not mean that non-military dimensions that have characterized modern, not to mention postmodern, war have necessarily become an integral part of operational art or should be treated as such.[38] Too broad an interpretation of operational art, which includes, for example, 'consciousness-shaping operations'—a concept spread by the OTRI against the backdrop of the second intifada,[39] which was aimed at both the enemy's and one's own society—blurs the distinction between operations and grand strategy. We have already witnessed similar attempts to offer too broad a meaning to security, which have caused the concept to lose much of its clarity.[40]

The ascendancy of firepower over manoeuvre as a major impediment

The ascendancy of firepower over manoeuvre on the Arab–Israeli battlefield in the post-1967 period was a result of technological changes that introduced to the scene precise, long-range, and much more destructive weapon systems, and an Arab effort to limit the IDF's manoeuvrability, which the Arab countries considered the major reason for their defeat in the Six Day War.

From an Israeli perspective, strengthened firepower has had three negative aspects. First, the increasing range and accuracy of modern weaponry have created a battlefield density that limits the scope for manoeuvre no less than the density stemming from the volume of force relative to space.[41] In the wake of their defeat in 1967, Arab armies have focused their efforts on neutralizing the freedom of action of Israeli armour and air power.[42] During the 1969–70 War of Attrition, it became evident that technological developments were limiting Israeli offensive capabilities. It seemed that, for the first time, the IAF was losing the battle against the Egyptian and Soviet missile belt.[43] Shortly after the August 1970 ceasefire came into effect, the Soviets deployed missile batteries along the Suez Canal. This was later referred to as the first practical Egyptian step towards the 1973 October War.[44]

In 1972, Israeli military officials started warning that the Arabs already possessed thousands of anti-tank missiles,[45] and that every single kilometre of the front was covered by dense Arab fire, consisting of large quantities of anti-tank weapons of various types, many of which were cheap and simple, and some 20 tanks, 2,000 anti-tank mines, 150–200 artillery guns, and other automatic weapons.[46] In the air, aptly described as a 'Maginot Line in the sky', a combined anti-aircraft system—consisting of SAM-2s, SAM-3s, SAM-6s, SAM-7s, and guns, the most effective of which was the ZPU-23-4—posed a serious threat to the IAF. The various components of this anti-aircraft system complemented each other in terms of range and altitude, thereby creating a very difficult-to-penetrate wall of fire.[47]

These developments were reflected in the heavy losses inflicted on the IAF during the initial stages of the 1973 October War. As the war started with an Arab initiative and the Israelis were caught by surprise, the IAF, instead of destroying Arab surface-to-air missiles (SAMs) before carrying out tactical missions on the battlefield, as required by its doctrine, was forced to reverse the sequence. The result was that most of the IAF's losses were caused by anti-aircraft weapon systems.

On the ground, Israeli tanks arrived at the front from the rear in small bursts. Instead of being operated in armour fists, as armoured warfare requires, they were thrown into battle in a dispersed manner, becoming easy prey for anti-tank hunters. By 14 October, the IDF had lost some 500 tanks on the Egyptian Front. At least 25 per cent of the attrition suffered by the Israeli-armoured corps was inflicted by anti-tank weapon systems, mostly Sagger missiles and rocket-propelled grenades (RPGs).[48] The attrition rates in 1973, however, were lower than the ones in 1967—23 per cent and 40 per cent, respectively—the reason being the IDF's tactical flexibility in coping with surprise and the resourcefulness of its commanders. Not only did Israeli tank crews apply new tactics for evading anti-tank missiles within a short period of time, they also dealt with the challenge in an inter-corps effort. Once they were joined by infantry and artillery, the problem was solved.[49] All this would have been unnecessary had the military and political echelons accepted Defence Minister Dayan's advice to retreat to the Gidi and Mitla Passes, and defend from there with small forces, until conditions were ripe to counter-attack in an organized and orderly manner.[50]

The traditional reason for battlefield density, that is, force-to-space ratio, continued to play a role as well. In 1973, density on the Southern Front was created as a result of the fact that the fighting took place along the 160-kilometre-long Suez Canal zone, where some 80 per cent of the Egyptian tanks were concentrated. And in Lebanon, in 1982, Israel concentrated a huge number of forces relative to space: two armoured divisions in a 160-by-30-kilometre terrain compartment in the Lebanon Mountains and two-and-a-half armoured divisions in a compartment of 30-by-10 kilometres in the Beka Valley.[51] The combination of high force-to-space ratios and mobility constraints due to the mountainous terrain created density that hardly enabled manoeuvring or employing great portions of the force. Whereas in 1956 and 1967 IDF troops advanced hundreds of kilometres a day, in 1973 and 1982 their advance could be measured by a few kilometres or dozens at most.

A second negative repercussion of the ascendancy of firepower has already been referred to: that is, the lesser effectiveness vis-à-vis LIC challenges. Firepower's destruction effect is usually more limited against an insurgency than against a regular army or a national infrastructure due to guerrillas' low signature. This was amply demonstrated during the Second Lebanon War, when both air power and artillery failed to deliver,[52] and Israel was forced by the United States to refrain from attacking Lebanese infrastructure targets, since the US administration considered Lebanon's pro-Western government one of its greatest achievements in the quest for democratization of the Middle East.

A third negative aspect of the ascendancy of firepower has been the temptation to conduct battles from headquarters and/or via plasma screens. Following the Second Lebanon War, both Chief of Staff Dan Halutz and former deputy chief of staff Matan Vilnai pointed to one of the reasons for the difficulties the IDF faced on the battlefield—the tendency of senior commanders to manage the battle not by leading their troops on the battlefield, but from their headquarters.[53] (For further discussion, see below.)

At the same time, the ascendancy of firepower has also had three positive aspects. First, it has the ability to transfer the war to the enemy's territory via fire (see discussion of offence below). Second, given the constraints on manoeuvre, it is no longer unimaginable to think in terms of firepower-facilitated manoeuvre, something that had previously been confined to the tactical level. And, indeed, as was proved by the IAF's attack on the Syrian SAM missiles in the Beka Valley in 1982, precision technology can effectively pave the way for ground manoeuvre. Third, technology can be mobilized for counter-terror missions, as was proven by Israeli-targeted killings during the second intifada.[54]

The positive aspects have, in recent years, been reflected in a new Israeli operational conception, which stipulates that firepower and the aerial dimension in general and stand-off fire in particular play a central role on the battlefield, decreasing friction, making traditional large-scale and deep ground manoeuvres as well as the capture of enemy territory much less necessary, if not obsolete, and avoiding the price entailed by a protracted presence in hostile territory.[55]

Post-heroic warfare and its repercussions

Another factor that has strongly worked against ground manoeuvres is the post-heroic state of mind that took hold of Israeli military operations from the late 1970s. Post-heroic warfare has two major rules: first, one is not allowed to get killed[56]; second, one is not allowed to kill enemy civilians. The explanation for the Israeli post-heroic attitude seems to be threefold: technological developments, the liberal-democratic values of the country, and the non-existential nature of LICs.

The IDF demonstrated early signs of adhering to the first rule of post-heroic warfare during the 1978 Litani operation against the Palestine Liberation Organization (PLO) on the Lebanese border, when it preferred using massive fire at the expense of quick manoeuvring on the ground in order to avoid or at least reduce its troop casualties.[57] During Operations Accountability (1993) and Grapes of Wrath (1996), Israel preferred responding to Hezbollah's high-trajectory fire by firepower rather than manoeuvre. It managed to maintain its presence in Lebanon for more than twenty years—from 1978 to 2000—thanks to the fact that the number of soldiers killed in battle, some twenty-five a year, was sustainable. A shift, however, started taking place after post-heroic warfare's first rule—avoid your own troop casualties—was broken in February 1997 when a helicopter crash over the Galilee claimed the lives of seventy-three Israeli troops on their way to Lebanon, and the casualties inflicted on Israeli troops in Wadi Saluki in August 1997 (five soldiers) and during the September 1997 elite commando unit operation in southern Lebanon (twelve soldiers). In 1999, Chief of Staff Shaul Mofaz admitted that the IDF was now relying on air activity against Hezbollah, rather than activities on the ground, so as to reduce Israeli casualties.[58] In 1996, the second rule was violated, when during Operation Grapes of Wrath some 100 Lebanese civilians were inadvertently killed by Israeli fire, which prompted a halt to the entire operation. After 1997, the voices calling for a withdrawal from southern Lebanon, spearheaded by the anti-war Four Mothers movement, were listened to attentively, and the door for the 2000 withdrawal was opened.

Likewise, during the intifadas, Israel behaved post-heroically. Engagement regulations were adapted so as to provide Israeli troops with the tools to cope with situations where unarmed civilians were involved.[59] The IDF also developed and used non-lethal and less lethal weapons. Since the mid-1990s, Research and Development (R&D) units in the Israeli Defence Ministry have focused on developing technologies to be used in asymmetric conflicts, whose main purpose is to increase the combat effectiveness of Israeli troops while reducing troop and enemy civilian casualties.[60] Israeli fighting tactics were also adapted to post-heroic warfare's rules. Notwithstanding the suicide bombings of the second intifada, Israel made an effort to uphold post-heroic warfare's second rule. Even targeted killings, which became a major counter-terror method, were compatible with the notion of discriminate use of force, with the number of innocent civilians killed during these actions dropping consistently over the years.[61]

The commitment to post-heroic warfare also cast its shadow over the Second Lebanon War, this time with a negative effect on Israeli operational effectiveness. According to an operational plan (Country Shield), which was prepared a few years before the outbreak of the Second Lebanon War, the IDF was supposed to take control of southern Lebanon from the Litani River south (the 'hammer') and from the Lebanon–Israel border north (the 'anvil'). This initial stage was to be followed by a two-week stage of controlling the territory via fire and small units. A six-week period seemed to be sufficient for neutralizing the Katyusha threat by hunting as many launchers as possible. Once completed, the IDF troops were to disengage and return to Israel. Bearing in mind Israeli society's loss aversion, Country Shield's planners aimed at crippling Hezbollah with minimal Israeli casualties.[62] The IDF also prepared an alternative plan (Ice Breaker), which tried to avoid a large-scale ground manoeuvre and focused on stand-off fire.[63]

When the war started, even the relatively moderate Country Shield plan was considered by the political and military echelons to be too costly. In cabinet meetings during the war, ministers warned against a ground operation due to its death toll.[64] Throughout the war, IAF fighter-bombers flew at high altitude in order to avoid pilot casualties.[65] Every casualty was reported to the chief of staff, and there was a case in which an entire battle was stopped because of one casualty.[66] An investigation committee, headed by General (ret.) Yoram Yair, found that, during the war, commanders' sense of responsibility for the lives of their troops overshadowed their commitment to fulfil their missions. Chief of Staff Dan Halutz admitted that a 'no-casualties' approach penetrated the Israeli military mentality as a result of the IDF's preoccupation with terror challenges.[67]

The decline of the IDF's traditional force multipliers

Once technology impinged on the IDF's force build-up and military operations, operational art was the first to pay the price. Former director of the research and development directorate at the Ministry of Defence, General Isaac Ben-Israel, advocated a technology-focused military doctrine, force design, and build-up, identifying military quality with hi-tech capabilities.[68] Similar views have been expressed by other Israeli military experts, such as Shmuel Gordon, who preached a fire-based substitute for Liddell Hart's indirect approach.[69]

And, indeed, each of Israel's traditional force multipliers has been affected by technological developments, particularly by the ascendancy of firepower over manoeuvre, as described below.

Offence/defence

Once manoeuvre became limited after 1967, a gap arose between the IDF's traditional unequivocal commitment to offence and its feasibility. In 1973, the strategic surprise by which Israel was caught, the saturation of the battlefield with forces and firepower, and the constraints on mobility as a result of the nature of the terrain, particularly the sandy Sinai Desert, caused great difficulty for air and ground offensives. At the same time, at least in principle, offence could benefit from improved firepower, particularly if the attacker—in this case, Israel—enjoyed dominance in battlefield knowledge (DBK), which could dramatically increase the level of attrition inflicted upon the Arab enemy while ensuring greater survivability for Israel's own troops.[70] Another positive option that emerged was the ability to transfer the war to the enemy's territory, attacking it via fire. These benefits, however, seemed to apply to HICs rather than LICs, as was proved in 2006, when the IDF's firepower superiority was not translated into battlefield success. But Israel has not waged pure HICs for more than thirty-five years now, so this has become much more than a temporary or one-off problem.

For the defender, the ascendancy of firepower has become an asset, again, first and foremost, if not only in HIC situations. As Prime Minister Ehud Olmert stated, 'once upon a time we were frightened by the idea that Syrian armoured divisions could just roll onto Israeli territory. Now we live in a new reality, having the tools for containing ground attack without capturing even one inch of Syrian land, and . . . capable of deciding such a campaign . . . from a distance'.[71]

Remnants of indirect approach

After the early 1970s, only little was left of the traditional Israeli indirect approach, which had been the jewel in the crown of its operational art. Its spirit, however, could occasionally still be found, particularly among the older generation of IDF commanders. It is no wonder, therefore, that two of the three following examples of the indirect approach—two successes and one failure—were connected to Ariel Sharon, who belonged to this generation. The first example is the crossing of the Suez Canal in October 1973. From a geographical/physical point of view, breaking through the Egyptians' deployment at a point where 80 per cent of their tanks were concentrated rather than operating in the empty spaces in their flanks and rear constituted a direct approach. The reason for the IDF crossing at the enemy's strongest point was a lack of sufficient crossing equipment, which made the outflanking of the Egyptian forces via the Red Sea unfeasible. Psychologically, though, the Israelis took advantage of the Egyptian failure to live up to Napoleon's thirty-fourth maxim, in which he warned against leaving 'intervals by which the enemy can penetrate between corps [. . .] unless it be to draw him into a snare'.[72] Attacking between the 2nd and 3rd Egyptian Armies—where the enemy was not expecting an attack—was compatible with the notion of the indirect approach. Once Israeli forces crossed the canal, taking advantage of the failure of the Egyptian 14 October offensive that had cost the Egyptians heavy losses, and reached manoeuvre spaces, the old 'package' of manoeuvrability, offence, and battlefield decision was revived.

The second example is the attempt to envelop Syrian troops in Lebanon during the 1982 war. It was again Ariel Sharon—this time not in uniform but as defence minister—who was responsible for the plan that reminded Prime Minister Menahem Begin of Hannibal's Battle of Cannae, during which the great Carthaginian commander applied a double envelopment of the Romans. Unlike Hannibal, who did not plan to give the enemy any chance to escape, Sharon was sure that the Syrians would withdraw after realizing that the Israelis were encircling them from three different directions—the Beka Valley (the 'anvil') and the central and western axes (the 'hammers'). There was one major problem, though: the Syrians did not cooperate with Sharon's plan.

The third example pertains to the battles waged by the paratrooper brigade under the command of Colonel Yoram Yair, also during the 1982 Lebanon War, which served the achievement of the operational objective. The paratroopers first outflanked the enemy by landing on the seashore near the mouth of the Awali River, and then advanced from south-west to north-east in the mountains, encircling Beirut and bypassing the seashore axis. Despite strong Syrian and Palestinian resistance, both in the mountains and in the streets of the Lebanese towns and villages on their way, the paratroopers coped with the challenges efficiently until they managed to take control of the Syrian outer defence belt around Beirut and accomplish the mission of joining up with the Christian-Lebanese allies north of the city.[73]

The 2006 war reflected a significant decline in the indirect approach. Israeli ground activity consisted of transparent manoeuvres, something that operational art does not tolerate, unless such manoeuvres are carried out for deception purposes. Had the IDF truly been committed to its sophisticated indirect-approach tradition, its ground operations would have opened by quickly outflanking and encircling the enemy and using the element of surprise to capture the northern parts of southern Lebanon first. An indirect approach *à la* Sun Tzu or Liddell Hart would have caused confusion among the enemy ranks and might have brought about its psychological collapse much better than the Clausewitzian direct approach, which enabled Hezbollah to recover and stand strong. Contrary to operational art's preference for a top-down effect, IDF ground troops were engaged in a Sisyphean effort to translate achievements in numerous battles into operational and strategic gains.

It may be true that the IDF had planned an operation based on a 'sophisticated blend of amphibious, airborne and ground penetrations to swiftly extend deep into the front, before rolling back, so as to destroy Hezbollah positions one by one from the rear, all the way back to the Israeli border'.[74] Given Israel's failure to incapacitate Hezbollah's political and ideological leadership, and based on the assumption that ground operations were inevitable in light of the war objectives, the air campaign during the initial stages of the war should have been followed by a large-scale ground operation aimed at achieving a battlefield decision or, at least, capturing the areas from which the Katyushas were fired.

Failure to concentrate forces at the strategic and operational levels in 1973

In 1973, the IDF found itself, for the first time, unable to concentrate force at the strategic level. The Arab coalition members took advantage of their quantitative superiority and their strategic surprise's effect in order to split the Israeli forces strategically between the Egyptian and the Syrian Fronts. Once the Peled Division—the ground forces' only reserve force—was allocated to the Northern Front at the early stages of the war, the IDF had no strategic reserves left. Given the longest interior lines Israel had ever been operating on, which stretched from the Suez Canal zone and the Golan Heights, reinforcing one of the fronts with a division engaged in fighting on another front would have meant that a significant force would be missing as a fighting force for no less than thirty-six hours—something that the IDF could not afford under the circumstances. At the operational level, the 8 October simultaneous counter-attack on the Northern and Southern Fronts, as well as the dispersed manner in which Israeli tanks were operating at the early stages of the war, were reflective of the failure to concentrate forces at that level, too.

Concentration of fire replacing concentration of forces

The ability to concentrate rapidly or disperse long-range and precise fire without any manoeuvre has made the dilemmas of concentration versus dispersion, typical of manoeuvre-oriented operations, much easier to solve. It has already caused the distinction between interior and exterior lines to lose much of its relevance. On the other hand, as was proved during the Second Lebanon War, in counter-insurgency operations a concentration of fire has a much smaller effect than ground manoeuvres, both physically (capturing territory) and psychologically. Moreover, the enemy, too, can concentrate fire, and if it launches rockets into the enemy's land—in this case, Israel—as did the Palestinians and Hezbollah from the early 1980s, then firepower may serve as a technological force multiplier for the weak, which can balance the stronger side's edge.

Prior to the Second Lebanon War, the notion of diffused warfare took hold of the IDF. Diffused warfare is based on the assumption made by many RMA thinkers that a fundamental shift has taken place from campaigns consisting of horizontal clashes between rival forces, which entail breaking through the opponent's layers of defence and proceeding along distinct lines with distinct start and finish lines, to diffused confrontation that takes place simultaneously on the entire battlespace, distributing the force's mass to a multitude of separate pressure points, rather than concentrating it on assumed centres of gravity.[75] Diffused warfare constitutes a challenge to the notion of concentration, which was typical of strategy at all levels, but failed to prove its effectiveness in 2006. It seems to have taken strategy back to the times when the accumulation of numerous tactical successes was supposed to be translated into operational or strategic success.

Other RMA-inspired notions adopted by the IDF were 'effects-based operations' (EBO)[76] and 'swarming'. Not only is the idea of 'effects' elusive,[77] but, by adopting it, senior IDF commanders distanced themselves from the old but simple notions, such as centre of gravity, which have united military thinkers and practitioners for centuries, except for the dilemma of where and against what it would be best to concentrate forces or fire in order to achieve a battlefield decision.[78]

Whereas EBO is not necessarily manoeuvre-based, as it can also count on shock and awe, 'swarming', that is coordinated attacks from different directions by small, dispersed, and networked units—another American concept that has also been enthusiastically embraced by the IDF—is manoeuvre-oriented.[79] Although it does reflect an intention to concentrate force, it seems to be alien to the notion of amassing as much force as necessary, against either a point of strength or a point of weakness, in the spirit of centre of gravity.

Lower likelihood of first strike and blitzkrieg

A basic problem Israel had to cope with when it planned a first strike was the time period required for mobilizing and deploying sufficient ground forces to that end. Considerably enhanced firepower capabilities have the potential to launch a first strike without exposing the preparations for it. Another positive development entailed in the significant strengthening of firepower capabilities is the option of near-real-time retaliation, which becomes relevant in case of a surprise attack or political constraints that make the launching of a first strike impossible. On the other hand, in a reality where weapons have longer ranges and are much more precise and destructive, the destruction inflicted as a result of absorbing the enemy's first strike might be even greater than before.

As for *blitzkrieg*, since the 1970s it has become a less-plausible option because it has required open spaces for manoeuvre—a rare resource in a reality of a saturated battlefield. This explains why in recent years the IDF has reorganized logistically, adopting a more centralized system, which is based on modularly structured area-logistics units.[80] During the Second Lebanon War, however, it became clear that the system may have improved control over logistical resources and may have saved manpower and stocks,[81] but at the same time it crippled the combat units' logistical autonomy and countered operational art's logic and spirit. It is doubtful whether it would have met operational requirements had the war involved large-scale ground manoeuvres.

Where have the great captains gone?

Ironically, while greater efforts have been made by the IDF in order to offer commanders better formal education and training, its operational art has been deteriorating, manifesting its weakness time and again.

Israeli technology-focused military thinking has produced a new species of commanders with blunted operational-art senses. IDF commanders have, in recent years, been suffering from two main problems. First, the technological age only strengthened their basic inclination to think in terms of technological force multipliers, such as smart weapons, rather than in terms of force multipliers based on smart doctrines and plans, which usually needs more abstract and paradoxical thinking. Commanders have tended to believe that on a battlefield where enemy forces can be destroyed by stand-off precision fire, optimal command and control is achieved from control centres, and operations and battles can be conducted via plasma screens.

More and more experts have claimed that classical war is over, accusing the older generation of IDF commanders of thinking as if they lived 'in the time of the War of Independence or the Sinai War', and 'in terms of tanks and ground operations . . . and all these worthless things'.[82] It is now clear that over-reliance on precision technology was one of the major reasons for the IDF malfunctioning in the Second Lebanon War, second only to the impact of policing missions in the territories.[83] Former deputy chief of staff Matan Vilnai rightly said that one could run McDonald's using plasma screens, but not a battle.[84] And General (ret.) Yossi Peled expressed a similar view, saying that 'a golden calf was created [before the Second Lebanon War] and named technology; many believed it could win the war'.[85]

IDF commanders have long been sympathetic to technology, but never to the degree of recent years. According to the *Maarachot* survey, the technological dimension of strategy was the most prevalent among *Maarachot* articles between 1948 and 2000, with 9.5 per cent of the articles. Other dimensions of war lagged behind—the operational with 2.5 per cent, the logistical with 3.5 per cent, and the societal with 1.5 per cent.[86]

The second problem IDF commanders have been suffering from in recent years stems from the tendency since the 1990s to equip commanders with managerial skills rather than grooming them to become great captains. This trend is alien to operational art's focus on generalship, and it reflects a misunderstanding of the difference between the non-linear, often paradoxical nature of military operations[87] and the more linear logic applied in a civilian environment. One of the expressions of the new trend was the general staff's reform called 'Aviv Neurim' (Spring of Youth) launched in the late 1990s. This was supposed to ensure greater efficiency in the organization, but in fact it paid relatively little attention to operational art. At the heart of that reform was greater authority to the arms and field units, unification of the command and budgetary authorities, the creation of a unitary body in charge of building up the ground forces, and a commitment to provide 'more security for each shekel spent'. In the late 1990s, Chief of Staff Shaul Mofaz distributed to IDF commanders Spencer Johnson's book, *Who Moved My Cheese?* whose natural target audience was managers, not military commanders. The intention was supposedly good; that is, helping commanders cope with changing realities. It, nevertheless, constituted a huge change from the past, when IDF commanders received a more traditional education and training.

CONCLUSION

A combination of reasons accounts for the fall of Israeli operational art after years of strong performance that was not based on formal education, but that manifested itself throughout three decades in the successful application of a series of force multipliers at all military levels of war, including the operational level. The establishment of the OTRI created the false impression that the IDF finally started taking operational art seriously, an idea that soon proved to be an illusion.

With LICs becoming the only type of war Israel has been engaged in since the 1980s, the importance of the operational level of war has decreased and experience in HICs, which has traditionally been the central source of inspiration for IDF commanders and their operational art, has almost disappeared.

Given the close linkage between operational art and manoeuvre, the ascendancy of firepower over manoeuvre has been detrimental to Israeli operational art. One of its by-products has been a greater tendency to think linearly at the expense of the non-linear, paradoxical thinking on which operational art has traditionally fed. The post-heroic state of mind that has characterized Israeli political and military echelons since the late 1970s has also taken the sting out of manoeuvre, as manoeuvre has been considered more likely to entail casualties than firepower.

The poor professionalism of IDF commanders—for reasons I have explained at length elsewhere—has not allowed commanders to become acquainted with the best theoretical materials on classical and modern military theory in general, and operational art in particular.[88] It has prevented them from criticizing imported, valued, and sometimes inadequate ideas that have been preached by a handful of charlatans who have taken advantage of IDF commanders' poor professional education, which failed to equip them with the necessary tools for challenging these ideas intellectually. The IDF's operational art is not a lost cause, however. It only takes military leadership that understands the value of a higher standard of professional education and training.

NOTES

1. 'Why the Israeli Army Loves Deleuze', <http://jdeanicite.typepad.com/i_cite/2006/09/why_the_israeli.html>; Eyal Weizman, 'Israeli Military Using Post-Structuralism as Operational Theory', *Infoshop News*, 1 August 2006, <http://www.infoshop.org/inews/article.php?story=20060801170800738>.
2. The Winograd Commission's final report, <http://www.vaadatwino.org.il/pdf/סופי%20דוח.pdf>, 318, 322.
3. Ibid., 274–5, 321.
4. Shimon Naveh, *Operational Art and the IDF: A Critical Study of a Command Culture* (Washington, DC: Center for Strategic and Budgetary Assessment, 2007).
5. Ibid., 52.
6. Ibid., 3, 35.
7. Eliot A. Cohen et al., *Knives, Tanks, and Missiles: Israel's Security Revolution* (Washington, DC: Washington Institute for Near East Policy, 1998), 74–6; Avi Kober, 'Israeli Military Thinking as Reflected in *Maarachot* Articles, 1948–2000', *Armed Forces and Society*, vol. 30, no. 1 (Fall 2003), 141–60; Avi Kober, 'What Happened to Israeli Military Thinking?', *Journal of Strategic Studies* (forthcoming).
8. Avi Kober, *Coalition Defection: The Dissolution of Arab Anti-Israeli Coalitions in War and Peace* (Westport, CT: Praeger, 2002), 60–3.

9. Amitzur Ilan, *Embargo, Power and Military Decision in the 1948 Palestine War* (Tel Aviv: MOD, 1995) [Hebrew].
10. Ibid.
11. Kober, *Coalition Defection*, 63–5.
12. J. F. C. Fuller, *Armament and History* (New York: Scribner, 1945), 7–8.
13. Avraham Ayalon, 'Comparing 1948, 1956 and 1967', *Maarachot*, 191–2 (June 1968), 8.
14. Edward Luttwak and Dan Horowitz, *The Israeli Army* (London: Allen Lane, 1975), 292–5.
15. Opinions have ranged from defence advocates (e.g. Clausewitz), to mixed-approach proponents (e.g. Bernhardi and Liddell Hart), to offence advocates (e.g. Napoleon, Jomini, Moltke, Schlieffen, and Fuller).
16. For Sun Tzu's and Liddell Hart's dream 'to subdue the enemy without fighting', or 'to produce a decision without any serious fighting', see Sun Tzu, *The Art of War*, trans. Samuel B. Griffith (New York: Oxford University Press, 1971), 77; B. H. Liddell Hart, *Strategy* (London: Faber & Faber, 1967), 338.
17. Brian Bond, *Liddell Hart: A Study of His Military Thought* (London: Cassell, 1977), 246.
18. Tuvia Ben-Moshe, 'Lidell Hart and the Israel Defense Forces: A Reappraisal', *Journal of Contemporary History*, vol. 16, no. 2 (April 1981), 369–91.
19. Kober, *Coalition Defection*, 63–5.
20. Jomini recommended that 'the principal mass of the force be moved against fractions of the enemy's, to attack them in succession'. Baron de Jomini, *The Art of War*, trans. G. H. Mendell and W. P. Craighill (1862; repr. Westport, CT: Greenwood, 1971), 331. Liddell Hart explained the logic of dispersion which precedes concentration: 'A concentrated effect can only be gained through an air of dispersion that causes the dispersal of the enemy's would-be concentration'. Basil H. Liddell Hart, *Thoughts on War* (London: Faber & Faber, 1943), 202.
21. Dan Schueftan, *A Jordanian Option* (Tel Aviv: Maarachot, 1986) [Hebrew], 81–3.
22. Tzu, *The Art of War*, 77–8.
23. For the meaning of the term and the levels of war it refers to, see William J. Fanning, 'The Origin of the Term *Blitzkrieg*: Another View', *Journal of Military History*, vol. 61 (April 1997), 283–302; Samuel J. Newland, 'Blitzkrieg in Retrospect', *Military Review*, vol. 84, no. 4 (July–August 2004), 86–9.
24. Luttwak and Horowitz, *The Israeli Army*, 175.
25. See, for example, Frederick II (the Great), The King of Prussia's Military Instruction to his Generals, Article VI, 'Of the Coup D'Oeil', <http://www.kw.igs.net/~tacit/artofwar/frederick.htm#VI>; Clausewitz, *On War*, 102.
26. The term 'practical soldiers' was coined by Liddell Hart. Liddell Hart, *Thoughts on War*, 96–7.
27. Israeli military psychologist Reuven Gal characterizes the Israeli commander as one lacking theoretical and historical knowledge, who is basing his professionalism on rich experience. Reuven Gal, *A Portrait of the Israeli Soldier* (Westport, CT: Greenwood, 1986), 116.
28. William S. Lind, *Maneuver Warfare Handbook* (Boulder, CO: Westview, 1985), 24.
29. Martin van Creveld, *The Sword and the Olive: A Critical History of the Israeli Defense Force* (New York: Public Affairs, 1998), 169.
30. Ibid.
31. Luttwak and Horowitz, *The Israeli Army*, 161, 174; Martin van Creveld, *Command in War* (Cambridge, MA: Harvard University Press, 1985), 196–8.

32. Avi Kober, 'The IDF in the Second Lebanon War: Why the Poor Performance?' *Journal of Strategic Studies*, vol. 31, no. 1 (February 2008).
33. Itay Bron, 'Where Has Maneuver Gone?' *Maarachot*, 420–1 (September 2008), 13.
34. Van Creveld, *The Sword and the Olive*, 362–3.
35. Ibid., 363.
36. Ibid., 131.
37. Avi Kober, *Israel's Wars of Attrition* (New York: Routledge, 2009), ch. 7.
38. See Shimon Naveh, *In Pursuit of Military Excellence* (London: Frank Cass, 1997). For the notion of 'moving ideas' or 'attacking the enemy's culture' as part of an operational conception or activity at the operational level, see 4GW's theorists Hammes and Lind et al. Thomas X. Hammes, 'War Evolves into the Fourth Generation', in Terry Terriff et al., *Global Insurgency and the Future of Armed Conflict* (New York: Routledge, 2008), 40; William S. Lind et al., 'The Changing Face of War', in ibid., 13–20.
39. Amir Rapaport, *Friendly Fire* (Tel Aviv: Maariv, 2007) [Hebrew], 80–1.
40. Benjamin Miller, 'The Concept of Security: Should It Be Redefined?' *Journal of Strategic_Studies*, vol. 24, no. 2 (June 2001), 13–42.
41. Eliot A. Cohen, 'A Revolution in Warfare', *Foreign Affairs*, vol. 75, no. 2 (March–April 1996), 45.
42. Avi-Shai, 'Planning for the Yom Kippur War: Egypt's War Objectives and Offensive Plan', *Maarachot*, 250 (July 1976), 17–18, 37–8.
43. Until recent years, this move was attributed to the Egyptians. Ezer Weizman, *On Eagles' Wings* (London: Weidenfeld and Nicolson, 1976), 281. New evidence, however, points to it as a Soviet move. See Boris Dolin, 'The Israeli–Soviet Campaign during the 1969–70 Israeli–Egyptian War of Attrition', MA thesis (Bar-Ilan University, 2008).
44. Weizman, *On Eagles' Wings*, 280.
45. Van Creveld, *The Sword and the Olive*, 232.
46. Avi Kober, *Battlefield Decision in the Arab–Israeli Wars, 1948–1982* (Tel-Aviv: Maarachot, 1995) [Hebrew], 365–9.
47. Ibid., 366.
48. Ibid., 367.
49. Meir Finkel, *On Flexibility* (Tel Aviv: MOD, 2007) [Hebrew], 194–207.
50. Chaim Herzog, *The Arab–Israeli Wars* (Jerusalem: Edanim, 1983) [Hebrew], 250.
51. Kober, *Battlefield Decision*, 413.
52. Meir Finkel, 'The Airpower Paradox: Enhanced Precision, Lesser Effectiveness', *Maarachot*, 420–1 (September 2008), 30–5; Yaacov Zigdon, 'Much Fire, Little Thought', in ibid., 44–53.
53. Ofer Shelah and Yoav Limor, *Captives in Lebanon* (Tel Aviv: Yediot Aharonot, 2007) [Hebrew], 385.
54. On Israeli-targeted killings during the second intifada, see Avi Kober, 'Targeted Killing During the Second Intifada: The Quest for Effectiveness', *Journal of Conflict Studies*, vol. 27, no. 1 (Summer 2007), <http://www.lib.unb.ca/Texts/JCS/bin/get.cgi?directory=Summer07/& filename=jcs27art06.html>.
55. The Winograd Commission's Final Report, <http://www.vaadatwino.org.il/pdf/סופי%20דוח.pdf>, 273–4; Shelah and Limor, *Captives in Lebanon*, 198.
56. Edward N. Luttwak, 'Where Are the Great Powers?' *Foreign Affairs*, vol. 73, no. 4 (July–August 1994), 23–8; 'Toward Post-Heroic Warfare', *Foreign Affairs*, vol. 74, no. 3 (May–June 1995), 109–22; 'A Post-Heroic Military Policy', *Foreign Affairs*, vol. 75, no. 4 (July–August 1996), 33–44.

57. Mordechai Gur, *Chief of the General Staff, 1974–1978* (Tel Aviv: Maarachot, 1998) [Hebrew], 404.
58. Interview on Israeli Radio, Channel 2, 6 October 1999.
59. <http://www.btselem.org/English/Publications/Full_Text/Illusions_of_Restraint>.
60. Chief of the Authority for Weapon Research and Development (AWRD) at the Israeli Defence Ministry, Major-General Isaac Ben-Israel, in an interview with *Haaretz*, 17 December 2001.
61. Kober, *Israel's Wars of Attrition.*
62. Shelah and Limor, *Captives in Lebanon*, 132–4.
63. Winograd Commission's Interim Report, <http://www.vaadatwino.org.il/pdf/מאוחד%20סופי%20לאינטרנט.pdf>, 56.
64. Ariella Ringel-Hoffman, 'This Is Not How a War Should Be Conducted', *Yediot Aharonot Weekend Supplement*, 23 March 2007; Scott Wilson, 'Israeli War Plan Had No Exit Strategy', <http://www.washingtonpost.com/wp-dyn/content/article/2006/10/20/AR2006102001688 _pf.html>.
65. Shelah and Limor, *Captives in Lebanon*, 244.
66. Israeli Radio, Channel 7, 2 November 2006, <http://www.inn.co.il/News/News.aspx/155971>.
67. Amir Bouchbout, 'Halutz's Swords Speech', <http://www.nrg.co.il/online/1/ART1/506/032.html>.
68. Isaac Ben-Israel, 'The Military Buildup's Theory of Relativity', *Maarachot*, 352–3 (August 1997), 33; 'Security, Technology, and Future Battlefield', in Haggai Golan (ed.), *Israel's Security Web: Core Issues of Israel's National Security in Its Sixth Decade* (Tel-Aviv: Maarachot, 2001) [Hebrew], 279.
69. Shmuel Gordon, *The Bow of Paris* (Tel Aviv: Poalim, 1997) [Hebrew], particularly 320–2.
70. See Steven Metz, *Armed Conflict in the 21st Century: The Information Revolution and Post-Modern Warfare* (Carlisle, PA: Strategic Studies Institute, April 2000), 31–3. The goals set out for the US military forces a decade into the twenty-first century by former secretary of defence Cohen and former chairman of the Joint Chiefs of Staff General Shalikashvili were that they possess 'dominant battlefield knowledge', 'full dimensional protection', 'dominant manoeuvre', and 'precision strike' ability from long distances. Michael O' Hanlon, *Technological Change and the Future of War* (Washington, DC: Brookings Institution, 2000). See also Gordon R. Sullivan and James M. Dubik, 'War in the Information Age', *Military Review*, vol. 74, no. 4 (April 1994), 55–6.
71. Nahum Barnea and Shimon Shiffer, interview with Prime Minister Ehud Olmert, *Yediot Aharonot New Year Supplement*, 29 September 2008.
72. *The Officer's Manual: Military Maxims of Napoleon*, trans. Colonel d'Aguillar (Dublin: Richard Milliken, 1831), 27.
73. Benny Mem, 'The Peace for Galilee War: Main Operations', *Maarachot*, 284 (September 1982), 24–48.
74. Edward N. Luttwak, 'Misreading the Lebanon War', *Jerusalem Post*, 21 August 2006.
75. Haim Assa and Yedidya Yaari, *Diffused Warfare* (Tel Aviv: Yediot Aharonot, 2005) [Hebrew].
76. Edward A. Smith, *Effects Based Operations: Applying Network Centric Warfare in Peace, Crisis, and War* (Washington, DC: Department of Defense Command and Control Research Program, 2002).
77. Effect is defined as 'the physical, functional, or psychological outcome, event, or consequence that results from specific military or non-military actions'. EBO is

defined as 'a process for obtaining a desired strategic outcome or effect on the enemy through the synergistic and cumulative application of the full range of military and non-military capabilities at all levels of conflict'. Lieutenant Colonel Allen W. Batschelet, *Effects-Based Operations: A New Operational Model?* (Carlisle, PA: US Army War College, 2002), 2.

78. The Winograd Commission's Interim Report, 49. For a recent criticism of EBO, see General John N. Mattis, 'Assessment of Effects Based Operations', <http://smallwarsjournal.com/documents/usjfcomebomemo.pdf>.
79. Sean J. A. Edwards, *Swarming on the Battlefield: Past, Present, and Future* (Santa Monica, CA: RAND, 2000); John Arquilla and David Ronfeldt, *Swarming and the Future of Conflict* (Santa Monica, CA: RAND, 2000); Amir Rapaport, *Friendly Fire* (Tel Aviv: Maariv, 2007) [Hebrew], 81.
80. Kober, 'The IDF in the Second Lebanon War', 29.
81. Amnon Barzilai, '[Chief of the IDF's Technology and Logistics Branch General Udi] Adam's Technological Revolution', *Haaretz*, 2 April 2004.
82. Barnea and Shiffer, interview with Prime Minister Ehud Olmert.
83. Amos Harel, 'A Flawed Operational Conception', *Haaretz*, 10 December 2006.
84. Amira Lam, 'We Betrayed Our Constituency', *Yediot Aharonot Weekend Supplement*, 1 September 2006.
85. Ari Shavit, interview with General (ret.) Yossi Peled, *Haaretz Weekend Supplement*, 20 October 2006.
86. Kober, 'Israeli Military Thinking as Reflected in *Maarachot* Articles', 156.
87. Aharon Zeevi, 'Aviv Ne'urim: The Vision and Its Implementation', *Maarachot*, 358 (April 1998), 3–6.
88. Kober, 'What Happened to Israeli Military Thinking?'

7

The Chinese Way of War

Andrew Scobell

INTRODUCTION

This chapter examines the Chinese Way of War over the span of several thousand years. Particular attention will be paid to military operations in theory and practice during the past ninety years—since the rise of the Communist movement in the 1920s and the founding of the People's Republic of China (PRC) in 1949. This period will hereafter be referred to as the 'contemporary era'. At the outset, it may be worthwhile to state what this chapter is not: it is not a military history of China; nor does it recount in chronological fashion the course of successive military campaigns. These can be found elsewhere.[1] Instead, this chapter explores what appear to be key enduring themes in Chinese military strategy through the centuries. This necessarily requires a short introduction to the larger topic of Chinese strategic thought and a brief survey of contemporary China's evolving military doctrine before focusing on what are widely considered the hallmarks of Chinese operational art.

The reader should be alerted to the fact that there are two contrasting interpretations of Chinese strategic thought. One emphasizes the uniqueness or 'Chineseness' of military strategy, while the second highlights the universalism of strategy and warfare stressing common themes and approaches among cultures. The former approach tends to dominate the thinking among both Chinese and non-Chinese soldiers, scholars, and analysts.[2] The latter approach is not as widespread, but it, nevertheless, has strong adherents.[3] This writer believes that there are key commonalities across strategic traditions, but he is also convinced that there are important and distinctive cultural elements within traditions. Throughout this chapter, attention will be drawn to universal themes and challenges in the operational art that are discernible in the Chinese case.

The underlying logic of the uniqueness approach stems from the fact that China possesses one of the world's great civilizations with arguably the most impressive and enduring record of writings on warfare and strategy. Indeed, the Chinese themselves are fond of observing that they are heirs to a civilization dating back 5,000 years. The Chinese are wont to point out that their country is the source of what is probably the world's oldest surviving treatise on military strategy—Sun Zi's (also transliterated as Sun Tzu) *The Art of War* which dates back more than 2,000 years to the Spring and Autumn Period (771–481 BC).

Moreover, according to leading strategists at the People's Liberation Army's (PLA) Academy of Military Sciences—China's most important military research institution—the country is home to an extensive array of ancient writings on strategy reportedly numbering in the thousands.[4] There are also a good number of novels and histories that contain considerable discussion of warfare and strategy and these are widely read by many Chinese to learn more about the military art. These include two novels dating from the Ming dynasty (1368–1644): *Romance of the Three Kingdoms* and *The Water Margin* (also called *Outlaws of the Marshes* and *All Men Are Brothers*). Mao Zedong (also transliterated as Mao Tse-tung), Chinese Communist leader and strategist, for example, remarked that in his youth he read and enjoyed famous works of Chinese literature, including these two novels. These books in particular, with tales of resourceful rebels and heroic generals, clearly influenced the evolution of military thinking, among not only the founding generation of Communist leaders, but subsequent ones as well.[5]

Those who insist upon the uniqueness of Chinese strategy point to certain putative cultural proclivities, such as a preference for harmony and peace over discord and conflict and an aversion to the use of force. Typically, these tendencies are attributed to the pervasive influence of Confucianism.[6] Despite this purported pacifist core in China's strategic tradition, this has not made the Chinese any less likely than any other ethnic group to wage wars or fight battles. According to statistics cited in an authoritative volume on strategy published by the PLA's most important research institute on military thought, China has witnessed 'more than 6,000 battles in 4,000 plus years since 26th Century B.C. . . . to the end of the Qing dynasty (1644–1911). This figure was more than one-third of the total numbers of battles that had happened around the world during the same period'.[7]

Others contend that Chinese strategy and warfare are strongly predisposed to the use of deception and stratagem. In fact, two analysts have dubbed the Chinese approach as 'strategy by stratagem'.[8] These tendencies are often associated with Sun Zi but can also be found in other writings, including tales about the legendary Chinese strategist Zhuge Liang (see below). Despite Sun Zi's widely cited preference for 'subduing the enemy without fighting' (*The Art of War*, chapter 3), this seems to be an ideal for which to strive rather than a realistic option for most military commanders. This point is underscored by the vast amount of advice in tomes on strategy, including *The Art of War* itself, on 'how to win by fighting'.[9]

The rest of this chapter will be divided into three parts. The first part will discuss the asymmetric dimension of Chinese military doctrine in the contemporary era. The second part will examine five widely assumed hallmarks of China's operational art. The third part will attempt to draw some tentative conclusions from the analysis and discussion.

ASYMMETRIC WARFARE: WEAPONS OF THE WEAK

Some contemporary observers in the United States and elsewhere write as if the Chinese invented asymmetric warfare and that somehow this was the unique product of the 'inscrutable' Oriental mind.[10] What these observers tend to overlook is the fact that attention to asymmetries has long been a staple in the conduct of war. This is especially true for the weaker side in a conflict that seeks to avoid fighting at a time and place of the adversary's choosing where the enemy can utilize its strengths and there is a high probability of defeat. Instead, a shrewd general plays to the strengths of his own forces and focuses his efforts on confronting the enemy in a manner, time, and place which would best exploit the weaknesses of his adversary. Indeed, the fundamental assumption of Mao Zedong's strategic principles of 'people's war' was that the Chinese Communists were far weaker militarily at the outset of the conflict than their adversaries and that this was likely to remain a reality for a considerable period of time. This was true when the Communist movement was an insurgent force seeking to defeat the ruling Kuomintang (KMT—also transliterated as Guomindang) or Nationalist regime of Chiang Kai-shek (also transliterated as Jiang Jieshi); it has also been true since the late 1940s when the Communists became the rulers of mainland China and in 1949 formally established the PRC, becoming a major power but one significantly weaker than the two superpowers, not just militarily, but economically and diplomatically as well. In both eras, the weaker Chinese Communist side adopted the principles of people's war in preparation to battle more powerful adversaries.

China has historically and traditionally been a continental military power. The focus of operational art has thus been on land warfare, although this began to change by the close of the twentieth century. This did not mean that maritime conflict was completely ignored, but it did mean that it tended to be seen as peripheral or an adjunct to operations on dry land.[11] Notable exceptions to the rule were the four voyages of Ming dynasty Admiral Zheng He in the early fifteenth century. As impressive as these expeditions were, they were less operations of a military nature to defeat adversaries and conquer new lands than they were voyages of discovery and exploration. It has only been during the last two decades or so that China's armed forces have begun to make sea power a national priority. Under the leadership of Admiral Liu Huaqing and others, the PRC commenced a sustained build-up of naval power. In the twenty-first century, the PLA has begun integrating maritime operations, including amphibious warfare, submarine warfare, mine warfare, as well as the use of short-range ballistic and cruise missiles. China's presumed adversary is the United States, and all these capabilities are intended to counter the more powerful and capable US navy, most likely in a Taiwan scenario.[12] The goal is to slow or deny US forces access to the theatre by leveraging China's more modest operational capabilities. The upshot, in the apt words of Thomas Christensen, is a Chinese military capable of 'posing problems [for the U.S. armed forces] without catching up'.[13]

In essence, the history of the operational art as studied and practised by China's Communist leaders is the evolution and adaptation of a strategy of weakness to counter the superior strength of successive adversaries in response to changing conditions.[14] The Chinese Communist Party (CCP) was formally founded in 1921 in the city of Shanghai and initially developed as an urban movement. However, within six years it was forced to reinvent itself as a rural movement and rapidly equip itself for simple self-preservation. The CCP's military arm, which later became known as the PLA, officially dates its founding as 1 August 1927. Whatever the precise circumstances and timing of its inception, the origins of the Chinese Communist armed forces were humble. Faced with a daunting predicament, Mao and other military thinkers formulated a strategy that became known as people's war. They made a virtue out of necessity to become a rural insurgency, focusing on gaining the support of the peasantry in rugged, inaccessible mountainous areas that promised a good measure of protection against the superior military capabilities of the movement's enemies. The primary adversary was the KMT. The Communists and the Nationalists forged a marriage of convenience in the mid-1920s. But following the success of the Northern Expedition of 1926–7, which succeeded at least nominally in unifying China, the KMT quickly turned on its erstwhile ally. The Nationalist Party under Chiang Kai-shek soon established itself as the dominant political power with the strongest military force in the country controlling the major cities and surrounding areas.

People's war in opposition

During the late 1920s, Mao began to sketch out a long-term strategy of protracted struggle with three phases to evolve as the movement became stronger and more capable militarily. The first phase was one of strategic defence in which the Communists would concentrate on building up their military strength. The second phase was strategic stalemate as the two sides reached roughly comparable strength and neither side clearly dominated the other. The third phase was envisioned as one of strategic counter-attack once the Communists had built up sufficient superior military power to fight and defeat the enemy in conventional warfare.[15]

The first phase lasted almost twenty years as military forces waged a mostly guerrilla war against the more powerful conventional forces of the KMT (1927–45) and Japan (in the years between 1937 and 1945). While hostilities between the CCP and the KMT were interrupted by extended periods of limited cooperation against Japanese invaders in the late 1930s and early 1940s, as well as short and uneasy ceasefires in the mid-1940s, the conflict was of a protracted nature. The most notable event of this period was the so-called Long March of 1934–5 in which the main force of Communist fighters in south-eastern China conducted a strategic withdrawal along a circuitous route across thousands of miles of hostile territory from its base area on the border between Jiangxi and Hunan Provinces to a new base area in Shaanxi Province in north-western China. The retreat has taken on mythical status in the military annals of Chinese Communism. The episode proved to be a turning point for the movement politically because it allowed Mao Zedong to establish himself as its foremost leader and the CCP to rejuvenate itself organizationally; moreover, the Long March earned the Communists a strategic pause, allowing the movement the opportunity to rebuild itself militarily, well inland and away from the invading Japanese imperial army, which succeeded in occupying vast swathes of China following the outbreak of the Sino-Japanese War in 1937 (labelled by Chinese Communists as the 'Anti-Japanese War').

The second phase of people's war began in 1945 as Communist armed forces gained combat strength and developed conventional military power. In that year, the CCP leadership decided that the PLA was sufficiently strong to begin to switch over to conventional military operations against their KMT adversaries (the only previous large-scale conventional operation was the so-called 'one hundred regiments campaign' conducted against the Japanese in the latter half of 1940). By the time of the Japanese surrender in mid-1945, the PLA was a more potent and battle-hardened force, albeit one lacking in conventional military campaign experience. Nevertheless, in August 1945, the decision was made to transform the core of the PLA 'from a guerrilla force to an army capable of large-scale mobile operations'. Thus, by the end of 1945, the best Communist troops had been reorganized into armies and brigades.[16]

Negotiations between the CCP and the KMT to end the Chinese Civil War, brokered by successive US emissaries, failed to reconcile the two sides and the conflict resumed in earnest. In June 1946, KMT forces launched wholesale attacks against Communist-controlled areas. After initially absorbing these strikes, the CCP began to mobilize the combined might of not just its military strength, but its political and propaganda resources as well, to break the strategic stalemate and take the war to KMT-controlled areas. The Communists continued to strengthen their conventional military capabilities by measures including recruiting more peasants into the ranks and arming its forces with more automatic weapons and artillery pieces. The CCP also ramped up its propaganda effort to explain its policies to the Chinese people, especially the agricultural reform programme.[17]

The third phase of people's war was under way by mid-1947 as the PLA initiated a strategic offensive. This time, military manoeuvres were more of a conventional nature instead of guerrilla warfare. Initially, offensive operations were conducted in rural areas controlled by the KMT, but, by mid-1948, PLA operations shifted to urban targets. Three large-scale operations—the Liao–Shen, the Ping–Jin, and Huai–Hai campaigns—resulted in the defeat of all major KMT military forces in northern China.[18] In less than five months, Communist forces emerged victorious on the battlefield; the KMT had lost approximately 1.5 million men (killed, wounded, and captured) and all the major cities in northern China, including Beiping (the city's name before it became the capital of the PRC and was renamed 'Beijing'), Shanghai, and Tianjin.[19] The Huai–Hai campaign (November 1948–January 1949) was the most decisive of the civil war involving more than one million troops. The Communist forces were able to soundly defeat their KMT adversaries in the field; moreover, they also prevented the withdrawal of some half a million well-armed troops southward across the Yangtze River and gained control of eastern China—including vital transportation routes (rivers and railways) as well as key cities, including Shanghai and the KMT capital, Nanjing (also transliterated as Nanking).[20] Thus, by April 1949, the CCP clearly had gained the upper hand, taking control of all the north and central Chinese heartland. By October 1949, the Communists felt sufficiently confident that victory was complete for Mao to proclaim the formal creation of the PRC. Chiang Kai-shek and a significant portion of his military forces abandoned the Chinese mainland and retreated to the island of Taiwan. By late 1949, the CCP controlled most of mainland China, with the exception of Tibet and other remote areas.

From people's war to local war

Following victory in the civil war, the CCP became focused on holding and consolidating state power. As a result, its strategy changed from that of an insurgent group intent on seizing power to one protecting itself against threats both foreign and domestic. People's war thus became a strategy of national defence. Beijing expected that war was likely to break out in the near future, and it would most probably be an all-out conflagration in which nuclear weapons would be used. During the 1950s, China assumed its adversary in such a war would be the United States, but, by the late 1960s, China anticipated that its enemy would be the Soviet Union. Playing to China's relative strengths in order to counter the country's significant weaknesses, the new Communist party-state adopted a strategy of luring the enemy deep in the event of war rather than trying to hold the enemy at the border. This sought to exploit China's strategic depth and large population. The country's vast size and substantial people power could be used to counteract the superior military power of any invading forces. In a protracted war, stubborn Chinese resistance would gradually wear down the attacker.

Despite the formal doctrine, the record of actual Chinese combat in the 1950s and 1960s was at odds with people's war. Campaigns by the PLA were all waged at or just beyond China's borders—notably the Korean War (1950–3), the Sino-Indian War (1962), and the Sino-Soviet border war (1969). Chinese forces did not practise 'protracted war' or attempt to 'lure the enemy deep'. Nevertheless, the spectre of China waging an all-out people's war against an invading army was sobering enough to serve as an effective deterrent to any would-be aggressor.

Following the death of Mao Zedong in 1976, China's military doctrine was in flux. Recognizing that the existing people's war doctrine did not suit China's changing security requirements, military leaders attempted to update their military strategy. Labelling the adaptation 'people's war under modern conditions', the PLA was prepared to fight a positional war seeking to hold an attacking army (expected to be the Soviet Red Army) at or near its borders and, if necessary, mobilizing the entire population in a guerrilla struggle to wear down the invader through a protracted war of defence in depth.

By the end of the 1970s, Beijing no longer expected a worldwide war was imminent; instead, smaller, more contained conflicts were expected to flare up; by the mid-1980s, Chinese strategists had concluded that their armed forces should be prepared for what they dubbed 'local wars'. Following the stunning success of the US-led coalition forces in the 1991 Persian Gulf War, the suffix 'under high-tech conditions' was added. Such conflicts would be waged against a technologically superior foe. While China had to do its utmost to modernize its military to fight these wars, inevitably it would find itself confronted by a far more potent military adversary. Then, in the first decade of the twenty-first century, the PLA tweaked its doctrine to recognize what was regarded as the revolution within a revolution. The core of the so-called revolution in military affairs (RMA) for Chinese soldiers was a revolution in information technology. Hence, as they look towards the second decade of the twenty-first century, China's armed forces are preparing to fight 'local wars under informatized conditions'. Thus, the PLA is striving to employ technology and information operations to counter a foe's asymmetric advantages rather than to attain pre-eminence for itself in those areas.

HALLMARKS OF THE CHINESE OPERATIONAL ART

Hallmarks of China's operational art have been identified. Frequently, Chinese operational art is depicted as emphasizing alternatives to the direct application of military force in a given situation. This image includes the contention that Chinese strategists and commanders prefer unorthodox approaches to direct force-on-force combat on the battlefield. This image also includes the presumption that Chinese generals have an ingrained preference for defensive operations rather than offensive measures. Moreover, some contend that the Chinese are disposed to positional warfare, although others insist the Chinese are more disposed to mobile operations. And still others claim that the Chinese stress that man is the decisive element in war and downplay technology. Furthermore, some argue that the Chinese evaluate battlefield success differently from non-Chinese.[21] Discussion of these hallmarks will be attempted with reference both to the writings of Chinese strategic thinkers and to the actual performance of Chinese military forces on the battlefield in the ancient and modern eras.

An analysis of the record reveals that successful Chinese generals have selected both orthodox and unorthodox methods in warfare, as well as are seeking a balance between the above-mentioned dichotomies. As Mao noted in December 1936: 'The problems of strategy include the following.... Giving proper consideration to the distinction ... between concentration and dispersion [of forces], between attack and defence ... between concealment and exposure ... between positional war and mobile war ... between military work and political work ...'.[22]

Orthodox and unorthodox

One important theme running through the writings of theorists from Sun Zi to the present day is the use of two kinds of strategies—orthodox and unorthodox. The former term in Chinese uses the character '*zheng*', while the latter uses the term '*qi*'. Orthodox refers to conventional and direct strategies, such as frontal assaults. Unorthodox refers to unconventional and indirect approaches, such as attacking in an unexpected way from an unexpected direction (i.e. from the rear).[23] The distinction between the two is not hard and fast; however, perhaps the simplest way to differentiate between *zheng* and *qi* is that the latter invariably contains the element of surprise or psychological warfare, while the former involves more straightforward kinetic warfare. The presumption of Chinese strategists is that, for a commander to emerge victorious, he must skilfully combine orthodox and unorthodox methods. Sun Zi says in *The Art of War* (chapter 5): 'In warfare the strategic configurations of power . . . do not exceed the unorthodox and orthodox, but the changes of the unorthodox and orthodox can never be completely exhausted. The unorthodox and orthodox mutually produce each other just like an endless cycle. Who can exhaust them?'[24] Indeed, one cannot exist without the other: thus, for example, exclusive reliance on the unorthodox would render one's methods orthodox.

Those who believe that China possesses a unique strategic tradition will tend to emphasize the unorthodox elements found in Chinese operational art, while those who believe China's strategic tradition is consistent with those of other states will tend to stress the orthodox elements. Here, it is worth making an obvious but important point—standard operational art around the globe is focused essentially on the same goal: wiping out the enemy while doing one's utmost to preserve one's own forces. Mao observed this in May 1938: 'All the guiding principles of military operations grow out of the one basic principle: to strive to the utmost to preserve one's own strength and destroy that of the enemy'.[25] This operational priority is discernible not only in the writings of Mao and Sun Zi, but also in non-Chinese theorists, such as Clausewitz and Jomini.[26]

One of the most famous cases of the successful use of unorthodox methods in Chinese military history, narrated in the *Romance of the Three Kingdoms* (chapter 95), involves Zhuge Liang—widely regarded in contemporary China as the greatest strategist of the pre-modern era. It is known as the 'empty fortress (or city)' stratagem. According to the story, the hero finds himself in a city commanding a token garrison with the majority of the state's armed forces elsewhere as a vastly superior enemy force rapidly approaches. Zhuge Liang feigns confidence and strength: he orders the gates of the city to be thrown open and his small contingent of soldiers to keep out of view. With this accomplished, he positions himself on the ramparts in full view of the invading force and calmly plays a traditional Chinese musical instrument. The invading generals are suspicious of the seemingly tranquil scene and apparently deserted city. They conclude that Zhuge Liang has set a cunning trap by concealing substantial forces, and they will be victims of an ambush if they attack. The upshot is that the enemy army withdraws without a fight. The important point to remember is that the success of the unorthodox method in this instance is contingent on two 'orthodox' facts being known to the enemy commanders. First, they know of Zhuge Liang's reputation as a cunning and skilled strategist; second, they know that he has sizeable and capable armed forces. Thus, in this case, the unorthodox would not succeed without an orthodox component.[27]

Both orthodox and unorthodox methods were used in imperial China. In the Ming dynasty (1368–1644), for example, during one of several campaigns against invading Japanese forces in China's tributary kingdom of Korea waged by imperial forces, Chinese generals employed a combination of bloody frontal assaults in broad daylight and surprise raids against key targets behind enemy lines under cover of darkness. The campaign, led by veteran Chinese commander Li Rusong, was hard fought, waged against battle-hardened Japanese troops. One of the most costly victories in the campaign was the capture of Pyongyang in 1593. On 8 February, in a ferocious urban one-day battle, Chinese forces unleashed a devastating 'combination of cannon fire and brutal street fighting' that succeeded in driving Japanese forces out of the city after inflicting an estimated 12,000 fatalities on the enemy (see also 'Man and Technology', below). In contrast, three months later, in mid-May 1593, Chinese forces captured the city of Seoul without any bloodshed. The dramatic victory was achieved by a stealth night-time foray on a major Japanese supply depot that was successfully destroyed. As a result, the Japanese garrison abandoned Seoul without a fight.[28]

Orthodox and unorthodox methods were used during Communist military campaigns to unify China following the end of the Second World War. Some Communist victories were won in brutal battles, while others were won in bloodless negotiated surrenders. Illustrative examples can be drawn from the Ping–Jin campaign noted above. The advance on the city of Tianjin involved 'a series of long, bloody battles'.[29] The capture of Tianjin was achieved on 17 January 1949 after three days of bitter fighting. The capture of Beiping, meanwhile, was achieved without firing a shot—a week later, on 20 January, the KMT commander General Fu Zuoyi (whose daughter was a Communist) negotiated a deal to surrender the garrison. By 27 January, KMT troops had completed a peaceful evacuation of the city.[30] However, the remarkably impressive unorthodox manner in which victory was achieved in the latter instance would almost certainly not have been possible without the hard-fought kinetic victory in the former instance. In other words, unless the steely resolve and combat capabilities of the besieging Communist force had been clearly demonstrated on nearby Tianjin, Beiping's defenders might have been more prepared to resist stubbornly and fight.[31]

Orthodox and unorthodox methods were also employed by commanders of the Chinese forces who participated in the Korean War. Elements of deception, surprise, and stealth were utilized to considerable effect, but were combined with orthodox methods, such as frontal assaults with massed artillery barrages. Deception was a hallmark of China's intervention in the Korean War from the very outset. The very title given to the forces dispatched to Korea was intended to deceive or, at least, provide Beijing a fig leaf of plausible denial. While the units that surreptitiously crossed the Yalu River under cover of darkness starting in mid-October 1950 were officially dubbed the 'Chinese People's Volunteers' (CPV), they were actually PLA units with their badges and patches carefully removed. Of course, no one believed that Chinese troops had intervened of their own volition, but the fiction of 'volunteerism' allowed Chinese soldiers to operate in Korea without requiring Beijing to declare itself formally a belligerent. Such a declaration of war, among other things, would have obligated the Soviet Union, under the terms of the January 1950 Sino-Soviet alliance treaty, to enter the conflict. The fig leaf suited all the de facto combatants because it prevented the war from escalating beyond the confines of the Korean Peninsula and/or into a more destructive conflagration between the superpowers. The Chinese maintained the element of surprise in their intervention because forces moved only under cover of darkness and remained hidden during daylight. Nevertheless, such measures did not negate the need for orthodox combat operations—vicious and hard-hitting campaigns of annihilation waged by the CPV against forces of the United Nations Command (UNC)—although the CPV retained a preference for night-time operations.[32] In all, more than 2.3 million troops and 600,000 civilian labourers served in Korea between 1950 and 1953. The Chinese suffered a total of more than a million casualties (killed, wounded, missing in action, and captured).[33]

Chinese troops also employed orthodox and unorthodox means against adversaries in other conflicts. The PLA used concentration of forces along with stealth and surprise in operations against Indian troops high in the Himalayas in 1962 and against Soviet troops along the Ussuri River in 1969. These combined methods proved more successfully implemented in the series of campaigns along the disputed southern border with India than it did seven years later against the Soviet Red Army on China's northern border.[34] Indeed, the Himalayan campaign is widely considered to be the PLA's most successful post-1949 military operation. The three-phase campaign waged in late 1962 was meticulously planned, skilfully executed, and bore most of the hallmarks of the Chinese operational art. PLA infantry numbering in the thousands manoeuvred well on high-altitude terrain, concentrating forces to launch surprise attacks on the scattered Indian army units, and always maintaining the initiative. In the first phase, they pushed their adversaries back across the demarcation line; in the second phase, they crossed the border and further punished Indian troops. After announcing a unilateral ceasefire, in the third phase, the PLA forces withdrew in good order, releasing Indian prisoners of war and captured equipment.[35]

Elements of surprise and deception were also employed by China in the 1979 war with Vietnam with modest success, but these aspects certainly did not prove decisive in the conflict. China sought to keep troop movements secret in the lead-up to the war, and then during the conflict Chinese forces tried to confuse their adversaries as to the main thrust of the attack as the PLA attacked at half a dozen points spread out along a broad front. The Chinese concentrated on orthodox invasion thrusts into Vietnam in two theatres of operations starting on 17 February. In the west, forces from the Kunming Military Region, commanded by General Yang Dezhi, attacked, while, in the east, forces from the Guangzhou Military Region, led by General Xu Shiyou, attacked. The operational goals were the destruction of Vietnamese military forces in the border area and the capture of several provincial capitals. The PLA utilized more than 300,000 troops arrayed in infantry, armour, and artillery units. These offensives were conventional manoeuvres that were poorly executed and Chinese forces became bogged down in the rugged mountainous terrain in bloody combat against stubborn, entrenched Vietnamese defenders. While the provincial capitals of Lao Cai and Cao Bang were eventually seized, these achievements took days instead of hours and were only accomplished with considerable bloodshed. Chinese forces did not attack the third geographical objective, Lang Son, until ten days after the war began, and, after four days of hard fighting, were only able to capture part of the city.[36] Shortly thereafter, in early March, the PLA began to withdraw from Vietnam practising a scorched-earth strategy. Thereupon, Beijing declared its military action had succeeded in teaching Hanoi a 'lesson'.

Thus, the orthodox and unorthodox methods have both been employed in Chinese campaigns over the centuries with varying degrees of success. The record clearly shows that one has not been neglected at the expense of the other.

Man and technology

Bravery, physical prowess, skill in combat, and strength in numbers—not to mention human ingenuity—have all been important in Chinese warfare. However, technology has never been ignored. Indeed, technological advances have proved dramatic on numerous occasions. Nevertheless, in ancient times, some discoveries, such as gunpowder (in approximately AD 1000), were never fully developed as instruments of war. In modern times, China has proved more adept at adapting to confront new technologies fielded by military adversaries. By the late twentieth century, although China was no longer a pioneer in military technology, it had become skilful at developing its own versions of modern weaponry, such as seagoing vessels, armour, nuclear weapons, and ballistic missiles.

Ancient China

Technological advances in agricultural productivity permitted greater wealth and, in turn, the creation of larger and more powerful states. By the Warring States Period (403–221 BC), the number of Chinese states had shrunk from many dozen to some twenty, a number of which had accumulated great wealth and were able to channel substantial resources into building armies numbering in the hundreds of thousands. The invention of cast iron and the crossbow dramatically transformed the conduct of and approach to warfare in China. Cast iron became widely used for weapons and implements in the fifth century BC, while the crossbow began to enjoy extensive use in the fourth century BC.[37] While there was really no such thing as operational art in the Spring and Autumn Period, during the Warring States Era the conduct of war professionalized with the widespread use of massed armies. Prior to these advancements in technology and state building, war fighting had been the province of noblemen battling each other from the platforms of horse-drawn chariots supported by small bands of foot soldiers—the equivalent of stylized combat between individual knights in Europe of the Middle Ages. These changes replaced ritualized contests between duelling aristocratic charioteers and heralded the emergence of military campaigns between sizeable forces from larger rival states. Not only was the conduct of war transformed, but a whole new field of intellectual study—the art of war—was created, replacing codes of chivalry.

Also in the Warring States Period, technological advances made walled cites more vulnerable and led to siege warfare becoming more sophisticated and more viable.[38] Prior to this time, if well stocked with provisions, the defenders of these fortresses typically could wait out besieging armies with the expectation that their attackers would eventually tire of waiting and/or run out of food before they did. Battering rams, catapults, and mobile towers could be put to good effect to capture a fortress.

The discovery of gunpowder led to the development of the world's earliest rockets and later to primitive artillery. This discovery did not have the dramatic impact on the nature of warfare in China the way that the introduction of the crossbow or even the stirrup did much earlier.[39] Yet, gunpowder and firearms did have significant impact in certain periods and specific campaigns. For example, artillery was effectively employed by China's armed forces during the Ming dynasty (1368–1644). In fact, the Ming was the first dynasty in China that 'systematically . . . produce[d] and deploy[ed] firearms throughout its military'. The Ming court found that the Portuguese had better weapons than the Chinese possessed so it obtained sample firearms and sought technological assistance. The result was improved arquebuses and cannon manufactured in Chinese armouries which the Ming armed forces put to good use. The Emperor Yongle (ruled 1403–25) began placing cannons in forts along the northern frontier to defend against raids by Central Asian nomads. The use of firearms likely gave the Ming an edge in dealing with the marauding Mongols and was 'unquestionably key' to the Ming's military victory in Korea against the Japanese (noted in the previous section). While the Japanese military had also adopted firearms, their focus was on arquebuses and, at least in Korea, Japanese forces were without artillery.[40] In this pre-modern round of campaign warfare of the late sixteenth century, the Chinese emerged victorious against the Japanese making better use of Western technology than their adversaries.

Nevertheless, the irony is that the civilization that had pioneered gunpowder centuries later became the victim of its invention, when modern artillery and firearms were used against the Chinese by European invaders who had successfully refined and developed this technology far beyond where the inventors had taken it.

Modern China

In the modern era, China has always seemed to be at a disadvantage technologically—always needing to counter the superiority of adversaries. In the early nineteenth century, it was European seafarers with superior maritime power; in the late nineteenth century and early twentieth century, it was the rapidly modernizing and expansionist Japanese with superior sea and land power; in the late twentieth century, it was the highly sophisticated arsenals and armies of the United States and the Soviet Union. But China did incorporate technology into warfare. Arguably, the first 'recognizably modern wars' fought on Chinese soil were in 1924 between the armies of rival warlords. The two conflicts—the

Jiangsu–Zhejiang War and the Zhili–Fengtian War—were waged 'in the style of the First World War'. The wars comprised campaigns of coordinated operations by infantry, cavalry, navy, and aircraft. There was considerable use of machine guns, modern artillery, barbed wire, and mines. Whenever possible, commanders made good use of railways to transport troops and equipment.[41]

Contemporary China first fully faced up to the vastness of the technological chasm in the 1950s in Korea. Here, large formations of well-trained and well-led, battle-hardened infantry confronted the awesome power of the world's most technologically advanced armed forces. US air power, firepower, and the spectre of atomic weaponry presented collectively a daunting and seemingly insurmountable hurdle to the Chinese forces.

Mao Zedong insisted:

> [t]he so-called theory that 'weapons decide everything'... [is] a subjective and one-sided view. Our view is opposed to this; we see not only weapons but also people. Weapons are an important factor in war, but not the decisive factor; it is people, not things, that are decisive. The contest of strength is not only a contest of military and economic power, but also a contest of human power and morale.[42]

He argued this in the late 1930s with reference to China facing the superior capabilities of Japan, but the same logic steeled China as it prepared to confront the far greater military might of the United States. Moreover, Chinese soldiers could draw comfort from the fact that the Communist movement had always faced Herculean challenges and vastly superior foes, and yet it had somehow managed to triumph. General Liu Zhen, the first commander of the newly created air arm of the CPV, on the eve of intervention in Korea felt overwhelmed by the magnitude of his mission. While experienced in land warfare, he confessed that air warfare was a complete 'mystery' and neither he nor any of his colleagues 'had any experience organizing or commanding air combat operations'. Moreover, Liu stated the obvious: '... in our levels of tactics and technology we were way, way below those of our enemy'. Nevertheless, what gave him inspiration was the 'resolute thought running through my mind... [that] the revolution had all along developed out of nothing, gone from small to big, developing as a brutal, difficult, death-defying struggle'.[43]

But the CPV grappled with the inescapable reality of US air-power dominance. It made for a logistical nightmare as soldiers and civilian workers struggled to maintain and repair roads and rail lines in the face of incessant bombing. Ensuring the flow of supplies and reinforcements to the Korean front was a constant struggle.[44] Chinese forces on the peninsula also operated under the threat of nuclear attack. While Mao publicly scoffed at the impact of nuclear weaponry, this masked a more serious concern. Although he was famously dismissive of nuclear weapons, dubbing them 'paper tigers', this did not stop him from later concluding that China must possess its own. After China had felt itself to be the victim of bullying and nuclear blackmail by the United States in Korea and the Taiwan Strait, Mao ordered the Chinese military, in 1955, to initiate its own nuclear programme to develop the bomb as quickly as possible.

China successfully detonated its first nuclear device in 1964.[45] Equally important was the decision in 1965 to develop a ballistic missile programme.[46] In sum, while man has been considered central in Chinese operational art, leveraging technology has been viewed as critical, especially in the contemporary era.

Offence and defence

The Great Wall is often interpreted as being emblematic of the defensive nature of Chinese strategy—the Chinese certainly insist this is the case.[47] While the wall might symbolize this at the strategic level—although it should be noted that there is significant scholarship suggesting that Chinese wall building has little, if anything, to do with a defensive strategic tradition—it does not appear to hold for the operational level.[48] The construction and maintenance of walls along imperial China's northern borders did not mean the end of offensive operations against the nomadic peoples of Central Asia.

What about China's operational art? Is it primarily defensive in character? The answer lies in the observation that, from ancient times, Chinese strategists have admonished commanders to seize the initiative and never relinquish it. Sun Zi certainly underscored this in chapter 6 of *The Art of War*, urging a commander to select the locations for battles and campaigns instead of permitting one's adversary to do so: 'Therefore, those skilled in war [must] bring the enemy to the field of battle and are not brought there by him'.[49]

In imperial China, generals sought to seize the initiative, which included both offensive and defensive military operations. What we now think of as the Great Wall and what most tourists see in locations near Beijing actually dates from the Ming dynasty (1368–1644).[50] Nevertheless, over the course of the 275 years of the Ming, China did not simply conduct defensive military operations. Many military expeditions were launched against the Mongols, the Vietnamese, the Japanese in Korea, as well as a variety of offensive operations to quell domestic rebellions and mutinies.

This included various Ming campaigns to deal with a perpetual scourge afflicting China's coastal regions: piracy. Pirates were routinely active all along the Chinese coast operating from bases in maritime south-eastern China. One of the most effective generals in dealing with the pirates was Qi Jiguang (1528–87) who focused on deploying several thousand carefully selected troops in both defensive and offensive operations on land and sea. With limited funding, Qi had to rely on simple weaponry and small ships. He focused the bulk of his energies on intensive drilling and modest junks each staffed by approximately fifty-five men. Then crew were divided into five units each assigned different tasks from handling artillery to firing arquebuses. The secret to Qi's success at anti-piracy operations appeared to be his dogged persistence along with readiness to shift quickly from a defensive stance into an offensive mode. This allowed him to wear down the less-disciplined pirates and ultimately defeat them.[51]

In modern times, Mao Zedong also urged his generals to maintain the initiative—even when on the strategic defensive during the initial phase of people's war. Mao advocated the operational principle of 'active defence'. While in the earliest stage of protracted people's war, Mao called for 'strategic defence', this did not mean surrendering the initiative. Moreover, while Mao advocated that his forces strike only after the enemy had struck, he did not mean simply waiting for an attack to come.

Strategic defence did not mean passive defence but included offensive operations. Thus, active defence did not condemn defenders to digging in and just waiting for the enemy to attack; rather, they could and should take the initiative as circumstances permitted.[52]

In the post-Mao era, active defence has altered its meaning to become an important strategic-level concept. Today, PLA strategists teach that the first battle is the decisive one and that he who strikes first has the advantage. In the twenty-first century, active defence does not preclude pre-emptive strikes.[53] According to Deng Xiaoping (also transliterated Teng Hsiao-ping), CCP leader and strategist, 'active defense is not merely defense per se, but also includes . . . our going out'. Senior Colonel Wang Naiming, writing in 1995, asserts that the principle of active defence epitomizes 'the organic integration of offense and defense'.[54] Whatever the meaning of the principle, it seems that Chinese soldiers are willing and able to employ both offensive and defensive operations. Thus, Mao's comments about operational art in the period of protracted revolutionary war made in the 1930s still resonate in the twenty-first century: 'Militarily speaking, our warfare consists of the alternate use of the defensive and the offensive'.[55]

Positional and mobile warfare

Consecutive dynasties and commanders have emphasized positional warfare. Indeed, China is famous for its sturdy and enduring fortifications, notably the legendary Great Wall of China. While successive Chinese rulers did engage in wall building, careful research has shown that the narrative of a massive fortification extending thousands of miles first constructed by the Emperor Qin Shihuang back in the second-century BC is a myth. The myth is potent because Qin is also credited with founding the first powerful unified Chinese state, and it is his tomb near present-day Xian which was unearthed in 1974 to reveal a massive army of terracotta warriors.

But Chinese generals have since ancient times engaged in mobile operations. This was true in the Spring and Autumn and the Warring States Periods. Generals employed chariots, cavalry, as well as massed infantry in campaigns against their adversaries. Mobile warfare continued into the dynastic era even as many emperors built and maintained mud, brick, or stone forts and walls as protection against northern nomadic peoples who launched raids against and even invasions of the northern Chinese plain. Furthermore, most cities were walled to protect against bandits and rival armies. For a significant period of Chinese history, until breakthroughs in siege warfare, these fortifications were quite effective in warding off enemies. But such fortifications did not negate the need for periodic expeditionary warfare against adversaries. Such structures provided locations for garrisoning troops and useful bases from which to launch mobile operations into the steppes.

While perhaps the most famous military legacy of the Ming dynasty is positional—the 'Great Wall' (see previous section)—this dynasty also engaged in a significant number of mobile campaigns. But as military engineers know, one well-constructed and sturdy fortification does not guarantee security. A system of fortifications was necessary—defence in depth—to protect China from nomadic raiders and invaders from the steppe. The Hongwu Emperor (1368–98) established a network of 'eight outer garrisons' as well as an inner line of forts. But construction of the 'Great Wall' would not happen for another 100 years.[56]

Wall building during the Ming was the result of domestic political compromise. Constructing fortifications was less expensive than all-out offensive operations against the Central Asian nomads. Following a court decision in 1472, a concerted initiative of wall building commenced. Two walls were completed in 1474, one 566 miles long and another 129 miles in length.[57] But periodic mobile operations into the steppe were also required as well as bribes and the granting of trading privileges. Thus, the Ming did not exclusively rely on walls; rather, a combination of positional warfare and mobile operations more or less succeeded in keeping the nomads at bay. Of course, these combined efforts required constant vigilance, attention, and a steady stream of resources, something that court politics made impossible to sustain indefinitely.[58]

Complete reliance on positional warfare is never advisable, especially for the weaker side. Mobile warfare, including operations to limit or curtail the mobility of one's adversary, was well worth attempting if possible. Napoleon is supposed to have remarked that armies march on their stomachs. Most Chinese military thinkers were clearly in agreement with this view, recognizing that campaigns of manoeuvre required extensive and well-conceived logistical operations. Sun Zi in chapter 2 of *The Art of War* suggested a ratio of one wagon of provisions for every 100 troops, and in chapter 7 he soberly observed '. . . that an army which lacks heavy equipment, fodder, food and stores will be lost'. Noting the difficulties and expense of provisioning one's forces, Sun Zi counselled (in chapter 2) that a 'wise general sees to it that his troops feed on the enemy' because 'enemy fodder' was far more cost-effective than bringing one's own supplies.[59] Located in the 'Provisions' section of *One Hundred Unorthodox Strategies*, one can find what Ralph Sawyer calls the 'most famous incendiary raid in Chinese history'. The episode took place in the Later Han (during the second century AD); General Ts'ao Ts'ao commanded a vastly outnumbered force that was exhausted and very low on supplies. Facing a desperate situation, they were suddenly handed a piece of vital intelligence by a defector: a vulnerable supply train of 10,000 wagons, guarded by a modest escort, was located nearby. Ts'ao Ts'ao decided to seize the enemy supplies. He led 5,000 cavalry disguised as enemy forces in a daring night-time operation. The audacious action achieved maximum surprise and shock value and was not only a great victory, but proved to be the 'turning point' of the entire campaign.[60]

Moreover, for much of its history, China has been plagued by banditry, piracy, and rebellion, often with a thin line separating them. Bandits could claim to be rebels, and outlaws could evolve into rebels. Both outlaws and rebels relied on superior mobility to survive larger and better-equipped forces of the ruling dynasty. One of the most famous pirates was Zheng Chenggong or Koxinga who proved a thorn in the side of the Manchu Qing dynasty during its early years (mid-seventeenth century) from his base on the island of Taiwan. Koxinga derived significant support from his claim to be fighting to restore the Ming dynasty by battling the Manchu invaders. A famous rebel was Hong Xiuquan, who spearheaded the Taiping Rebellion and waged a protracted fourteen-year-long armed insurrection against the Qing dynasty. Starting in 1850, Hong successfully wrested control over much of southern China establishing his capital in Nanjing. The Taipings were eventually defeated in 1864.

The Communists, of course, tapped into this tradition of insurgency and banditry for inspiration. Mao argued that Chinese history was a record of peasant uprisings and claimed that the CCP was heir to a glorious revolutionary tradition. It was precisely in the spirit of motivating and instructing his forces that Mao articulated the essence of his operational art as follows:

> The enemy advances, we retreat;
> The enemy camps, we harass;
> The enemy tires, we attack;
> The enemy retreats, we pursue.[61]

The pithy slogan encapsulated the mobile operations the Communists endeavoured to practise in a simple and straightforward way that uneducated peasants could easily grasp.

Mobility is especially important in guerrilla warfare so that units can quickly move and disperse forces in order to avoid posing as a big target and hence being visible and vulnerable to attack. Moreover, mobility enabled dispersed forces to rapidly concentrate at a decisive point for attack.[62]

Once the CCP had seized power and the insurgents had become the regime, positional warfare became more important. China's cities, infrastructure, and borders switched from targets for attack to facilities requiring protection. Still, this marked a change at the strategic level since the Communists did not have expansionist goals beyond the territory they claimed (Taiwan, Tibet, etc.) as being part and parcel of China historically.

What did not change was a Communist operational preference to be on the move and seizing the initiative. This penchant can be clearly seen in the first eight months (October 1950–May 1951) of China's intervention in Korea with the launching of a series of no less than five offensives. The initial two campaigns—launched in October and November 1950—yielded remarkable successes, with the CPV recapturing Pyongyang and pushing the UNC forces back to the 38th parallel. However, instead of recognizing that the CPV needed time to rest and regroup as well as the importance of Chinese generals needing to reassess operational imperatives, Mao insisted CPV commander Peng Dehuai press forward and win a quick victory. Aside from the simple matter of Chinese troops being exhausted from incessant marching and fighting in an alien land, just as serious was the fact that these forces had run low on food and ammunition. Logistics are a critical dimension in any kind of warfare, especially in mobile operations where forces are moving rapidly and further from their home base. The problem in Korea was particularly acute because logistics had not been given due attention, since, historically, supply had not been a monumental issue when Communist forces were operating inside China. During the Chinese Civil War, soldiers either operated in close proximity to a base area, could live off the land, and/or survived on captured enemy foodstuffs and equipment.[63] During the five mobile campaigns in Korea, poor logistics severely hampered operations. Soldiers did not get enough food, warm clothing, or ammunition.[64]

Eventually, the war became bogged down in a bloody positional conflict between massed infantry and high-powered artillery operating from heavily fortified positions. Ultimately, the war ended in a stalemate with neither side able to break through the other's intricate network of trenches and tunnels.

The same logistical inadequacies noted in Korea also emerged two decades later to hamper mobile operations during the attack on Vietnam. Soldiers reportedly had to go without food or drinking water for extended periods because of stretched supply lines. While, in 1950, Chinese armies were battle tested and experienced in matters of command, control, and communication from decades of guerrilla combat and years of large-scale conventional operations against Nationalist forces, the same was not true in 1979. In Vietnam, orders were confused, coordination between units was poor, and radios routinely did not function. The irony was that distances in the theatre of operations were far shorter—albeit along a 600-mile front—in 1979 than they had been in the 1950s in Korea.[65]

While Chinese operational art has revealed a preference for mobile warfare, positional warfare has proved to be an important dimension for successful Chinese commanders.

Theatrical production or waging real war?

How does one measure victory? Is the criterion of success inflicting a crushing defeat on your adversary or demonstrating one's steely resolve? Is Chinese war fighting more about 'saving face' or achieving overwhelming victory on the field of battle? Some scholars contend that, for the Chinese, war is all about symbolism and call to mind the drama and spectacle of Chinese opera.[66] Other scholars insist that Chinese military operations, at least in the contemporary era, are about battles of annihilation and wars of attrition.[67] The reality seems to be a combination. At times, the purpose of an artillery barrage or attack seems to be for propaganda—to put on a display of the regime's resolve for the benefit of the

Chinese people; at times, the goal appears to be to defeat enemy forces in a decisive manner on the field of battle; at other times, the goal may be both.

A famous instance in ancient Chinese history is how T'ien Tan rescued the state of Ch'i in the Warring States Period. The city of Chi-mo was besieged for five years. The situation was dire and the defenders were desperate. T'ien Tan made careful preparations for a surprise spectacle worthy of a Hollywood epic. He orchestrated a series of strange moves to puzzle and confuse the besieging army. The culmination was a consummate night-time performance complete with lights, flashy costumes, and sound effects. These theatrics were conducted with military precision and in deadly earnest, all to maximum effect. T'ien Tan instructed the people to dress a thousand cattle in bright red cloth decorated with 'five colored dragon veins'. Razor-sharp blades were securely attached to the horns of each beast and oil-soaked torches were firmly bound to their tails. The defenders quietly made multiple breaches in the city walls. Then, at the appointed hour one night, the cattle were sent stampeding out through the breaches with torches alight, closely pursued by silent soldiers ready for combat. The inhabitants in the city provided eerie background music by clanging metal implements together and beating drums. The supernatural spectacle of what appeared to be hundreds of dragons charging the stirring encampment and drawing blood from every sleepy soldier they came in contact with so terrified the besiegers that they fled in fear. This dramatic victory is listed as one of the *Thirty-Six Stratagems* and one of the *One Hundred Unorthodox Strategies*.[68]

Symbolic victory and military success were both important in dynastic China and ultimate triumph depended on campaign follow-through. Perhaps no more so than in the so-called Tumu incident of 1449 when the Ming emperor's chief adviser anticipated an easy victory over Mongol forces. This excessive optimism led Wang Zhen to persuade the Emperor Zhengtong (r. 1435–49) to come and witness the successful campaign first-hand. With an estimated half a million soldiers, the emperor set out from Beijing to the steppe. A series of costly mistakes and inept leadership resulted in a dramatic Mongol victory over the Chinese expeditionary force in August 1449. Instead of a symbolic Ming victory, the outcome was a Mongol battlefield victory in which the Chinese emperor was taken captive and his chief adviser killed. Yet complete victory in the campaign eluded the Mongols, who proved unable to leverage their important prisoner to any advantage. The Ming court did not capitulate; instead, it simply abandoned the captured emperor and enthroned a new one. Meanwhile, the Mongols swept down on Beijing in October but, unable to capture the Ming capital, they returned virtually empty-handed to the steppe.[69] Battlefield triumph and symbolic victory did not translate into campaign success in this instance.

In the contemporary era as well, war fighting was about spectacles as well as campaigns and battles of annihilation. The so-called border conflicts with India (1962), the Soviet Union (1969), and Vietnam (1979) were not so much about acquiring or defending disputed territory as they were about demonstrating China's resolve to an adversary. While border disputes did in each case significantly figure in Beijing's decision to go to war, the overriding goal behind each instance was a desire for the countries concerned to take China more seriously. Because Beijing believed it was perceived as weaker or less militarily prepared by each adversary, foremost in the minds of Chinese leaders was driving home the point that China must be taken seriously. The PLA would not back away from a fight. In none of these three combat operations was the purpose to seize and hold territory. Rather, Chinese forces attacked their adversaries in sharp and bloody engagements before eventually withdrawing from the disputed terrain.

Meanwhile, war fighting against the KMT forces on offshore islands in the Taiwan Strait during the early 1950s was a different story. Although these operations were certainly full of symbolism—demonstrating the CCP's intent to complete the unification of China and show unwavering commitment to achieve total victory against the Nationalists—the goal of these operations was the actual capture of selected offshore islands. Thus, the propaganda from Mao about Beijing allowing the KMT to hold these islands as part of a shrewd 'noose strategy' to allow Beijing to exert pressure on Chiang Kai-shek and maintain links between the mainland and Taiwan was an *ex post facto* rationale to cope with operational failure. By the late 1950s, Mao had given up on success on the battlefield and began in earnest to manipulate hostilities against the offshore islands for propaganda and political theatre.[70]

The 1995–6 Taiwan Strait crisis is best classified as a 'show of force' in which Beijing engaged in sabre-rattling to warn Taipei and Washington that China was seriously upset with the actions of both. The show was also an effort on the part of top political leader Jiang Zemin to assuage the PLA and the Chinese people, who were irate at what was widely perceived as the traitorous acts of Taiwanese authorities and the perfidy of the United States. The missile tests off the coast of Taiwan and the military exercises in late 1995 and early 1996 were calibrated to send messages to each audience.[71]

It must be stressed that, while symbolism and propaganda are important hallmarks of Chinese Communist warfare, so too are battles of annihilation. The PRC has not demonstrated any reluctance to use force when it is deemed necessary. Official pronouncements and doctrinal writings insist China only employs military means as a last resort. However, once a decision to conduct military operations has been made, there seems to be no turning back. Beijing has demonstrated a pattern of verbal warnings in the lead-up to employing military power discernible in cases such as Korea and India.[72] These verbal blasts have been read as signals of deterrence to be heeded by the adversary. Instead of being aimed at making the use of actual force unnecessary, this rhetoric appears to serve the purpose of rationalizing in Chinese minds that they had made every effort to use peaceful means before resorting to force. Moreover, the use of operational pauses has been interpreted by analysts as signalling a desire for negotiation; however, upon closer examination, these moves seem to have no strategic-level deterrent or compellence function, but are simply opportunities intended for Chinese forces to regroup and prepare for the next offensive. In Korea, for example, the break-off of contact by Chinese forces in November 1950 was not to signal restraint and a lost opportunity that the United States failed to read correctly at the time; rather, it was so that the

CPV could prepare for the next campaign. Beijing had decided that its strategic goal was the occupation of the entire Korean Peninsula and the operational goal was to sweep southwards all the way to Pusan.[73]

In Chinese conflicts since 1949 we have witnessed the carefully calibrated use of force, but these operations entailed significant calculated risks. While Beijing clearly intended in each case to keep the war limited, all of these instances entailed considerable risk of escalation. In the final analysis, while the Chinese believe they have used military force sparingly, in practice they have demonstrated little hesitation to use the repeated application of force, as deemed necessary.[74] The PLA has traditionally sought to concentrate superior numbers on a specific enemy force, isolate it, and attempt to annihilate the force.[75] These characteristics are evident in Chinese operations in Korea, India, and Vietnam. However, for the PRC, the ultimate criterion of victory is not operational success but geostrategic advantage.[76] Beijing's goal is not so much capturing territory or inflicting casualties and destruction on the enemy, but rather to make a larger point. This point can include demonstrating resolve to others and/or the Chinese people.

CONCLUSION

Chinese operational art is a combination of orthodox and unorthodox elements, a mixture of man and technology, a blend of offence and defence, as well as mobile and positional warfare. At times, Chinese soldiers are fighting for show; at times, they are fighting for military victory, and, at other times, for both. These dimensions are not merely evident in contemporary China but in earlier eras as well. How distinct is Chinese operational art compared to the operational arts of other countries? The above-mentioned hallmarks can be found in the operational manuals, strategic tomes, and military histories of other countries, as well as in practice on the fields of battle, although perhaps combined in somewhat different measures and variations. Nevertheless, the putative differences may be less evident in the actual practice of the operational art than they are often imagined to be. Moreover, these differences may be manifested more at the higher levels of strategy than at the operational level. It does seem clear that there are cultural distinctions in the way strategic thinkers approach matters of war and peace—beliefs about the efficacy of military force, and assumptions about their own strategic traditions. Certainly, Chinese strategists firmly believe this is so.[77] But whether these beliefs translate into real differences in how China's military conducts operations relative to the armed forces of other states cannot be answered conclusively in this short chapter.

How effective is Chinese operational art in the twenty-first century? There has been no major war since 1979 to show conclusively the state of the art. However, one can look at evolving PLA doctrine, performance in peacekeeping operations (PKOs), and execution in military exercises conducted in recent years, as well as the PLA's response to domestic crises, such as the popular protests of 1989, and natural disasters, such as the tragic 2008 Sichuan earthquake. Doctrinal development suggests refinements and increasing sophistication in combined and joint operations. Performances in PKOs reveal that the PLA is more capable. Of course, China sends its brightest commanders and best-trained forces abroad. These operations, at considerable distances from home, have involved relatively small units and in most cases, many functions, including overall command, control, and logistics, have been performed by the militaries of other countries. In recent years, the PLA has sought to make field exercises more realistic with opposition forces and live ammunition, for example. China has also conducted a growing number of multinational exercises, including a number beyond China's borders, with a variety of other countries, most notably with the militaries of member countries of the Shanghai Cooperation Organization.[78]

The PLA's operational response to the spring 1989 demonstrations in Beijing was mixed. On the one hand, this was not the kind of scenario for which the armed forces had trained or were equipped; on the other, the forces performed unevenly. However, in the final analysis, use of lethal force against unarmed civilians was caused less by the operational inadequacies of China's military than by glaring incompetence and acute paranoia on the part of China's political leaders.[79] Lastly, the PLA's response to the devastating earthquake that struck Sichuan Province in May 2008 showcased the heroics and muscle power of dedicated Chinese soldiers rather than any enhanced operational capabilities for humanitarian assistance or disaster relief. The PLA was found wanting in terms of the availability of appropriate technology, the ability swiftly to mobilize manpower and equipment and transport these promptly to the affected region. Taken together, these episodes reveal that China's armed forces are increasingly sophisticated and more capable operationally, while, at the same time, the PLA continues to be hamstrung by certain limitations, including inadequate force-projection capabilities even within China's own borders.[80]

In the first decade of the twenty-first century, Chinese operational art is on the cusp of change. Joint- and combined-arms operations are now taken seriously, although the use of air power has never been a critical factor in Chinese military conflict in the twentieth century. What has been a central preoccupation, however, is countering enemy air power, such as in Korea in the 1950s. This preoccupation continues today and, as a result, a significant element of the PLA air-force mission in the early twenty-first century is air defence.[81] Meanwhile, maritime operations are of increasing interest as China pays greater attention to the strategic significance of the seas. One indication of this is the PLA navy's dispatch of a small flotilla in December 2008 to engage in anti-piracy operations in the Gulf of Aden.

NOTES

1. For some excellent recent surveys of Chinese military history, see David Graff and Robin Higham (eds.), *A Military History of China* (Boulder, CO: Westview, 2002); Xiaobing Li, *A History of the Modern Chinese Army* (Lexington, KY: University Press of

Kentucky, 2007); Bruce A. Elleman, *Modern Chinese Warfare, 1795–1989* (London: Routledge, 2001); Peter Lorge, *War, Politics, and Society in Early Modern China, 900–1795* (London: Routledge, 2005); David A. Graff, *Medieval Chinese Warfare, 300–900* (London: Routledge, 2002). For an extremely comprehensive treatment of campaigns in China since the late 1940s, see Mark A. Ryan, David M. Finkelstein, and Michael A. McDevitt (eds.), *Chinese Warfighting: The PLA Experience Since 1949* (Armonk, NY: M. E. Sharpe, 2003).

2. See, for example, Geoffrey Parker (ed.), *Cambridge Illustrated History of Warfare: The Triumph of the West* (Cambridge: Cambridge University Press, 1995), 2; John Keegan, *A History of Warfare* (London: Hutchinson, 1993), 214–15.
3. See, for example, Michael I. Handel, *Masters of War: Classical Strategic Thought* (3rd rev. edn.; London: Routledge, 2007).
4. Peng Guangqian and Yao Youzhi (chief editors), *The Science of Military Strategy* (Beijing: Military Science Publishing House, 2005), 4. This is the official English translation of the 2001 Chinese-language book *Zhanlue xue* [Junshi Kexue Chubanshe]. Some of the most well-known of these ancient tomes can be found in Ralph D. Sawyer (trans.), *The Seven Military Classics of Ancient China* (Boulder, CO: Westview Press, 1993).
5. Mao noted the influence of such books to his first Western biographer. See Edgar Snow, *Red Star over China* (New York: Random House, 1938), 115–16. On the wider influence of *The Water Margin* and *Romance of the Three Kingdoms* on contemporary Chinese strategists, see Ralph D. Sawyer with Mei-Chun Lee Sawyer, *The Tao of Deception: Unorthodox Warfare in Historic and Modern China* (New York: Basic Books, 2007), 331–54.
6. See, for example, John K. Fairbank, 'Introduction: Varieties of the Chinese Military Experience', in Frank A. Kierman, Jr., and John K. Fairbank (eds.), *Chinese Ways in Warfare* (Cambridge, MA: Harvard University Press, 1974), 1–26. For a critical discussion of these contentions, see Andrew Scobell, *China's Use of Military Force: Beyond the Great Wall and the Long March* (New York: Cambridge University Press, 2003), ch. 2.
7. Peng and Yao, *The Science of Military Strategy*, 3.
8. Howard L. Boorman and Scott A. Boorman, 'Strategy and National Psychology in China', *Annals of the American Academy of Social and Political Science*, CLXX (1967), 143–55 (quote is on 152). For perhaps the most sustained treatment, see Sawyer with Sawyer, *The Tao of Deception.*
9. Handel, *Masters of War*, 25. Handel calls Sun Zi's approach to war an 'idealized paradigm' (ibid., 22).
10. This thinking pervades a number of works, including Ross Munro and Richard Bernstein, *The Coming Conflict with China* (New York: Alfred A. Knopf, 1997).
11. See, for example, Edward L. Dreyer, 'The Poyang Campaign, 1363: Inland Naval Warfare in the Founding of the Ming Dynasty', in Kierman, Jr., and Fairbank (eds.), *Chinese Ways in Warfare*, 202–42.
12. See, for example, Michael McDevitt, 'The Strategic and Operational Context Driving PLA Navy Building' and Bernard D. Cole, 'Right-Sizing the Navy: How Much Naval Force Will Beijing Deploy?' both in Roy Kamphausen and Andrew Scobell, *Right-Sizing the People's Liberation Army: Exploring the Contours of China's Military* (Carlisle Barracks, PA: Strategic Studies Institute, 2007), 481–556.
13. On Chinese anti-access strategies, see Roger Cliff, Mark Burles, Michael S. Chase, Derek Eaton, and Kevin Pollpeter, *Entering the Dragon's Lair: Chinese Antiaccess*

Strategies and Their Implications for the United States (Santa Monica, CA: RAND, 2007). On the PLA's threat to the US military, see Thomas J. Christensen, 'Posing Problems without Catching Up: China's Rise and Its Challenge for U.S. Security Policy', *International Security*, 25: 4 (Spring 2001), 5–40.

14. This point is also made by other students of Chinese strategy and war fighting, including Paul H. B. Godwin. See, for example, Paul H. B. Godwin, 'Change and Continuity in Chinese Military Doctrine, 1949–1999', in Ryan, Finkelstein, and McDevitt (eds.), *Chinese Warfighting*, 23.
15. 'On Protracted War' (May 1938), in *Selected Works of Mao Tse-tung*, vol. II (Beijing: Foreign Languages Press, 1967), 136–45.
16. Li, *A History of the Modern Chinese Army*, 72.
17. Ibid., 72–5.
18. Liao–Shen is short for Liaoxi–Shenyang campaign (12 September–2 November 1948); Ping–Jin is short for Beiping–Tianjin campaign (21 November 1948–31 January 1949); Huai–Hai is short for Huai River–Lunghai Railway (6 November 1948–10 January 1949).
19. Li, *A History of the Modern Chinese Army*, 75.
20. Gary J. Bjorge, *Moving the Enemy: Operational Art in the Chinese PLA's Huai Hai Campaign*, Leavenworth Paper no. 22 (Fort Leavenworth, KS: Combat Studies Institute Press, 2004).
21. For concise discussion of these asserted proclivities, see Andrew Scobell, 'Is There a Chinese Way of War?' *Parameters*, XXXV: 1 (Spring 2005), 118–22.
22. 'Problems of Strategy in China's Revolutionary War' (December 1936), in *Selected Works of Mao Tse-tung*, vol. I (Peking: Foreign Languages Press, 1967), 185–6. See also ten operational principles identified by Mao. These are located in 'The Present Situation and Our Tasks' (25 December 1947), in *Selected Works of Mao Tse-tung*, vol. IV (Peking: Foreign Languages Press, 1969), 161–2. These operational principles remain relevant in the twenty-first century. See Wang Houqing and Zhang Xingye (eds.), *Zhanyi Xue* [The Study of Campaigns] (Beijing: Guofang Daxue Chubanshe, 2000). While there is no official English translation of this volume, it has been the focus of a number of English-language analyses. See, for example, Christensen, 'Posing Problems without Catching Up' and Dennis J. Blasko, *The Chinese Army Today: Tradition and Transformation for the 21st Century* (London: Routledge, 2006), ch. 5.
23. Orthodox and unorthodox are the terms preferred by Ralph Sawyer. Sawyer with Sawyer, *The Seven Military Classics*, 164–5. Samuel Griffith prefers to translate *zheng* and *qi* as 'normal' and 'extraordinary', respectively. See Samuel Griffith (trans.), *Sun Tzu: The Art of War* (New York: Oxford University Press, 1963), 91.
24. This is the Sawyers' translation. See their *The Seven Military Classics*, 165. For more discussion on the meaning of 'unorthodox', see Sawyer with Sawyer, *The Tao of Deception*, 61–6.
25. 'Problems of Strategy in Guerrilla War against Japan' (May 1938), in *Selected Works of Mao Tse-tung*, vol. II (Peking: Foreign Languages Press, 1967), 81.
26. See, for example, the discussion in Handel, *Masters of War*, ch. 11.
27. This episode is summarized in Griffith (trans.), *Sun Tzu*, 97–8, and recounted in Sawyer with Sawyer, *The Tao of Deception*, 362–71.
28. Peter Lorge, *War, Politics and Society in Early Modern China, 900–1795* (London: Routledge, 2005), 134.
29. Larry M. Wortzel, 'The Beiping–Tianjin Campaign of 1948–1949', in Ryan, Finkelstein, and McDevitt (eds.), *Chinese Warfighting*, 57.

30. These different means of achieving victory are highlighted by Lieutenant General Li Jijun, former vice-president of the Academy of Military Science, in an address to the US Army War College in July 1997. See Li Jijun, *Traditional Military Thinking and the Defensive Strategy of China*, Letort Paper no. 1 (Carlisle Barracks, PA: Strategic Studies Institute, 1997), 5. General Li also notes the capture of a third city, Hohehot, by stratagem.
31. Larry Wortzel makes the same point. See Wortzel, 'The Beiping–Tianjin Campaign of 1948–1949', 67.
32. For a useful volume of analyses and selected translations of Chinese military memoirs, see Xiaobing Li, Allan R. Millett, and Bin Yu (trans. and eds.), *Mao's Generals Remember Korea* (Lawrence, KS: University Press of Kansas, 2001).
33. Li, *A History of the Modern Chinese Army*, 110–11.
34. See Thomas Robinson, 'The Sino-Indian Border Conflicts of 1969: New Evidence Three Decades Later', in Ryan, Finkelstein, and McDevitt (eds.), *Chinese Warfighting*, 198–216.
35. Cheng Feng and Larry M. Wortzel, 'PLA Operational Principles and Limited War: The Sino-Indian War of 1962', in Ryan, Finkelstein, and McDevitt (eds.), *Chinese Warfighting*, 173–97. See also Li Jijun, *Traditional Military Thinking and the Defensive Strategy of China*, 5.
36. Zhang Xiaoming, 'China's 1979 War with Vietnam: A Reassessment', *China Quarterly*, no. 184 (December 2005), 863–5. This account is largely consistent with the earlier one by Harlan Jencks. See Harlan W. Jencks, 'China's "Punitive" War on Vietnam: A Military Assessment', *Asian Survey*, 19 (August 1979), 801–15. Jencks also notes the very slow progress of operations against Lang Son (ibid., 811). See also Edward C. O'Dowd, *Chinese Military Strategy in the Third Indochina War: The Last Maoist War* (New York: Routledge, 2007).
37. On the date of the introduction of the crossbow, see Joseph Needham, Robin D. S. Yates with the collaboration of Krzysztof Gawlikowski, Edward McEwen, and Wang Ling, *Science and Civilization in China*, vol. 5, *Chemistry and Chemical Technology*, part. VI, *Military Technology: Missiles and Sieges* (Cambridge: Cambridge University Press, 1994), 139. For more on the crossbow, see 120–83.
38. For analyses of siege warfare in medieval China, see Herbert Franke, 'Siege and Defense of Towns in Medieval China', in Kierman, Jr., and Fairbank (eds.), *Chinese Ways of Warfare*, 151–201; and Needham et al., *Military Technology: Missiles and Sieges*, 241–485.
39. Edward L. Dreyer, 'Military Continuities: The PLA and Imperial China', in William W. Whitson (ed.), *The Military and Political Power in China in the 1970s* (New York: Praeger, 1971), 3–24.
40. Lorge, *War, Politics and Society in Early Modern China*, 125.
41. Arthur Waldron, *From War to Nationalism: China's Turning Point, 1924–1925* (New York: Cambridge University Press, 1995), 4.
42. 'On Protracted War', 143.
43. Liu Zhen, *Liu Zhen Huiyilu* [Memoirs of Liu Zhen] (Beijing: Jiefangjun Chubanshe, 1990), 337–8 and 342, quoted in Scobell, *China's Use of Military Force*, 90–1.
44. See, for example, Jonathan D. Pollack, 'The Korean War and Sino-American Relations', in Harry Harding and Yuan Ming (eds.), *Sino-American Relations, 1945–1955: A Joint Reassessment of a Critical Decade* (Wilmington, DE: Scholarly Resources, 1989), 226–7.
45. John W. Lewis and Xue Litai, *China Builds the Bomb* (Stanford, CA: Stanford University Press, 1988).

46. Li, *A History of the Modern Chinese Army*, 174.
47. Li Jijun, *Traditional Military Thinking and the Defensive Strategy of China*, 4.
48. On the history behind the myth of the construction of the Great Wall, see Arthur Waldron, *The Great Wall of China: From History to Myth* (New York: Cambridge University Press, 1990). See also Nicola Di Cosmo, *Ancient China and Its Enemies* (Cambridge: Cambridge University Press, 2002), ch. 4.
49. Griffith (trans.), *Sun Tzu*, 96.
50. Waldron, *The Great Wall of China*.
51. Lorge, *War, Politics and Society in Early Modern China*, 126–8.
52. 'Problems of Strategy in China's Revolutionary War' (September 1936), in *Selected Works of Mao Tse-tung*, vol. I, 204–8.
53. Scobell, *China's Use of Military Force*, 35.
54. The Deng quotation is from Chen Zhou, 'Differences between China's Theory of Modern Local War and America's Theory of Limited War', *Zhongguo Junshe Kexue*, 4 (1995), 46; and Wang Naiming, 'Adhere to Active Defense and Modern People's War', in Michael Pillsbury (ed.), *Chinese Views of Future Warfare* (Washington, DC: National Defense University Press, 1997), 37. Both quotations can be found in Scobell, *China's Use of Military Force*, 35.
55. 'Problems of Strategy in China's Revolutionary War', 208.
56. Waldron, *The Great Wall of China*, 76.
57. Ibid., 103, 105.
58. Ibid., chs. 7, 8, 9.
59. Griffith (trans.), *Sun Tzu*, 72, 104, 174.
60. Sawyer with Sawyer, *The Tao of Deception*, 146–50. *One Hundred Unorthodox Strategies* first appeared in China approximately 600 years ago. See Sawyer with Sawyer, *The Tao of Deception*, 291–5.
61. 'A Single Spark Can Start a Prairie Fire' (January 1930), *Selected Works of Mao Tse-tung*, vol. I, 121.
62. See, for example, guideline 4 of Mao's operational principles: 'Present Situation and Our Tasks', 161.
63. See guideline 9 of Mao's operational principles: 'Present Situation and Our Tasks', 162.
64. Li, *A History of the Modern Chinese Army*, 96–101; Pollack, 'The Korean War and Sino-American Relations', 224–5.
65. Zhang, 'China's 1979 War with Vietnam', 871; and Li, *A History of the Modern Chinese Army*, 254–7.
66. Jonathan Adelman and Chih-Yu Shih, *Symbolic War: The Chinese Use of Force, 1840–1980* (Taipei: Institute of International Relations, 1993).
67. Mark Ryan, David Finkelstein, and Michael McDevitt, 'Introduction: Patterns of PLA Warfighting', in Ryan, Finkelstein, and McDevitt (eds.), *Chinese Warfighting*, 9–10.
68. On this episode, see Sawyer with Sawyer, *The Tao of Deception*, 3–6. See also Sun Haichen, *The Wiles of War: 36 Military Strategies from Ancient China* (Beijing: Foreign Languages Press, 1993). For a discussion of the thirty-six stratagems, see Sawyer with Sawyer, *The Tao of Deception*, 354–9.
69. Lorge, *War, Politics and Society in Early Modern China*, 121–3.
70. Thomas J. Christensen, *Useful Adversaries: Grand Strategy, Domestic Mobilization, and Sino-American Conflict, 1947–1958* (Princeton, NJ: Princeton University Press, 1996), ch. 6.
71. Scobell, *China's Use of Military Force*, ch. 8.

72. Allen S. Whiting, *The Chinese Calculus of Deterrence: India and Indochina* (Ann Arbor, MI: University of Michigan Press, 1975).
73. The classic case was in Korea. While the CPV's pause in fighting in November 1950 has been interpreted by Whiting as Chinese signalling, Christensen has demonstrated that this lull was actually a strategic pause. See Christensen, *Useful Adversaries*, ch. 5.
74. Scobell, 'Is There a Chinese Way of War?', 119.
75. See guidelines 2, 3, 5, and 6 of Mao's operational principles: 'The Present Situation and Our Tasks', 161.
76. Scobell, 'Is There a Chinese Way of War?', 118. See also Ron Christman, 'How Beijing Evaluates Military Campaigns: An Initial Assessment', in Burkitt and Wortzel, *The Lessons of History*, 253–92.
77. For discussion and analysis of the beliefs of Chinese strategists about their own strategic traditions, see Scobell, *China's Use of Force*, ch. 2. For discussion of Chinese beliefs about US and Japanese strategic traditions, see Scobell, *China and Strategic Culture* (Carlisle Barracks, PA: Strategic Studies Institute, 2002), 14–23.
78. For more analysis, see Blasko, *The Chinese Army Today*, ch. 7; and Andrew J. Nathan and Andrew Scobell, *China's Search for Security* (New York: Columbia University Press, forthcoming 2011), ch. 11.
79. This case is complex. For a detailed examination, see Scobell, *China's Use of Military Force*, ch. 7.
80. See Nathan and Scobell, *China's Search for Security*, ch. 11.
81. John W. Lewis and Xue Litai, *Imagined Enemies: China Prepares for Uncertain War* (Stanford, CA: Stanford University Press, 2006), 38–9.

Conclusion

John Andreas Olsen and Martin van Creveld

This book has presented various perspectives on the evolution of operational art—the essential linkage between the higher level of strategy and the lower level of tactics—by scrutinizing how operational theory and practice have evolved in various armed forces over time. Operational art did not emerge all at once, but instead grew slowly and gradually. Ideas developed, they were tested in wars, and new ideas and concepts were built upon them. Over time, the theory and practice of operational art adapted to accord with contemporary circumstances, and it was these very adjustments and redefinitions of operational art that ensured its continuing relevance.

The authors of the various chapters differ in their interpretations of how armed forces have applied operational art in the past. However, all of them recognize history as a process subject to political, economic, and social changes on the one hand and military-technological advances on the other. Further, they share a view of operational art as interactive: in seeking victories in time and space operational art uses tactics as its *means* and serves strategy as its *end*, and even the most elegantly conceived operational plan will ultimately fail if it is paired with unrealistic war aims. Stated differently, the relationships among strategy, operational art, and tactics are more important to success than operational art in isolation. Only by understanding these relationships can a military leader adhere to Gerhard von Scharnhorst's dictum to 'consider the whole of war before its components'.[1] Strategy is the art of using available and sufficient means to attain the objective of the war; operational art is the theory and practice of planning and conducting operations; and tactics is the art of winning the actual battles. A somewhat simplistic, but nevertheless illustrative, way to capture this concept is that *strategy* is the art of war, *operational art* the art of campaigning, and *tactics* the art of battle.[2]

An extension of this conceptual framework leads to recognition that success in operational art depends on two other factors. First, a plan of campaign must include a termination phase. Termination represents an essential link between strategy and operational art; what is commonly termed an 'exit strategy' is in fact a goal and product of operational art. Political leaders and military commanders tend to devote far more time and effort to planning and preparing for war, and identifying the optimal timing for attack, than to visualizing the desired end state and the best way to achieve it. Yet, to state the obvious, 'every war must end', and success in warfare is determined by that ending. Second, as these case studies show, operational success depends on a plan that is logistically feasible. Logistical considerations must be an integral part of any plan of campaign, since the logistical component of the operation ensures sustainability. Many campaigns throughout history have failed simply because of logistical over-stretch.

This book's point of reference is campaigns, and these campaigns have typically been large-scale operations. But wars from the time of Napoleon to the end of the Second World War differ from the wars currently being fought in Afghanistan and Iraq. In today's world, insurgency and counter-insurgency have become the most common and, in many ways, most important forms of war—far more common than regular warfare between nation states. The relative infrequency of large-scale operations and the prevalence of smaller ones, often irregular and 'unruly' in nature, and often without the classic rear and front lines, have led analysts to question the current and future relevance of operational art.

While such scepticism is understandable, operational art is and will remain an important element in the cognitive process of planning and conducting campaigns, whether they target regular forces or insurgents. Just as the aim, scale, and scope of today's campaign plans differ from those seen in the days of Napoleon, so the aim, scale, and scope of operational art must change to reflect current realities. Hence, the appropriate question is not whether operational art is relevant to the future, but rather how we—theorists and practitioners alike—can make operational art relevant to the challenges at hand. It is easy to dismiss operational art as *passé*; it is more difficult, but far more interesting and useful, to make it applicable to today's and tomorrow's operations.

In accepting that *the times they are a-changin'* it is important to recognize new features that demand new responses. Dr Antulio Echevarria offers a useful distinction when he refers to war's 'first grammar'—the principles and procedures related to defeating an opponent by armed force—compared to war's 'second grammar'—the handling of insurgents, guerrillas, partisans, terrorists, and various forms of irregular warfare. General Sir Rupert Smith makes a similar distinction when he asserts that 'war amongst the people' has replaced traditional industrial war. In the epilogue to this book, he suggests that the new paradigm is best characterized by an ebb and flow between confrontation and conflict, where the objectives for military forces are no longer 'take, hold, destroy, defeat,' but, for example, 'create a safe and secure environment'. Under the old paradigm, the objective was to destroy the opponent; under the new paradigm, the objective is to alter the opponent's intentions. Where the old paradigm considered military force supreme, the new accords equal importance to diplomatic, political, economic, social, and legal measures.

In describing the trends that distinguish the new paradigm from industrial war, Sir Rupert suggests that success in operational art will require changes in mindsets as well as in military institutions, structures, and processes, as all are currently based on an outdated view of warfare. He concludes that if operational art is to be relevant and useful in the future, we must understand it as 'a combination of a free, creative, and original expression of the use of force and forces; a design; and direction, an expression of the character and aptitude of the artist'.

More than anything else, operational art is an intellectual framework. Though different armies at different times and places have taken and still take different views of the concept, ever since it emerged during the nineteenth century it has distinguished the master from the plodder, the successful commander from the mere butcher. On the one hand, no commander can guarantee victory simply by mastering operational art better than his opponents can, and history offers many examples that support this assertion. On the other hand, take away operational art in both defensive and offensive campaigns, and basically all that remains of warfare is the pursuit of destruction. Without operational art—the interplay of move and counter-move and the attempt to confuse the enemy, mislead him, alter his mental and physical balance, hit him where it hurts most, and exploit success most effectively—war would merely be a series of tactical actions with relative attrition as the measure of advance or retreat, success or failure.

The evolution of operational art has seemingly reached a critical point following almost two decades of strategic bewilderment caused by the end of the Cold War, exasperating peace operations, and 9/11. But regardless of the *form* that future conflicts may take, officers in national and international forces will find themselves tasked with translating short-term operations into a larger operational design that links their near-term actions to the strategic aim of the campaign. Military leaders who study and practice operational art will always need expertise in matching strategy with tactics; that is, in linking what should be achieved with what must be done. Such expertise comes about through general education, training, and wartime experience, but knowledge of how the concept evolved can further assist in developing professional excellence.

Undoubtedly, interpretations and applications of operational art will differ widely in accordance with each commander's mission, personality, and priorities. Yet there is a common thread: from a problem-solving perspective, operational art will make it possible to take an unstructured problem and give it sufficient structure to ensure that further planning can lead to useful action.[3] Understanding the operational level of war, operational art, and operational warfare improves the fundamental understanding of military operations per se, and therefore underlies all military successes. Consequently, whatever else officers may study and master—organization, leadership, intelligence, technology, logistics—they must have operational art at their fingertips.

At the very least, operational art will remain essential when recognized as a methodology that enables the effective planning and execution of all operations. At its best, operational art can play a pivotal role in military success when skilled leaders apply it in its full dimensions—functioning as true artists to give expression to a nation's strategic vision.

NOTES

1. Herbert Rosinski, 'Scharnhorst to Schlieffen: "The Rise and Decline of German Military Thought"', *Naval War College Review* (Summer 1976), 103, cited in Brig. Justin Kelly and Michael James Brennan, *Alien: How Operational Art Devoured Strategy* (Carlisle, PA: US Army War College, 2009), 6.
2. John English, 'The Operational Art: Developments in the Theories of War', in B. J. C. McKercher and Michael A. Hennessy (eds.), *The Operational Art: Developments in the Theories of War* (Westport, CT: Praeger, 1996), 7–28.
3. United States Army, 'Commander's Appreciation and Campaign Design,' *TRADOC Pamphlet 525-5-500*, version 1 (Fort Monroe, VA: Headquarters, U.S. Army, Training and Doctrine Command, 28 January 2008), 14.

Epilogue

General Sir Rupert Smith

DISTANT PAST

For as long as men have fought against one another in organized bands, we can see tactics and strategy in play. Ug in his cave was the leader because he was the best hunter, provider, and the best fighter and defender in the clan. He in his own interest was intent on advancing the interests of his clan. He realized that his tactical skill would only get him so far, so he needed a strategy. He made common cause with other nearby clans so as to increase his forces; marrying off his spare women to cement the links between the clans and sharing the better hunting grounds to ensure a degree of equality between the clans. He ensured there were reserve stocks of food not just for the hard winter but so that when the men were called upon to fight, rather than hunt, the people in the caves did not go hungry. He collected all the information he could about the hunting grounds and clans around him. He was careful to choose his targets and method to match his overall objective. If he needed more women and slaves he would seek to attack a weak clan, taking them by surprise so as to overwhelm them with the least amount of killing. For we must not kill what we want to work for us, he explained to his men. If, on the other hand, he wanted exclusive use of some hunting ground, perhaps to fish when the salmon were running, or of some defile through which the herds migrated, he could not afford to have his men fighting when they should be hunting. So he had now to decide whether to conduct a pre-emptive attack on the competitors, or to ambush them on their approach, but these methods, decisive as they appeared to some, risked the manpower necessary to gain the advantage he was after. So he considered a treaty with the nearest weaker clan in which it would receive a share of the hunting in return for helping guard the area.

In the early days of his leadership, Ug led the warriors of the clan in battle, and his tactical skill borne of and honed in the hunting field was better than or matched his opponent's. And by having a strategy, he usually arranged matters to his advantage before the battle, so that even when faced by a tactician of equal competence he won. As his clan grew in size, subordinate leaders sometimes led raids. He found that having a strategy was important to provide the context for the raid: to allow the subordinate to understand how he was to do what he was sent to do, and, should he fail, to limit the cost. Furthermore, he came to realize that strategy and tactics have no value in themselves; they can only have a value relative to the strategy and tactics of an opponent.

Ug and other successful clan leaders learnt that strategic thought and planning were a necessity if they and their people were to progress. While tactical excellence was also imperative, it was important only in the event of battle. The strategic plan was in operation before, during, and after the battle; it provided the context for the choice of objectives, the allocation of resources, the approach to battle, and the winning or losing of subsequent actions. Above all, it reduced the probability of a tactical defeat bringing disaster upon the clan.

Ug and his fellow leaders did not think in terms of strategy and tactics as being separate. Their thoughts were largely their own, and they did not need to put them into compartments so as to explain to others or to teach them. In particular, they did not need to explain how they thought about the linkage of their strategy to their tactics. Indeed, because strategic and tactical leadership lay with the one man, the thought process was more or less of a piece; I doubt there was any formal recognition of the linkage. Nevertheless, if we see now, as we do, that strategy and tactics are separate but related aspects of an endeavour, then we must suppose there is a linkage between the two. And if we can analyse, as I have above, the thought process of early man into strategy and tactics, then there too must have been a linkage. Nowadays, we call this linking activity the 'operational level of war' and the practice of commanders at this level 'operational art'.

Ug did not discuss this particular aspect for another reason: success at achieving this linkage was the practical expression of his 'magic', of what made him the winner and secure as the clan leader. The linkage, the essence of his magic as the leader, was expressed in terms of originality of interpretation, the creativity in the application of resource, the unexpected choice of effects, the economy of effort, the timing, the balance, and the coherence of the whole. His ability to do this on each occasion and to do something that was appropriate to that occasion meant that he could usually compensate for tactical and strategic shortcomings relative to the particular opponent, and still achieve his aim. He quickly came to realize that because he faced an opponent with a will of his own, the execution of his 'magic' was dynamic: he must be able to rearrange the pattern to his advantage as events unfolded. The strategy and tactics were relatively stable and took time to adjust; it was at the point of linkage between the two that there was freedom for dynamic creativity. He was in his time a great leader because of this ability. If this knowledge and understanding were shared at all, it was only with his heir, and then only as Ug's powers were waning. Just as he drew pictures on his cave wall for purposes we can only imagine and did not think of it as art, so he practised operational art.

As man progressed from the cave to the city, so armies grew in size. Societies were able to support the soldier or at least a warrior cast and the profession of arms began to take a recognizable form. The profession's attributes were fourfold: skill at arms, the disciplined application of force en masse, fortification, and the supply, maintenance, and movement of a force. All of these were essentially tactical and technical abilities. The strategy emanated from the kings and emperors advised by their courts. And it was often they who took to the field with their armies to put the strategy into effect. It was they who provided the linkage between their strategy and the tactics of their armies in the face of the opponent in the field. Even when a field commander was appointed, the choice of who to send was more often than not political rather than military. There were two reasons for this: the army represented the power of the ruler; he would only give such power to someone he trusted; and the field commander had to understand the strategic context of his actions to ensure their linkage. In short, the exercise of the operational art lay with the source of strategic direction or someone appointed by that source.

The legions of the Roman Republic and Empire give a good example. Their professionalism, discipline, and tactical skill gave rise to Flavius Josephus's description: 'Their drills were like bloodless battles, and their battles like bloody drills'.

This professionalism, the standard of training, the tactical skill, and the techniques were in the hands of the centurions. Senior to the centurions and providing all but the most senior officers were tribunes, the most senior of whom were political appointments. In command of the legion was a legate, appointed by the Senate, and only those of the senatorial class were eligible. The legates were responsible for linking the tactical excellence of their commands to the strategic purpose of their deployment—the exercise of the operational art.

These developments in man's progress gave rise to another way of understanding the practice of operational art. The Romans give us an example of this practice, but it would have existed for at least as long as there were large kingdoms and empires. Such was the size of the Roman Empire, legates more often than not conducted campaigns. They were allocated a force, an objective, and a space in which to achieve it; sometimes they were set a time in which to achieve the objective. In today's terms, the commander conducted a campaign in a theatre of operations to achieve an objective that maintained or altered the strategic situation to the advantage of the Empire as a whole. But his operational theatre was unique by virtue of its geography, the people in it, the local politics, and his objective. What was appropriate and successful in Palestine was not necessarily applicable in Britain. Just as he would have approved the adaptation of basic tactics and organization of forces by his subordinate leaders so as to defeat the particular enemy. So the particular circumstances of his theatre would have dictated a unique expression of the operational art, the campaign, to link those tactical acts to the achievement of the strategic goal.

It was found that conducting a campaign, particularly when distant from the strategic source, required skills that were not just those of the tactician. Nowadays, for example, we call these administrative, engineering, supply, and logistical skills. One might also add intelligence as a separate discipline. Frequently, alliances were made with local forces, requiring diplomatic and economic skills. The expression of the operational art was more often than not in terms of the excellence of these skills rather than in flair and imagination. What won the campaigns were the high standards of design, put into effect efficiently and with tactical skill. Flair, originality, and boldness were usually expressed in engineering and logistical terms.

At about the same time as the Roman Army was taking form, Sun-Tzu wrote *The Art of War.* In it, he describes how to think about strategy and the operational art in the circumstances that prevail at any given time in order to achieve a specific goal. His advice has stood the test of time. In particular, he explains that there are no formulas for the successful practice of the art of war. Rather, one must create or seize the favourable situation in the circumstances and in relation to the opponent at the time, allocating objectives to subordinates accordingly. The successful recognition or creation of this favourable situation is the expression of operational art.

So by the beginning of the first millennium, we can see the essential elements of the operational art and those responsible for exercising it. The critical test of any expression of operational art is in the defeat of the opponent. The commander in that linking position between the source of strategic direction and tactical command is the operational artist. With a deep understanding of the strategic objective and context, he creates, with a mixture of art and skill appropriate to the circumstances, a pattern of events to be achieved by his tactical commanders that defeats the opponent. The expression of the art is boundless and yet circumstantial; the commander is free within the circumstances he cannot change and in the face of the opponent. The choice of composition is his; what does he deploy, where, and to what purpose, where is he strong and where weak? He can and should practice illusion; what impression does he want the opponent to have and how to achieve it? And he can play with perspectives; he can choose how he uses time and space. With forces of any size and distance from the strategic source, the skills associated with the administration, supply, and movement of mass with economy of effort are required to express the art in a winning design.

With hindsight, for much of the next 1,500 years, the conduct of war and the expression of the operational art can be understood in these terms, for at the time they were thought of as one and the same. However, the use of gunpowder marks the start of a process that led to the operational art being seen as a separate activity.

RECENT PAST

Until cannon were available, the use of naval forces in war was largely to move and supply land forces. There had been battles at sea, but with the weapons of the day and with the exception of the galley that had a ram, these had been conducted ship to ship as though each was a small piece of rather unstable land. For example, the Romans had made extensive use of naval forces, but they were always a supporting arm of the army and generally kept close to the coast. The cannon allowed ships to fight as ships and the maritime nations began to develop warships and operate them in squadrons and fleets to gain control of the sea. One could now conduct naval operations in their own right far from one's coast, and what we would now call joint maritime operations became a possibility. Hitherto the use of naval and land forces were essentially sequential: now they could be used in concert. Under skilled hands, this could achieve a synergy of effects but their use in this way produced a complexity in planning and conducting the operation.

In 1588, the Spanish were at war with England. Seeking to invade England with an army being assembled in the Low Countries, the Spanish dispatched the Armada to transport the army across the Channel in the face of the English fleet and then to sustain it. The operation was defeated. The Armada failed to defeat the English fleet in the Channel and was badly mauled by the time it was anchored off Calais. The defeat turned into a catastrophe as the Armada headed north around the British Isles in storm-force winds. I give this example to show how these joint operations have an inherent complexity. The Spanish seem to have seen the operation as a series of discreet steps: assemble and sail the Armada, load the army, sail the army to the invasion beaches or port, support the army while it is established ashore, and then sustain it. All the steps would be resisted by the English. The Armada made no apparent effort to defeat the English fleet; the commander appears to have seen his primary effort as being to transport the army and presumably land it against opposition. Perhaps he thought this because if he had tried to bring the English fleet to battle, he would have lost ships and might not have had enough to carry out his other tasks while the English, being at home, would have been more likely to find replacements for any they had lost. In any event, he does not appear to have understood that gaining and maintaining control of the Channel was a necessary condition for a successful invasion in all its stages. Thus, the force as a whole is always divided by the separate environments of land and sea and the unique capabilities required to operate in them, and this introduces complexity. The complexity lies at its simplest in striking a balance between the allocation of resources and forces to apparently sequential events in the knowledge that the sequence is only measured in time and not effect. In other words, having gained control of the sea one must continue to maintain it. Thus, the allocation of resources or forces must be understood less as a subtraction from the whole but more as a division of capability. On the other hand, complexity has the potential advantage of being a multiplier of effects. The English were able to take advantage of the complexity. As much by the ineptness of the Spanish as their own actions, they were undefeated. The Armada sailed for home, unable to embark the army, transport it, and defeat the English simultaneously. The Spanish Army was rendered irrelevant, and the weather completed the destruction of the Spanish fleet. The English gained the product, not the sum, of the failure to defeat them in the Channel.

By the early nineteenth century, forces are larger, operating at ever greater distances from their strategic base, and wars are on occasions conducted in a number of separate but related campaigns. In order to describe what is happening or happened, phrases were used like 'grand strategy' to denote decisions and actions above the strategy of a campaign, or 'grand tactics' to denote something more than just tactical considerations. In each case, the user is seeking to define the particular that is different from strategy and tactics by either redefining strategy or naming it as a superior form of tactics. For many, the British being an example, these phrases have been adequate for their understanding of the conduct of war well into the twentieth century. Nevertheless, the point at which the operational art as a separate activity was practised was being recognized; the operational level was being defined.

To some extent, this need for definition was a result of the need to explain, instruct, and educate as the nature of war changed with revolution, conscription, the steamship, the railway, and industrialization. Armies became bigger and more strategically mobile. The staff work necessary to organize and maintain these forces became more important and more complex. Many of those operational-level skills mentioned earlier required well-trained staff to support the commander if they were to be carried out. It was the Germans soon after unification who first formally recognized the need for operational decision and staff work. The German strategy was to be prepared to fight a war on two fronts, East and West; each front with a different enemy, geography, and so on. Each needed a separate allocation of objectives, forces, resources, priorities, and so on. Each was an operation in its own right and could be influenced by the superior commander by the movement of forces from the strategic depth of Germany or from one operational front to the other. Thus, to a large extent, the Germans, following Napoleon, saw the operational art in terms of the movement of forces from strategic depth to mass effort on one front to defeat the opponent in time to mass again on the other front to defeat the second enemy. In moving their forces, they sought to strike the centre of the opponent's strength from an unexpected direction. The skill required to support the creativity of the design and the dynamics of its execution being essentially organizational and logistic.

In the first half of the twentieth century, two inventions, the internal combustion engine and radio communications, gave new opportunities for greater dynamism in the expression of the operational art. The former led to powered flight and cross-country fighting vehicles and the latter increased the ability of the commander to collect information, act on it, and control and decide on subsequent actions. By the middle of the Second World War, the Russians, who were probably the clearest in their nomenclature, were organized and capable of manoeuvre at the operational level. They had formed Operational Manoeuvre Groups (OMGs). These were used with devastating effect at the Battle of Kursk and halted the German offensive into Russia. The German accounts tell that nothing was the same after that. The Red Army attacked west to Berlin in a series of massive offensives conducted by a number of operational-level formations simultaneously, the commanders seeking always to release the OMGs into the rear of the German positions. The Western Allies were doing this too. For example, by 1944 in North-West Europe the independent armoured brigades in the Second British Army allocated to corps commanders and the firepower of the Artillery Groups at that level were intended to fulfil a similar purpose to an OMG.

The Western Allies made greater use of air power. Just as the development of warships created a capability for battles on the sea separate from those on land, so the airplane did the same for the air and, just as with the sea, actions in one environment could greatly enhance actions in the others. The Allies used their air forces strategically in discreet air campaigns to gain control of the air and to strike German and Japanese industrial capacity and the will of the people. Joint operations of all three capabilities were conducted to open new fronts in North Africa, Italy, North-West Europe, and, perhaps the best example, the US Pacific offensive to defeat Japan. Air power directly supported the battles on land; great firepower could be concentrated rapidly in one place, troops moved, and positions sustained. Naval victories were won by carrier-borne air power alone. There were bold attempts at operational manoeuvre from the air; for example, the airborne operation in September 1944 to seize crossings over the Rivers Maas, Waal, and lower Rhine was an attempt at operational manoeuvre that failed at Arnhem. The 1944 Chindit operation in the Japanese rear in Burma was another, more successful airborne operation.

All of these operations by their complexity and size were more like great constructions than expressions of art. The complexity already noted of maritime operations was increased with the addition of air operations, and the number of men and mass of materiel created a logistical inertia to movement. Skill in the construction and production of the operational design and originality in the development and use of new tools and techniques were at a premium. The development of radar and the concept for its use by Royal Air Force (RAF) Fighter Command and the subsequent operational victory in the Battle of Britain are a good example of this manifestation of the operational art.

These actions at the point of linkage between strategy and tactics were taken under the authority of a single man, the commander. He had to have the confidence of those at the strategic level, the confidence that he understood the strategic context of his objective and actions. If, as he often did, he had Allied contingents in his command, he had to have the confidence of their capitals as well. However much support he had from staff officers and subordinate commanders, he decided on the operational design, he commanded the operation to the end in the face of the resistance of his opponent. The choice of design, the nature of the influence he brought to bear on its conception, and the direction of its execution were his; he was the operational artist.

If in 1945, or soon after, the operational art was defined in today's terms we would have written something like:

> The operational commander directs his joint allied force along a path of tactical steps of his design to the strategic goal. The artfulness of his design and the skilfulness of his direction are measured in three ways: first, by success in the face of the opponent; second, by achieving the strategic goal; and third, in the economy of resource in achievement.

The practice of this art at the operational level through the ages and changes in the nature of warfare has certain characteristics. They were not necessarily how the practitioner understood or thought about what he was doing at the time, but they can be seen to a greater or lesser extent in the practice of the art.

The first is that there has to be an opponent; the operational art can only be expressed in relation to, and in the face of, an opponent practising his operational art. You should have a strategy before the war or operation commences, and you should have trained your forces in their skill at arms and tactics. But the operational art can only be practised in the event, and the art is effectively judged by the opponent.

The operational art is practised by one man. He is appointed to this responsibility by his superiors at the political and strategic levels, and he must retain their confidence. He is given or must assume the authority to discharge his art. In practising his art, he links the strategy within which his operation sits to the tactical acts his command performs. He seeks to achieve the product rather than the sum of the tactical acts so as to gain the operational objectives that either alter the strategic situation to his advantage or directly achieve the strategic goal. The totality of his art is expressed in a campaign in a theatre of operations.

Operational art can be understood in three ways. First, as a free, creative, and original expression of the use of force and forces. Where to concentrate and where to disperse, what is to appear ordinary and what extraordinary, what objectives to set and achieve in what order, how to lead the opponent into unwitting cooperation, and how to take advantage of time and space are all examples of where there is freedom of choice. Second, in the design of the operation. The larger the forces deployed and the greater the complexity of their employment, the greater the significance of operational design. Logistics, engineering, the use of technology, organization, and administration are examples of the factors to be considered in designing the operation. Third, in the direction of the operation to its successful conclusion. In large measure, this is an expression of the character and aptitude of the operational commander—the artist. His leadership, seen in the confident tactical skill and flair of his subordinates and the morale and discipline of his force, is essential. His presence at the right time and place; his calmness in crisis and fortitude; the balance, timing, and coherence of his decisions; his boldness and seizure of the moment—all these are manifestations of excellence in direction.

PRESENT

In 1945, as argued in *The Utility of Force*, war in the form of industrial war ceased to have utility and wars amongst the people made their appearance. The essential difference between the two was that in war amongst the people, military force is no longer used to decide the matter but to create a condition in which the strategic result is achieved; the strategic object being to alter the opponent's intentions rather than to destroy him. War is now a state of continual confrontation in which conflicts occur. The military acts in the conflict support the achievement of the desired outcome of the confrontation by other than military means—these include, for example, diplomatic, political, economic, social, and legal measures.

A confrontation occurs when two or more bodies in broadly the same circumstances are pursuing different outcomes. The confrontation is resolved when one or both parties adjust their desired outcomes to accommodate the other. Confrontations are decided to one's advantage or won by changing the other's intentions. Political affairs of all stripes, national and international, are about resolving confrontations. When the parties decide to work together or to abide by some rules or law, they are resolved. But when one or both sides cannot get their way and will not accept an alternative outcome, they sometimes seek to use military force to get it—they turn to conflict. With industrial war, military force was used to decide the confrontation directly; conflict was decisive strategically.

However, in war amongst the people force is used sub-strategically, usually only tactically. This is done for two reasons: the side that has small forces, if it is wise, does not play to the opponent's strengths, but rather follows the path of the guerrilla, avoiding set battle and the operationally or strategically decisive engagement, so as not to present the stronger opponent with opportunities to strike the mortal blows. The side that has large forces and possibly has nuclear weapons has too much to lose in using all of its strength. The costs to the economy of mobilizing society, such as in industrial war, are too great; the use of such force would be disproportionate and flout international law; and starting a nuclear war would have great political costs, quite apart from risking mankind and the environment.

The weaker side follows a generic strategy composed of the 'propaganda of the deed', the 'strategy of provocation', and the 'erosion of will' so as to advance their position in the overall confrontation. Sometimes the weak seek to replicate the strength of the stronger side rather than match it and, for example, develop a nuclear weapon, while following the same generic strategy. Those who might be supposed to be the stronger side because of having large and apparently strong forces find it difficult to gain advantage, to exert power. The philosopher Michel Foucalt said, 'power is a relationship not a possession'. Finding the way to establish that relationship to one's advantage is the strategic question of our time.

Note that just because the use of force is only tactical, it does not mean that there will not be big fights or that the future is one of urban terrorism. Nor is it to say that we will not fight for objectives to do with state sovereignty. It is to say that force will not achieve this directly or strategically; it may, if used well, establish a condition in which the objective is achieved by other means. We need to find a way to bring these other means to bear at the appropriate time and place in conjunction with the use of military force.

War amongst the people has six characteristics or trends that make it different from industrial war. In each particular case the trends are more or less so, their significance is different, and they are in a different balance. The six trends are as follows: (*a*) the ends or strategic objectives are changing from the hard, simple objectives of industrial war to soft or malleable conditional objectives, (*b*) they are conducted by non-state and multinational organizations, (*c*) they take place amongst the people, (*d*) they are timeless (protracted), (*e*) the parties fight so as to not lose the force, and (*f*) new uses are being found for old weapons and organizations.

The objectives for the use of military force in industrial war are hard and simple: 'take, hold, destroy, defeat' are the sort of words used. Success is measured in territory taken and forces destroyed. In war amongst the people, the objectives are malleable and complex, they describe a condition, which enables intentions to be changed or formed by other means; an example would be 'create a safe and secure environment'. And the more we seek to establish law and order, the more the will or intentions of the people become the objective. Indeed, the strategic objective is more often than not to capture the will of the people or at least render it neutral.

The next trend is that we tend to carry out these actions in a multinational grouping or in non-state groupings, and sometimes this applies to only one side. These coalitions need not be the formal ones, like the NATO alliance or the UN; they can be formed in the event such as in Iraq in 2008. The non-state nature of the operation is particularly evident in the theatre of operations; however formal the alliance, the force is composed only of contingents provided by the allies willing to contribute on the day, and they are in an informal alliance with the agencies representing the other means, usually other intergovernmental organizations (IGOs) and non-governmental organizations (NGOs). The non-state groupings are legion: Hezbollah, the Northern Alliance, the Taliban, and so on.

The third and most obvious trend is that war takes place amongst the people. First, the objective is the will of the people. Second, those operating to the tenets of the guerrilla depend on the people for concealment, for support, both moral and physical, and for information. Third, these conflicts take place amongst the people in another sense, through the media. Whoever coined the phrase 'the theatre of operations' was very prescient. We operate now as though we were in a theatre or Roman circus. The theatre commander needs to produce, write, act, and tell a more compelling story than his opponent in the minds of the people, both those in the circus pit and those in the stands. For the people, the strategic objective, every military act is part of a drama that in some cases directly involves them. Their understanding and support for what is happening are shaped by the context, timing, and presentation of the act. The military acts, the conflict with the opponent, are supporting elements of the drama of the confrontation. All measures, military and the others, must be concerted to achieving advantage in the overarching confrontation: to dislocate the opponent's military acts from his confrontational purpose in the minds of the people.

The fourth trend is that war amongst the people is timeless or protracted. We set out to win industrial wars quickly, because the whole of society was involved, and we wanted to get back to peace and have a normal life. In our new circumstances, timing is more important than doing things to time. The basic tactic is to engage only on one's own terms, when it is to your advantage to do so safely. And when our military objectives are to set conditions in which other instruments of power resolve the confrontation, then we must maintain the condition until they succeed.

The fifth trend is that we fight to preserve the force. No commander wants to suffer any more casualties to his men and equipment than he has to. But in industrial war, it was in the main possible to replace his losses. We developed the production lines to do this: conscription, the training depots, reserve formations, as well as those in industry for the equipment. In large measure, these production lines exist no longer. We are unable to replace our losses. We fight to preserve the force for other reasons. We have to sustain the operation, because it is not strategically decisive we have to maintain the condition, and to do that needs a continuous presence. And politicians at home, uncertain of the people's support for the multinational venture, wish to keep the costs to men and materiel within bounds that are politically sustainable in the circumstances.

The sixth and final trend is that new uses are being found for weapons and organizations acquired and developed for different purposes. NATO is not being used for its founding purpose and weapons and organizations are not being used for purposes or in the way originally intended. This is not to argue that commanders should not adapt their forces to the circumstances—they should—but if these changes are necessary, then something has changed to make them necessary. The original concept was of industrial war, it is war amongst the people that is demanding the change; if this was not the case, why is it necessary for the title 'operations other than war'?

These trends act on each other and fall into a different balance with each case. But whatever their particular combination, they have consequences for the exercise of operational art.

We have seen how the operational art links strategy to tactics. For any linkage to occur, there must be a strategy. There is ample historical evidence to show how difficult it is for states in an alliance or coalition to form and direct a strategy. As a rule, the more immediate and existential the threat, and the more dominant one ally, the simpler the problem, but it is always difficult to resolve. Complexity is a consequence of multinational endeavours—and it is increased when the objectives for the use of force are conditional, and the desired strategic outcome of the confrontation is to be achieved by other means that are not under the same hand as that using military force. For the non-state actor, matters are simpler; there is a single source of strategic direction largely free of the responsibilities and burdens of statehood that does not have to come from some hierarchical structured body. By adopting any strategy, particularly ones like the propaganda of the deed, and avoiding giving the opponent opportunities to use his strength, he has an immediate advantage over those unable or slow to form a strategy. This advantage is even more evident when it comes to providing strategic direction as the operation unfolds.

When one party has a strategy and the other does not, the tactical acts of whatever side, being common to both, are linked inevitably to the side with the strategy—regardless of outcome. The side with the strategy is able to exercise the operational art and, not least for want of opposition at that level, even turn its tactical failures to its advantage. It is this that gives rise to the observable phenomenon of 'winning every fight and losing the war'.

The forces and agencies deployed are usually provided by a number of different states, IGOs, and NGOs. Each has its own strategic reason for its contribution and an idea of the reward for it. Although clearly related to achieving the operation's purpose, these national goals are not the same as those of the multinational organization. As a result, the state providing a contribution will often restrict the use of its contribution to fulfilling its national goals rather than those of the multinational organization. Additionally, and contributing to this national bias, states are responsible for supporting their own contingents, their legitimacy, and sustaining their presence in the theatre. To make this manageable, states take on particular tasks, defined by area or function. This is as true of the agencies as it is of the military forces. Each state, IGO, and NGO maintains a linkage between its own strategy and its contribution. The linkage represents the interest of the state or organization in the rewards for it and the risks to be gained by their contribution, rather like a shareholder in a commercial company who has invested to gain income and capital rather than to trade in something. However, unlike the relationship of the shareholder and the company, the state retains considerable control over the use of its contribution by the organization it has charged with the venture. The result is that the multinational force cannot operate to a single purpose or even a set of priorities. This and the foregoing paragraphs also explain why it is so difficult to define success in these wars of confrontation and conflict.

These multinational deployments are not always organized as a piece. One organization may deal with military matters and another with development. Afghanistan is probably an extreme example of this fact. There are three military organizations, each receiving strategic direction from a different source: NATO's International Security Assistance Force (ISAF), a US Force (Operation Enduring Freedom), and the Afghan security forces. In addition, and apart from the Afghan government, there are the UN's agencies, the EU, national agencies such as the United Kingdom's Department for International Development (DfiD) or the United States Agency for International Development (USAID), and many NGOs, all seeking to support and develop the state. Whatever sources they have for strategic direction are not as a rule the same as the military. The result is incoherence in strategic direction and definition of objectives. There are ample examples in many deployments of these agencies and the military working together successfully at low tactical levels. Within the limits of language, training, equipment, and their national restraints, they cooperate effectively. But usually the results of their endeavours do not sit within a coherent pattern of achievement that amounts to a campaign. Indeed, because of the lack of strategic coherence, nobody or no agency is responsible for conducting the all-encompassing campaign to achieve coherence of action in the theatre of operations.

In war amongst the people, those engaged in operational art must reconcile the achievement of two objectives: that of the conflict and that of the confrontation. This is true to both armies and their opponents. The two conflictual objectives can be understood to be directly opposed—this is a battle in which each seeks to win—but this is not necessarily the case with the two confrontational objectives. For example, the opponent may want law and order and good roads, and you may also want him to have them. But he will not have them at the point of your bayonet or in the form and way that suit your cultural and social norms rather than his.

Reconciling the achievement of the confrontational objective with that of the conflict is not easy because each is achieved with different means. Ultimately, conflicts, battles, and fights are won by firepower, either applied directly to kill and destroy the opponent, or in such demonstrably evident potential that its imminent prospect leads to retreat or surrender. The currency of conflict is firepower. It is the business of the military to apply firepower. In a confrontation where one is seeking to change or form an opponent's intentions, the currency is information. All agencies, including the military, can transmit information by word and deed. For example, if we want to deter an attack, the opponent must be made to understand that we will fight to defend ourselves, that he will lose or at least lose more than he will gain by defeating us, that there are advantages to him in not attacking us, that we can find and hit that which he wishes to defend (which is not the same target as that which is attacking us), and that we will escalate if at first we do not succeed. We want the opponent to understand that this is our position and so form his intention not to attack us before the confrontation becomes a conflict. His understanding is shaped by information; the information may be transmitted by demonstrations of military forces, the acquisition of weapons, diplomacy, alliances, and so on.

In the confrontation just described, the relationship between information and firepower potential is simple and direct. But in cases where conflicts are already part of an overall confrontation, matters are more complex. The mind or minds of those in the confrontation are not necessarily those in the particular conflicts or fights. For example, in 1998–9, NATO was in confrontation with President Milosevic of Serbia over Kosovo, initially to deter murder and ill-treatment of the Kosovars, and subsequently to coerce him with the use of air power into withdrawing his forces and administration from Kosovo. The confrontation was with Milosevic and his henchmen, not the people of Serbia or their armed forces. The conflict was with the Serbian Air Defence Forces and these were suppressed quickly. But it proved difficult to find the objectives and targets that when hit created the condition and thereby the flow of information that directly threatened Milosevic's position sufficiently to persuade him to withdraw from Kosovo. The Serbian forces deployed and concealed presented few targets; infrastructure targets hit in Kosovo were ineffective, because the Serbians did not care for the Kosovars, and those hit in Serbia gained popular support for Milosevic, because they were seen as an attack not on him but on them. It was not until the Russians were persuaded to bring diplomatic pressure to bear on Milosevic that he conceded and NATO won the confrontation. To guarantee the victory, the Russians had to enter the theatre of operations. They became the other means, and they were persuaded to be so and acted in the condition created by NATO's bombing.

In war amongst the people, reconciling the two objectives to one's advantage takes place within the theatre of operations and as a result the criteria for defining the theatre are different to those of the past. In the past, the theatre was defined in terms of space, objective, opponent, forces, and resources allocated. While these remain viable criteria, others have now to be considered as a consequence of two characteristics of war amongst the people: the nature of the strategic objective and that it takes place amongst the people.

Defining the point at which the two objectives need reconciling can also be understood by considering where the currency changes, where the effect of firepower has to be translated into the effect of information if it is to have value in achieving the overall aim. Deciding the level of the fight is a mutual activity between opponents; it is the point they engage in the relationship of battle. In industrial war, the side that raised the largest amount of firepower dictated the level of the fight. In war amongst the people, developed from the antithesis of industrial war, the militarily weaker side deliberately operates below the utility of the stronger opponent's weapons and forces as he would wish to use them. If the opponent tries to use large amounts of force, he plays to the advantage of the weaker opponent's strategy and risks losing the confrontation rather than the conflict, and being unable to sustain the operation. He learns to adjust the level of the fight and its nature to somewhere much closer to that of his opponent. As a general rule, in Afghanistan and in Iraq, the level in terms of the command hierarchy is about that of a commander of a reinforced company. Thus, the point of currency exchange is at the level above that in the hierarchy; company commanders and below should deal in firepower for objectives to do with the conflict, while those above deal in information for objectives to do with the confrontation.

The strategic objective for military force is to create a condition in which other means alter intentions. Consider the metaphor of the Roman circus mentioned earlier when describing the trends of war amongst the people. You are the director of a gladiatorial contest and there is another production trying to go on at the same time. Your object is to have everyone follow your production, your narrative is to be the one used to understand the conflicting events in the pit, and yours is to be the one all remember. In addition to the two sets of gladiators who come and go in the pit, there are other people. Who are they? What are their relationships to the other gladiators, can these be altered, and if so how? Are they in disguise? Where do they stand in the confrontation? Which show did they buy tickets for? And in the stands, who is the audience? What show did they come to see or do they just want to be entertained? How are they to be communicated with and influenced? Who are the opinion formers and where are they sitting? Every gladiatorial act, whether of deployment, appearance in the pit, or employment against the other gladiators, affects the people's understanding. And always remember: the people are the home audience of an army. Lose their interest and support, and you lose the battle no less than if the opponent comes up with a master stroke. Those in the pit will have a different view and thus understanding to those in the stands. What storyline does the act support? What other means, lighting, scenery, and props are necessary? Who in the audience is the target for the message? As has been found with the operations in Afghanistan and more generally with the so-called war on terror, defining the theatre in terms of political boundaries does not help find the answers to these questions, let alone act on them.

Even as this chapter is being written, an example of this theatre is being acted out. The Indian security forces are dealing with an attack by a group of terrorists in Mumbai. The terrorists appear to have attacked the people in popular meeting places, hotels, and restaurants, searching for British and Americans in particular, and in addition singling out for attack a Jewish outreach centre, murdering the rabbi and other Jews therein. The targets were probably chosen for their symbolism as the apparent manifestation of globalization: growth, wealth, and technology, and of competing ideas such as Judaism and democracy. On live media the event unfolded to the global audience, but where is the boundary between the pit and the stands? Who is part of the drama and who is watching it? The audience is global but each radio and TV station is transmitting slightly different stories, personally and nationally tweaked. Nobody is countering the unspoken narrative of the attack as the propaganda of the deed; on the contrary, there is a search for whom to blame for not preventing the deed. Nobody is being positive about the reactions and deeds of the security forces.

In these new circumstances, we have yet to come to a useful definition of the theatre and of who is responsible for what within it. Not least amongst the reasons why is that our institutions of government, administration, and law are constructed to operate within a state. This makes it difficult when wars amongst the people are conducted by multinationals and non-states. Nevertheless, it is possible to see the outline solution. The pit of the theatre of operations should contain those engaged in the conflict, those involved in activities that serve the achievement of the confrontational goal and are directly related to the conflict, such as law and order, and the people directly affected by the conflict. In the ringside stands are those who are not directly affected by the conflict but are close enough to it to want to be assured that they will not be. The more distant seats belong to those who wish to be assured that they can live their lives as they wish to. And those who watch or listen to the broadcast are also part of the audience but are not in the theatre.

Earlier in this chapter, it was shown that in conflict the opponents were the judges of each other's operational art. In war amongst the people, the minds of those one is seeking to change have become the judges. Each of the opponents is seeking to alter the intentions of the other, but frequently the strategic objective is only reached when the minds of the people have been captured. The lower the level of the fight or conflicts, the more the issues are confrontational, the more the people are the judge. Put another way, while much has been made of late of the idea of the 'strategic corporal' always having an adverse effect on the execution of the plan, it is overblown. The reality is that the corporal and the sergeant are of the conflict, but their actions can affect the confrontation: they are on its coalface. The ubiquitous checkpoint is an example: every person delayed, humiliated, abused, or worse is a person on the way to conversion to the opponent's cause. Understanding the totality of the theatre and the audience is critical to the exercise of the operational art. It is the business of the operational commander to so position his tactical operation in its context, to set the tactical objectives and the way they are to be achieved, that the 'corporal' has the best chance of influencing the operational and strategic situation to advantage.

To summarize, the situation today is that the form of war has changed from industrial war to war amongst the people. All our institutions, and their structures and processes, have evolved to conduct industrial war successfully; they are unsuited to the conduct of war in the new paradigm of war amongst the people. The consequences of this change with the greatest significance for the practice of operational art are as explained above: (*a*) the difficulty of producing a strategy in a multinational organization and without a strategy there is no operational art; (*b*) where one side has a strategy and the other does not, all tactical acts of both sides are understood only in the context of the single strategy; (*c*) it is rare to find a single source of multinational strategic direction to those in the theatre of operations; (*d*) the forces and agencies in the theatre are not under one source of operational direction; (*e*) the difficulty in defining success; (*f*) the two objectives, that of the overall confrontation and that of the conflict, have to be reconciled in the theatre in the face of the opponent's reconciliation of his two objectives; (*g*) each objective is achieved by different means: firepower for conflict and information for the confrontation; (*h*) the reconciliation takes place in the theatre of operations and in terms of the hierarchy of command just above the level of the commander of those engaged in the fight; and (*i*) it is difficult to define the theatre.

These consequences may also help to explain some of the other characteristics of our current operations, such as (*a*) the shifting nature of the stated objectives for the operation as expectations are recalibrated in the face of the opponent's measures, (*b*) the difficulty governments of contributing states have in analysing operational events and explaining them to their people, (*c*) the difficulty in applying the law and the choice of the law to apply, and (*d*) the difficulty in foreseeing the consequence of tactical events on the confrontation.

Above all, these issues explain why there is little, if any, evidence of the practice of the operational art or design. In practice, the tactical acts in conflict, however successful in themselves, are conducted in a strategic vacuum, in which multiple sources of conflicting interests act more or less incoherently in an ill-defined theatre. The people amongst whom the fight is conducted, those in the pit, are fearful and wish to be without all who fight amongst them. But they cannot realize this wish, so they tend to give at least tacit authority to those who they think know them best and reward their allegiance.

FUTURE

On the assumption we wish to win our wars amongst the people, we must improve on how we conduct them. Some of the causes of the difficulties we face in the conduct of war amongst the people are a consequence of the position we hold in the overarching confrontation. For example, to act outside the law, whether treaty, humanitarian, or criminal, when the confrontational objective is in part at least to establish the rule of law, is to undermine one's own position, as the United States found with Abu Ghraib and Guantanamo. Other causes are in the form and nature of each state, its governmental institutions, and those formed by the states.

It is often tempting to think of achieving the overall objective as a serial process: first, win the fights and defeat the opponent, then deal with underpinning issues that gave rise to the confrontation in the first place. Our institutional structures help lead us into the temptation; the military, defence, ministries of defence, and NATO are deemed to win the conflict and the others, diplomats, the United Nations Development Programme (UNDP), the EU, the Organization for Security and Co-operation in Europe (OSCE), etc. will do the rest afterwards. This approach is folly; it plays directly to the strategy of the opponent to his advantage since on their own the military acts appear disproportionate to the population they are carried out within. The military acts must be firmly based within the measures to win the confrontation, thus guarding against adopting methods in conflict that, however successful in themselves, reinforce the opponent's position in the confrontation.

The change required of our state-based institutions, including those of the law, will take a long time to realize and on the evidence of history will probably only be forced by the war itself, particularly losing or being close to losing a war. The changes will be strategic and making them will involve more than the matters under discussion in this chapter. Nevertheless, we would do better in these multinational ventures if we provided for the absolute essentials for the exercise of the operational art: a strategy to link to the tactics, a designated authority responsible for the linkage in its totality, and a theatre in which to exercise this authority.

The example of a commercial venture helps show how we might do this with the institutional structures we have at present. A group of individuals undertake to collaborate to achieve a gain or reward; they invest cash and material assets in the venture. They are 'partners', and in their articles of association they agree their relationships: who is to be the senior partner, the division of rewards, and so on. Perhaps they need more funds and material resources. They could offer partnerships, associate partnerships, or go public and offer shares in the venture. In any event, the venture has a structure at its head that, while representing the interests of the partners and investors, allows for strategic decision and direction. The partners would appoint a chief executive to run the business day to day, perhaps one of their numbers would be picked or they might employ a suitable person. Depending on the business and its scope, they may have more than one business area, each with its own chief executive, or perhaps when the business areas are interdependent form a committee of the managing directors with one of them as chairman.

If this general concept was applied to the way we conduct our multinational warlike ventures, then those who had democratic accountability for forces on the ground would be partners. Partners in a structure formed to achieve a reward rather than one formed and then deciding on the reward to achieve. A structure formed to take strategic decisions and to provide a single source of strategic direction to its executive authority. The executive authority, a man or woman or a small committee, would be responsible for the operation or campaign as a whole. In return for adopting this idea and improving the probability of gaining the reward, each partner and shareholder would grant authority to the executive body over its contribution or investment and confine its strategic debate to the venture's strategic structure.

The executive authority would be responsible for confronting the opponent and forming the link between strategy and tactics, and has authority over all the forces and resources committed to the venture. The object is to win the confrontation and so this authority need not be vested in a military officer, indeed if it is he should understand he is not wielding only the military; he is not a military commander. In many cases, forming a small committee will be necessary; it will bring separate competencies together and may well be the only way, for legal and political reasons, to achieve a single source of operational direction. However, the committee will need a chairman, and he might be called the theatre director.

Defining the theatre, or business area, may well be easier than hitherto if this approach was adopted. Just as the relationships within the structure are decided with the object of the venture in mind, so the overall aim would help define the theatre. And by designating the authority to undertake the operation as a whole, the area, both physical and functional, has to be considered.

With these essential elements decided, operational art may well flourish in the face of that of the opponent. It will be of a different form than before, for as in art and design form follows function.

Operational art as argued can already be understood as a combination of a free, creative, and original expression of the use of force and forces; a design; and direction, an expression of the character, and aptitude of the artist.

The successful operation will use forces offensively in conflict in such a way as to dislocate the opponent's use of force from its confrontational purpose. The more the opponent's military acts are interpreted as senseless, purposeless violence for its own sake, the less the linkage. Defensively, the use of force must be firmly linked to advancing the achievement of the confrontational goals, all the agencies, military and civil, acting to a single logic. Maintaining and strengthening this pivotal linkage, translating the currencies of firepower and information to such effect that minds are changed, will define the acts in the theatre pit. The creativity will be given coherence and meaning much as a drama unfolds—the facts as displayed by all on the stage create a scene that is part of an act that leads to other scenes and acts to a dénouement.

The design will have little to do with manoeuvre. The driving design logic will be of information: information to learn the theatre and the opponent; information, its collection, analysis, and dissemination, whether as actionable intelligence in the conflict or in the theatre of the confrontation. Its structure will be informed by the needs of governance, law and order, and development.

And the need for direction, calm, resolute, and constant direction, will be as critical as before. This source of the campaign's driving logic must have the confidence of those at both the strategic and the tactical levels as before, but now the greater the confidence of the people in the theatre, the greater the art.

So, if in the future we had made these adaptations, we might define operational art as:

> the theatre director conducts his command of all forces, agencies, and resources in a scheme of orchestrated actions of his design to produce the strategic goal. The artfulness of his design and the skill as a conductor are measured: first, by success in the face of the opponent; second, by achieving the strategic goal; and third, in the economy of resource in achievement.

Notes on Contributors

Dr Antulio J. Echevarria II is associate professor and the director of research at the Strategic Studies Institute (SSI), US Army War College. He graduated from the US Military Academy in 1981, was commissioned as an armour officer, and held a variety of command and staff assignments in Germany and the United States prior to his retirement at the rank of lieutenant colonel. Dr Echevarria is a graduate of the US Army Command and General Staff College and the Army War College; he holds MA and Ph.D. degrees in History from Princeton University. He is the author of *After Clausewitz: German Military Thinkers before the Great War* (2001), *Imagining Future War* (2007), and *Clausewitz and Contemporary War* (2007). He has published articles and essays in a number of scholarly and professional journals, including monographs, such as 'Toward an American Way of War' (2004), 'Fourth-Generation War and Other Myths' (2005), 'Challenging Transformation's Clichés' (2007), and 'Wars of Ideas and the War of Ideas' (2008) for SSI. He has also lectured widely, both nationally and internationally, and has contributed to several book chapters.

Dr Jacob W. Kipp is adjunct professor of Russian Military History at the University of Kansas. In 2009, he retired from government service as Deputy Director of the School of Advanced Military Studies of the US Army, a post he held from 2006 to 2009. He received his MA and Ph.D. in History from Pennsylvania State University, taught Russian and military history at Kansas State University from 1971 to 1985, joined the Soviet Army Studies Office as a senior analyst in 1986, and became the director of the Foreign Military Studies Office in 2003. He is the author of a large number of articles and monographs on Soviet and Russian military history, operations, and doctrine. He is the editor of *Central European Security Concerns* (1993), *V. K. Triandafillov's 'The Nature of Operations of Contemporary Armies'* (1994), and *General Makhmut Gareev's 'If War Comes Tomorrow?'* (1998).

Dr Avi Kober earned his doctorate at the Hebrew University and is senior lecturer in political studies at Bar-Ilan University and senior research associate at the Begin–Sadat Center for Strategic Studies (BESA). His main areas of research are military theory and doctrine, Arab–Israeli wars, and low-intensity conflicts. Dr Kober is the author of *Coalition Defection: The Discussion of Arab Anti-Israel Coalitions in War and Peace* (2002) and *Israel's Wars of Attrition: Attrition Challenges to Democratic States* (2009). His recent publications also include 'Israeli Military Thinking as Reflected in Ma'arachot Articles, 1948–2000', *Armed Forces and Society*, vol. 30, no. 1 (Fall 2003); 'From *Blitzkrieg* to Attrition: Israel's Attrition Strategy and Staying Power', *Small Wars and Insurgencies*, vol. 16, no. 2 (2005); 'Does the Iraq War Represent a Phase Change in Warfare?' *Defense* *and Security Analysis*, vol. 21, no. 2 (June 2005); 'Great Power Involvement and Battlefield Success in the Arab–Israeli Wars, 1948–1982', *Journal of Cold War Studies*, vol. 8, no. 1 (Winter 2006); 'Targeted Killing during the Second Intifada: The Quest for Effectiveness', *Journal of Conflict Studies*, vol. 27, no. 1 (Summer 2007); 'The IDF in the Second Lebanon War: Why the Poor Performance?' *Journal of Strategic Studies*, vol. 31, no. 1 (February 2008); and 'Technological and Operational Incentives and Disincentives for Force Transformation', in Stuart A. Cohen (ed.), *The New Citizen Armies* (2009).

Colonel Dr John Andreas Olsen is the dean of the Norwegian Defence University College, head of the Division for Strategic Studies at the Norwegian Defence Command and Staff College, and visiting professor of operational art and tactics at the Swedish National Defence College. A serving officer, he is a graduate of the Norwegian Defence College (2008) and the German Command and Staff College (2005). Recent assignments include tours as the Norwegian liaison officer to the German Operational Command in Potsdam, as the military assistant to the attaché in Berlin, and as a tutor and researcher at the Norwegian Air Force Academy. Olsen has a doctorate in History and International Relations from De Montfort University, a master's degree in Contemporary British Literature and Politics from the University of Warwick, a master's degree in English (cand. philol.), and an engineering degree in Electronics from the University of Trondheim. He is the author of *John Warden and the Renaissance in American Air Power* (2007) and *Strategic Air Power in Desert Storm* (2003), and has written several editorials on military operations and air power. He is the editor of *On New Wars* (2006) and *A History of Air Warfare* (2010).

Dr Andrew Scobell is senior political scientist at the RAND Corporation in Washington, DC. Prior to that, he was a tenured faculty member for three years at the George H. W. Bush School of Government and Public Affairs at Texas A&M University in College Station, Texas. From 1999 until 2007, he was associate research professor at the Strategic Studies Institute at the US Army War College, and adjunct professor of political science at Dickinson College, both in Carlisle, Pennsylvania. Scobell earned a Ph.D. in Political Science from Columbia University. He is the author of *China's Use of Military Force: Beyond the Great Wall and the Long March* (2003), and co-author (with Andrew J. Nathan) of *China's Search for Security* (Columbia University Press, forthcoming 2011).

Professor Dennis Showalter is professor of history at Colorado College. He earned his MA and doctorate at the University of Minnesota, has been visiting professor at the US Air Force Academy, the US Military Academy, and the Marine Corps University, and was the president of the Society of Military History from 1997 to 2001. He has held numerous fellowships, served on a number of boards, and has since 1993 been the joint editor of the journal *War in History*. Professor Showalter has an extensive list of publications and several forthcoming books. He is the author of *Railroads and Rifles: Soldiers, Technology and the Unification of Germany* (1975, repr. in 2007), *The Wars of Frederick the Great* (1996), *The Wars* *of German Unification* (2004), *Patton and Rommel: Men of War in the Twentieth Century* (2005), and *Hitler's Panzers: The Lightning Attacks that Revolutionized Warfare* (2009). He has also co-authored, with William Astore, *Hindenburg: Icon of German Militarism* (2005) and *Soldiers' Lives through History: The Early Modern World* (2007). He is the editor or co-editor of *History in Dispute: World War I* (2002), *History in Dispute: The Second World War* (2000), and *History in Dispute: The Cold War* (2000).

General Sir Rupert Smith retired from the British army after forty years of service in 2002. His last appointment was Deputy Supreme Commander Allied Powers Europe, 1998–2001, covering NATO's Balkan operations, including the Kosovo bombing, and the development of the European Defence and Security Identity. Prior to that, he was the General Officer Commanding Northern Ireland, 1996–8; commander of the United Nations Protection Force (UNPROFOR) in Sarajevo, 1995 (including the establishment of the UN Rapid Reaction Force); the assistant chief of defence operations and security at the UK Ministry of Defence, 1992–4; and General Officer Commanding 1 (UK) Armoured Division, 1990–2, thus commanding that division in the Gulf War of 1991. A graduate of the Royal Military Academy at Sandhurst, he enlisted in 1962 and was commissioned into the Parachute Regiment in 1964. He has served in East and South Africa, Arabia, the Caribbean, Malaysia, and Europe. General Smith is a visiting professor at the University of Reading and the author of *The Utility of Force: The Art of War in the Modern World* (2005), a book on the changing character of war and its implications for future operations.

Professor Hew Strachan is Chichele Professor of the History of War, All Souls College, University of Oxford, and director of the Changing Character of War Programme. He is a life fellow of Corpus Christi College, University of Cambridge, where he earned his BA and MA degrees, and where he was successively appointed research fellow, admissions tutor, and senior tutor (1975–92). From 1992 to 2001, he was professor of modern history at the University of Glasgow and from 1996 to 2001 director of the Scottish Centre for War Studies. His books include *Wellington's Legacy: The Reform of the British Army, 1830–1854* (1984), *From Waterloo to Balaclava: Tactics, Technology and the British Army, 1815–1854* (1985), *European Armies and the Conduct of War* (1988), *The Politics of the British Army* (1997), *The First World War: Volume I. To Arms* (2001), *The First World War: A New Illustrated History* (2003), *The First World War in Africa* (2004), and *Clausewitz's On War: A Biography* (2007). Professor Strachan is a fellow of the Royal Society of Edinburgh and the Royal Historical Society, visiting professor at the Royal Norwegian Air Force Academy, and the joint editor of the journal *War in History*.

Professor Martin van Creveld was born in the Netherlands, but raised and educated in Israel. After receiving his master's degree at the Hebrew University, he did a Ph.D. in History at the London School of Economics and Political Science. Since 1971, he has been on the faculty of the history department at the Hebrew

University, from which he retired early in 2008. Van Creveld is one of the leading experts on military history and strategy, with a special interest in the future of war. He has authored twenty books, including *Supplying War* (1978), *Command in War* (1985), *The Transformation of War* (1991), *The Rise and Decline of the State* (1999), *The Changing Face of War: Lesson of Combat from the Marne to Iraq* (2006), and *The Culture of War* (2008). Between them, these books have been translated (or are being translated) into twenty languages. Professor Martin van Creveld has been a consultant for the defence establishments of several countries, and taught or lectured at practically every defence college, military and civilian, from Canada to New Zealand and from Norway to South Africa. He has appeared on countless television and radio programmes as well as written for, and been interviewed by, hundreds of papers and magazines around the world.

Selected Bibliography

Adams, Colin and Laurence, Ray, *Travel and Geography in the Roman Empire* (London: Taylor and Francis, 2007).

Adelman, Jonathan and Shih, Chih-Yu, *Symbolic War: The Chinese Use of Force, 1840–1980* (Taipei: Institute of International Relations, 1993).

Alberts, David S., Gartska, John J., and Stein, Frederick P., *Network Centric Warfare: Developing and Leveraging Information Superiority* (Washington, DC: C4ISR Cooperative Research Program, 1999).

American Military History (Washington, DC: Center of Military History, 1989).

Armstrong, Richard N., *Soviet Operational Deception: The Red Cloak* (Fort Leavenworth, KS: Combat Studies Institute, 1988).

Arquilla, John and Ronfeldt, David, *Swarming and the Future of Conflict* (Santa Monica, CA: RAND, 2000).

Ascoli, David, *A Day of Battle: Mars-la-Tour, 16 August 1870* (London: Harrap, 1987).

Austin, N. J. E. and Rankov, M. B., *Exploratio: Military and Political Intelligence in the Roman World from the Second Punic War to the Battle of Adrianople* (London: Routledge, 1995).

Avant, Deborah, *Political Institutions and Military Change: Lessons from Peripheral Wars* (Ithaca, NY: Cornell University Press, 1994).

Batschelet, Allen W., *Effects-Based Operations: A New Operational Model?* (Carlisle, PA: US Army War College, 2002).

Bayley, Tennant H., *Spy Wars: Moles, Mysteries and Deadly Games* (New Haven, CT: Yale University Press, 2007).

Beevor, Antony, *Inside the British Army* (London: Chatto and Windus, 1990).

—— *Stalingrad: The Fateful Siege, 1942–1943* (New York: Viking Books, 1998).

Bellum Africanum (London: Heinemann, Loeb Classical Library, 1946).

Bellum Civile (London: Heinemann, Loeb Classical Library, 1963).

Biddle, Stephen, *Afghanistan and the Future of Warfare: Implications for Army and Defense Policy* (Carlisle, PA: US Army War College, 2002).

Biddle, T. D., *Rhetoric and Reality in Air Warfare: The Evolution of British and American Ideas About Strategic Bombing, 1914–1945* (Princeton, NJ: Princeton University Press, 2002).

Bidwell, Shelford and Graham, Dominick, *Fire-Power: British Army Weapons and the Theories of War, 1904–1945* (London: Allen and Unwin, 1982).

Bjorge, Gary J., *Moving the Enemy: Operational Art in the Chinese PLA's Huai Hai Campaign*, Leavenworth Paper no. 22 (Fort Leavenworth, KS: Combat Studies Institute Press, 2004).

Blasko, Dennis J., *The Chinese Army Today: Tradition and Transformation for the 21st Century* (London: Routledge, 2006).

Blumenson, Martin, *Patton: The Man behind the Legend, 1885–1945* (New York: Morrow, 1985).

Bond, Brian, *The Victorian Army and the Staff College, 1854–1914* (London: Eyre Methuen, 1972).

—— *Liddell Hart: A Study of His Military Thought* (London: Cassell, 1977).

Boot, Max, *War Made New: Technology, Warfare, and the Course of History: 1500 to Today* (New York: Gotham, 2006).

Boraston, J. H. (ed.), *Sir Douglas Haig's Despatches (December 1915–April 1919)*, 2 vols. (London: Dent, 1919).

Botjer, George F., *Sideshow War: The Italian Campaign, 1943–45* (College Station, TX: Texas A&M University Press, 1996).

British Defence Doctrine: Joint Warfare Publication (JWP) 0-01 (London: Ministry of Defence, 1996).

Brodie, Bernard, *The Absolute Weapon* (New York: Harcourt Brace, 1946).

—— *War and Politics* (New York: Macmillan, 1973).

Brose, Eric Dorn, *The Kaiser's Army: The Politics of Military Technology during the Machine Age, 1870–1918* (Oxford: Oxford University Press, 2001).

Bucholz, Arden, *Moltke and the German Wars, 1864–1871* (New York: Palgrave, 2001).

Burdick, C. and Jacobsen, H.A. (eds.), *The Halder War Diary, 1939–1942* (Novato, CA: Presidio, 1988).

Chandler, David G., *The Campaigns of Napoleon* (New York: Macmillan, 1966).

Christensen, Thomas J., *Useful Adversaries: Grand Strategy, Domestic Mobilization, and Sino-American Conflict, 1947–1958* (Princeton, NJ: Princeton University Press, 1996).

Citino, Robert, *The Path to Blitzkrieg: Doctrine and Training in the German Army, 1920–1939* (Boulder, CO: Lynne Rienner, 1999).

—— *Quest for Decisive Victory: From Stalemate to Blitzkrieg in Europe, 1899–1940* (Lawrence, KS: University Press of Kansas, 2002).

—— *The German Way of War: From the Thirty Years' War to the Third Reich* (Lawrence, KS: University Press of Kansas, 2005).

Clausewitz, Carl von, *On War*, ed. and trans. by Michael Howard and Peter Paret (Princeton, NJ: Princeton University Press, 1976).

Cliff, Roger, Burles, Mark, Chase, Michael S., Eaton, Derek, and Pollpeter, Kevin, *Entering the Dragon's Lair: Chinese Antiaccess Strategies and Their Implications for the United States* (Santa Monica, CA: RAND, 2007).

Cohen, Eliot A. et al., *Knives, Tanks, and Missiles: Israel's Security Revolution* (Washington, DC: Washington Institute for Near East Policy, 1998).

Corum, James, *The Roots of Blitzkrieg* (Lawrence, KS: University Press of Kansas, 1992).

Cosmo, Nicola Di, *Ancient China and Its Enemies* (Cambridge: Cambridge University Press, 2002).

Creveld, Martin van, *Command in War* (Cambridge, MA: Harvard University Press, 1985).

—— *Technology and War: From 2000 B.C. to the Present* (New York: Free Press, 1989).

—— *The Sword and the Olive: A Critical History of the Israeli Defense Force* (New York: Public Affairs, 1998).

—— *The Culture of War* (New York: Presidio, 2008).

Deist, Wilhelm, *The Wehrmacht and German Rearmament* (London: Macmillan, 1981).

Department of the Army, *FM 100–5 Operations*, 20 August 1982 (Washington, DC: GPO, 1982).

—— *FM 100–5 Operations*, 14 June 1993 (Washington, DC: GPO, 1993).

—— *FM 3–24 Counterinsurgency*, 15 December 2006 (Washington, DC: GPO, 2006).

Design for Military Operations—The British Military Doctrine, prepared under the direction of the Chief of the General Staff (London: HMSO, 1989).

DiNardo, Richard L., *Germany's Panzer Arm* (Westport, CT: Praeger, 1997).

Doughty, Robert, *The Breaking Wave: Sedan and the Fall of France, 1940* (Hamden, CT: Shoe String Press, 1990).
Duffy, Christopher, *Frederick the Great: A Military Life* (London: Routledge, 1985).
Echevarria, Antulio, *After Clausewitz: German Military Thinkers Before the Great War* (Lawrence, KS: University Press of Kansas, 2000).
Edwards, Sean J. A., *Swarming on the Battlefield: Past, Present, and Future* (Santa Monica, CA: RAND, 2000).
Elleman, Bruce A., *Modern Chinese Warfare, 1795–1989* (London: Routledge, 2001).
Elting, John R., *Swords around a Throne: Napoleon's Grande Armee* (New York: Free Press, 1988).
Epstein, Robert M., *Napoleon's Last Victory and the Emergence of Modern War* (Lawrence, KS: University Press of Kansas, 1994).
Fergusson, James, *A Million Bullets: The Real Story of the British Army in Afghanistan* (London: Transworld, 2006).
Freedman, Lawrence and Karsh, Efraim, *The Gulf Conflict, 1990–1991: Diplomacy and War in the New World Order* (Princeton, NJ: Princeton University Press, 1991).
French, David, *Raising Churchill's Army: The British Army and the War Against Germany, 1919–1945* (Oxford: Oxford University Press, 2000).
Frieser, Karl-Heinz with Greenwood, John T., *Blitzkrieg Legend: The 1940 Campaign in the West* (Annapolis, MD: Naval Institute Press, 2005).
Fuller, John F. C., *The Reformation of War* (London: Hutchinson, 1923).
—— *The Foundations of the Science of War* (London: Hutchinson, 1926).
—— *Lectures on F.S.R. II* (London: Sifton Praed, 1931).
—— *Lectures on F.S.R. III (Operations Between Mechanized Forces)* (London: Sifton Praed, 1932).
—— *Armament and History* (New York: Scribner, 1945).
Gal, Reuven, *A Portrait of the Israeli Soldier* (Westport, CT: Greenwood, 1986).
Gat, Azar, *Fascist and Liberal Visions of War: Fuller, Liddell Hart, Douhet and Other Modernists* (Oxford: Oxford University Press, 1998).
—— *British Armour Theory and the Rise of the Panzer Arm: Revising the Revisionists* (New York: St. Martin's Press, 2000).
General Service Schools, *General Tactical Functions of Larger Units* (Fort Leavenworth, KS: General Service Schools, 1926).
General Staff, War Office, *Field Service Regulations Part I: Operations. 1909* (reprinted with amendments; London: HMSO, 1914).
—— *Field Service Regulations Part II: Organization and Administration* (London: HMSO, 1909; reprinted with amendments to October 1914).
—— *Field Service Regulations, Volume II: Operations. 1920. Provisional* (London: HMSO, 1920).
Germains, Victor Wallace, *The 'Mechanization' of War* (London: Sifton Praed, 1927).
Glantz, David M. (ed.), *The Initial Period of the War on the Eastern Front, 22 June–August 1941* (London: Frank Cass, 1993).
—— *Zhukov's Greatest Defeat: The Red Army's Epic Disaster in Operation Mars, 1942* (Lawrence, KS: University Press of Kansas, 1999).
—— and House, Jonathan, *When Titans Clashed: How the Red Army Stopped Hitler* (Lawrence, KS: University Press of Kansas, 1995).
Gooch, John, *Plans of War: The General Staff and British Military Strategy, c.1900–1916* (London: Routledge, 1974).
Graff, David A., *Medieval Chinese Warfare, 300–900* (London: Routledge, 2002).

—— and Higham, Robin (eds.), *A Military History of China* (Boulder, CO: Westview, 2002).
Graham, Dominick, *Tug of War: The Battle for Italy, 1943–1945* (New York: St. Martin's Press, 1986).
Guangqian, Peng and Youzhi, Yao (chief editors), *The Science of Military Strategy* (Beijing: Military Science Publishing House, 2005).
Guderian, Heinz, *Panzer Leader*, trans. C. Fitzgibbon (New York: Dutton, 1952).
Gudmundsson, Bruce, *Stormtroop Tactics: Innovation in the German Army, 1914–1918* (Westport, CT: Praeger, 1989).
Habeck, Mary R., *Storm of Steel: The Development of Armor Doctrine in Germany and the Soviet Union, 1919–1939* (Ithaca, NY: Cornell University Press, 2003).
Hagemeister, Stacy and Solon, Jenny, *Operation Just Cause: Lessons Learned*, 3 vols. (Fort Leavenworth, KS: Center for Army Lessons Learned, 1990).
Haichen, Sun, *The Wiles of War: 36 Military Strategies from Ancient China* (Beijing: Foreign Languages Press, 1993).
Hamley, Edward Bruce, *The Operations of War Explained and Illustrated* (Edinburgh: Blackwood, 1866).
—— *Operations of War* (7th edn., Edinburgh: Blackwood, 1922).
Handel, Michael I., *Masters of War: Classical Strategic Thought* (3rd rev. edn., London: Routledge, 2007).
Hargreaves, Reginald, *Blitzkrieg Unleashed: The German Invasion of Poland, 1939* (Barnsley: Pen & Sword, 2008).
Harris, J. P., *Men, Ideas and Tanks: British Military Thought and Armoured Forces, 1903–1939* (Manchester: Manchester University Press, 1995).
—— *Douglas Haig and the First World War* (Cambridge: Cambridge University Press, 2008).
Hart, B. H. Liddell, *The Decisive Wars of History: A Study in Strategy* (London: Bell, 1929).
—— *Thoughts on War* (London: Faber & Faber, 1943).
—— *Strategy* (London: Faber & Faber, 1967).
Hart, Russell A., *How the Allies Won in Normandy* (Norman, OK: University of Oklahoma Press, 2004).
Heller, C. E. and Stoft, W. A. (eds.), *America's First Battles, 1776–1965* (Lawrence, KS: University Press of Kansas, 1986).
Henderson, George F. R., *The Science of War: A Collection of Essays and Lectures, 1891–1903* (1st edn., 1906; London: Longmans, Green, 1919).
Herodotus, *The Histories* (London: Heinemann, Loeb Classical Library, 1961–6).
Herring, George, *America's Longest War: The United States and Vietnam, 1950–1975* (New York: Alfred A. Knopf, 1979).
Hewes, James E., Jr., *From Root to McNamara: Army Organization and Administration, 1900–1963* (Washington, DC: GPO, 1975).
Hines, John C., Mishulovich, Ellis M., and Shull, John F., *Soviet Intentions, 1965–1985: Soviet Post–Cold War Testimonial Evidence* (McLean, VA: BDM Corporation, 1995).
Hofschröer, Peter, *Leipzig 1813: The Battle of the Nations* (Oxford: Osprey, 1993).
—— *1815: The Waterloo Campaign*, 2 vols. (Oxford: Osprey, 1998–9).
—— *Lützen and Bautzen 1813: The Turning Point* (Oxford: Osprey, 2001).
Hooker, Richard, Jr. (ed.), *Maneuver Warfare: An Anthology* (Novato, CA: Presidio, 1993).
Howard, Michael, *The Franco-Prussian War: The German Invasion of France, 1870–1871* (London: Rupert Hart-Davis, 1960).

Ignatieff, Michael, *Virtual War: Kosovo and Beyond* (New York: Metropolitan, 2000).
James, D. Clayton and Wells, Anne Sharp, *Refighting the Last War: Command and Crisis in Korea, 1950–1953* (New York: Free Press, 1993).
Jarymowycz, Roman, *Cavalry from Hoof to Track* (Westport, CT: Praeger Security International, 2008).
Joint Publication, *JP 3-07. Joint Doctrine for Military Operations Other Than War* (Washington, DC: GPO, 16 June 1995).
—— *JP 3-0. Joint Operations* (Washington, DC: GPO, 2006).
—— *5-0. Joint Operation Planning* (Washington, DC: GPO, 2006).
Jomini, Antoine Henri, *The Art of War*, trans. G. H. Mendell and W. P. Craighill (Philadelphia, PA: Lippincott, 1862).
Kagan, Frederick R., *The End of the Old Order: Napoleon and Europe, 1801–1805* (New York: First Da Capo Press, 2006).
Kahn, Herman, *On Thermonuclear War* (Princeton, NJ: Princeton University Press, 1960).
—— *On Escalation: Metaphors and Scenarios* (New York: Praeger, 1965).
Keegan, John, *A History of Warfare* (London: Hutchinson, 1993).
—— *Six Armies in Normandy: From D-Day to the Liberation of Paris* (New York: Penguin, 1994).
Kelly, Brig. Justin and Brennan, Michael J., *Alien: How Operational Art Devoured Strategy* (Carlisle, PA: US Army War College, 2009).
Kitchen, Martin, *The German Offensives of 1918* (Stroud: Tempus, 2001).
Kitson, Frank, *Warfare as a Whole* (London: Faber, 1987).
Kobbe, William A., *Notes on Strategy and Logistics* (Fort Monroe, VA: Artillery School Press, 1896).
Kober, Avi, *Coalition Defection: The Dissolution of Arab Anti-Israeli Coalitions in War and Peace* (Westport, CT: Praeger, 2002).
—— *Israel's Wars of Attrition* (New York: Routledge, 2009).
Krause, Michael D. and Phillips, R. Cody, *Historical Perspectives on the Operational Art* (Washington, DC: Center of Military History, United States Army, 2005).
Krepenevich, Andrew Jr., *The Army and Vietnam* (Baltimore: Johns Hopkins University Press, 1986).
Leggiere, Michael, *Napoleon and Berlin: The Franco-Prussian War in North Germany, 1813* (Norman, OK: University of Oklahoma Press, 2002).
Lewis, John W. and Litai, Xue, *China Builds the Bomb* (Stanford, CA: Stanford University Press, 1988).
—— *Imagined Enemies: China Prepares for Uncertain War* (Stanford, CA: Stanford University Press, 2006).
Li, Xiaobing, *A History of the Modern Chinese Army* (Lexington, KY: University Press of Kentucky, 2007).
—— Millett, Allan R., and Yu, Bin (trans. and eds.), *Mao's Generals Remember Korea* (Lawrence, KS: University Press of Kansas, 2001).
Lider, Julian, *British Military Thought after World War II* (Aldershot: Gower, 1985).
Lind, William S., *Maneuver Warfare Handbook* (Boulder, CO: Westview, 1985).
Lorge, Peter, *War, Politics, and Society in Early Modern China, 900–1795* (London: Routledge, 2005).
Luttwak, Edward and Horowitz, Dan, *The Israeli Army* (London: Allen Lane, 1975).
Luvaas, Jay, *The Education of an Army: British Military Thought, 1815–1940* (London: Cassell, 1965).

Mackenzie, J. J. G. and Reid, Brian Holden (eds.), *The British Army and the Operational Level of War* (London: Tri-Service Press, 1989).

Mäder, Markus, *In Pursuit of Conceptual Excellence: The Evolution of British Military-Strategic Doctrine in the Post–Cold War Era, 1989–2002* (Bern: Peter Lang, 2004).

Majdalany, Fred, *The Battle of El Alamein: Fortress in the Sand* (Philadelphia, PA: University of Pennsylvania Press, 2003).

Manstein, Erich von, *Lost Victories* (Chicago, IL: Regnery, 1958).

Marder, Arthur J. (ed.), *Fear God and Dread Nought: The Correspondence of Admiral of the Fleet Lord Fisher of Kilverstone*, 3 vols. (London: Cape, 1952–9).

Marsden, Eric W., *Greek and Roman Artillery* (Oxford: Clarendon Press, 1971).

Marshall, S. L. A., *Men Against Fire: The Problem of Battle Command in Future War* (3rd edn., New York: Wm Morrow, 1966).

Maude, F. N., *The Jena Campaign* (London: Sonnenschein, 1909).

Maurice, John Frederick, *War* (London: Macmillan, 1891).

—— *British Strategy: A Study of the Applications of the Principles of War* (London: Constable, 1929).

McInnes, Colin, *Hot War, Cold War: The British Army's Way in Warfare, 1945–95* (London: Brassey's, 1996).

McKercher, B. J. C. and Hennessy, Michael A. (eds.), *The Operational Art: Developments in the Theories of War* (Westport, CT: Praeger, 1996).

Mearsheimer, John J., *Conventional Deterrence* (Ithaca, NY: Cornell University Press, 1983).

Megargee, Geoffrey P., *War of Annihilation: Combat and Genocide on the Eastern Front* (Lanham, MD: Rowman and Littlefield, 2005).

Meilinger, Phillip S., *Paths of Heaven: The Evolution of Airpower Theory* (Maxwell AFB, AL: Air University Press, 1997).

Mellenthin, Friedrich W., *Panzer Battles* (Norman, OK: University of Oklahoma Press, 1956).

Meretskov, Kirill, *Serving the People* (Moscow: Progress, 1971).

Metz, Steven, *Armed Conflict in the 21st Century: The Information Revolution and Post-Modern Warfare* (Carlisle, PA: Strategic Studies Institute, April 2000).

—— *Learning from Iraq: Counterinsurgency in Iraq* (Carlisle, PA: US Army War College, 2007).

Munro, Ross and Bernstein, Richard, *The Coming Conflict with China* (New York: Alfred A. Knopf, 1997).

Murray, Williamson and Millett, Allan R., *A War to Be Won: Fighting the Second World War* (Cambridge, MA: Belknap, 2000).

Nagl, John, *Learning to Eat Soup with a Knife: Counterinsurgency Lessons from Malaya and Vietnam* (Chicago, IL: University of Chicago Press, 2002).

Nathan, Andrew J. and Scobell, Andrew, *China's Search for Security* (New York: Columbia University Press, 2010).

Naveh, Shimon, *In Pursuit of Military Excellence: The Evolution of Operational Theory* (London: Frank Cass, 1997).

—— *Operational Art and the IDF: A Critical Study of a Command Culture* (Washington, DC: Center for Strategic and Budgetary Assessment, 2007).

Naylor, William K., *The Principles of Strategy* (Fort Leavenworth, KS: General Service Schools, 1920).

Needham, Joseph, Yates, Robin D. S. with the collaboration of Gawlikowski, Krzysztof, McEwen, Edward, and Ling, Wang, *Science and Civilization in China*, vol. 5, *Chemistry*

and Chemical Technology, Part VI, *Military Technology: Missiles and Sieges* (Cambridge: Cambridge University Press, 1994).
Niepold, Gerd, *Battle for White Russia: The Destruction of Army Group Centre, June 1944* (London: Brassey's, 1987).
Notes on the Battle of Jena, by an Officer of the R. Staff Corps (London: Naval and Military Press, n.d. [1827]).
Odom, William E., *The Collapse of the Soviet Military* (New Haven, CT: Yale University Press, 1998).
—— *After the Trenches: The Transformation of the U.S. Army, 1918–1939* (College Station, TX: Texas A&M University Press, 1999).
O'Dowd, Edward C., *Chinese Military Strategy in the Third Indochina War: The Last Maoist War* (New York: Routledge, 2007).
O'Hanlon, Michael, *Technological Change and the Future of War* (Washington, DC: Brookings Institution, 2000).
Olsen, John Andreas, *John Warden and the Renaissance of American Air Power* (Washington, DC: Potomac, 2007).
Osgood, Robert E., *Limited War: The Challenge to American Strategy* (Chicago, IL: University of Chicago Press, 1957).
Overy, Richard J., *Why the Allies Won* (New York: Norton, 1997).
—— *The Air War, 1939–1945* (Washington, DC: Potomac, 2005).
Owens, Admiral Bill, *Lifting the Fog of War* (New York: Farrar, Strauss, and Giroux, 2000).
Palazzo, Albert, *Seeking Victory on the Western Front: The British Army and Chemical Warfare in World War I* (Lincoln, NB: University of Nebraska Press, 2000).
—— *Moltke to Bin Laden: The Relevance of Doctrine in the Contemporary Military Environment* (Canberra: Land Warfare Studies Centre, September 2008).
Parker, G., *The Army of Flanders and the Spanish Road, 1567–1659* (Cambridge: Cambridge University Press, 1972).
—— (ed.), *Cambridge Illustrated History of Warfare: The Triumph of the West* (Cambridge: Cambridge University Press, 1995).
Place, Timothy Harrison, *Military Training in the British Army, 1940–1944* (London: Frank Cass, 2000).
Poseck, Maximilian von, *The German Cavalry in 1914 in Belgium and France*, ed. J. Howe (Berlin: Mittler, 1923).
Procopius, *Anecdota* (London: Heinemann, Loeb Classical Library, 1953–4).
Raus, Erhard (ed.), *Panzer Operations: The Eastern Front Memoir of General Raus, 1941–1945*, trans. S. Newton (Cambridge, MA: Da Capo Press, 2003).
Reid, Brian Holden, *J. F. C. Fuller: Military Thinker* (Basingstoke: Macmillan, 1987).
—— *Studies in British Military Thought: Debates with Fuller and Liddell Hart* (Lincoln, NB: University of Nebraska Press, 1999).
Robertson, William, *From Private to Field Marshal* (London: Constable, 1921).
Ryan, Mark A., Finkelstein, David M., and McDevitt, Michael A., *Chinese Warfighting: The PLA Experience Since 1949* (Armonk, NY: M. E. Sharpe, 2003).
Samuelson, Lennart, *Soviet Defence Industry Planning: Tukhachevskii and Military-Industrial Mobilization, 1926–1937* (Stockholm: Stockholm Institute of East European Economies, 1996).
—— *Plans for Stalin's War Machine: Tukhachevskii and Military-Economic Planning, 1925–1941* (Basingstoke: Macmillan, 2000).
Sawyer, Ralph D. (trans.), *The Seven Military Classics of Ancient China* (Boulder, CO: Westview Press, 1993).

—— with Sawyer, Mei-Chun Lee, *The Tao of Deception: Unorthodox Warfare in Historic and Modern China* (New York: Basic Books, 2007).

Saxe, M. de, *Reveries on the Art of War* (Mineola, NY: Dover, [1757]/2007).

Schelling, Thomas C., *Arms and Influence* (New Haven, CT: Yale University Press, 1966).

Schneid, Frederick, *Napoleon's Conquest of Europe: The War of the Third Coalition* (Westport, CT: Praeger, 2005).

Schroeder, Paul, *Austria, Great Britain, and the Crimean War: The Destruction of the European Concert* (Ithaca, NY: Cornell University Press, 1972).

Scobell, Andrew, *China and Strategic Culture* (Carlisle Barracks, PA: Strategic Studies Institute, 2002).

—— *China's Use of Military Force: Beyond the Great Wall and the Long March* (New York: Cambridge University Press, 2003).

Scott, Henry L., *Military Dictionary* (New York: D. Van Nostrand, 1864).

Seeckt, Hans von, *Thoughts of a Soldier*, trans. G. Waterhouse (London: Ernest Benn, 1930).

Showalter, Dennis E., *Tannenberg: Clash of Empires* (Hamden, CT: Archon, 1991).

—— *The Wars of Frederick the Great* (London: Pearson Education, 1996).

—— *The Wars of German Unification* (London: Edward Arnold, 2004).

—— *Patton and Rommel: Men of War in the Twentieth Century* (New York: Berkeley Caliber, 2006).

Simms, Brendan, *The Impact of Napoleon: Prussian High Politics, Foreign Policy, and the Crisis of the Executive, 1797–1806* (Cambridge: Cambridge University Press, 1997).

Simpkin, Richard, *Race to the Swift: Thoughts on Twenty-First Century Warfare* (London: Brassey's, 1985).

Smith, Edward A., *Effects Based Operations: Applying Network Centric Warfare in Peace, Crisis, and War* (Washington, DC: Department of Defense Command and Control Research Program, 2002).

Snow, Edgar, *Red Star over China* (New York: Random House, 1938).

Stahel, David, *Operation Barbarossa and German Military Defeat in the East* (New York: Cambridge University Press, 2009).

Stoecker, Sally W., *Forging Stalin's Army: Marshal Tukhachevsky and the Politics of Military Innovation* (Boulder, CO: Westview Press, 1998).

Strachan, Hew, *From Waterloo to Balaclava: Tactics, Technology and the British Army, 1815–1854* (Cambridge: Cambridge University Press, 1985).

—— *Carl von Clausewitz's On War: A Biography* (London: Atlantic Books, 2007).

Sudoplatov, Pavel et al., *Special Tasks* (New York: Little, Brown, 1994).

Sumida, Jon Tetsuro, *Decoding Clausewitz: A New Approach to 'On War'* (Lawrence, KS: University Press of Kansas, 2008).

Summers, Harry G., Jr., *On Strategy: A Critical Analysis of the Vietnam War* (Novato, CA: Presidio, 1982).

Svechin, Aleksandr A., *Strategy*, trans. and ed. Kent D. Lee (Minneapolis, MN: Eastview Press, 1992).

Szabo, Franz, *The Seven Years War in Europe, 1756–1763* (London: Pearson Education, 2007).

Tacitus, *The Histories* (London: Penguin, 1986).

Telp, Claus, *The Evolution of Operational Art, 1740–1813: From Frederick the Great to Napoleon* (London: Routledge, 2005).

The Fundamentals of British Maritime Doctrine. BR 1806 (London: HMSO, 1995).

The Officer's Manual: Military Maxims of Napoleon, trans. Colonel d'Aguillar (Dublin: Richard Milliken, 1831).

The Principles of Strategy for an Independent Corps or Army in a Theater of Operations (Fort Leavenworth, KS: Command and General Staff College, 1936).

Tzu, Sun, *Sun Tzu: The Art of War*, trans. Samuel B. Griffith (New York: Oxford University Press, 1963).

US Joint Chiefs of Staff, *Joint Vision 2010* (Washington, DC: GPO, 1996).

—— *Joint Vision 2020* (Washington, DC: GPO, 2000).

Van Dyke, Carl, *The Soviet Invasion of Finland, 1939–1940* (London: Frank Cass, 1997).

Vego, Milan, *Joint Operational Warfare*, I-16 (Newport, RI: US Naval War College, 2007).

Waldron, Arthur, *The Great Wall of China: From History to Myth* (New York: Cambridge University Press, 1990).

—— *From War to Nationalism: China's Turning Point, 1924–1925* (New York: Cambridge University Press, 1995).

Wawro, Geoffrey, *The Franco-Prussian War* (Cambridge: Cambridge University Press, 2003).

Weigley, Russell F., *The American Way of War: A History of United States Military Strategy and Policy* (Bloomington, IN: Indiana University Press, 1977).

Weizman, Ezer, *On Eagles' Wings* (London: Weidenfeld and Nicolson, 1976).

Whiting, Allen S., *The Chinese Calculus of Deterrence: India and Indochina* (Ann Arbor, MI: University of Michigan Press, 1975).

Xenopohon, *Cyropaedia* (London: Heinemann, Loeb Classical Library, 1949).

Yardley, Michael and Sewell, Dennis, *A New Model Army* (London: W. H. Allen, 1989).

Zabecki, David, *Steel Wind: Colonel Georg Bruchmüller and the Birth of Modern Artillery* (Westport, CT: Praeger, 1994).

—— *The German 1918 Offensives: A Case Study in the Operational Level of War* (New York: Routledge, 2008).

Zaloga, Steven J., *Bagration, 1944: The Destruction of Army Group Centre* (Oxford: Osprey, 1996).

—— *Poland 1919: The Birth of Blitzkrieg* (Oxford: Osprey, 2002).

Zetterling, Niklas and Frankson, Anders, *Kursk 1943: A Statistical Analysis* (London: Frank Cass, 2005).

Zuber, Terence, *Inventing the Schlieffen Plan: German War Planning, 1871–1914* (Oxford: Oxford University Press, 2002).

—— *The Moltke Myth: German War Planning, 1857–1871* (Lanham, MD: University Press of America, 2008).

Index